$400.00

Know all men by these present that I Chilly McIntosh of the Creek Nation do bargain and sell unto Wesy Hardridge of the same Nation for a certain Negro Woman by the name of Mary about twenty five years old ~~which~~ ~~I warrant and defend~~ for an incideration of the Sum of four hundred Dollors to me in hand paid by Sora Wesy Hardridge. Which property I warrent and defend from all claim or Claimants Whatsoever given under my hand above writen this 30th day of September 1831

Witness
Benjamin Hawkins

Chilly McIntosh

FACSIMILE OF NEGRO BILL OF SALE
Slightly reduced

The American Indian in the Civil War, 1862–1865

BY

ANNIE HELOISE ABEL

Introduction to the Bison Book Edition
by Theda Perdue and Michael D. Green

University of Nebraska Press
Lincoln and London

First Bison Book printing: 1992
Most recent printing indicated by the last digit below:
10   9   8   7   6   5   4   3

Library of Congress Cataloging-in-Publication Data
Abel, Annie Heloise, 1873–
The American Indian in the Civil War, 1862–1865 / by Annie Heloise
Abel: introduction by Theda Perdue and Michael D. Green.
p. cm.
Reprint. Originally published: Cleveland: A. H. Clark Co., 1919. Origi-
nally published as v. 2 in author's series: The Slaveholding Indian.
Includes bibliographical references and index.
ISBN 0-8032-5919-0 (pa)
1. Indians of North America—History—Civil War, 1862–1865.   2.
United States—History—Civil War, 1862–1865—Participation, In-
dian.   3. Indians of North America—Indian Territory—History.   I.
Title.
E540.I3A17   1993
973.7′4—dc20
92-11003   CIP

Reprinted from the original edition titled *The American Indian as Partici-*
pant in the Civil War and published in 1919 by the Arthur H. Clark Company, Cleveland

CONTENTS

ILLUSTRATIONS

INTRODUCTION
By Theda Perdue and Michael D. Green

The Civil War was a major event in the lives of southern Indians who had been removed to Indian Territory in the antebellum period. Early attempts to remain neutral crumbled under pressure from their Arkansas and Texas neighbors, clever Confederate diplomacy, and indifference from a United States concerned with more pressing problems. By the fall of 1861, the Cherokees, Chickasaws, Choctaws, Creeks, and Seminoles had signed Confederate treaties and organized military companies to serve as a home guard. Thus the southern Indians became a part of the bloodiest war in United States history. Their participation in the conflict is the subject of the second volume in Annie Heloise Abel's *Slaveholding Indians*.

The Civil War opened old wounds among three of the southern Indian nations. Factionalism dated back to the removal era when some citizens favored emigration to the west and others preferred to remain on their ancestral lands. As Civil War approached, many southern Indians wanted little to do with those states that had forced them from their homeland, nor did they want to follow the lead of the highly acculturated Indians who promoted the Confederate cause. Antagonism stemmed from complex political, economic, and cultural tensions that varied from nation to nation, but the result was that significant numbers of Cherokees, Creeks, and Seminoles wanted nothing to do with the Confederacy.[1]

The first battles of the Civil War in Indian Territory occurred in November and December of 1861 when the Confederate Creek Regiment tracked down and attacked Opothle Yoholo and some eight thousand Creek, Seminole, and black followers who were attempting to escape to Union lines in Kansas. In two sharply fought engagements, Opothle Yoholo and his people slipped away, but the third, the Battle of Chustenalah, was devastating. The neutrals, by now bitterly anti-Confederate, lost everything but the clothes on their backs. In a blinding snow storm they stumbled, afoot, exhausted and freezing, into Kansas.[2] Desperately in need of food and shelter, they suffered terribly. The Union army in Kansas simply was not prepared to deal with refugees.[3] The problem continued throughout the war as other Indians defected from the Confederacy and joined the Kansas refugees. Many enlisted in the Union Indian Brigade and ultimately helped liberate their nations.[4] Among the inductees were many southern Indians, particularly Cherokees, who originally had joined the Confederate army. Recognizing that they had far more in common with Opothle Yoholo than the slaveholding planters who had promoted the Confederate alliance, they defected and became unionists. After the Battle of Pea Ridge in 1862, the Confederacy disbanded an entire Cherokee regiment because most of its members had gone over to the Union.[5]

The problem of refugees was a serious one throughout the Civil War. In addition to the people who fled to Kansas, many southern sympathizers took refuge in Texas.[6] Afraid that periodically invading Union troops would liberate their slaves, they took their chattels with them, rented land, and raised crops. As the war ground on, however, they too began to suffer severe deprivation. The slaves, forcibly taken from familiar surroundings and perhaps even family members, had to labor under even more difficult conditions, and as supplies grew scarce, they felt the pinch of hunger first. Some managed to escape to Union lines, but others awaited the war's end in bondage. Following the war, masters often abandoned these freedmen in Texas, far from their homes and from the citizenship that Reconstruction treaties required southern Indians to grant them.[7]

The Battle of Pea Ridge is important to Abel because it was the only major engagement in which Indian Territory forces participated. Fought in March 1862 in northwestern Arkansas, it was a bloody disaster for the Confederates but a glorious moment for Colonel Stand Watie and his Cherokee Mounted Rifles. In one of the few Confederate successes, Watie's men captured and stilled the Union artillery batteries, thereby permitting an orderly Confederate retreat.

But withdrawal into Indian Territory simply relocated the conflict. Unfortunately, it also transformed it into a partisan struggle in which Confederate and Union Indian forces fought guerilla actions against one another, the land, and the non-combatants who had not joined the others in refugee camps. The trials suffered by those who remained in Indian Territory were extreme. Old animosities surfaced and produced civil wars with little connection to the conflagration in the United States. Some residents of Indian Territory seized this opportunity to settle old scores while others simply took advantage of unattended property to loot and vandalize. The lack of effective governments in the Indian nations meant that such crimes went largely

unpunished. Furthermore, the vacuum of law and order enticed non-Indian deserters, outlaws, and oppor-
tunists from other areas to Indian Territory, where
they helped themselves to what those fleeing the violence had left behind. Periodic raids by Union and
Confederate forces contributed to the turmoil.[8] The
Creek and Cherokee nations were the most grievously
devastated, while the Choctaws struggled to feed and
house thousands of refugees who could not make it to
Texas.

The deteriorating relationship of the southern Indians with the Confederacy is the chief concern of this
book. Although one reviewer of the first volume concluded that "the author is of British ancestry and so
presumably is free from sectional prejudice,"[9] the emphasis is on the Confederacy. Perhaps the existence of
Wiley Britton's study, which had a more unionist fla-
vor, influenced Abel's decision.[10] Furthermore, she
considered the Union handling of Indian issues to be
particularly inept.[11]

In this volume, Abel describes the military engagements and administrative difficulties of coping with
Native American forces and refugees. This derives
primarily from the nature of her sources. Relying on
Bureau of Indian Affairs documents and similar administrative records from the Confederacy, she uses
virtually no Native sources. At the time in which Abel
wrote, however, no one had made use of the records
on which this study is based, and few Native records
had come to light. Consequently, she establishes a
framework in which modern historians can now exploit other documents to write a more complete story
of Native southerners in the Civil War.

Since the appearance of Abel's work, several primary documents that give insight into the Civil War ex-

periences of Native peoples have been published. *Cherokee Cavaliers: Forty Years of Cherokee History as Told in the Correspondence of the Ridge-Watie-Boundinot Family* presents the views of the leaders of the Confederate Cherokees, who enlisted in the Confederate army, and their families, who took refuge in Texas.[12] The papers of John Ross, the chief of the Cherokees during the Civil War, demonstrates the conflicting emotions confronting Native people who had to chose between the Confederacy and the Union.[13] The diary of Hannah Hicks, daughter of a missionary and widow of a prominent Cherokee politician, illustrates how very difficult life in the Cherokee Nation was for those who stayed behind.[14] The diary of George W. Grayson reveals the experiences of a Creek Confederate officer.[15] In addition to these published sources, Native sources at the University of Oklahoma, Gilcrease Institute, and the Oklahoma Historical Society present the Indians' point of view. Particularly useful are the Indian-Pioneer papers housed at the Oklahoma Historical Society and the Western History Collection of the University of Oklahoma. This collection of interviews conducted during the 1930s with residents of Oklahoma before statehood contains many reminiscences of life during the Civil War.[16]

Access to Native sources would have produced a different book, one that still needs to be written.[17] These sources might also have served to temper Abel's ethnocentric perspective and racist language. Offensive as these are, Abel's characterizations of Native people usually makes them genuine actors in their own histories. The alleged atrocities at Pea Ridge, for example, "showed that the red men were quite equal to making their own plans in fighting and were not to be relied upon to do things decently and in order" (p. 33). That

such comments were typical of the time in which Abel
wrote does not excuse the attitudes they reveal but it
does force us to look beyond the offensive language to
a view of Native peoples that is quite modern. No mere
pawns of white men, the Indians portrayed by Abel
make rational decisions based on the evidence they
have available.

Annie Heloise Abel was born in England in 1873.[18]
At the age of twelve, she emigrated with her family to
Kansas. She received her undergraduate and master's
degrees from the University of Kansas and studied for
a year at Cornell University. In 1893 she became the
first woman to receive Yale's Bulkley Fellowship; Yale
awarded her Ph.D. in 1905. Her dissertation, "The
History of Events Resulting in Indian Consolidation
West of the Mississippi," appeared in the *Annual Report
of the American Historical Association* in 1906.[19] In that
year, she moved from her first job at Wells College to
Women's College of Baltimore, now Goucher College,
where she remained until 1915. While she was living in
Baltimore, Abel had easy access to Indian Bureau records in Washington. She began to investigate the role
of Indians in the Civil War, and published an article on
the subject in 1910.[20] In 1915, the year the first volume
of *Slaveholding Indians* appeared, Abel moved to Smith
College. She developed an interest in British policy towards Native peoples and in 1921 she went to Australia on her sabbatical to research aboriginal policy. Abel
married while she was in Australia and resigned her
position at Smith. She used her husband's name, Henderson, but after they separated permanently in 1927,
she adopted a hyphenated surname, Abel-Henderson.
She taught briefly at Sweetbriar College and the University of Kansas before retiring in 1930 and moving
to Aberdeen, Washington, to live with her sister. When

she died in 1947, Abel left a substantial body of work on Native peoples. In addition to her studies of southern Indians, she meticulously edited the records of travelers, fur traders, and Indian agents.[21]

Abel's major legacy, however, is her trilogy *The Slaveholding Indians*. In this work, she charts the diplomatic maneuvers that led to the Confederate alliances, the participation of Native soldiers in military operations which brought devastation to Indian Territory, and the impact of Confederate defeat on the nations that had repudiated their treaties with the United States. The story is a tragic one, but leaving it untold would be a greater tragedy. Native southerners shared the experience of civil war with other Americans, and their involvement in that upheaval had as profound an effect on their subsequent history. Abel's was the first serious telling of that story.

NOTES

1. Moris L. Wardell, *A Political History of the Cherokee Nation, 1838–1907* (Norman: University of Oklahoma Press, 1938); Arrell M. Gibson, *The Chickasaws* (Norman: University of Oklahoma Press, 1971); Stephen Steacy, "The Chickasaw Nation on the Eve of the Civil War," *Chronicles of Oklahoma* 49 (1971) 51–75; Paul Bonnifield, "The Choctaw Nation on the Eve of the Civil War," *Journal of the West* 12 (1973): 386–402; Angie Debo, *Rise and Fall of the Choctaw Republic* (Norman: University of Oklahoma Press, 1934); Andre Paul du Chateau, "The Creek Nation on the Eve of the Civil War," *Chronicles of Oklahoma* 52 (1974): 290–315; Angie Debo, *The Road to Disappearance* (Norman: University of Oklahoma Press, 1941); Edwin C. McReynolds, *The Seminoles* (Norman: University of Oklahoma Press, 1957).

2. Edwin C. Bearss, "The Civil War Comes to Indian Territory, 1861: The Flight of Opothleyoholo," *Journal of the West* 11 (1972): 9–42; Carter Blue Clark, "Opthleyohola and the Creeks during the Civil War," in *Indian Leaders: Oklahoma's First Statesmen*, ed. H. Glen Jordan and Thomas M. Holm (Oklahoma City: Oklahoma Historical Society, 1979), pp. 49–63.

3. Dean Banks, "Civil War Refugees from Indian Territory in the North, 1861–1864," *Chronicles of Oklahoma* 41 (1963–64): 442–49; Edmund Danziger, "The Office of Indian Affairs and the Problem of Civil War Refugees," *Kansas Historical Quarterly* 35 (1969): 257–75.

4. Wiley Britton, *The Union Indian Brigade in the Civil War* (Kansas City, Mo.: Franklin Hudson Publishing Company, 1922).

5. Kenny A. Franks, *Stand Watie and the Agony of the Cherokee Nation* (Memphis State University Press, 1979); W. Craig Gaines, *The Confederate Cherokees: John Drew's Regiment of Mounted Rifles* (Baton Rouge: Louisiana State University Press, 1989).

6. LeRoy H. Fisher and William L. McMurry, "Confederate Refugees from Indian Territory," *Chronicles of Oklahoma* 57 (1979): 451–62; Angie Debo, "Southern Refugees of the Cherokee Nation," *Southwestern Historical Quarterly* 35 (1932): 255–66.

7. Daniel F. Littlefield, *The Chickasaw Freedmen*; Littlefield, *The Cherokee Freedmen*. These treaties are the subject of the third volume of Abel's trilogy, *American Indian under Reconstruction*.

8. Gary N. Heath, "The First Federal Invasion of Indian Territory," *Chronicles of Oklahoma* 44 (1966–67): 409–419; William J. Willey, "The Second Federal Invasion of Indian Territory," *Chronicles of Oklahoma* 44 (1966–67): 420–30; Larry C. Rampp and Donald L. Rampp, *The Civil War in Indian Territory* (Austin, Tex.: Presidial Press, 1975); LeRoy H. Fischer, *The Civil War Era in Indian Territory* (Los Angeles: Lorrin L. Morrison, 1974).

9. *Journal of Negro History* 1 (1916): 339.

10. *The Civil War on the Border* (2 vols., New York: Putnam, 1891–99).

11. While David A. Nichols accuses Abel of contributing historigraphically to the "compartmentalization" of Indian affairs, he does not disagree with her depiction of Union Indian policy. *Lincoln and the Indians: Civil War Policy and Politics* (Columbia: University of Missouri Press, 1978).

12. Edward Everett Dale and Gaston Litton, eds. (Norman: University of Oklahoma Press, 1939).

13. Gary Moulton, ed., *The Papers of John Ross* (2 vols., Norman: University of Oklahoma Press, 1985).

14. "The Diary of Hannah Hicks," *The American Scene* 13 (1972).

15. George W. Grayson, *A Creek Warrior for the Confederacy: The Autobiography of Chief G.W. Grayson*, ed. W. David Baird (Norman: University of Oklahoma Press, 1988).

16. For an example, see Theda Perdue, *Nations Remembered: An Oral History of the Five Civilized Tribes* (Westport, Conn.: Greenwood Press, 1980).

17. Charles Royster and Reid Mitchell's work could provide good models. Royster, *A Revolutionary People at War* (New York: Norton, 1982); Mitchell, *Civil War Soldiers* (New York: Viking, 1988).

18. This biographical sketch is condensed from Harry Kelsey, "A Dedication to the Memory of Annie Heloise Abel Henderson, 1873–1947," *Arizona and the West* 15 (1973): 1–4.

19. *Annual Report of the American Historical Association* 1 (1906) 235–450.

20. "The Indians in the Civil War," *American Historical Review* 15 (1910): 281–96.

21. *The Official Correspondence of James S. Calhoun While Indian Agent at Santa Fe and Superintendent of Indian Affairs in New Mexico* (Washington, D.C.: U.S. Government Printing Office, 1915); "The Journal of John Greiner," *Old Santa Fe* 3 (1916): 189–243; *A Report from Natchitoches in 1807 by Dr. John Sibley* (New York: Museum of the American Indian, 1922); *Chardron's Journal at Fort Clark, 1834–1839* (Pierre: South Dakota Department of History, 1932); *Tabeau's Narrative of Loisel's Expedition to the Upper Missouri* (Norman: University of Oklahoma Press, 1939); "Indian Affairs in New Mexico under the Administration of William Carr Lane; from the Journal of John Ward," *New Mexico Historical Review* 16 (1941): 106–32, 328–58.

THE AMERICAN INDIAN
IN THE CIVIL WAR, 1862–1865

I. THE BATTLE OF PEA RIDGE, OR ELK-HORN, AND ITS MORE IMMEDIATE EFFECTS

The Indian alliance, so assiduously sought by the Southern Confederacy and so laboriously built up, soon revealed itself to be most unstable. Direct and unmistakable signs of its instability appeared in connection with the first real military test to which it was subjected, the Battle of Pea Ridge or Elkhorn, as it is better known in the South, the battle that stands out in the history of the War of Secession as being the most decisive victory to date of the Union forces in the West and as marking the turning point in the political relationship of the State of Missouri with the Confederate government.

In the short time during which, following the removal of General Frémont, General David Hunter was in full command of the Department of the West — and it was practically not more than one week — he completely reversed the policy of vigorous offensive that had obtained under men, subordinate to his predecessor.[1] In southwest Missouri, he abandoned the advanced position of the Federals and fell back upon Sedalia and Rolla, railway termini. That he did this at the suggestion of President Lincoln[2] and with the tacit approval of General McClellan[3] makes no differ-

---

[1] *The Century Company's War Book*, vol. i, 314-315.

[2] *Official Records*, first ser., vol. iii, 553-554. Hereafter, except where otherwise designated, the *first series* will always be understood.

[3] — *Ibid.*, 568.

ence now, as it made no difference then, in the consideration of the consequences; yet the consequences were, none the less, rather serious. They were such, in fact, as to increase very greatly the confusion on the border and to give the Confederates that chance of recovery which soon made it necessary for their foes to do the work of Nathaniel Lyon all over again.

It has been most truthfully said [4] that never, throughout the period of the entire war, did the southern government fully realize the surpassingly great importance of its Trans-Mississippi District; notwithstanding that when that district was originally organized, [5] in January, 1862, some faint idea of what it might, peradventure, accomplish did seem to penetrate, [6] although ever so vaguely, the minds of those then in authority. It was organized under pressure from the West as was natural, and under circumstances to which meagre and tentative reference has already been made in the first volume of this work. [7] In the main, the circumstances were such as developed out of the persistent refusal of General McCulloch to coöperate with General Price.

There was much to be said in justification of McCulloch's obstinacy. To understand this it is well to recall that, under the plan, lying back of this first

[4] *Official Records*, vol. liii, supplement, 781-782; Edwards, *Shelby and His Men,* 105.

[5] — *Ibid.*, vol. viii, 734.

[6] It is doubtful if even this ought to be conceded in view of the fact that President Davis later admitted that Van Dorn entered upon the Pea Ridge campaign for the sole purpose of effecting "a diversion in behalf of General Johnston" [*Rise and Fall of the Confederate Government,* vol. ii, 51]. Moreover, Van Dorn had scarcely been assigned to the command of the Trans-Mississippi District before Beauregard was devising plans for bringing him east again [Greene, *The Mississippi,* 11; Roman, *Military Operations of General Beauregard,* vol. i, 240-244].

[7] Abel, *American Indian as Slaveholder and Secessionist,* 225-226 and footnote 522.

appointment to the Confederate command, was the expectation that he would secure the Indian Territory. Obviously, the best way to do that was to occupy it, provided the tribes, whose domicile it was, were willing. But, if the Cherokees can be taken to have voiced the opinion of all, they were not willing, notwithstanding that a sensationally reported[8] Federal activity under Colonel James Montgomery,[9] in the neighborhood of the frontier posts, Cobb, Arbuckle, and Washita, was designed to alarm them and had notably influenced, if it had not actually inspired, the selection and appointment of the Texan ranger.[10]

Unable, by reason of the Cherokee objection thereto, to enter the Indian country; because entrance in the face of that objection would inevitably force the Ross faction of the Cherokees and, possibly also, Indians of other tribes into the arms of the Union, McCulloch intrenched himself on its northeast border, in Arkansas, and there awaited a more favorable opportunity for accomplishing his main purpose. He seems to have desired the Confederate government to add the contiguous portion of Arkansas to his command, but in that he was disappointed.[11] Nevertheless, Arkansas early interpreted his presence in the state to imply that he was there primarily for her defence and, by the middle of June, that idea had so far gained general acceptance that C. C. Danley, speaking for the Arkansas Military Board, urged President Davis "to meet

---

[8] *Official Records*, vol. liii, supplement, 679.

[9] The name of Montgomery was not one for even Indians to conjure with. James Montgomery was the most notorious of bushwhackers. For an account of some of his earlier adventures, see Spring, *Kansas*, 241, 247-250, and for a characterization of the man himself, Robinson, *Kansas Conflict*, 435.

[10] *Official Records*, vol. liii, supplement, 682.

[11] Snead, *Fight for Missouri*, 229-230.

the exigent necessities of the State" by sending a second general officer there, who should command in the northeastern part.[12]

McCulloch's relations with leading Confederates in Arkansas seem to have been, from the first, in the highest degree friendly, even cordial, and it is more than likely that, aside from his unwillingness to offend the neutrality-loving Cherokees, the best explanation for his eventual readiness to make the defence of Arkansas his chief concern, instead of merely a means to the accomplishment of his original task, may be found in that fact.   On the twenty-second of May, the Arkansas State Convention instructed Brigadier-general N. Bart Pearce, then in command of the state troops, to coöperate with the Confederate commander "to the full extent of his ability"[13] and, on the twenty-eighth of the same month, the Arkansas Military Board invited that same person, who, of course, was Ben McCulloch, to assume command himself of the Arkansas local forces.[14]   Sympathetic understanding of this variety, so early established, was bound to produce good results and McCulloch henceforth identified himself most thoroughly with Confederate interests in the state in which he was, by dint of untoward circumstances, obliged to bide his time.

It was far otherwise as respected relations between McCulloch and the Missouri leaders.   McCulloch had little or no tolerance for the rough-and-ready methods of men like Claiborne Jackson and Sterling Price.   He regarded their plans as impractical, chimerical, and their warfare as after the guerrilla order, too much like

---

[12] *Official Records*, vol. liii, supplement, 698-699.

[13] — *Ibid.*, 687.

[14] — *Ibid.*, 691.

that to which Missourians and Kansans had accustomed themselves during the period of border conflict, following the passage of the Kansas-Nebraska Bill. McCulloch himself was a man of system. He believed in organization that made for efficiency. Just prior to the Battle of Wilson's Creek, he put himself on record as strongly opposed to allowing unarmed men and camp followers to infest his ranks, demoralizing them.[15] It was not to be expected, therefore, that there could ever be much in common between him and Sterling Price. For a brief period, it is true, the two men did apparently act in fullest harmony; but it was when the safety of Price's own state, Missouri, was the thing directly in hand. That was in early August of 1861. Price put himself and his command subject to McCulloch's orders.[16] The result was the successful engagement, August 10 at Wilson's Creek, on Missouri soil. On the fourteenth of the same month, Price reassumed control of the Missouri State Guard[17] and, from that time on, he and McCulloch drifted farther and farther apart; but, as their aims were so entirely different, it was not to be wondered at.

Undoubtedly, all would have been well had McCulloch been disposed to make the defence of Missouri his only aim. Magnanimity was asked of him such as the Missouri leaders never so much as contemplated showing in return. It seems never to have occurred to either Jackson or Price that coöperation might, perchance, involve such an exchange of courtesies as would require Price to lend a hand in some project that McCulloch might devise for the well-being of his own particular

[15] *Official Records*, vol. liii, supplement, 721.
[16] — *Ibid.*, 720.
[17] — *Ibid.*, 727.

charge. The assistance was eventually asked for and refused, refused upon the ground, familiar in United States history, that it would be impossible to get the Missouri troops to cross the state line. Of course, Price's conduct was not without extenuation. His position was not identical with McCulloch's. His force was a state force, McCulloch's a Confederate, or a national. Besides, Missouri had yet to be gained, officially, for the Confederacy. She expected secession states and the Confederacy itself to force the situation for her. And, furthermore, she was in far greater danger of invasion than was Arkansas. The Kansans were her implacable and dreaded foes and Arkansas had none like them to fear.

In reality, the seat of all the trouble between McCulloch and Price lay in particularism, a phase of state rights, and, in its last analysis, provincialism. Now particularism was especially pronounced and especially pernicious in the middle southwest. Missouri had always more than her share of it. Her politicians were impregnated by it. They were interested in their own locality exclusively and seemed quite incapable of taking any broad survey of events that did not immediately affect themselves or their own limited concerns. In the issue between McCulloch and Price, this was all too apparent. The politicians complained unceasingly of McCulloch's neglect of Missouri and, finally, taking their case to headquarters, represented to President Davis that the best interests of the Confederate cause in their state were being glaringly sacrificed by McCulloch's too literal interpretation of his official instructions, in the strict observance of which he was keeping close to the Indian boundary.

President Davis had personally no great liking for

Price and certainly none for his peculiar method of fighting. Some people thought him greatly prejudiced[18] against Price and, in the first instance, perhaps, on nothing more substantial than the fact that Price was not a Westpointer.[19] It would be nearer the truth to say that Davis gauged the western situation pretty accurately and knew where the source of trouble lay. That he did gauge the situation and that accurately is indicated by a suggestion of his, made in early December, for sending out Colonel Henry Heth of Virginia to command the Arkansas and Missouri divisions in combination.[20] Heth had no local attachments in the region and "had not been connected with any of the troops on that line of operations."[21] Unfortunately, for subsequent events his nomination[22] was not confirmed.

Two days later, December 5, 1861, General McCulloch was granted[23] permission to proceed to Richmond, there to explain in person, as he had long wanted to do, all matters in controversy between him and Price. On the third of January, 1862, the Confederate Congress called[24] for information on the subject, doubtless under pressure of political importunity. The upshot of it all was, the organization of the Trans-Mississippi District of Department No. 2 and the appointment of Earl Van Dorn as major-general to command it. Whether or no, he was the choice[25] of General A. S. Johnston, department commander, his appointment bid fair, at the

---

[18] *Official Records*, vol. liii, supplement, 816-817.
[19] — *Ibid.*, 762.
[20] — *Ibid.*, vol. viii, 725.
[21] — *Ibid.*, 701.
[22] Wright, *General Officers of the Confederate Army*, 33, 67.
[23] *Official Records*, vol. viii, 702.
[24] *Journal of the Congress of the Confederate States*, vol. i, 637.
[25] Formby, *American Civil War*, 129.

time it was made, to put an end to all local disputes and to give Missouri the attention she craved. The ordnance department of the Confederacy had awakened to a sense of the value of the lead mines [26] at Granby and Van Dorn was instructed especially to protect them.[27] His appointment, moreover, anticipated an early encounter with the Federals in Missouri. In preparation for the struggle that all knew was impending, it was of transcendent importance that one mind and one interest should control, absolutely.

The Trans-Mississippi District would appear to have been constituted and its limits to have been defined without adequate reference to existing arrangements. The limits were, "That part of the State of Louisiana north of Red River, the Indian Territory west of Arkansas, and the States of Arkansas and Missouri, excepting therefrom the tract of country east of the Saint Francis, bordering on the Mississippi River, from the mouth of the Saint Francis to Scott County, Missouri. . ."[28] Van Dorn, in assuming command of the district, January 29, 1862, issued orders in such form that Indian Territory was listed last among the limits[29] and it was a previous arrangement affecting Indian Territory that was most ignored in the whole scheme of organization.

It will be remembered that, in November of the preceding year, the Department of Indian Territory had been created and Brigadier-general Albert Pike assigned to the same.[30] His authority was not explicitly

---

[26] *Official Records,* vol. liii, supplement, 767, 774.

[27] Van Dorn's protection, if given, was given to little purpose; for the mines were soon abandoned [Britton, *Memoirs of the Rebellion on the Border, 1863,* 120].

[28] *Official Records,* vol. viii, 734.

[29] — *Ibid.,* 745.

[30] — *Ibid.,* 690.

superseded by that which later clothed Van Dorn and yet his department was now to be absorbed by a military district, which was itself merely a section of another department. The name and organization of the Department of Indian Territory remained to breed confusion, disorder, and serious discontent at a slightly subsequent time. Of course, since the ratification of the treaties of alliance with the tribes, there was no question to be raised concerning the status of Indian Territory as definitely a possession of the Southern Confederacy. Indeed, it had, in a way, been counted as such, actual and prospective, ever since the enactment of the marque and reprisal law of May 6, 1861.[31]

Albert Pike, having accepted the appointment of department commander in Indian Territory under somewhat the same kind of a protest—professed consciousness of unfitness for the post—as he had accepted the earlier one of commissioner, diplomatic, to the tribes, lost no time in getting into touch with his new duties. There was much to be attended to before he could proceed west. His appointment had come and had been accepted in November. Christmas was now near at hand and he had yet to render an account of his mission of treaty-making. In late December, he sent in his official report[32] to President Davis and, that done, held himself in readiness to respond to any interpellating call that the Provincial Congress might see fit to make. The intervals of time, free from devotion to the completion of the older task, were spent by him in close attention to the preliminary details of the newer, in securing funds and in purchasing supplies and equipment

---

[31] Richardson, *Messages and Papers of the Confederacy,* vol. i, 105.

[32] The official report of Commissioner Pike, in manuscript, and bearing his signature, is to be found in the Adjutant-general's office of the U.S. War Department.

generally, also in selecting a site for his headquarters. By command of Secretary of War, Judah P. Benjamin, Major N. B. Pearce[33] was made chief commissary of subsistence for Indian Territory and Western Arkansas and Major G. W. Clarke,[34] depot quartermaster. In the sequel of events, both appointments came to be of a significance rather unusual.

The site chosen for department headquarters was a place situated near the junction of the Verdigris and Arkansas Rivers and not far from Fort Gibson.[35] The fortifications erected there received the name of Cantonment Davis and upon them, in spite of Pike's decidedly moderate estimate in the beginning, the Confederacy was said by a contemporary to have spent "upwards of a million dollars."[36] In view of the ostensible object of the very formation of the department and of Pike's appointment to its command, the defence of Indian Territory, and, in view of the existing location of enemy troops, challenging that defence, the selection of the site was a reasonably wise one; but, as subsequent pages will reveal, the commander did not retain it long as his headquarters. Troubles came thick and fast upon him and he had barely reached Cantonment Davis before they began. His delay in reaching that place, which he did do, February 25,[37] was caused by various occurrences that made it difficult for him to get his materials together, his funds and the like. The very difficulties presaged disaster.

Pike's great purpose – and, perhaps, it would be no exaggeration to say, his only purpose – throughout the

[33] *Official Records,* vol. liii, supplement, 764.
[34] — *Ibid,* 770.
[35] — *Ibid,* 764.
[36] Britton, *Memoirs of the Rebellion on the Border,* 72.
[37] *Official Records,* vol. viii, 286.

full extent of his active connection with the Confederacy was to save to that Confederacy the Indian Territory. The Indian occupants in and for themselves, unflattering as it may seem to them for historical investigators to have to admit it, were not objects of his solicitude except in so far as they contributed to his real and ultimate endeavor. He never at any time or under any circumstances advocated their use generally as soldiers outside of Indian Territory in regular campaign work and offensively.[38] As guerrillas he would have used them.[39] He would have sent them on predatory expeditions into Kansas or any other near-by state where pillaging would have been profitable or retaliatory; but never as an organized force, subject to the rules of civilized warfare because fully cognizant of them.[40] It is doubtful if he would ever have allowed them, had he consulted only his own inclination, to so much as cross the line except under stress of an attack from without. He would never have sanctioned their joining an unprovoked invading force. In the treaties

---

[38] The provision in the treaties to the effect that the alliance consummated between the Indians and the Confederate government was to be both offensive and defensive must not be taken too literally or be construed so broadly as to militate against this fact: for to its truth Pike, when in distress later on and accused of leading a horde of tomahawking villains, repeatedly bore witness. The keeping back of a foe, bent upon regaining Indian Territory or of marauding, might well be said to partake of the character of offensive warfare and yet not be that in intent or in the ordinary acceptation of the term. Everything would have to depend upon the point of view.

[39] A restricted use of the Indians in offensive guerrilla action Pike would doubtless have permitted and justified. Indeed, he seems even to have recommended it in the first days of his interest in the subject of securing Indian Territory. No other interpretation can possibly be given to his suggestion that a battalion be raised from Indians that more strictly belonged to Kansas [*Official Records*, vol. iii, 581]. It is also conceivable that the force he had reference to in his letter to Benjamin, November 27, 1861 [*ibid.*, vol. viii, 698] was to be, in part, Indian.

[40] Harrell, *Confederate Military History*, vol. x, 121-122.

which he negotiated he pledged distinctly and explicitly the opposite course of action, unless, indeed, the Indian consent were first obtained.[41]   The Indian troops, however and wherever raised under the provisions of those treaties, were expected by Pike to constitute, primarily, a home guard and nothing more.   If by chance it should happen that, in performing their function as a home guard, they should have to cross their own boundary in order to expel or to punish an intruder, well and good; but their intrinsic character as something resembling a police patrol could not be deemed thereby affected.   Moreover, Pike did not believe that acting alone they could even be a thoroughly adequate home force.   He, therefore, urged again and again that their contingent shoud be supplemented by a white force and by one sufficiently large to give dignity and poise and self-restraint to the whole, when both forces were combined, as they always ought to be.[42]

At the time of Pike's assumption of his ill-defined command, or within a short period thereafter, the Indian force in the pay of the Confederacy and subject to his orders may be roughly placed at four full regiments and some miscellaneous troops.[43]   The dispersion [44] of Colonel John Drew's Cherokees, when about to attack Opoeth-le-yo-ho-la, forced a slight reörganization and that, taken in connection with the accretions to the command that came in the interval before the Pea Ridge campaign brought the force approximately to four full

---

[41] In illustration of this, take the statement of the Creek Treaty, article xxxvi.

[42] Aside from the early requests for white troops, which were antecedent to his own appointment as brigadier-general, Pike's insistence upon the need for the same can be vouched for by reference to his letter to R. W. Johnson, January 5, 1862 [*Official Records,* vol. liii, supplement, 795-796].

[43] Pike to Benjamin, November 27, 1861, *ibid,* vol. viii, 697.

[44] *Official Records,* vol. viii, 8, 17-18.

regiments, two battalions, and some detached companies. The four regiments were, the First Regiment Choctaw and Chickasaw Mounted Rifles under Colonel Douglas H. Cooper, the First Creek Regiment under Colonel D. N. McIntosh, the First Regiment Cherokee Mounted Rifles under Colonel John Drew, and the Second Regiment Cherokee Mounted Rifles under Colonel Stand Watie. The battalions were, the Choctaw and Chickasaw and the Creek and Seminole, the latter under Lieutenant-colonel Chilly McIntosh and Major John Jumper.

Major-general Earl Van Dorn formally assumed command of the newly created Trans-Mississippi District of Department No. 2, January 29, 1862.[45] He was then at Little Rock, Arkansas. By February 6, he had moved up to Jacksonport and, a week or so later, to Pocahontas, where his slowly-assembling army was to rendezvous. His call for troops had already gone forth and was being promptly answered,[46] requisition having been made upon all the state units within the district, Missouri, Arkansas, Louisiana, also Texas. Indian Territory, through Pike[47] and his subordinates,[48] was yet to be communicated with; but Van Dorn had, at the moment, no other plan in view for Indian troops than to use them to advantage as a means of defence and as a corps of observation.[49] His immediate object, according to his own showing and according to the circumstances that had brought about the formation of the district, was to protect Arkansas[50] against

---

[45] *Official Records*, vol. viii, 745-746.

[46] — *Ibid.*, vol. liii, supplement, 776-779, 783-785, 790, 793-794.

[47] — *Ibid.*, vol. viii, 749, 763-764.

[48] — *Ibid.*, 764-765.

[49] Van Dorn to Price, February 14, 1862, *ibid.*, 750.

[50] Arkansas seemed, at the time, to be but feebly protected. R. W. Johnson deprecated the calling of Arkansas troops eastward. They were

invasion and to relieve Missouri; his plan of operations was to conduct a spring campaign in the latter state, "to attempt St. Louis," as he himself put it, and to drive the Federals out; his ulterior motive may have been and, in the light of subsequent events, probably was, to effect a diversion for General A. S. Johnston; but, if that were really so, it was not, at the time, divulged or so much as hinted at.

Ostensibly, the great object that Van Dorn had in mind was the relief of Missouri. And he may have dreamed, that feat accomplished, that it would be possible to carry the war into the enemy's country beyond the Ohio; but, alas, it was his misfortune at this juncture to be called upon to realise, to his great discomfiture, the truth of Robert Burns' homely philosophy,

> The best-laid schemes o' mice and men
> Gang aft a-gley.

His own schemes and plans were all rendered utterly futile by the unexpected movement of the Federal forces from Rolla, to which safe place, it will be remembered, they had been drawn back by order of General Hunter. They were now advancing by forced marches via Springfield into northwestern Arkansas and were driving before them the Confederates under McCulloch and Price.

The Federal forces comprised four huge divisions and were led by Brigadier-general Samuel R. Curtis. Towards the end of the previous December, on Christmas Day in fact, Curtis had been given "command of the Southwestern District of Missouri, including the

---

needed at home, not only for the defence of Arkansas, but for that of the adjoining territory [*Official Records,* vol. liii, supplement, 781-782]. There were, in fact, only two Arkansas regiments absent and they were guarding the Mississippi River [*ibid,* 786]. By the middle of February, or thereabouts, Price and McCulloch were in desperate straits and were steadily "falling back before a superior force to the Boston Mountains" [*ibid.,* 787].

country south of the Osage and west of the Meramec River."[51]   Under orders of November 9, the old Department of the West, of which Frémont had had charge and subsequently Hunter, but for only a brief period, had been reorganized and divided into two distinct departments, the Department of Missouri with Halleck in command and the Department of Kansas with Hunter.   Curtis, at the time when he made his memorable advance movement from Rolla was, therefore, serving under Halleck.

In furtherance of Van Dorn's original plan, General Pike had been ordered to march with all speed and join forces with the main army.   At the time of the issuance of the order, he seems to have offered no objections to taking his Indians out of their own territory. Disaster had not yet overtaken them or him and he had not yet met with the injustice that was afterwards his regular lot.   If his were regarded as more or less of a puppet command, he was not yet aware of it and, oblivious of all scorn felt for Indian soldiers, kept his eye single on the assistance he was to render in the accomplishment of Van Dorn's object.   It was anything but easy, however, for him to move with dispatch.   He had difficulty in getting such of his brigade as was Indian and as had collected at Cantonment Davis, a Choctaw and Chickasaw battalion and the First Creek Regiment, to stir.   They had not been paid their money and had not been furnished with arms and clothing as promised.   Pike had the necessary funds with him, but time would be needed in which to distribute them, and the order had been for him to move promptly.   It was something much more easily said than done.   Nevertheless, he did what he could, paid outright the Choctaws and Chickasaws, a performance that occupied

---

[51] *Official Records*, vol. liii, supplement, vol. viii, 462.

three precious days, and agreed to pay McIntosh's Creek regiment at the Illinois River. To keep that promise he tarried at Park Hill one day, expecting there to be overtaken by additional Choctaws and Chickasaws who had been left behind at Fort Gibson. When they did not appear, he went forward towards Evansville and upward to Cincinnati, a small town on the Arkansas side of the Cherokee line. There his Indian force was augmented by Stand Watie's regiment[52] of Cherokees and at Smith's Mill by John

---

[52] Watie's regiment of Cherokees was scarcely in either marching or fighting trim. The following letter from John Ross to Pike, which is number nine in the John Ross *Papers* in the Indian Office, is elucidative. It is a copy used in the action against John Ross at the close of the war. The italics indicate underscorings that were probably not in the original.

EXECUTIVE DEPARTMENT, PARK HILL, Feby 25th, 1862.
To BRIG. GEN^L. A. PIKE, Com^dy Indian Department.

SIR: I have deemed it my duty to address you on the present occasion— You have doubtless ere this received my communication enclosing the action of the National Council with regard to the final ratification of our Treaty— Col. Drew's Regiment promptly took up the line of march on the receipt of your order from Fort Smith towards Fayetteville. *I accompanied the Troops some 12 miles East of this and I am happy to assure you in the most confident manner that in my opinion this Regiment will not fail to do their whole duty, whenever the Conflict with the common Enemy shall take place.* There are so many conflicting reports as to your whereabouts and consequently much interest is felt by the People to know where the Head Qrs. of your military operations will be established during the present emergencies— *I had intended going up to see the Troops of our Regiment; also to visit the Head Qrs of the Army at Cane Hill in view of affording every aid in any manner within the reach of my power to repel the Enemy.* But I am sorry to say I have been dissuaded from going at present in consequence of some unwarrantable conduct on the part of many *base, reckless and unprincipled persons belonging to Watie's Regiment who are under no subordination or restraint of their leaders in domineering over and trampling upon the rights of peaceable and unoffending citizens.* I have at all times in the most unequivocal manner assured the People that you will not only promptly discountenance, but will take steps to put a stop to such proceedings for the protection of their persons and property and to *redress their wrongs*— This is not the time for *crimination* and *recrimination*; at a proper time *I have certain specific complaints to report for your investigation.* Pardon me for again reiterating that

Drew's.[53] The Cherokees had been in much confusion all winter. Civil war within their nation impended.[54] None the less, Pike, assuming that all would be well when the call for action came, had ordered all the Cherokee and Creek regiments to hurry to the help of McCulloch.[55] He had done this upon the first intimation of the Federal advance. The Cherokees had proceeded only so far, the Creeks not at all, and the main body of the Choctaws and Chickasaws, into whose minds some unscrupulous merchants had instilled mercenary motives and the elements of discord generally, were lingering far in the background. Pike's white force was, moreover, ridiculously small, some Texas cavalry, dignified by him as collectively a squadron, Captain O. G. Welch in command. There had as yet not been even a pretense of giving him the three regiments of white men earlier asked for. Toward the close of the afternoon of March 6, Pike "came up with the rear of McCulloch's division,"[56] which proved to be the very division he was to follow, but he was one day late for the fray.

The Battle of Pea Ridge, in its preliminary stages, was already being fought. It was a three day fight, counting the skirmish at Bentonville on the sixth between General Franz Sigel's detachment and General Sterling Price's advance guard as the work of the first day.[57] The real battle comprised the engagement at

the mass of the People *are all right in Sentiment for the support of the Treaty of Alliance with the Confederate States.* I shall be happy to hear from you — I have the honor to be your ob^t Servt

JOHN ROSS, *Prin^l Chief*, Cherokee Nation.

[53] Pike's Report, March 14, 1862, *Official Records*, vol. viii, 286-292.

[54] James McIntosh to S. Cooper, January 4, 1862, *ibid.*, 732; D. H. Cooper to Pike, February 10, 1862, *ibid.*, vol. xiii, 896.

[55] — *Ibid.*, 819.

[56] — *Ibid.*, vol. viii, 287.

[57] — *Ibid.*, 208-215, 304-306.

Leetown on the seventh and that at Elkhorn Tavern[58] on the eighth. At Leetown, Pike's Cherokee contingent[59] played what he, in somewhat quixotic fashion, perhaps, chose to regard as a very important part. The Indians, then as always, were chiefly pony-mounted, "entirely undisciplined," as the term discipline is usually understood, and "armed very indifferently with common rifles and ordinary shot-guns."[60] The ponies, in the end, proved fleet of foot, as was to have been expected, and, at one stage of the game, had to be tethered in the rear while their masters fought from the vantage-ground of trees.[61] The Indian's most effective work was done, throughout, under cover of the woods. Indians, as Pike well knew, could never be induced to face shells in the open. It was he who advised their climbing the trees and he did it without discounting, in the slightest, their innate bravery.[62] There came a time, too, when he gave countenance to another of their

---

[58] The Elkhorn Tavern engagement is sometimes referred to, and most appropriately, as the Sugar Creek [Phisterer, *Statistical Record*, 95]. Colonel Eugene A. Carr of the Third Illinois Cavalry, commanding the Fourth Division of Curtis's army, described the tavern itself as "situated on the west side of the Springfield and Fayetteville road, at the head of a gorge known as Cross Timber Hollow (the head of Sugar Creek) . . ." [*Official Records*, vol. viii, 258]. "Sugar Creek Hollow," wrote Curtis, "extends for miles, a gorge, with rough precipitate sides . . ." [*ibid.*, 589]. It was there the closing scenes of the great battle were enacted.

[59] The practice, indulged in by both the Federals and the Confederates, of greatly overestimating the size of the enemy force was resorted to even in connection with the Indians. Pike gave the number of his whole command as about a thousand men, Indians and whites together [*Official Records*, vol. viii, 288; xiii, 820] notwithstanding that he had led Van Dorn to expect that he would have a force of "about 8,000 or 9,000 men and three batteries of artillery" [*ibid.*, vol. viii, 749]. General Curtis surmised that Pike contributed five regiments [*ibid.*, 196] and Wiley Britton, who had excellent opportunity of knowing better because he had access to the records of both sides, put the figures at "three regiments of Indians and two regiments of Texas cavalry" [*Civil War on the Border*, vol. i, 245].

[60] *Official Records*, vol. xiii, 819.

[61] —*Ibid.*, vol. viii, 288.

[62] —*Ibid.*

peculiarities. He allowed Colonel Drew's men to fight in a way that was "their own fashion," [63] with bow and arrow and with tomahawk. [64] This, as was only meet it should, called down upon him and them the opprobrium of friends and foes alike. [65] The Indian warwhoop was indulged in, of itself enough to terrify. It was hideous.

The service that the Cherokees rendered at different times during the two days action was not, however, to be despised, even though not sufficiently conspicuous to be deemed worthy of comment by Van Dorn. [66] At Leetown, with the aid of a few Texans, they managed to get possession of a battery and to hold it against repeated endeavors of the Federals to regain. The death of McCulloch and of McIntosh made Pike the ranking officer in his part of the field. It fell to him to rally

[63] *Official Records*, vol. viii, 289.

[64] — *Ibid.*, 195.

[65] The northern press took up the matter and the New York *Tribune* was particularly virulent against Pike. In its issue of March 27, 1862, it published the following in bitter sarcasm:

"The Albert Pike who led the Aboriginal Corps of Tomahawkers and Scalpers at the battle of Pea Ridge, formerly kept school in Fairhaven, Mass., where he was indicted for playing the part of Squeers, and cruelly beating and starving a boy in his family. He escaped by some hocus-pocus law, and emigrated to the West, where the violence of his nature has been admirably enhanced. As his name indicates, he is a ferocious fish, and has fought duels enough to qualify himself to be a leader of savages. We suppose that upon the recent occasion, he got himself up in good style, war-paint, nose-ring, and all. This new Pontiac is also a poet, and wrote 'Hymns to the Gods' in *Blackwood;* but he has left Jupiter, Juno, and the rest, and betaken himself to the culture of the Great Spirit, or rather of two great spirits, whisky being the second."

[66] Van Dorn did not make his detailed official report of this battle until the news had leaked out that the Indians had mangled the bodies of the dead and committed other atrocities. He was probably then desirous of being as silent as he dared be concerning Indian participation, since he, in virtue of his being chief in command, was the person mainly responsible for it. In October of the preceding year, McCulloch had favored using the Indians against Kansas [*Official Records*, vol. iii, 719, 721]. Cooper objected strongly to their being kept "at home" [*ibid.*, 614] and one of the leading chiefs insisted that they did not intend to use the scalping knife [*ibid.*, 625].

McCulloch's broken army and with it to join Van
Dorn. On the eighth, Colonel Watie's men under
orders from Van Dorn took position on the high ridges
where they could watch the movements of the enemy
and give timely notice of any attempt to turn the Confederate left flank. Colonel Drew's regiment, meanwhile, not having received the word passed along the
line to move forward, remained in the woods near Leetown, the last in the field. Subsequently, finding themselves deserted, they drew back towards Camp Stephens,
where they were soon joined by "General Cooper,
with his regiment and battalion of Choctaws and Chickasaws, and" by "Colonel McIntosh with 200 men of his
regiment of Creeks."[67] The delinquent wayfarers
were both fortunate and unfortunate in thus tardily
arriving upon the scene. They had missed the fight
but they had also missed the temptation to revert to
the savagery that was soon to bring fearful ignominy
upon their neighbors. To the very last of the Pea
Ridge engagement, Stand Watie's men were active.
They covered the retreat of the main army, to a certain
extent. They were mostly half-breeds and, so far as
can be definitely ascertained, were entirely guiltless of
the atrocities charged against the others.

General Pike gave the permission to fight "in their
own fashion" specifically to the First Cherokee Mounted Rifles, who were, for the most part, full-blooded Indians; but he later confessed that, in his treaty negotiations with the tribes, they had generally stipulated that
they should, if they fought at all, be allowed to fight
as they knew how.[68] Yet they probably did not mean,
thereby, to commit atrocities and the Cherokee National Council lost no time, after the Indian shortcomings

[67] *Official Records*, vol. viii, 292.
[68] — *Ibid.*, vol. xiii, 819.

at the Battle of Pea Ridge had become known, in putting itself on record as standing opposed to the sort of thing that had occurred,

> *Resolved,* That in the opinion of the National Council, the war now existing between the said United States and the Confederate States and their Indian allies should be conducted on the most humane principles which govern the usages of war among civilized nations, and that it be and is earnestly recommended to the troops of this nation in the service of the Confederate States to avoid any acts toward captured or fallen foes that would be incompatible with such usages. [69]

The atrocities committed by the Indians became almost immediately a matter for correspondence between the opposing commanders. The Federals charged mutilation of dead bodies on the battle-field and the tomahawking and scalping of prisoners. The Confederates recriminated as against persons "alleged to be Germans." The case involving the Indians was reported to the joint committee of Congress on the *Conduct of the Present War*;[70] but at least one piece of evidence was not, at that time, forthcoming, a piece that, in a certain sense, might be taken to exonerate the whites. It came to the knowledge of General Blunt during the summer and was the Indians' own confession. It bore only indirectly upon the actual atrocities but showed that the red men were quite equal to making their own plans in fighting and were not to be relied upon to do things decently and in order. Drew's men, when they deserted the Confederates after the skirmish of July third at Locust Grove, confided to the Federals the intelligence "that the killing of the white rebels by the Indians in" the Pea Ridge "fight was determined

---

[69] *Official Records,* vol. xiii, 826.

[70] By vote of the committee, General Curtis had been instructed to furnish information on the subject of the employment of Indians by the Confederates [*Journal,* 92].

upon before they went into battle." [71]   Presumptively, if the Cherokees could plot to kill their own allies, they could be found despicable enough and cruel enough to mutilate the dead, [72] were the chance given them and that without any direction, instruction, or encouragement from white men being needed.

The Confederate defeat at Pea Ridge was decisive and, as far as Van Dorn's idea of relieving Missouri was concerned, fatally conclusive. As early as the twenty-first of February, Beauregard had expressed a wish to have him east of the Mississippi [73] and March had not yet expired before Van Dorn was writing in such a way as to elicit the consummation of the wish. The Federals were in occupation of the northern part of Arkansas; but Van Dorn was very confident they would not be able to subsist there long or "do much harm in the west."   In his opinion, therefore, it was incumbent upon the Confederates, instead of dividing their strength between the east and the west, to concentrate on the saving of the Mississippi. [74]   To all appearances, it was there that the situation was most critical. In due time, came the order for Van Dorn to repair eastward and to take with him all the troops that might be found available.

The completeness of Curtis's victory, the loss to the Southerners, by death or capture, of some of their best-loved and ablest commanders, McCulloch, McIntosh, Hébert, and the nature of the country through which the Federals pursued their fleeing forces, to say nothing of the miscellaneous and badly-trained character of

---

[71] *Official Records,* vol. xiii, 486.

[72] The same charge was made against the Indians who fought at Wilson's Creek [Leavenworth *Daily Conservative,* August 24, 1861].

[73] Roman, *Military Operations of General Beauregard,* vol. i, 240.

[74] *Official Records,* vol. viii, 796.

those forces, to which, by the way, Van Dorn ascribed[75] much of his recent ill-success, all helped to make the retirement of the Confederates from the Pea Ridge battle-ground pretty much of a helter-skelter affair. From all accounts, the Indians conducted themselves as well as the best. The desire of everybody was to get to a place of safety and that right speedily. Colonel Watie and his regiment made their way to Camp Stephens,[76] near which place the baggage train had been left[77] and where Cooper and Drew with their men had found refuge already. Some two hundred of Watie's Indians were detailed to help take ammunition back to the main army.[78] The baggage train moved on to Elm Springs, the remainder of the Indians, under Cooper, assisting in protecting it as far as that place.[79] At Walnut Grove, the Watie detail, having failed to deliver the ammunition because of the departure of the army prior to their arrival, rejoined their comrades and all moved on to Cincinnati, where Pike, who with a few companions had wandered several days among the mountains, came up with them.[80]

In Van Dorn's calculations for troops that should accompany him east or follow in his wake, the Indians had no place. Before his own plans took final shape and while he was still arranging for an Army of the West, his orders for the Indians were, that they should make their way back as best they could to their own country and there operate "to cut off trains, annoy the enemy in his marches, and to prevent him as far as possible from supplying his troops from Missouri and

---

[75] *Official Records*, vol. viii, 282.

[76] — *Ibid.*, 291.

[77] — *Ibid.*, 317.

[78] — *Ibid.*, 318.

[79] — *Ibid.*; Britton, *Civil War on the Border*, vol. i, 273.

[80] *Official Records*, vol. viii, 292.

Kansas." [81]   A little later, but still anterior to Van Dorn's summons east, more minute particulars of the programme were addressed to Pike.   Maury wrote,

> The general commanding has decided to march with his army against the enemy now invading the northeastern part of the State.   Upon you, therefore, will devolve the necessity of impeding his advance into this region.   It is not expected that you will give battle to a large force, but by felling trees, burning bridges, removing supplies of forage and subsistence, attacking his trains, stampeding his animals, cutting off his detachments, and other similar means, you will be able materially to harass his army and protect this region of country.   You must endeavor by every means to maintain yourself in the Territory independent of this army.   In case only of absolute necessity you may move southward.   If the enemy threatens to march through the Indian Territory or descend the Arkansas River you may call on troops from Southwestern Arkansas and Texas to rally to your aid.   You may reward your Indian troops by giving them such stores as you may think proper when they make captures from the enemy, but you will please endeavor to restrain them from committing any barbarities upon the wounded, prisoners, or dead who may fall into their hands. You may purchase your supplies of subsistence from wherever you can most advantageously do so.   You will draw your ammunition from Little Rock or from New Orleans via Red River.   Please communicate with the general commanding when practicable. [82]

It was an elaborate programme but scarcely a noble one.   Its note of selfishness sounded high.   The Indians were simply to be made to serve the ends of the white men.   Their methods of warfare were regarded as distinctly inferior.   Pea Ridge was, in fact, the first and last time that they were allowed to participate in the war on a big scale.   Henceforth, they were rarely ever anything more than scouts and skirmishers and that was all they were really fitted to be.

---

[81] *Official Records*, vol. viii, 282, 790; vol. liii, supplement, 796.
[82] — *Ibid.*, vol. viii, 795-796.

II. LANE'S BRIGADE AND THE INCEPTION OF THE INDIAN

The Indian Expedition had its beginnings, fatefully or otherwise, in "Lane's Kansas Brigade." On January 29, 1861, President Buchanan signed the bill for the admission of Kansas into the Union and the matter about which there had been so much of bitter controversy was at last professedly settled; but, alas, for the peace of the border, the radicals, the extremists, the fanatics, call them what one may, who had been responsible for the controversy and for its bitterness, were still unsettled. James Lane was chief among them. His was a turbulent spirit and it permitted its owner no cessation from strife. With President Lincoln's first call for volunteers, April 15, 1861, Lane's martial activities began. Within three days, he had gathered together a company of warriors,[83] the nucleus, psychologically speaking, of what was to be his notorious, jayhawking, marauding brigade. His enthusiasm was infectious. It communicated itself to reflective men like Carl Schurz[84] and was probably the secret of Lane's

[83] John Hay records in his *Diary*, "The White House is turned into barracks. Jim Lane marshaled his Kansas warriors to-day at Willard's and placed them at the disposal of Major Hunter, who turned them to-night into the East Room. It is a splendid company — worthy such an armory. Besides the Western Jayhawkers it comprises some of the best *material* in the East. Senator Pomeroy and old Anthony Bleecker stood shoulder to shoulder in the ranks. Jim Lane walked proudly up and down the ranks with a new sword that the Major had given him. The Major has made me his aid, and I labored under some uncertainty, as to whether I should speak to privates or not." — THAYER, *Life and Letters of John Hay*, vol. i, 92.

[84] It would seem to have communicated itself to Carl Schurz, although Schurz, in his *Reminiscences*, makes no definite admission of the fact. Hay

mysterious influence with the temperate, humane, just, and so very much more magnanimous Lincoln, who, in the first days of the war, as in the later and the last, had his hours of discouragement and deep depression. For dejection of any sort, the wild excitement and boundless confidence of a zealot like Lane must have been somewhat of an antidote, also a stimulant.

The first Kansas state legislature convened March 26, 1861, and set itself at once to work to put the new machinery of government into operation. After much political wire-pulling that involved the promise of spoils to come,[85] James H. Lane and Samuel C. Pomeroy[86] were declared to be elected United States senators, the term of office of each to begin with the first session of the thirty-seventh congress. That session was

---

says, "Going into Nicolay's room this morning, C. Schurz, and J. Lane were sitting. Jim was at the window, filling his soul with gall by steady telescopic contemplation of a Secession flag impudently flaunting over a roof in Alexandria. 'Let me tell you,' said he to the elegant Teuton, 'we have got to whip these scoundrels like hell, C. Schurz. They did a good thing stoning our men at Baltimore and shooting away the flag at Sumter. It has set the great North a-howling for blood, and they'll have it.'

" 'I heard,' said Schurz, 'you preached a sermon to your men yesterday.'

" 'No, sir! this is not time for preaching. When I went to Mexico there were four preachers in my regiment. In less than a week I issued orders for them all to stop preaching and go to playing cards. In a month or so, they were the biggest devils and best fighters I had.'

"An hour afterwards, C. Schurz told me he was going home to arm his clansmen for the wars. He has obtained three months' leave of absence from his diplomatic duties, and permission to raise a cavalry regiment. He will make a wonderful land pirate; bold, quick, brilliant, and reckless. He will be hard to control and difficult to direct. Still, we shall see. He is a wonderful man." — THAYER, *Life and Letters of John Hay,* vol. i, 102-103.

[85] In Connelley's *James Henry Lane, the "Grim Chieftain" of Kansas,* the following is quoted as coming from Lane himself:

"Of the fifty-six men in the Legislature who voted for Jim Lane, five-and-forty now wear shoulder-straps. Doesn't Jim Lane look out for his friends?"

[86] John Brown's rating of Pomeroy, as given by Stearns in his *Life and Public Services of George Luther Stearns,* 133-134, would show him to have been a considerably less pugnacious individual than was Lane.

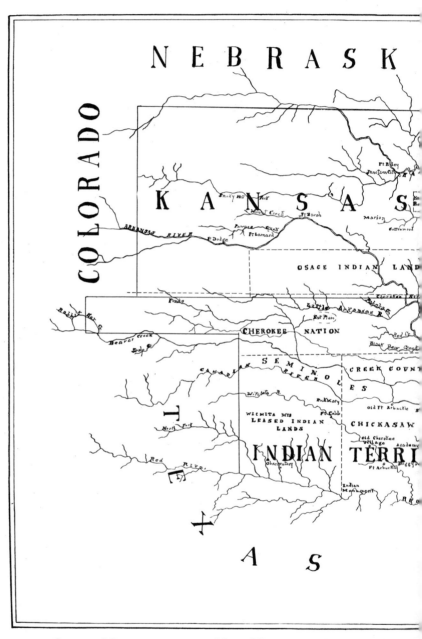

SKETCH MAP SHOWING THE MAIN THEATRE OF BORDER WARFAR

AND THE LOCATION OF TRIBES WITHIN THE INDIAN COUNTRY

the extra one, called for July, 1861. Immediately, a difficulty arose due to the fact that, subsequent to his election to the senatorship and in addition thereto, Lane had accepted a colonelcy tendered by Oliver P. Morton[87] of Indiana, his own native state.[88] Lane's friends very plausibly contended that a military commission from one state could not invalidate the title to represent another state in the Federal senate. The actual fight over the contested seat came in the next session and, quite regardless of consequences likely to prejudice his case, Lane went on recruiting for his brigade. Indeed, he commended himself to Frémont, who, in his capacity as major-general of volunteers and in charge of the Western Military District, assigned him to duty in Kansas, thus greatly complicating an already delicate situation and immeasurably heaping up difficulties, embarrassments, and disasters for the frontier.

The same indifference towards the West that characterized the governing authorities in the South was exhibited by eastern men in the North and, correspondingly, the West, Federal and Confederate, was unduly sensitive to the indifference, perhaps, also, a trifle unnecessarily alarmed by symptoms of its own danger. Nevertheless, its danger was real. Each state gave in its adherence to the Confederacy separately and, therefore, every single state in the slavery belt had a problem to solve. The fight for Missouri was fought

[87] Morton, war governor of Indiana, who had taken tremendous interest in the struggle for Kansas and in the events leading up to the organization of the Republican party, was one of the most energetic of men in raising troops for the defence of the Union, especially in the earliest stages of the war. See Foulke's *Life of Oliver P. Morton,* vol. i.

[88] Some doubt on this point exists. John Speer, Lane's intimate friend and, in a sense, his biographer, says Lane claimed Lawrenceburg, Indiana, as his birthplace. By some people he is thought to have been born in Kentucky.

on the border and nowhere else. The great evil of squatter-sovereignty days was now epidemic in its most malignant form. Those days had bred intense hatred between Missourian and Kansan and had developed a disregard of the value of human life and a ruthlessness and brutality in fighting, concomitant with it, that the East, in its most primitive times, had never been called upon to experience. Granted that the spirit of the crusader had inspired many a free-soiler to venture into the trans-Missouri region after the Kansas-Nebraska bill had become law and that real exaltation of soul had transformed some very mercenary and altogether mundane characters unexpectedly into martyrs; granted, also, that the pro-slavery man honestly felt that his cause was just and that his sacred rights of property, under the constitution, were being violated, his preserves encroached upon, it yet remains true that great crimes were committed in the name of great causes and that villains stalked where only saints should have trod. The irregular warfare of the border, from fifty-four on, while it may, to military history as a whole, be as unimportant as the quarrels of kites and crows, was yet a big part of the life of the frontiersman and frightful in its possibilities. Sherman's march to the sea or through the Carolinas, disgraceful to modern civilization as each undeniably was, lacked the sickening phase, guerrilla atrocities, that made the Civil War in the West, to those at least who were in line to experience it at close range, an awful nightmare. Union and Confederate soldiers might well fraternize in eastern camps because there they so rarely had any cause for personal hostility towards each other, but not in western. The fight on the border was constant and to the death.

The leaders in the West or many of them, on both sides, were men of ungovernable tempers, of violent and unrestrained passions, sometimes of distressingly base proclivities, although, in the matter of both vices and virtues, there was considerable difference of degree among them. Lane and Shelby and Montgomery and Quantrill were hardly types, rather should it be said they were extreme cases. They seem never to have taken chances on each other's inactivity. Their motto invariably was, to be prepared for the worst, and their practice, retaliation.

It was scarcely to be supposed that a man like Lane, who had never known moderation in the course of the long struggle for Kansas or been over-scrupulous about anything would, in the event of his adopted state's being exposed anew to her old enemy, the Missourian, be able to pose contentedly as a legislator or stay quietly in Washington, his role of guardian of the White House being finished.[89] The anticipated danger to Kansas visibly threatened in the summer of 1861 and the critical moment saw Lane again in the West, energetic beyond precedent. He took up his position at Fort Scott, it being his conviction that, from that point and from the line of the Little Osage, the entire eastern section of the state, inclusive of Fort Leavenworth, could best be protected.[90]

---

[89] As Villard tells us [*Memoirs,* vol. i, 169], Lane was in command of the "Frontier Guards," one of the two special patrols that protected the White House in the early days of the war. There were those, however, who resented his presence there. For example, note the diary entry of Hay, "Going to my room, I met the Captain. He was a little boozy and very eloquent. He dilated on the troubles of the time and bewailed the existence of a garrison in the White House 'to give *éclat* to Jim Lane.'" — THAYER, op. cit., vol. i, 94. The White House guard was in reality under General Hunter [*Report of the Military Services of General David Hunter,* 8].

[90] *Official Records,* vol. iii, 453, 455.

Fort Scott was the ranking town among the few Federal strongholds in the middle Southwest.   It was within convenient, if not easy, distance of Crawford Seminary which, situated to the southward in the Quapaw Nation, was the headquarters of the Neosho Agency; but no more perturbed place could be imagined than was that same Neosho Agency at the opening of the Civil War.   Bad white men, always in evidence at moments of crisis, were known to be interfering with the Osages, exciting them by their own marauding to deviltry and mischief of the worst description.[91]   As a

---

[91] A letter from Superintendent W. G. Coffin of date, July, 30, 1861 [Indian Office Special Files, no. 201, *Schools*, C. 1275 of 1861] bears evidence of this as bear also the following letters, the one, private in character, from Augustus Wattles, the other, without specific date, from William Brooks:

PRIVATE

MR. DOLE   MONEKA, KANSAS, May 20, 1861.

Dear Sir, A messenger has this moment left me, who came up from the Osages yesterday – a distance of about forty miles. The gentleman lives on the line joining the Osage Indians, and has, since my acquaintance with him about three years.

A short time ago, perhaps three weeks, a number of lawless white men went into the Nation and stole a number of ponies. The Indians made chase, had a fight and killed several, reported from three to five, and retook their ponies.

A company of men is now getting up here and in other counties, to go and fight the Indians. I am appealed to by the Indians to act as their friend.

They represent that they are loyal to the U.S. Government and will fight for their Great Father, at Washington, but must be protected from bad white men at home. The Government must not think them enemies when they only fight thieves and robbers.

Rob[t] B. Mitchell, who was recently appointed Maj. General of this State by Gov. Robinson, has resigned, and is now raising volunteers to fight the Indians. He has always been a Democrat in sympathy with the pro-slavery party, and his enlisting men now to take them away from the Missouri frontier, when we are daily threatened with an attack from that State, and union men are fleeing to us for protection from there, is certainly a very questionable policy. It could operate no worse against us, if it were gotten up by a traitor to draw our men off on purpose to give the Missourians a chance when we are unprepared.

I presume you have it in your power to prevent any attack on the

tribe, the Osages were not very dependable at the best
of times and now that they saw confusion all around

Indians in Kansas till such time as they can be treated with. And
such order to the Commander of the Western Division of the U.S.
Army would stop further proceedings.

I shall start to-morrow for Council Grove and meet the Kansas
Indians before General Mitchell's force can get there. As the point
of attack is secret, I fear it may be the Osages, for the purpose of
creating a necessity for a treaty with himself by which he can secure
a large quantity of land for himself and followers. He is acquainted
with all the old Democratic schemes of swindling Indians.

The necessity for prompt action on the part of the Indian Department increases every day. The element of discord in the community here now, was once, the pro-slavery party. I see their intention
to breed disturbances with the Indians is malicious and selfish. They
are active and unscrupulous, and must be met promptly and decisively.

I hope you will excuse this, as it appears necessary for me to step
a little out of my orders to notify you of current events. I am very
respectfully Your Ob^t Ser^vt   AUGUSTUS WATTLES, *Special Agent*
[Indian Office Special Files, no. 201.]

GRAND FALLS, NEWTON CO., MO.
COM. INDIAN AFFAIRS
    Washington, D. C.

Hon. Sir: Permit me to inform you, by this means, of the efforts
that have been and are now being made in Southern Kansas to arouse
both the "Osages" and "Cherokees" *to rebel*, and bear arms against
the U.S. Government— At a public meeting near the South E. corner
of the "Osage Nation" called by the settlements for the devising of
some means by which to protect themselves from "unlawful characters," Mr. John Mathis, who resides in the Osage Nation and has
an Osage family, also Mr. "Robert Foster" who lives in the Cherokee
Nation and has a Cherokee family endeavored by public speeches and
otherwise to induce "Osages", "Cherokees", as well as Americans who
live on the "Neutral Lands" to bear arms against the U.S. Government—*aledging that there was no U.S. Government*. There was 25
men who joined them and they proceeded to organise a *"Secession
Company"* electing as Capt R. D. Foster and 1st Lieutenant James
Patton— This meeting was held June 4th 1861—at "McGhees Residence"— The peace of this section of country requires the removal
of these men from the Indian country, or some measures that will
restrain them from exciting the Indians in Southern Kansas.

Yours Respectfully   WM. BROOKS.

You will understand why you are addressed by a private individual
on this subject instead of the Agent, since A. J. Dorn, the present
Indian Agent, is an avowed "Secessionist" and consequently would
favor, rather than suppress the move.   WM. BROOKS.
[*Ibid., Southern Superintendency*, B567 of 1861]

them their most natural inclination was to pay back old scores and to make an alliance where such alliance could be most profitable to themselves. The "remnants" of tribes, Senecas, Shawnees, and Quapaws, associated with them in the agency, Neosho, that is, although not of evil disposition, were similarly agitated and with good reason. Rumors of dissensions among the Cherokees, not so very far away, were naturally having a disquieting effect upon the neighboring but less highly organized tribes as was also the unrest in Missouri, in the southwestern counties of which, however, Union sentiment thus far dominated.[92]   Its continuance would undoubtedly turn upon military success or failure and that, men like Lyon and Lane knew only too well.

As the days passed, the Cherokee troubles gained in intensity, so much so that the agent, John Crawford, even then a secessionist sympathiser, reported that internecine strife might at any hour be provoked.[93]   So confused was everything that in July the people of southeastern Kansas were generally apprehensive of an attack from the direction of either Indian Territory or Arkansas.[94]   Kansas troops had been called to Missouri; but, at the same time, Lyon was complaining that men from the West, where they were greatly needed, were being called by Scott to Virginia.[95]   On August 6 two emergency calls went forth, one from Frémont for a brigade from California that could be stationed at El Paso and moved as occasion might require, either upon San Antonio or into the Indian Territory,[96]

---

[92] Branch to Mix, June 22, 1861, enclosing letter from Agent Elder, June 15, 1861 [Indian Office Files, *Neosho*, B 547 of 1861].

[93] —*Ibid., Cherokee*, C 1200 of 1861.

[94] *Official Records*, vol. iii, 405.

[95] —*Ibid.*, 397, 408.

[96] —*Ibid.*, 428.

the other from Congressmen John S. Phelps and Francis P. Blair junior, who addressed Lincoln upon the subject of enlisting Missouri troops for an invasion of Arkansas in order to ward off any contemplated attack upon southwestern Missouri and to keep the Indians west of Arkansas in subjection.[97]   On August 10 came the disastrous Federal defeat at Wilson's Creek.   It was immediately subsequent to that event and in anticipation of a Kansas invasion by Price and McCulloch that Lane resolved to take position at Fort Scott.[98]

The Battle of Wilson's Creek, lost to the Federals largely because of Frémont's failure to support Lyon, was an unmitigated disaster in more than one sense. The death of Lyon, which the battle caused, was of itself a severe blow to the Union side as represented in Missouri; but the moral effect of the Federal defeat upon the Indians was equally worthy of note.   It was instantaneous and striking.   It rallied the wavering Cherokees for the Confederacy[99] and their defection was something that could not be easily counterbalanced and was certainly not counterbalanced by the almost coincident, cheap, disreputable, and very general Osage offer, made towards the end of August, of services to the United States in exchange for flour and whiskey.[100]

The disaster in its effect upon Lane was, however, little short of exhilarating.   It brought him sympathy, understanding, and a fair measure of support from people who, not until the eleventh hour, had really comprehended their own danger and it inspired him to redouble his efforts to organize a brigade that should ade-

---

[97] *Official Records*, vol. iii, 430.
[98] — *Ibid.*, 446.
[99] *The Daily Conservative* (Leavenworth), October 5, 1861.
[100] — *Ibid.*, August 30, 1861, quoting from the Fort Scott *Democrat*.

quately protect Kansas and recover ground lost.   Prior
to the battle, "scarcely a battalion had been recruited
for each" of the five regiments, the Third, Fourth, Fifth,
Sixth, and Seventh Kansas, which he had been empowered by the War Department to raise.[101]   It was in the
days of gathering reinforcements, for which he made an
earnest plea on August 29,[102] that he developed a disposition to utilize the loyal Indians in his undertaking.
The Indians, in their turn, were looking to him for
much needed assistance.   About a month previous to
the disaster of August 10, Agent Elder had been obliged
to make Fort Scott, for the time being, the Neosho
Agency headquarters, everything being desperately in-
secure at Crawford's Seminary.[103]

[101] Britton, *Civil War on the Border,* vol. i, 122.

[102] *Official Records,* vol. iii, 465.

[103] The following letter, an enclosure of a report from Branch to Dole,
August 14, 1861, gives some slight indication of its insecurity:

OFFICE OF NEOSHO AGENCY

Fort Scott, July 27, 1861.

SIR – I deem it important to inform the Department of the situation of this Agency at this time.   After entering upon the duties of
this office as per instructions – and attending to all the business that
seemed to require my immediate attention – I repaired to Franklin Co.
Kan. to remove my family to the Agency.

Leaving the Agency in care of James Killebrew Esq the Gov^t
Farmer for the Quapaw Nation.   Soon after I left I was informed by
him that the Agency had been surrounded by a band of armed men,
and instituted an inquiry for "*that Abolition Superintendent and
Agent.*"   After various interrogatories and answers they returned in
the direction of Missouri and Arkansas lines from whence they were
supposed to have come.   He has since written me and Special Agent
Whitney and Superintendent Coffin told me that it would be very
unsafe for me to stay at that place under the present excited state of
public feeling in that vicinity.   I however started with my family on
the 6th July and arrived at Fort Scott on the 9th intending to go
direct to the Agency.   Here I learned from Capt. Jennison commanding a detachment of Kansas Militia, who had been scouting in that
vicinity, that the country was full of marauding parties from Gov.
Jackson's Camp in S.W. Mo.   I therefore concluded to remain here
and watch the course of events believing as I did the Federal troops

Lane, conjecturing rightly that Price, moving north-westward from Springfield, which place he had left on the twenty-sixth of August, would threaten, if he did not actually attempt, an invasion of Kansas at the point of its greatest vulnerability, the extreme southeast, hastened his preparations for the defence and at the very end of the month appeared in person at Fort Scott, where all the forces he could muster, many of them refugee Missourians, had been rendezvousing. On the second of September, the two armies, if such be not too dignified a name for them, came into initiatory action at Dry Wood Creek,[104] Missouri, a reconnoitering party of the Federals, in a venture across the line, having

would soon repair thither and so quell the rebellion as to render my stay here no longer necessary. But as yet the Union forces have not penetrated that far south, and Jackson with a large force is quartered within 20 or 25 miles of the Agency— I was informed by Mr. Killebrew on the 23d inst. that everything at the Agency was safe—but the house and roads were guarded— Hence I have assumed the responsibility of establishing my office here temporarily until I can hear from the department.

And I most sincerely hope the course I have thus been compelled to pursue will receive the approval of the department.

I desire instructions relative to the papers and a valuable safe (being the only moveables there of value) which can only be moved *at present* under the protection of a guard. And also instructions as to the course I am to pursue relative to the locality of the Agency.

I feel confident that the difficulty now attending the locality at Crawford Seminary will not continue long—if not then I shall move directly there unless instructions arrive of a different character.

All mail matter should be directed to Fort Scott for the Mail Carrier has been repeatedly arrested—and the mails may be robbed— Very respectfully your Obedient Servant

PETER P. ELDER, *U.S. Neosho Agent.*

H. B. BRANCH ESQ, Superintendent of Ind. Affairs C.S.

St. Joseph, Mo.

[Indian Office Files, *Neosho*, B 719 of 1861].

[104] For additional information about the Dry Wood Creek affair and about the events leading up to and succeeding it, see *Official Records*, vol. liii, supplement, 436; Britton, *Civil War on the Border*, vol. i, chapter x; Connelley, *Quantrill and the Border Wars*, 199.

fallen in with the advance of the Confederates and, being numerically outmatched, having been compelled to beat a retreat.   In its later stages, Lane personally conducted that retreat, which, taken as a whole, did not end even with the recrossing of the state boundary, although the pursuit did not continue beyond it.   Confident that Price would follow up his victory and attack Fort Scott, Lane resolved to abandon the place, leaving a detachment to collect the stores and ammunition and to follow him later.   He then hurried on himself to Fort Lincoln on the north bank of the Little Osage, fourteen miles northwest.   There he halted and hastily erected breastworks of a certain sort.[105]   Meanwhile, the citizens of Fort Scott, finding themselves left in the lurch, vacated their homes and followed in the wake of the army.[106]   Then came a period, luckily short, of direful confusion.   Home guards were drafted in and other preparations made to meet the emergency of Price's coming.   Humboldt was now suggested as suitable and safe headquarters for the Neosho Agency;[107] but, most opportunely, as the narrative will soon show, the change had to wait upon the approval of the Indian Office, which could not be had for some days and, in the meantime, events proved that Price was not the menace and Fort Scott not the target.

It soon transpired that Price had no immediate intention of invading Kansas.[108]   For the present, it was

[105] In ridicule of Lane's fortifications, see Spring, *Kansas,* 275.

[106] As soon as the citizens, panic-stricken, were gone, the detachment which Lane had left in charge, under Colonel C. R. Jennison, commenced pillaging their homes [Britton, *Civil War on the Border,* vol. i, 130.]

[107] H. C. Whitney to Mix, September 6, 1861, Indian Office Consolidated Files, *Neosho,* W 455 of 1861.

[108] By the fifth of September, Lane had credible information that Price had broken camp at Dry Wood and was moving towards Lexington [Britton, *Civil War on the Border,* vol. i, 144].

enough for his purpose to have struck terror into the
hearts of the people of Union sentiments inhabiting
the Cherokee Neutral Lands, where, indeed, intense
excitement continued to prevail until there was no
longer any room to doubt that Price was really gone
from the near vicinity and was heading for the Missouri River. Yet his departure was far from meaning
the complete removal of all cause for anxiety, since
marauding bands infested the country roundabout and
were constantly setting forth, from some well concealed
lair, on expeditions of robbery, devastation, and murder. It was one of those marauding bands that in this
same month of September, 1861, sacked and in part
burnt Humboldt, for which dastardly and quite unwarrantable deed, James G. Blunt, acting under orders
from Lane, took speedy vengeance; and the world was
soon well rid of the instigator and leader of the outrage, the desperado, John Matthews.[109]

[109] (a)   FT. LINCOLN, SOUTHERN KANSAS.
                                             Sept. 25, 1861.
HON. WM. P. DOLE, Com. of Ind. Af^rs

Dear Sir, We have just returned from a successful expedition
into the Indian Country, And I thought you would be glad to hear
the news.

Probably you know that Mathews, formerly an Indian Trader
amongst the Osages has been committing depredations at the head of
a band of half breed Cherokees, all summer.

He has killed a number of settlers and taken their property; but
as most of them were on the Cherokee neuteral lands I could not
tell whether to blame him much or not, as I did not understand the
condition of those lands.

A few days ago he came up to Humbolt and pillaged the town.
Gen. Lane ordered the home guards, composed mostly of old men,
too old for regular service, to go down and take or disperse this
company under Mathews.

He detailed Lieut. Col. Blunt of Montgomery's regiment to the
command, and we started about 200 strong. We went to Humbolt
and followed down through the Osage as far as the Quapaw Agency
where we came up with them, about 60 strong.

Mathews and 10 men were killed at the first fire, the others re-

As soon as Lane had definite knowledge that Price had turned away from the border and was moving northward, he determined to follow after and attack

treated. We found on Mathews a Commission from Ben. McCulloch, authorizing him to enlist the Quapaw and other Indians and operate on the Kansas frontier.

The Osage Indians are loyal, and I think most of the others would be if your Agents were always ready to speak a word of confidence for our Government, and on hand to counteract the influence of the Secession Agents.

There is no more danger in doing this than in any of the Army service. If an Agent is killed in the discharge of his duty, another can be appointed the same as in any other service. A few prompt Agents, might save a vast amount of plundering which it is now contemplated to do in Kansas.

Ben. McCulloch promises his rangers, and the Indians that he will winter them in Kansas and expel the settlers.

I can see the Indians gain confidence in him precisely as they loose it in us. It need somebody amongst them to represent our power and strength and purposes, and to give them courage and confidence in the U.S. Government.

There is another view which some take and you may take the same, i.e. let them go – fight and conquer them – take their lands and stop their annuities.

I can only say that whatever the Government determines on the people here will sustain. The President was never more popular. He is the President of the Constitution and the laws. And notwithstanding what the papers say about his difference with Fremont, every heart reposes confidence in the President.

So far as I can learn from personal inquiry, the Indians are not yet committed to active efforts against the Gov.   AUG. WATTLES.
[Indian Office Special Files, no. 201, *Central Superintendency,* W 474 of 1861.]

(b)   SACK AND FOX AGENCY, Dec. 17th 1861.
HON. W. P. DOLE, Commissioner of Indian Affairs

Dear Sir: After receiving the cattle and making arrangements for their keeping at Leroy I went and paid a visit to the Ruins of Humboldt which certainly present a gloomy appearance. All the best part of the town was burnt. Thurstons House that I had rented for an office tho near half a mile from town was burnt tho his dwelling and mill near by were spared. All my books and papers that were there were lost. My trunk and what little me and my son had left after the sacking were all burnt including to Land Warrents one 160 acres and one 120. Our Minne Rifle and ammunition Saddle bridle, etc. . . About 4 or 5 Hundred Sacks of Whitney's Corn were burnt. As soon as I can I will try to make out a list of the Papers from the

him, if possible, in the rear. Governor Robinson was much opposed [110] to any such provocative and apparently purposeless action, no one knowing better than he Lane's vindictive mercilessness. Lane persisted notwithstanding Robinson's objections and, for the time being, found his policies actually endorsed by Prince at Fort Leavenworth.[111] The attack upon Humboldt, having revealed the exposed condition of the settlements north of the Osage lands, necessitated his leaving a much larger force in his own rear than he had intended.[112] It also made it seem advisable for him to order the building of a series of stockades, the one of most immediate interest being at Leroy.[113] By the fourteenth of September, Lane found himself within twenty-four miles of Harrisonville but Price still far ahead. On the twenty-second, having made a detour for the purpose of destroying some of his opponent's stores, he performed the atrocious and downright inexcusable exploit of burning Osceola.[114] Lexington, besieged, had fallen into Price's hands two days before. Thus had the foolish Federal practice of acting in detach-

Department [that] were burnt. As I had some at Leavenworth I cannot do so til I see what is there. As Mr. Hutchinson is not here I leave this morning for the Kaw Agency to endeavour to carry out your Instructions there and will return here as soon as I get through there. They are building some stone houses here and I am much pleased with the result. The difference in cost is not near so much as we expected but I will write you fully on a careful examination as you requested. Very respectfully your obedient Servant

W. G. COFFIN, *Superintendent of Indian Affairs*
Southern Superintendency

[Indian Office Files, *Southern Superintendency*, C 1432 of 1861].

[110] *Official Records*, vol. iii, 468-469.

[111] — *Ibid.*, 483.

[112] — *Ibid.*, 490.

[113] — *Ibid.*

[114] — *Ibid.*, 196; vol. liii, supplement, 743; Britton, *Civil War on the Border*, vol. i, 147-148; Connelley, *Quantrill and the Border Wars*, 208-209, 295.

ments instead of in force produced its own calamitous result. There had never been any appreciable coördination among the parts of Frémont's army. Each worked upon a campaign of its own. To some extent, the same criticism might be held applicable to the opposing Confederate force also, especially when the friction between Price and McCulloch be taken fully into account; but Price's energy was far in excess of Frémont's and he, having once made a plan, invariably saw to its accomplishment. Lincoln viewed Frémont's supineness with increasing apprehension and finally after the fall of Lexington directed Scott to instruct for greater activity. Presumably, Frémont had already aroused himself somewhat; for, on the eighteenth, he had ordered Lane to proceed to Kansas City and from thence to coöperate with Sturgis.[115] Lane slowly obeyed[116] but managed, while obeying, to do considerable marauding, which worked greatly to the general detestation and lasting discredit of his brigade. For a man, temperamentally constituted as Lane was, warfare had no terrors and its votaries, no scruples. The grim chieftain as he has been somewhat fantastically called, was cruel, indomitable, and disgustingly licentious, a person who would have hesitated at nothing to accomplish his purpose. It was to be expected, then, that he would see nothing terrible in the letting loose of the bad white man, the half-civilized Indian, or the wholly barbarous negro upon society. He believed that the institution of slavery should look out for itself[117] and, like Governor Robinson,[118] Senator Pomeroy, Secretary Cameron, John

[115] *Official Records,* vol. iii, 500.
[116] —*Ibid.,* 505-506.
[117] —*Ibid.,* 516.
[118] Spring, *Kansas,* 272.

Cochrane,[119] Thaddeus Stevens,[120] and many another, fully endorsed the principle underlying Frémont's abortive Emancipation Proclamation. He advocated immediate emancipation both as a political and a military measure.[121]

There was no doubt by this time that Lane had it in mind to utilize the Indians. In the dog days of August, when he was desperately marshaling his brigade, the Indians presented themselves, in idea, as a likely military contingent. The various Indian agents in Kansas were accordingly communicated with and Special Agent Augustus Wattles authorized to make the needful preparations for Indian enlistment.[122] Not much could be done in furtherance of the scheme while Lane was engaged in Missouri but, in October, when he was back in Kansas, his interest again manifested itself. He was then recruiting among all kinds of people, the more hot-blooded the better. His energy was likened to frenzy and the more sober-minded took alarm. It was the moment for his political opponents to interpose and Governor Robinson from among them did interpose, being firmly convinced that Lane, by his intemperate zeal and by his guerrilla-like fighting was provoking Missouri to reprisals and thus precipitating upon Kansas the very troubles that he professed to wish to ward off. Incidentally, Robinson, unlike Frémont, was vehemently opposed to Indian enlistment.

Feeling between Robinson and Lane became exceedingly tense in October. Price was again moving sus-

---

[119] *Daily Conservative*, November 22, 1861.

[120] Woodburn, *Life of Thaddeus Stevens*, 183.

[121] Lane's speech at Springfield, November 7, 1861 [*Daily Conservative*, November 17, 1861].

[122] For a full discussion of the progress of the movement, see Abel, *American Indian as Slaveholder and Secessionist*, 227 ff.

piciously near to Kansas. On the third he was known
to have left Warrensburg, ostensibly to join McCulloch
in Bates County[123] and, on the eighth, he was reported
as still proceeding in a southwestwardly direction, possibly to attack Fort Scott.[124] His movements gave opportunity for a popular expression of opinion among
Lane's adherents. On the evening of the eighth, a
large meeting was held in Stockton's Hall to consider
the whole situation and, amidst great enthusiasm, Lane
was importuned to go to Washington,[125] there to lay the
case of the piteous need of Kansas, in actuality more
imaginary than real, before the president. Nothing
loath to assume such responsibility but not finding it
convenient to leave his military task just then, Lane
resorted to letter-writing. On the ninth, he complained[126] to Lincoln that Robinson was attempting to
break up his brigade and had secured the coöperation
of Prince to that end.[127] The anti-Robinson press[128]
went farther and accused Robinson and Prince of not
being big enough, in the face of grave danger to the
commonwealth, to forget old scores.[129] As a solution
of the problem before them, Lane suggested to Lincoln
the establishment of a new military district that should
include Kansas, Indian Territory, and Arkansas, and
be under his command.[130] So anxious was Lane to be

---

[123] *Official Records,* vol. iii, 525, 526, 527.

[124] — *Ibid,* 527.

[125] *Daily Conservative,* October 9, 10, 1861.

[126] *Official Records,* vol. iii, 529.

[127] *Daily Conservative,* October 9, 15, 1861.

[128] Chief among the papers against Robinson, in the matter of his long-
standing feud with Lane, was the *Daily Conservative* with D. W. Wilder as
its editor. Another anti-Robinson paper was the Lawrence *Republican.*
The Cincinnati *Gazette* was decidedly friendly to Lane.

[129] *Daily Conservative,* October 15, 1861.

[130] *Official Records,* vol. iii, 529-530. Lane outlined his plan for a separate department in his speech in Stockton's Hall [*Daily Conservative,*

identified with what he thought was the rescue of Kansas that he proposed resigning his seat in the senate that he might be entirely untrammelled.[131] Perchance, also, he had some inkling that with Frederick P. Stanton[132] contesting the seat, a bitter partisan fight was in prospect, a not altogether welcome diversion.[133] Stanton, prominent in and out of office in territorial days, was an old political antagonist of the Lane faction and one of the four candidates whose names had been before the legislature in March. In the second half of October, Lane's brigade notably contributed to Frémont's show of activity and then, anticipatory perhaps to greater changes, it was detached from the main column and given the liberty of moving independently down the Missouri line to the Cherokee country.[134]

Lane's efforts towards securing Indian enlistment did not stop with soliciting the Kansas tribes. Thoroughly aware, since the time of his sojourn at Fort Scott, if not before, of the delicate situation in Indian Territory, of the divided allegiance there, and of the despairing cry for help that had gone forth from the Union element to Washington, he conceived it eminently fitting and practicable that that same Union element should have its loyalty put to good uses and be itself induced to take up arms in behalf of the cause it affected so ardently to endorse. To an ex-teacher among the Seminoles, E. H. Carruth, was entrusted the task of recruiting.

The situation in Indian Territory was more than deli-

October 9, 1861]. Robinson was opposed to the idea [*ibid.,* November 2, 6, 1861].

[131] *Official Records,* vol. iii, 530.

[132] Martin, *First Two Years of Kansas,* 24; *Biographical Congressional Directory,* 1771-1903.

[133] *Daily Conservative,* November 1, 1861, gives Robinson the credit of inciting Stanton to contest the seat.

[134] *Daily Conservative,* October 30, 1861.

cate. It was precarious and had been so almost from the beginning. The withdrawal of troops from the frontier posts had left the Territory absolutely destitute of the protection solemnly guaranteed its inhabitants by treaty with the United States government. Appeal[135] to the War Department for a restoration of what was a sacred obligation had been without effect all the summer. Southern emissaries had had, therefore, an entirely free hand to accomplish whatever purpose they might have in mind with the tribes. In September,[136] the Indian Office through Charles E. Mix, acting commissioner of Indian affairs in the absence of William P. Dole, who was then away on a mission to the Kansas tribes, again begged the War Department[137] to look into matters so extremely urgent. National honor would of itself have dictated a policy of intervention before

---

[135] Secretary Cameron's reply to Secretary Smith's first request was uncompromising in the extreme and prophetic of his persistent refusal to recognize the obligation resting upon the United States to protect its defenceless "wards." This is Cameron's letter of May 10, 1861:

"In answer to your letter of the 4th instant, I have the honor to state that on the 17th April instructions were issued by this Department to remove the troops stationed at Forts Cobb, Arbuckle, Washita, and Smith, to Fort Leavenworth, leaving it to the discretion of the Commanding Officer to replace them, or not, by Arkansas Volunteers.

"The exigencies of the service will not admit any change in these orders." [Interior Department Files, *Bundle no. 1 (1849-1864) War.*]

Secretary Smith wrote to Cameron again on the thirtieth [Interior Department *Letter Press Book*, vol. iii, 125], enclosing Dole's letter of the same date [Interior Department, *File Box, January 1 to December 1, 1861*; Indian Office *Report Book*, no. 12, 176], but to no purpose.

[136] Indian Office *Report Book*, no. 12, 218-219.

[137] Although his refusal to keep faith with the Indians is not usually cited among the things making for Cameron's unfitness for the office of Secretary of War, it might well and justifiably be. No student of history questions to-day that the appointment of Simon Cameron to the portfolio of war, to which Thaddeus Stevens had aspirations [Woodburn, *Life of Thaddeus Stevens*, 239], was one of the worst administrative mistakes Lincoln ever made. It was certainly one of the four cabinet appointment errors noted by Weed [*Autobiography*, 607].

the poor neglected Indians had been driven to the last desperate straits. The next month, October, nothing at all having been done in the interval, Dole submitted[138] to Secretary Smith new evidence of a most alarmingly serious state of affairs and asked that the president's attention be at once elicited. The apparent result was that about the middle of November, Dole was able to write with confidence – and he was writing at the request of the president – that the United States was prepared to maintain itself in its authority over the Indians at all hazards.[139]

Boastful words those were and not to be made good until many precious months had elapsed and many sad regrettable scenes enacted. In early November occurred the reorganization of the Department of the West which meant the formation of a Department of Kansas separate and distinct from a Department of Missouri, an arrangement that afforded ample opportunity for a closer attention to local exigencies in both states than had heretofore been possible or than, upon trial, was subsequently to be deemed altogether desirable. It necessarily increased the chances for local patronage and exposed military matters to the grave danger of becoming hopelessly entangled with political.

The need for change of some sort was, however, very evident and the demand for it, insistent. If the southern Indians were not soon secured, they were bound to menace, not only Kansas, but Colorado[140] and to help materially in blocking the way to Texas, New Mexico,

---

[138] Indian Office *Report Book* no. 12, 225.

[139] Dole to Hunter, November 16, 1861, *ibid., Letter Book,* no. 67, pp. 80-82.

[140] On conditions in Colorado Territory, the following are enlightening: *ibid., Consolidated Files,* C 195 of 1861; C 1213 of 1861; C 1270 of 1861; C 1369 of 1861; V 43 of 1861; *Official Records,* vol. iv, 73.

and Arizona. Their own domestic affairs had now reached a supremely critical stage.[141]   It was high time

141 In addition to what may be obtained on the subject from the first volume of this work, two letters of slightly later date furnish particulars, as do also the records of a council held by Agent Cuther with certain chiefs at Leroy.

(a).   LAWRENCE KANSAS, Dec. 14th, 1861.

HON. W. P. DOLE, Commissioner of Ind. Affairs

Dear Sir, It is with reluctance that I again intrude on your valuable time. But I am induced to do so by the conviction that the subject of our Indian relations is really a matter of serious concern: as involving the justice and honor of our own Government, and the deepest interests – the very existence, indeed – of a helpless and dependent people. And knowing that it is your wish to be furnished with every item of information which may, in any way, throw light on the subject, I venture to trouble you with another letter.

Mico Hat-ki, the Creek man referred to in my letter of Oct. 31st has been back to the Creek Nation, and returned about the middle of last month. He was accompanied, to this place, by one of his former companions, but had left some of their present company at LeRoy. They were expecting to have a meeting with some of the Indians, at LeRoy, to consult about the proper course to be pursued, in order to protect the loyal and peaceable Indians, from the hostility of the disaffected, who have become troublesome and menacing in their bearing.

With this man and his companion, I had considerable conversation, and find that the Secessionists and disaffected Half-breeds are carrying things with a high hand. While the loyal Indians are not in a condition to resist them, by reason of the proximity of an overwhelming rebel force.

From them (repeating their former statements, regarding the defection of certain parties, and the loyalty of others, with the addition of some further particulars) I learn the following facts: Viz. That M Kennard, the Principal Chief of the Lower Creeks, most of the McIntoshes, George Stidham, and others have joined the rebels, and organized a military force in their interest; for the purpose of intimidating and harrassing the loyal Indians. They name some of the officers, but are not sufficiently conversant with military terms to distinguish the different grades, with much exactness. Unee McIntosh, however, is the highest in rank, (a Colonel I presume) and Sam Cho-co-ti, George Stidham, Chilly McIntosh, are all officers in the Lower Creek rebel force.

Among the Upper Creeks, John Smith, Timiny Barnet and Wm. Robinson, are leaders.

Among the Seminoles, John Jumper, the Principal Chief, is on the side of the rebels. Pas-co-fa, the second chief, stands neutral. Fraser McClish, though himself a Chickasaw, has raised a company

for the Federal government to do something to attest
its own competency. There was need for it to do that,

among the Seminoles in favor of the rebellion. They say the full
Indians will kill him.

The Choctaws are divided in much the same way as the other
Tribes, the disaffected being principally among the Half-breeds.

The Chickasaw Governor, Harris, is a Secessionist; and so are
most, if not all, the Colberts. The full Indians are loyal to the Government, as are some of the mixed bloods also, and here, I remark,
from my own knowledge, that this Governor Harris was the first to
propose the adoption of concerted measures, among the Southern
Tribes, on the subject of Secession. This was instantly and earnestly
opposed by John Ross, as being out of place, and an ungrateful violation of the Treaty obligations, by which the Tribes had placed themselves under the exclusive protection of the United States; and, under
which, they had enjoyed a long course of peace and prosperity.

They say, there are about four hundred Secessionists, among the
Cherokees. But whether organized or not, I did not understand. I
presume they meant such as were formerly designated by the term
Warriors, somewhat analogous to the class among ourselves, who are
fit for military duty, though they may or may not be actually organized and under arms. So that the *Thousands* of *Indians* in the secession papers, as figuring in the armies, are enormous exaggerations;
and most of them sheer fabrications.

Albert Pike, of Little Rock, boasts of having visited and made
treaty alliances with the Comanches, and other tribes, on behalf of
the "Confederate States," but the Indians do not believe him. And,
in blunt style, say "he tells lies."

They make favorable mention of O-poth-le-yo-ho-lo, an ex-Creek
Chief, a true patriot of former days. But, it seems, he has been molested and forced to leave his home to avoid the annoyance and violence of the rebel party. There are, however, more than three
thousand young men, of the warrior class, who adhere to his principles, and hold true faith and allegiance to the United States.

They say also that John Ross is not a Secessionist, and that there
are more than four thousand patriots among the Cherokees, who are
true to the Government of the United States. This agrees, substantially, with my own personal knowledge, unless they have changed
within a very short time, which is not at all probable, as the Cherokees, of this class, are pretty fully and correctly informed about the
nature of the controversy. And I may add, that much of their information is, through one channel and another, communicated to the
Creeks, and much of their spirit too.

On the whole, judging from the most reliable information, I have
been able to obtain, I feel assured that the Full Indians of the Creeks,
Cherokees, Seminoles, and the small bands living in the Creek Nation,
are faithful to the Government. And the same, to a great extent, is

moreover, on recognizably loyal ground, causes for dissatisfaction among Kansas emigrant tribes to be re-

true of the Choctaws and Chickasaws. And were it not for the proximity of the rebel force, the loyal Indians would put down the Secession movement among themselves, at once. Or rather, they would not
have suffered it to rise at all.

The loyal Indians say, they wish "to stand by their Old Treaties."
And they are as persistent in their adherence to these Treaties, as
we are, to our Constitution. And I have no doubt that, as soon as
the Government can afford them protection, they will be ready, at the
first call, to manifest, by overt action, the loyalty to which they are
pledged.

They are looking, with great anxiety and hope, for the coming of
the great army. And I have no doubt that a friendly communication
from the Government, through the Commissioner of Indian Affairs,
would have a powerful effect in removing any false impressions,
which may have been made, on the ignorant and unwary, by the
emissaries of Secession, and to encourage and reassure the loyal friends
of the Government, who, in despair of timely aid, may have been compelled to yield any degree of submission, to the pressure of an overwhelming force. I was expecting to see these Indians again, and to
have had further conversation with them. But I am informed by
Charles Johnnycake that they have gone to Fort Leavenworth and
expect to go on to Washington. Hearing this, I hesitated about
troubling you with this letter at all, as, in that case, you would see
them yourself. But I have concluded to send it, as affording me an
opportunity to express a few thoughts, with which it would hardly
be worth while to occupy a separate letter.

Hoping that the counsels and movements of the Government may
be directed by wisdom from above, and that the cause of truth and
right may prevail, I remain with great respect, Dear Sir, Your Obedient Ser^v EVAN JONES.

P.S. I rec. a note from Mr. Carruth, saying that he was going
to Washington, with a delegation of Southern Indians, and I suppose
Mico Hatki and his companions are that Delegation, or at least a
part of them.

I will just say in regard to Mr. Carruth that I was acquainted with
him, several years ago, as a teacher in the Cherokee Nation. He afterwards went to the Creek Nation, *I think*, as teacher of a Government school, and I believe, has been there ever since. If so, he must
know a good deal about the Creeks. Mr. Carruth bore a good character. I think he married one of the Missionary ladies of the Pres-
byterian Mission.

[Indian Office Special Files, no. 201, *Southern Superintendency,* J 530 of 1861.]

(b).   WICHITA AGENCY, L.D., December 15, 1861.

All well and doing well. Hear you are having trouble among
yourselves – fighting one another, but you and we are friendly. Our

moved and drastic measures taken with the indigenous of the plains.

The appointment of Hunter to the command of the

brothers the Comanches and all the other tribes are still your friends. Mode Cunard and you were here and had the talk with Gen. Pike; we still hold to the talk we made with Gen. Pike, and are keeping the treaty in good faith, and are looking for him back again soon. We look upon you and Mode Cunard and Gen. Pike as brothers. Gen. Pike told us at the council that there were but few of us here, and if any thing turned up to make it necessary he would protect them. We are just as we were when Gen. Pike was up here and keeping the treaty made with him. Our brothers the wild Comanches have been in and are friendly with us.

All the Indians here have but one heart. Our brothers, the Texans, and the Indians are away fighting the cold weather people. We do not intend to go North to fight them, but if they come down here, we will all wait to drive them away. Some of my people are one-eyed and a little crippled, but if the enemy comes here they will all jump out to fight him. Pea-o-popicult, the principal Kiowa chief, has recently visited the reserve, and expressed friendly intentions, and has gone back to consult the rest of his people, and designs returning.

HOSECA X MARIA ⎫
KE-HAD-A-WAH ⎬ *Chiefs of the Camanches*
BUFFALO HUMP ⎭
TE-NAH
GEO. WASHINGTON
JIM POCKMARK

[Indian Office, *Confederate Papers,* Copy of a letter to John Jumper, certified as a true copy by A. T. Pagy.]

(c).　　　　　　　　LEROY, COFFEY CO., KANSAS, Nov. 4, 1861.
HON. WM. P. DOLE, COMᴿ INDIAN AFFAIRS,
　　　　　Washington, D. C.

Dear Sir: Enclosed I send you a statement of delegation of Creeks, Chickasaw, and Kininola who are here for assistance from the Government. You will see by the enclosed that I have held a Council with them the result of which I send *verbatim.* They have travelled some 300 or 400 miles to get here, had to take an unfrequented road and were in momentary fear of their lives not because the secessionists were stronger than the Union party in their nation, but because the secessionists were on the alert and were determined that there should be no communication with the Government.

They underwent a great many privations in getting here, had to bear their own expenses, which as some of them who were up here a short time ago have travelled in coming and going some 900 miles was considerable.

I am now supplying them with everything they need on my own responsibility. They dare not return to their people unless troops

Department of Kansas was open to certain objections, no doubt; but, to Lane, whose forceful personality had

are sent with them and they assure me the moment that is done, a large portion of each of the tribes will rally to the support of the Government and that their warriors will gladly take up arms in its defence.

I write to you from Topeka and urge that steps be taken to render them the requisite protection. I am satisfied that the Department will see the urgent necessity of carrying out the Treaty stipulations and giving these Indians who are so desirous of standing firm by the Government and who have resisted so persistently all the overtures of the secessionists, the assistance and protection which is their due. I am informed by these Indians that John Ross is desirous of standing by the Government, and that he has 4000 warriors who are willing to do battle for the cause of the Union.

They also inform me, that the Washitas, Caddos, Tenies, Wakoes, Tewakano, Chiekies, Shawnees, and Kickapoos are almost unanimously Union. Gen. Lane is anxious to do something to relieve the Union Indians in the southern tribes, by taking prompt and energetic steps at this time – it can be done with little expense and but little trouble, while the benefit to be derived will be incalculable. Let me beg of you and more that the matter be laid before the Department and the proper steps be taken to give the Indians that protection which is their due and at the same time take an important step in sustaining the supremacy of the Government. Your obedient Servant,   GEO. A. CUTLER, *agent* for the Indians of the Creek agency.

ENCLOSURES

At a Council of the Creeks, held at Leroy in Coffey County, Kansas, at the house of the Agent of said Indians, Maj. Geo. A. Cutler, who was unable to visit their Country owing to the rebellion existing in the Country, the following talk was had by the Chiefs of said nation, eight in number – Four Creeks, Two Seminoles, Two Chickasaws.

Oke-Tah-hah-shah-haw-choe, Chief of Creek Upper District says, he will talk short words this time – wants to tell how to get trouble in Creek nation. First time Albert Pike come in he made great deal trouble. That man told Indian that the Union people would come and take away property and would take away land – now you sleep, you ought to wake up and attend to your own property. Tell them there ain't no U.S. – ain't any more Treaty – all be dead – Tell them as there is no more U.S. no more Treaty that the Creeks had better make new Treaty with the South and the Southern President would protect them and give them their annuity – Tell them if you make Treaty with southern President that he would pay you more annuity and would pay better than the U.S. if they the Indians would help the Southern President – Mr. Pike makes the half

impressed itself, for good or ill, upon the trans-Missouri region, it was, to say the least, somewhat discon-

breeds believe what he says and the half breeds makes some of the full blood Indians believe what he says that they (the Indians) must help the secessionists. Then that is so – but as for himself he dont believe him yet. Then he thought the old U.S. was alive yet and the Treaty was good. Wont go against the U.S. himself – That is the reason the Secessions want to have him – The Secessionists offered 5000$ for his head because he would not go against the U.S. Never knew that Creek have an agent here until he come and see him and that is why I have come among this Union people. Have come in and saw my agent and want to go by the old Treaty. Wants to get with U.S. Army so that I can get back to my people as Secessionists will not let me go. Wants the Great Father to send the Union Red people and Troops down the Black Beaver road and he will guide them to his country and then all his people will be for the Union – That he cannot get back to his people any other way – Our Father to protect the land in peace so that he can live in peace on the land according to the Treaty – At the time I left my union people I told them to look to the Beaver Road until I come. Promised his own people that the U.S. Army would come back the Beaver Road and wants to go that way – The way he left his country his people was in an elbow surrounded by secessions and his people is not strong enough against them for Union and that is the reason he has come up for help – Needed guns, powder, lead to take to his own people. Own people for the Union about 3350 warriors all Creeks – Needed now clothing, tents for winter, tools, shirts, and every thing owned by whites, – wants their annuity as they need it now – The Indians and the Whites among us have done nothing against any one but the Secessionists have compelled us to fight and we are willing to fight for the Union. Creek half breeds joined secessionists 32 head men and leaders – 27 towns for the Union among Creeks

Signed: OKE-TAH-HAH-SHAH-HAW CHOE
his X mark.

Talk of Chickasaw Chief, Toe-Lad-Ke

Says – Will talk short words – have had fever and sick – Secessionists told him no more U.S. no more Treaty – all broken up better make new Treaty with Secessionists – Although they told him all this did not believe them and that is reason came up to see if there was not still old U.S. – Loves his country – loves his children and would not believe them yet – That he did not believe what the Secessionists told him and they would not let him live in peace and that is the reason he left his country – The secessionists want to tie him – whip him and make him join them – but he would not and he left.

100 warriors for secession –
2240 do " Union

certing, not because Lane was hostile to Hunter personally – the two men had long had a friendly acquaintance

The secessionists plague him so much talk he asks for his country
that the army go down and that is what his people wants same as
Creek and Seminole – Have seen the agent of the Creeks but have
not seen our agent but want to see him – wants agent sent – He has
always done no wrong – Secessionists would not let him live in
peace – and if have to fight all his people will fight for Union – That
is all the chance that he can save his lands and property to children –
by old U.S. and Treaty – Chickasaw – Seminoles and Creeks all in
no difference – all for the Union – all want annuity and have had none
for some time – Now my Great Father you must remember me and
my people and all our wants   *Signed*: TOE-LAD-KE, his X mark.

Talk of Seminole Chief, Choo-Loo-Foe-Lop-hah-Choe

Says: Pike went among the Seminoles and tell them the same as
he told the Creek   The talk of Pike he did not believe and told him
so himself – Some of my people did believe Pike and did join the
secessionists also he believed the old U.S. is alive and Treaty not
dead and that is the reason he come up and had this talk – Never had
done any thing against Treaty and had come to have Great Father
protect us – Secession told him that Union men was going to take
away land and property – could get no annuity old U.S. all gone –
come to see – find it not so – wants President to send an agent dont
know who agent is – wants to appoint agent himself as he knows who
he wants.   Twelve towns are for the Union
            500 warriors for the Union
            100   do   " Secession
All people who come with Billy Bowlegs are Union – Chief in place
of Billy Bowlegs Shoe-Nock-Me-Koe this is his name – Need everything that Creeks need – arms clothing, etc etc. wants to go with
army same way and same road with Creek – This is what we ask of
our Great Father live as the Treaty says in peace – and all Seminole
warriors will fight for the Union.   This is the request of our people
of our Great Father   They need their annuity have not had any for
nearly a year and want it sent
            Signed: CHOO-LOO-FOE-LOP-HAH-CHOE, his X mark.
We the Chiefs of the three nations Creeks, Chickasaws and
Seminoles who are of this delegation and all for the Union and the
majority of our people are for the Union and agree in all that has
been said by the Chiefs who have made this talk, and believe all they
have said to be true –

OKE-TAH-HAH-SHAH-HAW-CHOE	his X mark	Creek
WHITE CHIEF	his X mark	
BOB DEER	his X mark	Creek
PHIL DAVID	his X mark	

with each other [142] – but because he had had great hopes of receiving the post himself.[143] The time was now drawing near for him to repair to Washington to resume his senatorial duties since Congress was to convene the second of December.

To further his scheme for Indian enlistment, Lane had projected an inter-tribal council to be held at his own headquarters. E. H. Carruth worked especially to that end. The man in charge of the Southern Superintendency, W. G. Coffin, had a similar plan in mind for less specific reasons. His idea was to confer with the representatives of the southern tribes with reference to Indian Territory conditions generally. It was part of the duty appertaining to his office. Humboldt [144] was the place selected by him for the meeting; but Leroy, being better protected and more accessible, was soon substituted. The sessions commenced the six-

Toe-Lad-Ke	his X mark	} Chickasaw
Chap-pia-ke	his X mark	
Choo-Loo-Foe-Lop-hah-Choe	his X mark	} Seminole
Oh-Chen-Yah-hoe-lah	his X mark	

Witness: C. F. Currier
W. Whistler

Leroy, Coffey Co. Kan., Nov. 4 1861.
I do certify that the within statement of the different chiefs were taken before me at a council held at my house at the time stated and that the talk of the Indian was correctly taken down by a competent clerk at the time.

Geo. A. Cutler, *Agent* for the Creek Indians.
[Indian Office Special Files, no. 201, *Southern Superintendency*, C 1400 of 1861.]

[142] Their acquaintance dated, if not from the antebellum days when Hunter was stationed at Fort Leavenworth and was not particularly magnanimous in his treatment of Southerners, then from those when he had charge, by order of General Scott, of the guard at the White House. *Report of the Military Services of General David Hunter*, pp. 7, 8.

[143] *Daily Conservative*, November 13, 1861.

[144] Coffin to Dole, October 2, 1861, Commissioner of Indian Affairs, *Report*, 1861, p. 39.

teenth[145] of November and were still continuing on the twenty-third.[146] It had not been possible to hold them earlier because of the disturbed state of the country and the consequent difficulty of getting into touch with the Indians.

Upon assuming command of the Department of Kansas, General Hunter took full cognizance of the many things making for disquietude and turmoil in the country now under his jurisdiction. Indian relations became, of necessity, matters of prime concern. Three things bear witness to this fact, Hunter's plans for an inter-tribal council at Fort Leavenworth, his own headquarters; his advocacy of Indian enlistment, especially from among the southern Indians; and his intention, early avowed, of bringing Brigadier-general James W. Denver into military prominence and of entrusting to him the supervisory command in Kansas. In some respects, no man could have been found equal to Denver in conspicuous fitness for such a position. He had served as commissioner of Indian affairs[147] under Buchanan and, although a Virginian by birth, had had a large experience with frontier life – in Missouri, in the Southwest during the Mexican War, and in California. He had also measured swords with Lane. It was in squatter-sovereignty days when, first as secretary and then as governor of Kansas Territory, he had been in a position to become intimately acquainted with the intricacies of Lane's true character and had had both occasion and opportunity to oppose some of that worthy's autocratic and thoroughly lawless maneu-

---

[145] *Daily Conservative*, November 17, 1861.

[146] — *Ibid.*, November 23, 1861.

[147] Denver was twice appointed Commissioner of Indian Affairs by Buchanan. For details as to his official career, see *Biographical Congressional Directory*, 499, and Robinson, *Kansas Conflict*, 424.

vers.[148]   As events turned out, this very acquaintance
with Lane constituted his political unfitness for the control that Hunter,[149] in December, and Halleck,[150] in the
following March, designed to give him. With the
second summons to command, came opportunity for
Lane's vindictive animosity to be called into play. His-
torically, it furnished conclusive proof, if any were
needed, that Lane had supreme power over the distribution of Federal patronage in his own state and exercised that power even at the cost of the well-being and
credit of his constituency.

When Congress began its second session in December, the fight against Lane for possession of his seat in
the Senate proceeded apace; but that did not, in the
least, deter him from working for his brigade. His
scheme now was to have it organized on a different
footing from that which it had sustained heretofore.
His influence with the administration in Washington
was still very peculiar and very considerable, so much
so, in fact, that President Lincoln, without taking ex-
pert advice and without consulting either the military
men, whose authority would necessarily be affected, or
the civil officials in Kansas, nominated him to the Senate as brigadier-general to have charge of troops in that
state.[151]   Secretary Cameron was absent from the city

[148] Robinson, *op. cit.*, 378 ff., 424 ff.

[149] *Official Records*, vol. viii, 456.

[150] — *Ibid.*, 832.

[151] The Leavenworth *Daily Conservative* seemed fairly jubilant over the
prospect of Lane's early return to military activity. The following extracts from its news items and editorials convey some such idea:

"General Lane of Kansas has been nominated to the Senate and unanimously confirmed, as Brigadier General, to command Kansas troops; the
express understanding being that General Lane's seat in the Senate shall not
be vacated until he accepts his new commission, which he will not do until
the Legislature of Kansas assembles, next month. He has no idea of doing
anything that shall oblige Governor Robinson and his appointee (Stanton)

at the time this was done and apparently, when apprised of it, made some objections on the score, not so much of an invasion of his own prerogative, as of its probable effect upon Hunter. Cameron had his first consultation with Lane regarding the matter, January second, and was given by him to understand that everything had been done in strict accordance with Hunter's own wishes.[152] The practical question of the relation of Lane's brigade to Hunter's command soon, however, presented itself in a somewhat different light and its answer required a more explicit statement from the president than had yet been made. Lincoln, when appealed to, unhesitatingly repudiated every suggestion of the idea that it had ever been his intention to give Lane an independent command or to have Hunter, in any sense, superseded.[153]

The need for sending relief to the southern Indians, which, correctly interpreted meant, of course, reasserting authority over them and thus removing a menacing and impending danger from the Kansas border, had been one of Lane's strongest arguments in gaining his way with the administration. The larger aspect of his purpose was, however, the one that appealed to Commissioner Dole, who, as head of the Indian Bureau, seems fully to have appreciated the responsibility that

who has been in waiting for several months to take the place." — *Daily Conservative*, January 1, 1862.

"Rejoicing in Neosho Battalion over report that Lane appointed to command Kansas troops." — *Ibid.*, January 4, 1862.

"General Lane will soon be here and General Denver called to another command." — *Ibid.*, January 7, 1862.

[152] Cameron to Hunter, January 3, 1862, *Official Records,* vol. liii, supplement, 512-513.

[153] Martin F. Conway, the Kansas representative in Congress, was under no misapprehension as to Lane's true position; for Lincoln had told him personally that Lane was to be under Hunter [*Daily Conservative*, February 6, 1862].

assuredly rested in all honor upon the government, whether conscious of it or not, to protect its wards in their lives and property. From the first intimation given him of Lane's desire for a more energetic procedure, Dole showed a willingness to coöperate; and, as many things were demanding his personal attention in the West, he so timed a journey of his own that it might be possible for him to assist in getting together the Indian contingent that was to form a part of the "Southern Expedition." [154]

The urgency of the Indian call for help [155] and the

[154] Lane's expedition was variously referred to as "the Southern Expedition," "the Cherokee Expedition," "the great jayhawking expedition," and by many another name, more or less opprobrious.

[155] Representations of the great need of the Indians for assistance were made to the government by all sorts of people. Agent after agent wrote to the Indian Office. The Reverend Evan Jones wrote repeatedly and on the second of January had sent information, brought to him at Lawrence by two fugitive Cherokees, of the recent battle in which the loyalists under Opoeth-le-yo-ho-la had been worsted, at the Big Bend of the Arkansas [Indian Office Special Files, no. 201, *Southern Superintendency, J* 540 of 1862]. In the early winter, a mixed delegation of Creeks and others had made their way to Washington, hoping by personal entreaty to obtain succor for their distressed people, and justice. Hunter had issued a draft for their individual relief [*ibid.*, J523 of 1861], and passes from Fort Leavenworth to Washington [*ibid.*, C1433 of 1861]. It was not so easy for them to get passes coming back. Application was made to the War Department and referred back to the Interior [*ibid.*, A434 of 1861]. The estimate, somewhat inaccurately footed up, of the total expense of the return journey as submitted by agents Cutler and Carruth was,

"11 R.R. Tickets to Fort Leavenworth by way of New York City
$48 ....$ 528.00
11 men $2 ea (incidental expenses) 22.00
2½ wks board at Washington $5 .... 137.50
Expenses from Leavenworth to Ind. Nat. 50.00
Pay of Tecumseh for taking care of horses...................... 25.00
                                                              ─────────
[*Ibid.*, C1433 of 1861]. $ 960.50"

Dole had not encouraged the delegation to come on to Washington. He pleaded lack of funds and the wish that they would wait in Fort Leavenworth and attend Hunter's inter-tribal council so that they might go back to their people carrying definite messages of what was to be done [Indian

evident readiness of the government to make answer to that call before it was quite too late pointed auspiciously to a successful outcome for Senator Lane's endeavors; but, unfortunately, Major-general Hunter had not been sufficiently counted with.   Hunter had previously shown much sympathy for the Indians in their distress [156] and also a realization of the strategic importance

Office *Letter Book*, no. 67, p. 107]. Dole had been forwarned of their intention to appear in Washington by the following letter:

FORT LEAVENWORTH, KAN., Nov. 23rd 1861.
HON. WM. P. DOLE, Com. Indian Affs.

Sir: On my arrival in St. Louis I found Gen¹ Hunter at the Planters House and delivered the message to him that you had placed in my hands for that purpose. He seemed fully satisfied with your letter and has acted on it accordingly. I recd from Gen¹ Hunter a letter for Mr. Cutler, and others of this place, all of which I have delivered. Having found Cutler here, he having been ordered by Lane to move the council from Leroy to Fort Scott. But from some cause (which I have not learned) he has brought the chiefs all here to the Fort, where they are now quartered awaiting the arrival of Gen¹ Hunter. He has with him six of the head chiefs of the Creek, Seminole and Cherokee Nations, and tells me that they are strong for the Union. He also says that John Ross (Cherokee) is all right but dare not let it be known, and that he will be here if he can get away from the tribe.

These chiefs all say they want to fight for the Union, and that they will do so if they can get arms and ammunition. Gen¹ Hunter has ordered me to await his arrival here at which time he will council with these men, and report to you the result. I think he will be here on Tuesday or Wednesday. Cutler wants to take the Indians to Washington, but I advised him not to do so until I could hear from you. When I met him here he was on his way there.

You had better write to him here as soon as you get this, or you will see him there pretty soon.

I have nothing more to write now but will write in a day or two.
Yours Truly   R. W. DOLE.
P.S. Coffin is at home sick, but will be here soon. Branch is at St. Joe but would not come over with me, cause, too buissie to attend to business.

[Indian Office Special Files, no 201, *Southern Superintendency*, D 410 of 1861].

[156] In part proof of this take his letter to Adjutant-general Thomas, January 15, 1862.

"On my arrival here in November last I telegraphed for permission to

of Indian Territory. Some other explanation, therefore, must be found for the opposition he advanced to
Lane's project as soon as it was brought to his notice.
It had been launched without his approval having been
explicitly sought and almost under false pretences.[157]
Then, too, Lane's bumptiousness, after he had accomplished his object, was naturally very irritating. But,
far above every other reason, personal or professional,
that Hunter had for objecting to a command conducted
by Lane was the identical one that Halleck,[158] Robinson, and many another shared with him, a wholesome
repugnance to such marauding[159] as Lane had permitted his men to indulge in in the autumn. It was to
be feared that Indians under Lane would inevitably
revert to savagery. There would be no one to put any
restraint upon them and their natural instincts would
be given free play. Conceivably then, it was not mere
supersensitiveness and pettiness of spirit that moved
General Hunter to take exception to Lane's appointment but regard for the honor of his profession, perchance, also, a certain feeling of personal dignity that

muster a Brigade of Kansas Indians into the service of the United States,
to assist the friendly Creek Indians in maintaining their loyalty. Had this
permission been promptly granted, I have every reason to believe that the
present disastrous state of affairs, in the Indian country west of Arkansas,
could have been avoided. I now again respectfully repeat my request." —
Indian Office General Files, *Southern Superintendency,* 1859-1862.

[157] To the references given in Abel, *The American Indian as Slaveholder
and Secessionist,* add Thomas to Hunter, January 24, 1862, *Official Records,*
vol. viii, 525.

[158] The St. Louis *Republican* credited Halleck with characterizing Hunter's
command, indiscriminately, as "marauders, bandits, and outlaws" [*Daily
Conservative,* February 7, 1862]. In a letter to Lincoln, January 6, 1862,
Halleck said some pretty plain truths about Lane [*Official Records,* vol. vii,
532-533]. He would probably have had the same objection to the use of
Indians that he had to the use of negroes in warfare [*Daily Conservative,*
May 23, 1862, quoting from the Chicago *Tribune*].

[159] On marauding by Lane's brigade, see McClellan to Stanton, February
11, 1862 [*Official Records,* vol. viii, 552-553].

legitimately resented executive interference with his rights. His protest had its effect and he was informed that it was entirely within his prerogative to lead the expedition southward himself. He resolved to do it. Lane was, for once, outwitted.

The end, however, was not yet. About the middle of January, Stanton became Secretary of War and soon let it be known that he, too, had views on the subject of Indian enlistment. As a matter of fact, he refused to countenance it.[160] The disappointment was the most keen for Commissioner Dole. Since long before the day when Secretary Smith had announced [161] to him that the Department of War was contemplating the employment of four thousand Indians in its service, he had hoped for some means of rescuing the southern tribes from the Confederate alliance and now all plans had come to naught. And yet the need for strenuous action of some sort had never been so great.[162] Opoeth-le-yo-ho-la and his defeated followers were refugees on the Verdigris, imploring help to relieve their present

---

[160] Note this series of telegrams [Indian Office Special Files, no. 201, *Southern Superintendency*, D 576 of 1862]:

"Secretary of War is unwilling to put Indians in the army. Is to consult with President and settle it today." — SMITH to Dole, February 6, 1862.

"President cant attend to business now. Sickness in the family. No arrangements can be made now. Make necessary arrangements for relief of Indians. I will send communication to Congress today." — Same to Same, February 11, 1862.

"Go on and supply the destitute Indians. Congress will supply the means. War Department will not organize them." — Same to Same, February 14, 1862.

[161] Smith to Dole, January 3, 1862 [Indian Office Special Files, no. 201, *Central Superintendency*, I 531 of 1862; Commissioner of Indian Affairs, *Report*, 1862, p. 150].

[162] On the second of January, Agent Cutler wired from Leavenworth to Dole, "Heopothleyohola with four thousand warriors is in the field and needs help badly. Secession Creeks are deserting him. Hurry up Lane." — Indian Office Special Files, no. 201, *Southern Superintendency*, C 1443 of 1862.

necessities and to enable them to return betimes to their own country.[163]   Moreover, Indians of northern antecedents and sympathies were exhibiting unwonted enthusiasm for the cause[164] and it seemed hard to have to repel them.   Dole was, nevertheless, compelled to do it.   On the eleventh of February, he countermanded the orders he had issued to Superintendent Coffin and thus a temporary quietus was put upon the whole affair of the Indian Expedition.

---

[163] Their plea was expressed most strongly in the course of an interview which Dole had with representatives of the Loyal Creeks and Seminoles, Iowas and Delawares, February 1, 1862.   Robert Burbank, the Iowa agent, was there.   White Cloud acted as interpreter [*Daily Conservative,* February 2, 1862].

[164] Some of these had been provoked to a desire for war by the inroads of Missourians.   Weas, Piankeshaws, Peorias, and Miamies, awaiting the return of Dole from the interior of Kansas, said, "they were for peace but the Missourians had not left them alone" [*ibid.,* February 9, 1862].

III. THE INDIAN REFUGEES IN SOUTH-
ERN KANSAS

The thing that would most have justified the military
employment of Indians by the United States government, in the winter of 1862, was the fact that hundreds
and thousands of their southern brethren were then
refugees because of their courageous and unswerving
devotion to the American Union. The tale of those
refugees, of their wanderings, their deprivations, their
sufferings, and their wrongs, comparable only to that
of the Belgians in the Great European War of 1914, is
one of the saddest to relate, and one of the most disgraceful, in the history of the War of Secession, in its
border phase.

The first in the long procession of refugees were
those of the army of Opoeth-le-yo-ho-la who, after their
final defeat by Colonel James McIntosh in the Battle
of Chustenahlah, December 26, 1861, had fled up the
valley of the Verdigris River and had entered Kansas
near Walnut Creek. In scattered lines, with hosts of
stragglers, the enfeebled, the aged, the weary, and the
sick, they had crossed the Cherokee Strip and the Osage
Reservation and, heading steadily towards the northeast, had finally encamped on the outermost edge of the
New York Indian Lands, on Fall River, some sixty
odd miles west of Humboldt. Those lands, never having been accepted as an equivalent for their Wisconsin
holdings by the Iroquois, were not occupied throughout
their entire extent by Indians and only here and there

encroached upon by white intruders, consequently the impoverished and greatly fatigued travellers encountered no obstacles in settling themselves down to rest and to wait for a much needed replenishment of their resources.

Their coming was expected. On their way northward, they had fallen in, at some stage of the journey, with some buffalo hunters, Sacs and Foxes of the Mississippi, returning to their reservation, which lay some distance north of Burlington and chiefly in present Osage County, Kansas. To them the refugees reported their recent tragic experience. The Sacs and Foxes were most sympathetic and, after relieving the necessities of the refugees as best they could, hurried on ahead, imparting the news, in their turn, to various white people whom they met. In due course it reached General Denver, still supervising affairs in Kansas, and William G. Coffin, the southern superintendent.[165] It was the first time, since his appointment the spring before, that Coffin had had any prospect of getting in touch with any considerable number of his charges and he must have welcomed the chance of now really earning his salary. He ordered all of the agents under him— and some[166] of them had not previously entered officially upon their duties—to assemble at Fort Roe, on the Verdigris, and be prepared to take charge of their

---

[165] These facts were obtained chiefly from a letter, not strictly accurate as to some of its details, written by Superintendent Coffin to Dole, January 15, 1862 [Indian Office Special Files, no. 201, *Southern Superintendency*, C 1474 of 1862].

[166] For instance, William P. Davis, who had been appointed Seminole Agent, despairing of ever reaching his post, had gone into the army [Dole to John S. Davis of New Albany, Indiana, April 5, 1862, Indian Office *Letter Book*, no. 68, p. 39]. George C. Snow of Parke County, Indiana, was appointed in his stead [Dole to Snow, January 13, 1862, *ibid.*, no. 67, p. 243].

several contingents; for the refugees, although chiefly Creeks, were representative of nearly every one of the non-indigenous tribes of Indian Territory.

It is not an easy matter to say, with any show of approach to exact figures, how many the refugees numbered.[167]   For weeks and weeks, they were almost continually coming in and even the very first reports bear suspicious signs of the exaggeration that became really notorious as graft and peculation entered more and more into the reckoning.   Apparently, all those who, in ever so slight a degree, handled the relief funds, except, perhaps, the army men, were interested in making the numbers appear as large as possible.   The larger the need represented, the larger the sum that might, with propriety, be demanded and the larger the opportunity for graft.   Settlers, traders, and some government agents were, in this respect, all culpable together.

There was no possibility of mistake, however, intentional or otherwise, about the destitution of the refugees.   It was inconceivably horrible.   The winter weather of late December and early January had been most inclement and the Indians had trudged through it, over snow-covered, rocky, trailless places and desolate prairie, nigh three hundred miles.   When they started out, they were not any too well provided with clothing; for they had departed in a hurry, and, before they got to Fall River, not a few of them were absolutely naked.   They had practically no tents, no bed-coverings, and no provisions.   Dr. A. B. Campbell, a surgeon sent out by General Hunter,[168] had reached them

---

[167] Compare the statistics given in the following: Commissioner of Indian Affairs, *Report*, 1861, p. 151; 1862, pp. 137, 157; Indian Office Special Files, no. 201, *Southern Superintendency*, C 1525 of 1862; General Files, *Southern Superintendency*, C 1602 of 1862.

[168] The army furnished the first relief that reached them. In its issue

towards the end of January and their condition was then so bad, so wretched that it was impossible for him to depict it. Prairie grasses were "their only protection from the snow" upon which they were lying "and from the wind and weather scraps and rags stretched upon switches." Ho-go-bo-foh-yah, the second Creek chief, was ill with a fever and "his tent (to give it that name) was no larger than a small blanket stretched over a switch ridge pole, two feet from the ground, and did not reach it by a foot from the ground on either side of him." Campbell further said that the refugees were greatly in need of medical assistance. They were suffering "with inflammatory diseases of the chest, throat, and eyes." Many had "their toes frozen off," others, "their feet wounded." But few had "either shoes or moccasins." Dead horses were lying around in every direction and the sanitary conditions were so bad that the food was contaminated and the newly-arriving refugees became sick as soon as they ate.[169]

Other details of their destitution were furnished by Coffin's son who was acting as his clerk and who was among the first to attempt alleviation of their misery.[170] As far as relief went, however, the supply was so out of proportion to the demand that there was never any time that spring when it could be said that they were fairly comfortable and their ordinary wants satisfied. Campbell frankly admitted that he "selected the nakedest of the naked" and doled out to them the few articles he

of January 18, 1862, the *Daily Conservative* has this to say: "The Kansas Seventh has been ordered to move to Humboldt, Allen Co. to give relief to Refugees encamped on Fall River. Lt. Col. Chas. T. Clark, 1st Battalion, Kansas Tenth, is now at Humboldt and well acquainted with the conditions."

[169] Commissioner of Indian Affairs, *Report*, 1862, pp. 151-152.

[170] O. S. Coffin to William G. Coffin, January 26, 1862, Indian Office Special Files, no. 201, *Southern Superintendency,* C 1506 of 1862.

had. When all was gone, how pitiful it must have been for him to see the "hundreds of anxious faces" for whom there was nothing! Captain Turner, from Hunter's commissary department, had similar experiences. According to him, the refugees were "in want of every necessary of life." That was his report the eleventh of February.[171] On the fifteenth of February, the army stopped giving supplies altogether and the refugees were thrown back entirely upon the extremely limited resources of the southern superintendency.

Dole[172] had had warning from Hunter[173] that such would have to be the case and had done his best to be prepared for the emergency. Secretary Smith authorized expenditure for relief in advance of congressional appropriation, but that simply increased the moral obligation to practice economy and, with hundreds of loyal Indians on the brink of starvation,[174] it was no

---

[171] Commissioner of Indian Affairs, *Report,* 1862, pp. 152-154.

[172] Dole had an interview with the Indians immediately upon his arrival in Kansas [Moore, *Rebellion Record,* vol. iv, 59-60, Doc. 21].

[173] Hunter to Dole, February 6, 1862, forwarded by Edward Wolcott to Mix, February 10, 1862 [Indian Office General Files, *Southern Superintendency,* 1859-1862, W 513 and D 576 of 1862; Commissioner of Indian Affairs, *Report,* 1862, p. 150].

[174] Agent G. C. Snow reported, February 13, 1862, on the utter destitution of the Seminoles [Indian Office General Files, *Seminole,* 1858-1869] and, on the same day, Coffin [*ibid., Southern Superintendency,* 1859-1862, C 1526] to the same effect about the refugees as a whole. They were coming in, he said, about twenty to sixty a day. The "destitution, misery and suffering amongst them is beyond the power of any pen to portray, it must be seen to be realised — there are now here over two thousand men, women, and children entirely barefooted and more than that number that have not rags enough to hide their nakedness, many have died and they are constantly dying. I should think at a rough guess that from 12 to 15 hundred dead Ponies are laying around in the camp and in the river. On this account so soon as the weather gets a little warm, a removal of this camp will be indespensable, there are perhaps now two thousand Ponies living, they are very poor and many of them must die before grass comes which we expect here from the first to the 10th of March. We are issuing a little corn to

time for economy. The inadequacy of the Indian service and the inefficiency of the Federal never showed up more plainly, to the utter discredit of the nation, than at this period and in this connection.

Besides getting permission from Secretary Smith to go ahead and supply the more pressing needs of the refugees, Dole accomplished another thing greatly to their interest. He secured from the staff of General Lane a special agent, Dr. William Kile of Illinois,[175] who had formerly been a business partner of his own[176] and, like Superintendent Coffin, his more or less intimate friend. Kile's particular duty as special agent was to be the purchasing of supplies for the refugees[177] and he at once visited their encampment in order the better to determine their requirements. His investigations more than corroborated the earlier accounts of their sufferings and privations and his appointment under the circumstances seemed fully justified, notwithstanding that on the surface of things it appeared very suggestive of a near approach to nepotism, and of nepotism Dole, Coffin, and many others were unquestionably guilty. They worked into the service just as many of their own relatives and friends as they conveniently and safely could. The official pickings were considered by them as their proper perquisites. "'Twas ever thus" in American politics, city, county, state, and national.

The Indian encampment upon the occasion of

the Indians and they are feeding them a little. . . " See also Moore, *Rebellion Record*, vol. iv, 30.

[175] Dole was from Illinois also, from Edgar County; Coffin was from Indiana [Indian Office Miscellaneous Records, no. 8, p. 432].

[176] *Daily Conservative*, February 8, 1862.

[177] Indian Office Consolidated Files, *Southern Superintendency*, D 576 of 1862; *Letter Book*, no. 67, pp. 450-452.

Kile's[178] visit was no longer on Fall River. Gradually, since first discovered, the main body of the refugees had moved forward within the New York Indian Lands to the Verdigris River and had halted in the neighborhood of Fort Roe, where the government agents had received them; but smaller or larger groups, chiefly of the sick and their friends, were scattered all along the way from Walnut Creek.[179] Some of the very belated exiles were as far westward as the Arkansas, over a hundred miles distant. Obviously, the thing to do first was to get them all together in one place. There were reasons why the Verdigris Valley was a most desirable location for the refugees. Only a very few white people were settled there and, as they were intruders and had not a shadow of legal claim to the land upon which they had squatted, any objections that they might make to the presence of the Indians could be ignored.[180]

For a few days, therefore, all efforts were directed, at large expense, towards converting the Verdigris Valley, in the vicinity of Fort Roe, into a concentration camp; but no precautions were taken against allowing unhygienic conditions to arise. The Indians themselves were much diseased. They had few opportunities for personal cleanliness and less ambition. Some of the food doled out to them was stuff that the army had condemned and rejected as unfit for use. They were emaciated, sick, discouraged. Finally, with

---

[178] Indian Office Land Files, 1855-1870, *Southern Superintendency,* K 107 of 1862.

[179] Some had wandered to the Cottonwood and were camped there in great destitution. Their chief food was hominy [*Daily Conservative,* February 14, 1862].

[180] For an account of the controversy over the settlement of the New York Indian Lands, see Abel, *Indian Reservations in Kansas and the Extinguishment of their Title,* 13-14.

the February thaw, came a situation that soon proved intolerable. The "stench arising from dead ponies, about two hundred of which were in the stream and throughout the camp," [181] unburied, made removal imperatively necessary.

The Neosho Valley around about Leroy presented itself as a likely place, very convenient for the distributing agents, and was next selected. Its advantages and disadvantages seemed about equal and had all been anticipated and commented upon by Captain Turner.[182] It was near the source of supplies – and that was an item very much to be considered, since transportation charges, extraordinarily high in normal times were just now exorbitant, and the relief funds very, very limited. No appropriation by Congress had yet been made although one had been applied for.[183] The great disadvantage of the location was the presence of white settlers and they objected, as well they might, to the near proximity of the inevitable disease and filth and, strangely enough, more than anything else, to the destruction of the timber, which they had so carefully husbanded. The concentration on the Neosho had not been fully accomplished when the pressure from the citizens became so great that Superintendent Coffin felt obliged to plan for yet another removal. Again the sympathy of the Sacs and Foxes of Mississippi manifested itself and most opportunely. Their reservation

---

[181] Annual Report of Superintendent Coffin, October 15, 1862, Commissioner of Indian Affairs, *Report,* 1862, p. 136. Compare with Coffin's account given in a letter to Dole, February 13, 1862.

[182] February 11, 1862, Commissioner of Indian Affairs, *Report,* 1862, p. 153; Indian Office Special Files, no. 201, *Southern Superintendency,* D 576 of 1862.

[183] *Congressional Globe,* 37th congress, second session, part 1, pp. 815, 849. Dole's letter to Smith, January 31, 1862, describing the destitution of the refugees, was read in the Senate, February 14, 1862, in support of joint resolution S. no. 49, for their relief.

lay about twenty-five miles to the northward and they generously offered it as an asylum.[184]   But the Indians balked.   They were homesick, disgusted with official mismanagement[185] and indecision, and determined to go no farther.   They complained bitterly of the treatment that they had received at the hands of Superintendent Coffin and of Agent Cutler and, in a stirring appeal[186] to President Lincoln, set forth their injuries, their grievances, and their incontestable claim upon a presumably just and merciful government.[187]

The Indians were not alone in their rebellious attitude.   There was mutiny seething, or something very like it, within the ranks of the agents.[188]   E. H. Carruth

---

[184] Coffin to Dole, March 28, 1862 [Indian Office Special Files, no. 201, *Southern Superintendency,* C 1565 of 1862].

[185] Mismanagement there most certainly had been. In no other way can the fact that there was absolutely no amelioration in their condition be accounted for. Many documents that will be cited in other connections prove this point and Collamore's letter is of itself conclusive. George W. Collamore, known best by his courtesy title of "General," went to Kansas in the critical years before the war under circumstances, well and interestingly narrated in Stearns' *Life and Public Services of George Luther Stearns,* 106-108. He had been agent for the New England Relief Society in the year of the great drouth, 1860-1861 [*Daily Conservative,* October 26, 1861] and had had much to do with Lane, in whose interests he labored, and who had planned to make him a brigadier under himself as major-general [Stearns, 246, 251]. He became quartermaster-general of Kansas [*Daily Conservative,* March 27, 1862] and in that capacity made, in the company of the Reverend Evan Jones, a visit of inspection to the refugee encampment. His discoveries were depressing [*ibid.,* April 10, 1862]. His report to the government [Indian Office General Files, *Southern Superintendency,* C 1602 of 1862] is printed almost *verbatim* in Commissioner of Indian Affairs, *Report,* 1862, 155-158.

[186] Coffin's letter to Dole of April 21, 1862 [Indian Office General Files, *Wichita,* 1862-1871, C 1601 of 1862] seems to cast doubt upon the genuineness of some of the signatures attached to this appeal and charges Agent Carruth with having been concerned in making the Indians discontented.

[187] Opoeth-le-yo-ho-la and other prominent refugees addressed their complaints to Dole, March 29, 1862 [Indian Office Land Files, *Southern Superintendency,* 1855-1870, O 43 of 1862] and two days later to President Lincoln, some strong partisan, supposed by Coffin to be Carruth, acting as scribe.

[188] On the way to the Catholic Mission, whither he was going in order

who had been so closely associated with Lane in the concoction of the first plan for the recovery of Indian Territory, was now figuring as the promoter of a rising sentiment against Coffin and his minions, who were getting to be pretty numerous. The removal to the Sac and Fox reservation would mean the getting into closer and closer touch with Perry Fuller,[189] the contractor, whose dealings in connection with the Indian refugees were to become matter, later on, of a notoriety truly disgraceful. Mistrust of Coffin was yet, however, very vague in expression and the chief difficulty in effecting the removal from the Neosho lay, therefore, in the disgruntled state of the refugees, which was due, in part, to their unalleviated misery and, in part, to domestic

---

to coöperate with Agent Elder in negotiating with the Osages, Coffin heard of "a sneaking conspiracy" that was "on foot at Iola for the purpose of prejudicing the Indians against us [himself and Dole, perhaps, or possibly himself and the agents]." The plotters, so Coffin reported, "sent over the Verdigris for E. H. Carruth who" was "deep in the plot," which was a scheme to induce the Indians to lodge complaint against the distributers of relief. One of the conspirators was a man who had studied law under Lane and who had wanted a position under Kile. Lane had used his influence in the man's behalf and the refusal of Coffin to assign him to a position was supposed to be the cause of all the trouble. Coffin learned that his enemies had even gone so far as to plan vacancies in the Indian service and to fill them. They had "instructed Lane, Pomeroy, and Conway accordingly," leaving graciously to Lane the choice of superintendent. A Mr. Smith, correspondent of the Cincinnati *Gazette* was their accredited secretary [Coffin to Dole, April 2, 1862, Indian Office Consolidated Files, *Southern Superintendency*, C 1571 of 1862].

Further particulars of the disaffection came to Coffin's ears before long and he recounted them to Dole in a letter of April 9, 1862 [*ibid.*, General Files, *Southern Superintendency*, 1859-1862].

189 Perry Fuller had been in Kansas since 1854 [U. S. House *Reports*, 34th congress, first session, no. 200, p. 8 of "Testimony"]. The first time that his name is intimately used in the correspondence, relative to the affairs of the refugees, is in a letter from Kile to Dole, March 29, 1862 [Indian Office Consolidated Files, *Southern Superintendency*, K 113 of 1862, which also makes mention of the great unwillingness of the Indians to move to the Sac and Fox reservation.

tribal discord. There was a quarrel among them over leadership, the election of Ock-tah-har-sas Harjo as principal chief having aroused strong antagonistic feeling among the friends of Opoeth-le-yo-ho-la.[190] Moreover, dissatisfaction against their agent steadily increased and they asked for the substitution of Carruth; but he, being satisfied with his assignment to the Wichitas,[191] had no wish to change.[192]

---

[190] Carruth gave particulars of this matter to Dole, April 20, 1862 [Indian Office General Files, *Wichita*, 1862-1871, C 1601 of 1862].

[191] Dole to Carruth, March 18, 1862 [Indian Office *Letter Book*, no. 67, pp. 493-494].

[192] Carruth to Dole, April 10, 1862 [*ibid.*, General Files, *Wichita*, 1862-1871, C 1588 of 1862; *Letters Registered*, vol. 58].

IV. THE ORGANIZATION OF THE FIRST
INDIAN EXPEDITION

Among the manifold requests put forward by the
refugees, none was so insistent, none so dolefully sincere, as the one for means to return home. It is a mistake to suppose that the Indian, traditionally laconic
and stoical, is without family affection and without that
noblest of human sentiments, love of country. The
United States government has, indeed, proceeded upon
the supposition that he is destitute of emotions, natural
to his more highly civilized white brother, but its files
are full to overflowing with evidences to the contrary.
Everywhere among them the investigator finds the
exile's lament. The red man has been banished so often from familiar and greatly loved scenes that it is a
wonder he has taken root anywhere and yet he has.
Attachment to the places where the bones of his people
lie is with him the most constant of experiences and his
cry for those same sacred places is all the stronger and
the more sorrowful because it has been persistently ignored by the white man.

The southern Indians had not been so very many
years in the Indian Territory, most of them not more
than the span of one generation, but Indian Territory
was none the less home. If the refugees could only get
there again, they were confident all would be well with
them. In Kansas, they were hungry, afflicted with disease, and dying daily by the score.[193] Once at home

---

[193] And yet they did have their amusements. Their days of exile were
not filled altogether with bitterness. Coffin, in a letter to the *Daily Conser-*

all the ills of the flesh would disappear and lost friends be recovered. The exodus had separated them cruelly from each other. There were family and tribal encampments within the one large encampment,[194] it is true, but there were also widely isolated groups, scattered indiscriminately across two hundred miles of bleak and lonely prairie, and no amount of philanthropic effort on the part of the government agents could mitigate the misery arising therefrom or bring the groups together. The task had been early abandoned as, under the circumstances, next to impossible; but the refugees went on begging for its accomplishment, notwithstanding that they had neither the physical strength nor the means to render any assistance themselves. Among them the wail of the bereaved vied in tragic cadence with the sad inquiry for the missing.

When Dole arrived at Leavenworth the latter part of January, representatives of the loyal Indians interviewed him and received assurances, honest and well-meant at the time given, that an early return to Indian Territory would be made possible. Lane, likewise interviewed,[195] was similarly encouraging and had every reason to be; for was not his Indian brigade in process of formation? Much cheered and even exhilarated in spirit, the Indians went away to endure and to wait. They had great confidence in Lane's power to accomplish; but, as the days and the weeks passed and he did not come, they grew tired of waiting. The waiting

vative, published April 16, 1862, gives, besides a rather gruesome account of their diseases, some interesting details of their camp life.

[194] On their division into tribal encampments, see Kile to Dole, April 10, 1862 [Indian Office General Files, *Southern Superintendency*, 1859-1862, K 119 of 1862].

[195] They had their interview with Lane at the Planters' House while they were awaiting the arrival of Dole. Opoeth-le-yo-ho-la (Crazy Dog) and a Seminole chief, Aluktustenuke (Major Potatoes) were among them [*Daily Conservative*, January 28, February 8, 1862].

Portrait of Colonel W. A. Phillips

seemed so hopeless to them miserable, so endlessly long. Primitive as they were, they simply could not understand why the agents of a great government could not move more expeditiously. The political and military aspects of the undertaking, involved in their return home, were unknown to them and, if known, would have been uncomprehended. Then, too, the vacillation of the government puzzled them. They became suspicious; for they had become acquainted, through the experience of long years, with the white man's bad faith and they had nothing to go upon that would counteract the influence of earlier distrust. And so it happened, that, as the weary days passed and Lane's brigade did not materialize, every grievance that loomed up before them took the shape of a disappointed longing for home.

So poignant was their grief at the continued delay that they despaired of ever getting the help promised and began to consider how they could contrive a return for themselves. And yet, quite independent of Lane's brigade, there had been more than one movement initiated in their behalf. The desire to recover lost ground in Indian Territory, under the pretext of restoring the fugitives, aroused the fighting instinct of many young men in southern Kansas and several irregular expeditions were projected.[196] Needless to say they came to nothing. In point of fact, they never really developed, but died almost with the thought. There was no adequate equipment for them and the longer the delay, the more necessary became equipment; because after the Battle of Pea Ridge, Pike's brigade had been set free to operate, if it so willed, on the Indian Territory border.

---

[196] In addition to those referred to in documents already cited, the one, projected by Coffin's son and a Captain Brooks, is noteworthy. It is described in a letter from Coffin to Dole, March 24, 1862.

Closely following upon the Federal success of March 6 to 8, came numerous changes and readjustments in the Missouri-Kansas commands; but they were not so much the result of that success as they were a part of the general reorganization that was taking place in the Federal service incident to the more efficient war administration of Secretary Stanton. By order of March 11, three military departments were arranged for, the Department of the Potomac under McClellan, that of the Mountain under Frémont, and that of the Mississippi under Halleck. The consolidation of Hunter's Department of Kansas with Halleck's Department of Missouri was thus provided for and had long been a consummation devoutly to be wished.[197] Both were naturally parts of the same organic whole when regarded from a military point of view. Neither could be operated upon independently of the other. Moreover, both were infested by political vultures. In both, the army discipline was, in consequence, bad; that is, if it could be said to be in existence at all. If anything, Kansas was in a worse state than Missouri. Her condition, as far as the military forces were concerned, had not much improved since Hunter first took command and it was then about the worst that could possibly be imagined. Major Halpine's description[198] of it, made by him in his capacity as assistant adjutant-general, officially to Halleck, is anything but flattering. Hunter was probably well rid of his job and Halleck, whom Lincoln much admired because he was "wholly for the service,"[199] had asked for the entire command.[200]

---

[197] Halleck, however, had not desired the inclusion of Kansas in the contemplated new department because he thought that state had only a remote connection with present operations.

[198] *Official Records*, vol. viii, 615-617.

[199] Thayer, *Life and Letters of John Hay*, vol. i, 127-128.

[200] Badeau, *Military History of U. S. Grant*, vol. i, 53, *footnote*.

Halleck's plans for remodeling the constituent elements of his department were made with a thorough comprehension of the difficulties confronting him. It is not surprising that they brought General Denver again to the fore. Hunter's troubles had been bred by local politics. That Halleck well knew; but he also knew that Indian relations were a source of perplexity and that there was no enemy actually in Kansas and no enemy worth considering that would threaten her, provided her own jay-hawking hordes could be suppressed. Her problems were chiefly administrative.[201] For the work to be done, Denver seemed the fittest man available and, on the nineteenth, he, having previously been ordered to report to Halleck for duty,[202] was assigned [203] to the command of a newly-constituted District of Kansas, from which the troops,[204] who were guarding the only real danger zone, the southeastern part of the state, were expressly excluded. The hydra-headed evil of the western world then asserted itself, the meddling, particularistic spoils system, with the result that Lane and Pomeroy, unceasingly vigilant whenever and wherever what they regarded as their preserves were likely to be encroached upon, went to President Lincoln and protested against the preferment of Denver.[205] Lincoln weakly yielded and wired to Halleck to suspend

---

[201] Halleck to Stanton, March 28, 1862, *Official Records*, vol. viii, 647-648.

[202] — *Ibid.*, 612.

[203] — *Ibid.*, 832.

[204] Those troops, about five thousand, were left under the command of George W. Deitzler, colonel of the First Kansas (*ibid.*, 614), a man who had become prominent before the war in connection with the Sharpe's rifles episode (Spring, *Kansas*, 60) and whose appointment as an Indian agent, early in 1861, had been successfully opposed by Lane (Robinson, *Kansas Conflict*, 458). There will be other occasions to refer to him in this narrative. He is believed to have held the secret that induced Lane to commit suicide in 1866 [*ibid.*, 457-460].

[205] Stanton to Halleck, March 26, 1862 [*Official Records*, vol. liii, supplement, 516].

the order for Denver's assignment to duty until further notice.[206]   Stanton, to whom Halleck applied [207] for an explanation, deprecated [208] the political interference of the Kansas senators and the influence it had had with the chief executive, but he, too, had to give way.   So effective was the Lane-Pomeroy objection to Denver that even a temporary [209] appointment of him, resorted [210] to by Halleck because of the urgent need of some sort of a commander in Kansas, was deplored by the president.[211]   Denver was then sent to the place where his abilities and his experience would be better appreciated, to the southernmost part of the state, the hinterland of the whole Indian country.[212]   Official indecision and personal envy pursued him even there, however, and it was not long before he was called eastward.[213]   The man who succeeded him in command of the District of Kansas [214] was one who proved to be his ranking officer [215] and his rival, Brigadier-general S. D. Sturgis.   Blunt succeeded him at Fort Scott.

[206] Lincoln to Halleck, March 21, 1862, *Official Records*, vol. liii, supplement, 516.

[207] Halleck to Stanton, March 26, 1862, *ibid.*

[208] "Deprecated" is, perhaps, too mild a word to describe Stanton's feeling in the matter.   Adjutant-general Hitchcock is authority for the statement that Stanton threatened "to leave the office" should the "enforcement" of any such order, meaning the non-assignment of Denver and the appointment of a man named Davis [Davies?], believed by Robinson to be a relative of Lane [*Kansas Conflict*, 446], be attempted [Hitchcock to Halleck, March 22, 1862, *Official Records*, vol. viii, 832-833].

[209] — *Ibid.*, vol. liii, supplement, 519.

[210] — *Ibid.*, vol. viii, 647-648.

[211] — *Ibid.*, vol. liii, supplement, 519.

[212] Concerning the work, mapped out for Denver, see Halleck to Sturgis, April 6, 1862 [*Official Records*, vol. viii, 668] and Halleck to Stanton, April 7, 1862 [*ibid.*, 672].

[213] May 14, 1862 [*ibid.*, vol. lii, part i, supplement, 249].

[214] — *Ibid.*, vol. liii, supplement, 520.

[215] "It is stated that the commission of Gen. Sturgis is dated April 10 and that of Gen. Denver Aug. 14 and consequently Gen. Sturgis is the ranking officer in this military District." — *Daily Conservative*, April 10, 1862.

The elimination of Kansas as a separate department marked the revival of interest in an Indian expedition. The cost of supporting so huge a body of refugees had really become a serious proposition and, as Colonel C. R. Jennison [216] had once remarked, it would be economy to enlist them. [217]   Congress had provided that certain Indian annuity money might be diverted to their maintenance, [218] but that fund was practically exhausted before the middle of March. [219]   As already observed, the refugees very much wished to assist in the recovery of Indian Territory. [220]   In fact they were determined to go south if the army went and their disappointment was likely to be most keen in the event of its and their not going. [221]   It was under circumstances such as these that Commissioner Dole recommended to Secretary Smith, March 13, 1862, that he

> Procure an order from the War Department detailing two Regiment of Volunteers from Kansas to go with the Indians to their homes and to remain there for their protection as long (as) may be necessary, also to furnish two thousand stand of arms and ammunition to be placed in the hands of the loyal Indians.

Dole's unmistakable earnestness carried the day. Within less than a week there had been promised [222] him all that he had asked for and more, an expedition-

---

[216] Jennison, so says the *Daily Conservative*, March 25, 1862, had been ordered with the First Cavalry to repair to Humboldt at the time the Indian Expedition was under consideration the first of the year and was brevetted acting brigadier for the purpose of furthering Dole's intentions.

[217] *Daily Conservative*, February 18, 1862.

[218] *Congressional Globe*, 37th congress, second session, part i, 835, 878.

[219] Dole to Smith, March 13, 1862 [Indian Office *Report Book*, no. 12, 331-332].

[220] Coffin to Dole, March 3, 1862 [*ibid.*, Consolidated Files, *Southern Superintendency*, C 1544 of 1862; *Letters Registered*, no. 58].

[221] *Daily Conservative*, March 5, 1862.

[222] Commissioner of Indian Affairs, *Report*, 1862, 148.

ary force of two white regiments and two [223] thousand Indians, appropriately armed. To expedite matters and to obviate any difficulties that might otherwise beset the carrying out of the plan, a semi-confidential agent, on detail from the Indian Office, was sent west with despatches [224] to Halleck and with an order [225] from the Ordnance Department for the delivery, at Fort Leavenworth, of the requisite arms. The messenger was Judge James Steele, who, upon reaching St. Louis, had already discouraging news to report to Dole. He had interviewed Halleck and had found him in anything but a helpful mood, notwithstanding that he must, by that time, have received and reflected upon the following communication from the War Department:

WAR DEPARTMENT,
WASHINGTON CITY, D. C., March 19, 1862.
MAJ. GEN. H. W. HALLECK,
Commanding the Department of Mississippi:

General: It is the desire of the President, on the application of the Secretary of the Interior and the Commissioner of Indian Affairs, that you should detail two regiments to act in the Indian country, with a view to open the way for the friendly Indians who are now refugees in Southern Kansas to return to their homes and to protect them there. Five thousand friendly Indians will also be armed to aid in their own protection, and you will please furnish them with necessary subsistence.

Please report your action in the premises to this Department. Prompt action is necessary.

By order of the Secretary of War:

L. THOMAS, *Adjutant-general.*[226]

---

[223] Two thousand was most certainly the number, although the communication from the War Department gives it as five.

[224] Dole to Halleck, March 21, 1862 [Indian Office *Letter Book*, no. 67, 516-517].

[225] — *Ibid.*, 517-518.

[226] *Official Records*, vol. viii, 624-625.

Steele inferred from what passed at the interview with Halleck that the commanding general was decidedly opposed to arming Indians. Steele found him also non-committal as to when the auxiliary force would be available.[227] Dole's letter, with its seeming dictation as to the choice of a commander for the expedition, may not have been to Halleck's liking. He was himself at the moment most interested in the suppression of guerrillas and jayhawkers, against whom sentence of outlawry had just been passed. As it happened, that was the work in which Dole's nominee, Colonel Robert B. Mitchell,[228] was to render such signal service[229] and, anticipating as much, Halleck may have objected to his being thought of for other things. Furthermore, Dole had no right to so much as cast a doubt upon Halleck's own ability to select a proper commander.

A little perplexed but not at all daunted by Halleck's lack of cordiality, Steele proceeded on his journey and, arriving at Leavenworth, presented his credentials to Captain McNutt, who was in charge of the arsenal. Four hundred Indian rifles were at hand, ready for him, and others expected.[230] What to do next, was the question? Should he go on to Leroy and trust to the auxiliary force's showing up in season or wait for it? The principal part of his mission was yet to be executed. The Indians had to be enrolled and everything got in train for their expedition southward. Their homes

[227] Steele to Dole, March 27, 1862 [Indian Office General Files, *Southern Superintendency*, 1859-1862, S 537 of 1862].

[228] Robert B. Mitchell was colonel, first of the Second Kansas Infantry, then of the Second Kansas Cavalry. He raised the former, in answer to President Lincoln's first call, 1861 [Crawford, *Kansas in the Sixties*, 20], chiefly in Linn County, and the latter in 1862.

[229] Connelley, *Quantrill and the Border Wars*, 236 ff.

[230] Steele to Dole, March 26, 1862 [Indian Office General Files, *Southern Superintendency*, 1859-1862].

once recovered, they were to be left in such shape as to be able to "protect and defend themselves."[231]

Halleck's preoccupation, prejudice, or whatever it was that prevented him from giving any satisfaction to Steele soon yielded, as all things sooner or later must, to necessity; but not to the extent of sanctioning the employment of Indians in warfare except as against other "Indians or in defense of their own territory and homes." The Pea Ridge atrocities were probably still fresh in his mind. On the fifth of April, he instructed[232] General Denver with a view to advancing, at last, the organization of the Indian expedition and Denver, Coffin, and Steele forthwith exerted all their energies in coöperating effort.[233] Some time was spent in inspecting arms[234] but, on the eighth, enough for two thousand Indians went forward in the direction of Leroy and Humboldt[235] and on the sixteenth were delivered to the superintendent.[236] Coffin surmised that new complications would arise as soon as the distribution began; for all the Indians, whether they intended to enlist or not, would try to secure guns. Nothing had yet been said about their pay and nothing heard of an auxiliary force.[237] Again the question was, what,

---

[231] Dole to Steele, March 21, 1862, Indian Office *Letter Book*, no. 67, 508-509.

[232] *Official Records*, vol. viii, 665.

[233] Dole's name might well be added to this list; for he had never lost his interest or relaxed his efforts. On the fifth of April, he communicated to Secretary Smith the intelligence that he had issued instructions to "the officers appointed to command the two Regiments of Indians to be raised as Home Guard to report at Fort Leavenworth to be mustered into service. . ."—Indian Office *Report Book*, no. 12, 357.

[234] Steele to Dole, April 7, 1862 [*ibid.*, General Files, *Southern Superintendency*, 1859-1862, S 538 of 1862].

[235] Denver to Halleck, April 8, 1862 [*Official Records*, vol. viii, 679].

[236] Commissioner of Indian Affairs, *Report*, 1862, 148.

[237] ". . . I fear we shall have trouble in regard to the guns as many will take guns that will not go and whether they will give up their arms is doubtful. I had a long talk with Opothly – Oholo on that point and told

in the event of its not appearing, should the Indian agents do?[238]

The time was propitious for starting the expedition; for not the shadow of an enemy had been lately seen in the West, unless count be taken of Indians returning home or small roving bands of possible marauders that the people of all parties detested.[239] But the order for the supplanting of Denver by Sturgis had already been issued, April sixth,[240] and Sturgis's policy was not yet

him you could only get 2000 guns and you wanted every one to go and an Indian with it and that if any of them got guns that did not go they must give up their guns to those that would go but I know enough of the Indian character to know that it will be next thing to an impossibility to get a gun away from one when he once gets it and I shall put off the distribution of the guns till the last moment and it would be best to send them on a day or two before being distributed but that would make them mad and they would not go at all and how we are to know how many to look out for from others than those we have here I am not able to see but we will do all that we can but you may look out for dificulty in the matter   they all seem anxious now to go and make no objections as yet nor have they said anything about their pay but as they were told before when we expect them to go into the Hunter Lane expedition that they would get the same pay as white troops and set off a part of it for their families it was so indelibly impressed upon their minds that I fear we will have a blow up on that score when it comes up   we hear nothing yet of any troops being ordered to this service and I very much fear they will put off the matter so long that there will be no crop raised this season. . .   the mortality amongst them is great more since warm weather has set in than during the cold weather   they foolishly physic themselves nearly to death danc [dance] all night and then jump into the river just at daylight to make themselves bullet proof   they have followed this up now every night for over two weeks and it has no doubt caused many deaths   Long Tiger the Uchee Chief and one of the best amongst them died to-day – yesterday we had 7 deaths and there will not be less to-day" – COFFIN to Dole, April 7, 1862, Indian Office General Files, *Southern Superintendency*, 1859-1862, C 1578 of 1862.

[238] This was the query put to Dole by Steele in a letter of the thirteenth of April, which acknowledged Dole's of the third and ventured the opinion that Postmaster-general Blair "must be imitating General McClellan and practicing strategy with the mails." Steele further remarked, "Genl Denver, Maj. Wright and I are in the dark as to the plans of the Indian Expedition. Gen. Denver thinks I should proceed at once to Leroy without waiting for your instructions." – *Ibid.*, S 539 of 1862.

[239] Curtis to Halleck, April 5, 1862 [*Official Records*, vol. viii, 662].

[240] Sturgis, upon the receipt of orders of this date, assumed command of

known. It soon revealed itself, however, and was hostile to the whole project that Dole had set his heart upon. Apparently that project, the moment it had been taken up by Denver, had ceased to have any interest for Lane on the score of its merits and had become identified with the Robinson faction in Kansas politics. At any rate, it was the anti-Robinson press that saw occasion for rejoicing in the complete removal of Denver from the scene, an event which soon took place.[241]

The relieving of Denver from the command of the District of Kansas inaugurated [242] what contemporaries described as "Sturgis' military despotism," [243] in amplification of which it is enough to say that it attempted the utter confounding, if not the annihilation, of the Indian Expedition, a truly noble undertaking to be sure, considering how much was hoped for from that expedition, how much of benefit and measure of justice to a helpless, homeless, impoverished people and considering, also, how much of time and thought and

the District of Kansas; but Denver was not called east until the fourteenth of May. On the twenty-first of April, it was still expected that he would lead an expedition "down the borders of Arkansas into the Indian country." [KELTON to Curtis, April 21, 1862, *ibid.*, vol. xiii, 364].

[241] The *Daily Conservative*, for instance, rejoiced over this telegram from Sidney Clark of May 2, which gave advanced information of Denver's approaching departure: "Conservative: The Department of Kansas is reinstated. Gen. Blunt takes command. Denver reports to Halleck; Sturgis here." The newspaper comment was, "We firmly believe that a prolongation of the Denver-Sturgis political generalship, aided as it was by the corrupt Governor of this State, would have led to a revolution in Kansas . . ." – *Daily Conservative*, May 6, 1862.

[242] General Sturgis assumed command, April 10, 1862 [*Official Records*, vol. viii, 683], and Denver took temporary charge at Fort Scott [*ibid.*, 668].

[243] Quoted from the *Daily Conservative* of May 20; but not with the idea of subscribing thereby to any verdict that would bear the implication that all of Sturgis's measures were arbitrary and wrong. Something strenuous was needed in Kansas. The arrest of Jennison and of Hoyt [*ibid.*, April 19, 23, 1862] because of their too radical anti-slavery actions was justifiable. Jennison had disorganized his regiment in a shameful manner [*ibid.*, June 3, 1862].

energy, not to mention money, had already been expended upon it.

Sturgis's policy with reference to the Indian Expedition was initiated by an order,[244] of April 25, which gained circulation as purporting to be in conformity with instructions from the headquarters of the Department of the Mississippi, although in itself emanating from those of the District of Kansas. It put a summary stop to the enlistment of Indians and threatened with arrest anyone who should disobey its mandate. Superintendent Coffin, in his inimitable illiteracy, at once entered protest [245] against it and coolly informed Sturgis that, in enrolling Indians for service, he was acting under the authority, not of the War, but of the Interior Department. At the same sitting, he applied to Commissioner Dole for new instructions.[246]

---

[244] *Official Records*, vol. xiii, 365.

[245]   LE ROY COFFEE COUNTY, KANSAS, April 29th 1862.
BRIG. GENL S. D. STURGIS, Fort Leavenworth Kansas

Dear Sir: A Special Messenger arrived here last night from Fort Leavenworth with your orders No. 8 and contents noted. I would most respectfully inform you that I am acting under the controle and directions of the Interior and not of the War Department. I have been endeavoring to the best of my humble ability to carry out the instructions and wishes of that Department, all of which I hope will meet your aprobation.

Your Messenger reports himself Straped, that no funds were furnished him to pay his expenses, that he had to beg his way down here. I have paid his bill here and furnished him with five dollars to pay his way back. Very respectfully your Obedient Servant

W. G. COFFIN, *Supt. of Indian Affairs*, Southern Superintendency.
[Indian Office Special Files, no. 201, *Southern Superintendency*, C 1612 of 1862].

[246]   LEROY COFFEY CO., KANSAS, April 29th, 1862.

SIR: Enclosed please find a communication from Brigadier General Sturgis in regard to the organising of the Indians and my reply to the same, the officers are here, or at least four of them. Col Furnace Agutant Elithurp Lieutenant Wattles and Agutant Dole I need scarcely say to you that we shall continue to act under your Instructions til further orders, the Officers above alluded to have been untiring in their efforts to get acquainted with and get the permanent

Colonel John Ritchie [247] of the inchoate Second Regiment Indian Home Guards did the same. [248]

The reëstablishment [249] of the Department of Kansas, at this critical moment, while much to be regretted as indicative of a surrender to politicians [250] and an abandonment of the idea, so fundamentally conducive to military success, that all parts must contribute to the good of the whole, had one thing to commend it, it restored vigor to the Indian Expedition. The department was reëstablished, under orders [251] of May second, with James G. Blunt in command. He entered upon his duties, May fifth, and on that selfsame day authorized the issue of the following most significant instructions, in toto, a direct countermand of all that Sturgis had most prominently stood for:

> organization of the Indians under way and have made a fine impression upon them, and I should very much regret any failure to carry out the programe as they have been allready so often disappointed that they have become suspicious and it all has a tendency to lessen their confidence in us and to greatly increase our dificulties All of which is most Respectfully Submitted by your obedient Servant
>
> W G COFFIN, Supt of Indian Affairs.

[Indian Office Special Files, no. 201, *Southern Superintendency*, C 1612 of 1862].

[247] For an inferential appraisement of Ritchie's character and abilities, see Kansas *Historical Collections*, vol. iii, 359-366.

[248] Ritchie to Dole, April 26, 1862 [Indian Office Miscellaneous Files, 1858-1863].

[249] The reëstablishment, considered in the light of the first orders issued by Blunt, those set out here, was decidedly in the nature of a reflection upon the reactionary policy of Halleck and Sturgis; but Halleck had no regrets. Of Kansas, he said, "Thank God, it is no longer under my command." [*Official Records*, vol. xiii, 440.] Ever since the time, when he had been urged by the administration in Washington, peculiarly sensitive to political importunities, not to retain, outside of Kansas, the Kansas troops if he could possibly avoid it, there had been more or less of rancor between him and them. His opinion of them was that they were a "humbug" [*ibid.*, vol. viii, 661].

[250] Almost simultaneously, Schofield was given independent command in Missouri, a similar surrender to local political pressure.

[251] *Official Records*, vol. xiii, 368-369.

General Orders,   HDQRS. DEPARTMENT OF KANSAS,
No. 2.   Fort Leavenworth, Kans., May 5, 1862.

I. General Orders, No. 8, dated Headquarters District of Kansas, April 25, 1862, is hereby rescinded.

II. The instructions issued by the Department at Washington to the colonels of the two Indian regiments ordered to be raised will be fully carried out, and the regiments will be raised with all possible speed.

By order of Brig. Gen. James G. Blunt,[252]

THOS. MOONLIGHT, *Captain
and Assistant Adjutant-general.*[253]

The full extent, not only of Sturgis's failure to coöperate with the Indian Office, but also of his intention utterly to block the organization of the Indian Expedition, is revealed in a letter[254] from Robert W. Furnas, colonel commanding the First Regiment Indian Home Guards, to Dole, May 4, 1862. That letter best explains itself. It was written from Leroy, Kansas, and reads thus:

> Disclaiming any idea of violating "Regulations" by an "Official Report" to you, permit me to communicate certain facts extremely embarrassing, which surround the Indian Expedition.
>
> In compliance with your order of Ap¹ 5th. I reported myself "forthwith" to the U. S. mustering officer at Ft. Leavenworth and was "mustered into the service" on the 18th. of April. I "awaited the orders from Gen¹ Halleck" as directed but rec'd none. On the 20th. Ap¹ I rec'd detailed instruc-

---

[252] The promotion of Blunt to a brigadier-generalship had caused surprise and some opposition. Referring to it, the *Daily Conservative*, April 12, 1862, said, "Less than three months ago Mr. Lincoln informed a gentleman from this State that no Kansas man would be made a Brigadier 'unless the Kansas Congressional delegation was unanimously and strenuously in his favor' . . . Either the President has totally changed his policy or Lane, Pomeroy and Conway are responsible for this most unexpected and unprecedented appointment. . ."

[253] *Official Records*, vol. xiii, 370.

[254] Indian Office General Files, *Southern Superintendency*, 1859-1862, F 363 of 1862.

tions from Adjt. Gen¹ Thomas, authorizing me to proceed and raise "from the loyal Indians now in Kansas a Regiment of Infantry." I immediately repaired to this place and in a very few days enrolled a sufficient number of Indians to form a minimum [255] Regiment. I am particularly indebted to the Agts. Maj. Cutler of the Creeks and Maj. Snow of the Seminoles, for their valuable services. Immediately after the enrolling, and in compliance with my instructions from Adjt. Gen¹ Thomas, I notified Lieut. Chas. S. Bowman U. S. mustering officer at Ft. Leavenworth of the fact, to which I have rec'd no answer.

At this point in my procedure a special messenger from Gen¹ Sturgis reached this place with a copy of his "Order No. 8," a copy of which I herewith send you. On the next day Maj. Minor in command at Iola, Kansas, and who had been furnished with a copy of General Sturgis' "Order" came with a company of Cavalry to this place "to look into matters." I showed him my authority, and informed him what I had done. He made no arrest, seeming utterly at a loss to understand the seemingly *confused* state of affairs. Whether Gen¹ Sturgis will on the reception of my notice at the Fort arrest me, or not, I know not. I have gone to the limits of my instructions and deem it, if not my duty, prudent at least to notify *you* of the condition of affairs, that you may be the better enabled to remove obstacles, that the design of the Department may be fully and promptly executed. . .[256]

---

[255] The regiment, according to the showing of the muster roll, comprised one thousand nine men. Fifteen hundred was the more usual number of a regiment, which, normally, had three battalions with a major at the head of each.

[256] The remainder of the letter deals with the muster roll of the First Regiment Indian Home Guards, which was forwarded to Dole, under separate cover, the same day, and of which Dole acknowledged the receipt, May 16, 1862 [Indian Office *Letter Book*, no. 68, pp. 240-241]. The roll shows the captain and number of each company as here:

Company A............Billy Bowlegs...............................106
    "   B............A-ha-luk-tus-ta-na-ke 100
    "   C............Tus-te-nu-ke-ema-ela 104
    "   D............Tus-te-nuk-ke 100
    "   E............Jon-neh (John)............................101
    "   F............Mic-co-hut-ka (White Chief).................103
    "   G............Ah-pi-noh-to-me 103

It soon developed that General Halleck had been equally at fault in disregarding the wishes of the government with respect to the mustering in of the loyal Indians. He had neglected to send on to Kansas the instructions which he himself had received from Washington.[257] It was incumbent, therefore, upon Blunt to ask for new. He had found the enlisted Indians with no arms, except guns, no shot pouches, no powder horns, although they were attempting to supply themselves as best they could.[258] Blunt thought they ought to be furnished with sheath, or bowie, knives; but the Indian Office had no funds for such a purpose.[259] The new instructions, when they came, were found to differ in no particular from those which had formerly been issued. The Indian Home Guards were to constitute an irregular force and were to be supported by such white troops, as Blunt should think necessary. They were to be supplied with transportation and subsistence and Blunt was to "designate the general to command." Blunt's own appointment was expected to remove all difficulties that had stood in the way of the Indian Expedition while under the control of Halleck.[260]   On

Company H............Lo-ga-po-koh 94
  "   I............Jan-neh (John)...........................100
  "   J............Lo-ka-la-chi-ha-go 98

[257] Coffin to Dole, May 8, 1862, *Indian Office General Files, Southern Superintendency*, 1859-1862.

[258] Same to Same, May 13, 1862, *ibid.*, Land Files, *Southern Superintendency*, 1855-1870.

[259] Dole to Coffin, May 20, 1862, *ibid., Letter Book*, no. 68, p. 252.

[260] "I visited the War Department today to ascertain what orders had been forwarded to you and your predecessor relative to the organization of two thousand Indians as a home guard, which when so organized would proceed to their homes in the Indian country in company with a sufficient number of white troops to protect them at their homes.

"I learn from Adjutant General Thomas that all necessary orders have been forwarded to enable you to muster these Indian Regiments into the service as an irregular force; and to send such white force with them as

May 8 came the order from Adjutant-general Thomas, "Hurry up the organization and departure of the two Indian regiments,"[261] which indicated that there was no longer any question as to endorsement by the Department of War.

As a matter of fact, the need for hurry was occasioned by the activity of secessionists, Indians and white men, in southwest Missouri, which would, of itself, suggest the inquiry as to what the Indian allies of the Confederacy had been about since the Battle of Pea Ridge. Van Dorn had ordered them to retire towards their own country and, while incidentally protecting it, afford assistance to their white ally by harassing the enemy, cutting off his supply trains, and annoying him generally. The order had been rigidly attended to and the Indians had done their fair share of the irregular warfare that terrorized and desolated the border in the late spring of the second year of the war. Not all of them, regularly enlisted, had participated in it, however; for General Pike had, with a considerable part of his brigade, gone away from the border as far as possible and had intrenched himself at a fort of his own planning, Fort McCulloch, in the Choctaw Nation, on the Blue River, a branch of the Red.[262]   Furthermore,

---

in your judgment may be deemed necessary, also that the difficulties we experienced while the expedition was under the control of Genl Halleck are now removed by your appointment, and that you will designate the general to command the whole expedition and see that such supplies for the transportation and subsistence as may be necessary are furnished to the whole expedition (Indians as well as whites). Lieut. Kile informs me that there was doubt whether the Quarter Master would be expected to act as Commissary for the Regiment. I suppose that you fully understand this was the intention. . ."–Dole to Blunt, May 16, 1862, Indian Office *Letter Book*, no. 68, pp. 241-242.

[261] *Daily Conservative*, May 9, 1862.

[262] ". . . General Albert Pike retreated from the battle of Pea Ridge, Arkansas, a distance of 250 miles, and left his new-made wards to the mercy

Colonel Drew and his men, later converts to secession-
ism, had, for a good part of the time, contented themselves with guarding the Cherokee Nation,[263] thus leaving Colonel Cooper and Colonel Stand Watie, with
their commands, to do most of the scouting and skir-

of war, stringing his army along through the Cherokee, Creek and Choctaw
Nations, passing through Limestone Gap, on among the Boggies, and halted
at Carriage Point, on the Blue, 'away down along the Chickasaw line.'
Cherokee Knights of the Golden Circle followed Pike's retreat to Texas. . ." – Ross, *Life and Times of Hon. William P. Ross*, p. viii.

[263] These two letters from John Ross are offered in evidence of this.
They are taken from Indian Office Miscellaneous Files, John Ross *Papers*:

(a)   EXECUTIVE DEPARTMENT, PARK HILL, March 21st, 1862.
   SIR: I am in receipt of your favor of the 23rd. inst. I have no
doubt that forage can be procured for Col. Drew's men in this vicinity by hauling it in from the farms of the surrounding Districts. The
subject of a Delegate in Congress shall be attended to so soon as arrangements can be made for holding an election. I am happy to learn
that Col. Drew has been authorized to furlough a portion of the men
in his Regiment to raise corn. I shall endeavor to be correctly informed of the movements of the enemy and advise you of the same.
And I shall be gratified to receive any important information that
you may have to communicate at all times. I am very respectfully and
truly, Yours, etc.   JOHN ROSS, *Prin^l Chief*, Cherokee Nation.

(b).   EXECUTIVE DEPARTMENT, C.N. PARK HILL, April 10th, 1862.
   SIR: I beg leave to thank you for your kind response to my letter
of the 22nd ulto and your order stationing Col. Drew's Regiment in
this vicinity. Though much reduced by furloughs in number it will
be useful for the particular purposes for which it was ordered here.
The unprotected condition of the country however is a source of
general anxiety among the People, who feel that they are liable to be
overrun at any time by small parties from the U.S. Army which remains in the vicinity of the late Battle Ground. This is more particularly the case since the removal of the Confederate Forces under your
command and those under Major Genl Price. Without distrusting
the wisdom that has prompted these movements, or the manifestation of
any desire on my part to enquire into their policy it will be nevertheless a source of satisfaction to be able to assure the people of the
country that protection will not be withheld from them and that they
will not be left to their own feeble defense. Your response is respectfully requested, I have the honor to be Sir with high regards,
Your Obt Servt.   JOHN ROSS, *Prin^l Chief*, Cherokee Nation.
To Brig. Genl A. Pike Com^dg,
   Department Indian Territory, Head Qrs. Choctaw Nation.

mishing. So kindly did the Indians take to that work that Colonel Cooper recommended [264] their employment as out-and-out guerrillas. That was on May 6 and was probably suggested by the fact that, on April 21, the Confederate government had definitely authorized the use of partisan rangers. [265] A good understanding of Indian military activity, at this particular time, is afforded by General Pike's report [266] of May 4,

. . . The Cherokee [267] and Creek troops are in their respective countries. The Choctaw troops are in front of me, in their country, part on this side of Boggy and part at Little Boggy, 34 miles from here. These observe the roads to Fort Smith and by Perryville toward Fort Gibson. Part of the Chickasaw battalion is sent to Camp McIntosh, 11 miles this side of the Wichita Agency, and part to Fort Arbuckle, and the Texan company is at Fort Cobb.

I have ordered Lieutenant-colonel Jumper with his Seminoles to march to and take Fort Larned, on the Pawnee Fork of the Arkansas, where are considerable stores and a little garrison. He will go as soon as their annuity is paid.

The Creeks under Colonel McIntosh are about to make an extended scout westward. Stand Watie, with his Cherokees, scouts along the whole northern line of the Cherokee country from Grand Saline to Marysville, and sends me information continually of every movement of the enemy in Kansas and Southwestern Missouri.

The Comanches, Kiowas, and Reserve Indians are all peaceable and quiet. Some 2,000 of the former are encamped about three days' ride from Fort Cobb, and some of them come in at intervals to procure provisions. They have sent to me to know

---

264 Cooper to Van Dorn, May 6, 1862, *Official Records*, vol. xiii, 823-824.

265 *Journal of the Congress of the Confederate States*, vol. v, 285.

266 *Official Records*, vol. xiii, 819-823.

267 This situation, so eminently satisfactory to John Ross, did not continue long, however, and on May 10, the Cherokee Principal Chief had occasion to complain that his country had been practically divested of a protecting force and, at the very moment, too, when the Federals were showing unwonted vigor near the northeastern border [Ross to Davis, May 10, 1862, *Official Records*, vol. xiii, 824-825].

if they can be allowed to send a strong party and capture any trains on their way from Kansas to New Mexico, to which I have no objection. To go on the war-path somewhere else is the best way to keep them from troubling Texas. . .

Stand Watie's scouting had brought him, April 26,[268] into a slight action with men of the First Battalion First Missouri Cavalry at Neosho, in the vicinity of which place he lingered many days and where his men[269] again fought, in conjunction with Colonel Coffee's, May 31.[270] The skirmish of the later date was disastrous to the Federals under Colonel John M. Richardson of the Fourteenth Missouri State Militia Cavalry and proved to be a case where the wily and nimble Indian had taken the Anglo-Saxon completely by surprise.[271] From Neosho, Stand Watie moved down, by slow and destructive stages, through Missouri and across into Indian Territory. His next important engagement was at Cowskin Prairie, June 6.

Meanwhile, the organization of the Indian Expedition, or Indian Home Guard, as it was henceforth most commonly styled, was proceeding apace.[272] The com-

---

[268] *Official Records*, vol. xiii, 61-63; Britton, *Civil War on the Border*, vol. i, 281-282.

[269] Stand Watie's whole force was not engaged and he, personally, was not present. Captain Parks led Watie's contingent and was joined by Coffee.

[270] *Official Records*, vol. xiii, 90-92, 94-95.

[271] — *Ibid.*, 92-94, 409. Watie, although not present, seems to have planned the affair [*ibid.*, 95]. Lieutenant-colonel Mills, who reported upon the Neosho engagement, was of the opinion that "the precipitate flight" of the Federals could be accounted for only upon the supposition that the "screaming and whooping of the Indians" unnerved them and "rendered their untrained horses nearly unmanageable." — *Ibid.*, 93.

[272] The progress in organization is indicated by these communications to the Indian Office:

(a). The enrollment, organizing etc. etc. of the Indians, and preparations for their departure, are progressing satisfactorily, though as I anticipated, it will be difficult to raise two Regiments, and I have some fears of our success in getting the full number for the 2nd Regiment. But if we get one full company of Delawares and Shawnees,

pletion of the first regiment gave little concern. It was composed of Creeks and Seminoles, eight companies of the former and two of the latter. The second regiment was miscellaneous in its composition and took longer to

as promised, and four companies of Osages, which the chiefs say they can raise, I think we shall succeed.

Two Regiments of white troops and Rabb's Battery have already started and are down by this time in the Cherokee Nation. Col. Doubleday, who is in command, has notified the officers here to prepare with all possible despatch, for marching orders. We are looking for Allens Battery here this week and if it comes I hope to make considerable addition to the Army from the loyal Refugee Indians here, as they have great confidence in *"them waggons that shoot,"* this has been a point with them all the time.

We were still feeding those that are mustered in and shall I suppose have to do so until the requisitions arive. The Dellawares and Shaw-nees also, I had to make arrangements to feed from the time of their arrival at the Sac and Fox Agency. But from all the indications now we expect to see the whole Expedition off in ten days or two weeks. – COFFIN to Dole, June 4, 1862, Indian Office General Files, *Southern Superintendency,* 1859-1862, C 1661.

(b). It has been some time since I wrote you and to fill my promise I again drop you a line. I presume you feel a lively interest in whatever relates to the Indians. The 1st. Regt. is now mustered into the service and will probably to-day number something over a minimum Regt. It is composed entirely of Creeks and Seminoles, eight companys of the former and two of the latter.

I have understood that the report of the Creek Agent gave the number of Creek men at 1990 – If this is a fact it is far from a correct statement – The actual number of Creek men over 14 years of age (refugees) will not number over 900. Some of these are unable to be soldiers. The actual number of Seminoles (men) will not excede 300 over 14 years of age, many of them are old and disabled as soldiers. Thus you will see that but one Regt. could be raised from that quarter. You are aware that the Creeks and Seminoles speak one language nearly and are thus naturally drawn together and they were not willing to be divided.

The second regt. is now forming from the various other tribes and I have no doubt will be filled, it would have been filled long ago, but Col. Ritchie did not repair here for a long time in fact not till after our Regt. was raised – Adjutant Dole came here promptly to do his duty – but in the absence of his Col. could not facilitate his regt. without assuming a responsibility that would have been unwise. I regret that he could not have been placed in our regt. for he will prove a faithful and reliable officer and should I be transfered to

organize, largely because its prospective commander, Colonel John Ritchie, who had gone south to persuade the Osages to enlist,[273] was slow in putting in an appearance at Humboldt. The Neosho Agency, to which the Osages belonged, was in great confusion, partly due to

any other position which I am strongly in hopes I may be, I hope you will exercise your influence to transfer him to my place, this will be agreable to all the officers of the 1st. regiment and desirable on his part.

The condition of the Indians here at the present writing is very favorable, sickness is abating and their spirits are reviving. I think I have fully settled the fact of the Indians capability and susceptibility to arive at a good state of military disiplin. You would be surprised to see our Regt. move. They accomplish the feat of regular time step equal to any white soldier, they form in line with dispatch and with great precission; and what is more they now manifest a great desire to learn the entire white man's disiplin in military matters. That they will make brave and ambitious soldiers I have no doubt. Our country may well feel proud that these red men have at last fell into the ranks to fight for our flag, and aid in crushing treason. Much honor is due them. I am sory that Dr. Kile did not accept the appointment of Quartermaster but owing to some misunderstanding with Col. Ritchie he declines.

You will please remember me to Gen¹ Lane and say that I have not heard from him since I left Washington. – A. C. ELLITHORPE to Dole, June 9, 1862, Indian Office General Files, *Southern Superintendency*, 1859-1862, C 1661.

(c). The Indian Brigade, consisting of about one thousand Creeks and Seminoles, sixty Quapaws, sixty Cherokees and full companies of wild Delawares, Kechees, Ironeyes, Cadoes, and Kickapoos, left this place (Leroy) yesterday for Humboldt, at which place I suppose they will join the so much talked of Indian expedition. Although I have not as yet fully ascertained the exact number of each Tribe, represented in said Brigade, but they may be estimated at about Fifteen Hundred, all of the Southern Refugee Indians who have been fed here by the Government, besides sixty Delawares from the Delaware Reservation, and about two Hundred Osages, the latter of which I have been assured will be increased to about four or five hundred, ere they get through the Osage Nation. . .

The news from the Cherokee Nation is very cheering and encouraging; it has been reported that nearly Two Thousand Cherokees will be ready to join the expedition on its approach into that country . . . – COFFIN to Dole, June 15, 1862, *ibid.*, C 1684.

[273] Coffin to Dole, June 4, 1862, *ibid., Neosho*, C 1662 of 1862. See also Carruth to Coffin, September 19, 1862, Commissioner of Indian Affairs, *Report*, 1862, 164-166.

the fact that, at this most untoward moment, the Osages were being approached for a cession of lands, and partly to the fact that Indians of the neighborhood, of unionist sympathies, Cherokees and Delawares [274] from the Cherokee country, Shawnees, Quapaws, [275] and Seneca-Shawnees, were being made refugees, partly, also, to the fact that Agent Elder and Superintendent Coffin were not working in harmony with each other. Their differences dated from the first days of their official relationship. Elder had been influential, for reasons most satisfactory to himself and not very complimentary to Coffin, in having the Neosho Agency transferred to the Central Superintendency. [276] Coffin had vigorously objected and with such effect that, in March, 1862, a retransfer had been ordered; [277] but not before Coffin had reported [278] that everything was now amicable between him and Elder. Elder was evidently of a different opinion and before long was asking to be allowed again to report officially to Superintendent Branch at St. Joseph. [279] There was a regular tri-weekly post between that place and Fort Scott, Elder's present headquarters, and the chances were good that Branch would be in a position to attend to mail more promptly than was Coffin. [280] The counter arguments

---

[274] F. Johnson to Dole, April 2, 1862, Indian Office, *Central Superintendency*, Delaware, J 627 of 1862.

[275] The propriety of permitting the refugee Quapaws to "return to their homes by accompanying the military expedition" was urged upon the Indian Office in a letter from Elder to Coffin, May 29, 1862 [Coffin to Dole, June 4, 1862, *ibid., Southern Superintendency*, Neosho, C 1663 of 1862].

[276] Office letter of June 5, 1861.

[277] Mix to Branch, March 1, 1862, Indian Office *Letter Book*, no. 67.

[278] Coffin to Dole, February 28, 1862, *ibid.*, General Files, *Southern Superintendency*, 1859-1862, C 1541 of 1862.

[279] Elder to Dole, May 16, 1862, *ibid.*, Neosho, E 106 of 1862.

[280] Coffin was spending a good deal of his time at Leroy. Leroy was one hundred twenty-five miles, so Elder computed, from Leavenworth, where he

of Coffin[281] were equally plausible and the request for transfer refused.

The outfit for the Indians of the Home Guard was decidedly inferior. Opoeth-le-yo-ho-la wanted batteries, "wagons that shoot." [282] His braves, many of them, were given guns that were worthless, that would not shoot at all.[283] In such a way was their eagerness to learn the white man's method of fighting and to acquire his discipline rewarded. The fitting out was done at Humboldt, although Colonel William Weer[284] of the Tenth Kansas Infantry, who was the man finally selected to command the entire force, would have preferred it done at Fort Scott.[285] The Indians had a thousand and one excuses for not expediting matters. They seemed to have a deep-seated distrust of what the Federal intentions regarding them might be when

directed his mail, and sixty or seventy from Fort Scott. His communications were held up until Coffin happened to go to Leavenworth. Moreover, Coffin was then expecting to go soon "into the Indian country."

[281] Coffin complained that Elder neglected his duties. It was Coffin's intention to remove the headquarters of the Southern Superintendency from Fort Scott to Humboldt. It would then be very convenient for Elder to report to him, especially if he would go back to his own agency headquarters and not linger, as he had been doing, at Fort Scott [Coffin to Dole, June 10, 1862, *ibid.*, C 1668 of 1862.

[282] *Daily Conservative*, May 10, 1862.

[283] Weer to Doubleday, June 6, 1862, *Official Records*, vol. xiii, 418; Coffin to Dole, June 17, 1862, Indian Office General Files, *Southern Superintendency*, 1859-1862.

[284] Weer was one of the men in disfavor with Governor Robinson [*Daily Conservative*, May 25, 1862]. He had been arrested and his reinstatement to command that came with the appearance of Blunt upon the scene was doubtless the circumstance that afforded opportunity for his appointment to the superior command of the Indian Expedition. Sturgis had refused to reinstate him. In December, 1861, a leave of absence had been sought by Weer, who was then with the Fourth Kansas Volunteers, in order that he might go to Washington, D.C., and be a witness in the case involving Lane's appointment as brigadier-general [Thomas to Hunter, December 12, 1861, *Congressional Globe*, 37th congress, second session, part i, 128].

[285] Weer to Moonlight, June 6, 1862, *Official Records*, vol. xiii, 419.

once they should be back in their own country. They begged that some assurance be given them of continued protection against the foe and in their legal rights. And, in the days of making preparations, they asked again and again for tangible evidence that white troops were really going to support them in the journey southward.

The main portion of the Indian Expedition auxiliary white force had all this time been more or less busy, dealing with bushwhackers and the like, in the Cherokee Neutral Lands and in the adjoining counties of Missouri. When Blunt took command of the Department of Kansas, Colonel Frederick Salomon [286] of the Ninth Wisconsin Volunteer Infantry was in charge at Fort Scott and the troops there or reporting there were, besides eight companies of his own regiment, a part of the Second Ohio Cavalry under Colonel Charles Doubleday, of the Tenth Kansas Infantry under Colonel William F. Cloud, and the Second Indiana Battery.[287] Blunt's first thought was to have Doubleday [288] lead the Indian Expedition, the auxiliary white force of which was to be selected from the regiments at Fort Scott. Doubleday accordingly made his plans, rendezvoused his men, and arranged that the mouth of Shoal Creek should be a rallying point and temporary headquarters; [289] but events were already in train for Colonel

---

[286] Salomon was born in Prussia in 1826 [Rosengarten, *The German Soldier in the Wars of the United States*, 150]. He had distinguished himself in some of the fighting that had taken place in Missouri in the opening months of the war and, when the Ninth Wisconsin Infantry, composed solely of German-Americans, had been recruited, he was called to its command [Love, *Wisconsin in the War of the Rebellion*, 578].

[287] *Official Records*, vol. xiii, 371-372, 377.

[288] For an account of Doubleday's movements in April that very probably gained him the place, see Britton, *Civil War on the Border*, vol. i, 296.

[289] *Official Records*, vol. xiii, 397, 408.

Weer to supersede him and for his own assignment to the Second Brigade of the expedition.

Previous to his supersedure by Weer, Doubleday conceived that it might be possible to reach Fort Gibson with ease,[290] provided the attempt to do so should be undertaken before the various independent secessionist commands could unite to resist.[291] That they were planning to unite there was every indication.[292] Doubleday[293] was especially desirous of heading off Stand Watie who was still hovering around in the neighborhood of his recent adventures, and was believed now to have an encampment on Cowskin Prairie near Grand River. Accordingly, on the morning of June 6, Doubleday started out, with artillery and a thousand men, and, going southward from Spring River, reached the Grand about sundown.[294] Watie was three miles away and, Doubleday continuing the pursuit, the two forces came to an engagement. It was indecisive,[295] however, and Watie slipped away under

[290] Doubleday to Moonlight, May 25, 1862, *Official Records*, vol. xiii, 397.

[291] Doubleday to Blunt, June 1, 1862, *ibid.*, 408.

[292] General Brown reported on this matter, June 2 [*ibid.*, 409] and June 4 [*ibid.*, 414], as did also General Ketchum, June 3 [*ibid.*, 412]. They all seem to have had some intimation that General Pike was to unite with Stand Watie as well as Coffee and others, and that was certainly General Hindman's intention. On May 31, the very day that he himself assumed command, Hindman had ordered Pike to advance from Fort McCulloch to the Kansas border. The order did not reach Pike until June 8 and was repeated June 17 [*ibid.*, 40].

[293] The idea seems to have obtained among Missourians that Doubleday was all this time inactive. They were either ignorant of or intent upon ignoring the Indian Expedition. June 4, Governor Gamble wrote to Secretary Stanton asking that the Second Ohio and the Ninth Wisconsin, being at Fort Scott and unemployed, might be ordered to report to Schofield [*ibid.*, 414, 438], who at the instance of politicians and contrary to the wishes of Halleck [*ibid.*, 368] had been given an independent command in Missouri.

[294] Doubleday to Weer, June 8, 1862 [*ibid.*, 102].

[295] Doubleday reported to Weer that it was a pronounced success, so did Blunt to Schofield [*ibid.*, 427]; but subsequent events showed that it was

cover of the darkness. Had unquestioned success crowned Doubleday's efforts, all might have been well; but, as it did not, Weer, who had arrived at Fort Scott[296] a few days before and had been annoyed to find Doubleday gone, ordered him peremptorily to make no further progress southward without the Indians. The Indian contingent had in reality had a set-back in its preparations. Its outfit was incomplete and its means for transportation not forthcoming.[297] Under such circumstances, Weer advised the removal of the whole concern to Fort Scott, but that was easier said than done, inasmuch, as before any action was taken, the stores were *en route* for Humboldt.[298] Nevertheless, Weer was determined to have the expedition start before Stand Watie could be reinforced by Rains.[299] Constant and insistent were the reports that the enemy was massing its forces to destroy the Indian Expedition.[300]

anything but that and the *Daily Conservative* tried to fix the blame upon Weer [Weer to Moonlight, June 23, 1862, *ibid.*, 446]. The newspaper account of the whole course of affairs may be given, roughly paraphrased, thus: Doubleday, knowing, perhaps, that Weer was to supersede him and that his time for action was short, "withdrew his detachment from Missouri, concentrated them near Iola, Kansas, and thence directed them to march to the mouth of Shoal Creek, on Spring River, himself taking charge of the convoying of a train of forty days supplies to the same place . . ." He arrived June 4. Then, "indefatigible in forwarding the preparations for a blow upon the camp of organization which the rebels had occupied unmolested on Cowskin Prairie," he made his plans for further advance. At that moment came the news that Weer had superseded him and had ordered him to stop all movement south. He disregarded the order and struck, even though not fully prepared [*Daily Conservative*, June 13, 1862].

[296] Weer to Moonlight, June 5, 1862, *Official Records*, vol. xiii, 418.

[297] — *Ibid.*; Weer to Doubleday, June 6, 1862, *ibid.*, 418-419.

[298] Weer to Moonlight, June 13, 1862, *ibid.*, 430.

[299] Same to same, June 7, 1862, *ibid.*, 422.

[300] The destruction of the Indian Expedition was most certainly the occasion for the massing, notwithstanding the fact that Missourians were apprehensive for the safety of their state only and wanted to have Weer's white troops diverted to its defence. Curtis, alone, of the commanders in Missouri seems to have surmised rightly in the matter [Curtis to Schofield, *ibid.*, 432].

Weer, therefore, went on ahead to the Osage Catholic Mission and ordered the Fort Scott troops to meet him there. His purpose was to promote the enlistment of the Osages, who were now abandoning the Confederate cause.[301] He would then go forward and join Doubleday, whom he had instructed to clear the way.[302]

Weer's plans were one thing, his embarrassments, another. Before the middle of June he was back again at Leroy,[303] having left Salomon and Doubleday[304] at Baxter Springs on the west side of Spring River in the Neutral Lands, the former in command. Weer hoped by his presence at Leroy to hurry the Indians along; for it was high time the expedition was started and he intended to start it, notwithstanding that many officers were absent from their posts and the men of the Second Indian Regiment not yet mustered in. It was absolutely necessary, if anything were going to be done with Indian aid, to get the braves away from under the influence of their chiefs, who were bent upon delay and determent. By the sixteenth he had the warriors all ready at Humboldt,[305] their bullet-proof medicine taken, their grand war dance indulged in. By the twenty-first, the final packing up began,[306] and it was not long thereafter before the Indian Expedition, after having experienced so many vicissitudes, had definitely materialized and was on its way south. Accompanying Weer were the Reverend Evan Jones, entrusted with

---

[301] Weer to Moonlight, June 13, 1862.

[302] Weer to Doubleday, June 6, 1862.

[303] Weer to Moonlight, June 13, 1862.

[304] On the twentieth, General Brown requested Salomon to send Doubleday to southwest Missouri [*Official Records*, vol. xiii, 440] and Salomon so far complied with the request as to post some companies of Doubleday's regiment, under Lieutenant-colonel Ratliff, at Neosho [*ibid.*, 445, 459].

[305] — *Ibid.*, 434.

[306] — *Ibid.*, 441.

a confidential message[307] to John Ross, and two special Indian agents, E. H. Carruth, detailed at the instance of the Indian Office, and H. W. Martin, sent on Coffin's own responsibility, their particular task being to look out for the interests and welfare of the Indians and, when once within the Indian Territory, to take careful stock of conditions there, both political and economic.[308] The Indians were in fine spirits and, although looking

---

[307] The message, addressed to "Mutual Friend," was an assurance of the continued interest of the United States government in the inhabitants of Indian Territory and of its determination to protect them [Coffin to Ross, June 16, 1862, Indian Office General Files, *Southern Superintendency*, 1859-1862, C 1684].

[308] ". . . You will assure all loyal Indians in the Indian Territory of the disposition and the ability of the Government of the United States to protect them in all their rights, and that there is no disposition on the part of said government to shrink from any of its Treaty Obligations with all such of the Indian Tribes, who have been, are now, and remaining loyal to the same. Also that the government will, at the earliest practicable period, which is believed not to be distant, restore to all loyal Indians the rights, privileges, and immunities, that they have enjoyed previous to the present unfortunate rebellion.

"If, during the progress of the Army you should find Indians in a suffering condition whose loyalty is *beyond doubt*, you will, on consultation with the officers, render such assistance, as you may think proper, with such aid as the officers may render you.

"You will carefully look into the condition of the country, ascertain the quantity of Stock, Hogs, and Cattle, also the quantity of Corn, wheat etc. which may be in the hands of the loyal Indians, and the amount of the crops in the ground the present season, their condition and prospects.

"You are requested to communicate with me at this office at every suitable opportunity on all the above mentioned points, in order to enable me to keep the Hon. Com^r of Indian Aff^rs well advised of the condition of affairs in the Indian Territory, and that the necessary steps may be taken at the earliest possible moment, consistent with safety and economy, to restore the loyal Indians now in Kansas to their homes.

"Should any considerable number of the Indians, now in the Army, remain in the Indian Territory, or join you from the loyal Indians, now located therein you will very probably find it best, to remain with them, until I can get there with those, who are now here. But of these matters you will be more able to judge on the ground." – Extract from Coffin's instructions to Carruth, June 16, 1862, *ibid.* Similar instructions, under date of June 23, 1862, were sent to H. W. Martin.

somewhat ludicrous in their uniforms,[309] were not much behind their comrades of the Ninth and Tenth Kansas [310] in earnestness and in attention to duty.[311] Nevertheless, they had been very reluctant to leave their families and were, one and all, very apprehensive as to the future.

---

[309] "I have just returned from Humboldt – the army there under Col. Weer consisting of the 10th Kansas Regiment 4 Companys of the 9th Kansas Allens Battery of Six Tenths Parrot Guns and the first and second Indian Regements left for the Indian Territory in good stile and in fine spirits the Indians with their new uniforms and small Military caps on their Hugh Heads of Hair made rather a Comecal Ludecrous apperance   they marched off in Columns of 4 a breast singing the war song all joining in the chourse and a more animated seen is not often witnessed.   The officers in command of the Indian Regements have labored incessantly and the improvement the Indians have made in drilling is much greater than I supposed them capabell of and I think the opinion and confidence of all in the eficency of the Indian Regements was very much greater when they left than at any previous period and I have little doubt that for the kind of service that will be required of them they will be the most efecient troops in the Expedition." – Coffin to Dole, June 25, 1862, Indian Office General Files, *Southern Superintendency*, 1859-1862, C 1684.

[310] Weer took with him as white anxiliary "the Tenth Kansas, Allen's battery, three companies Ninth Kansas . . ." [*Official Records*, vol. xiii, 441]. It seems to have been his intention to take the Second Kansas also; but that regiment was determined to stay at Humboldt until it had effected a change in its colonels in favor of Owen A. Bassett [*ibid.*, 434].

[311] Weer was disgusted with conditions surrounding his white force. This is his complaint, on the eve of his departure:

"Commissions to officers from the Governor are pouring in daily. I am told that the Tenth is rapidly becoming a regiment of officers. To add to these difficulties there are continual intrigues, from colonels down, for promotions and positions of command. Officers are leaving their posts for Fort Leavenworth and elsewhere to engage in these intrigues for more prominent places. The camps are filled with rumors of the success of this or that man. Factions are forming, and a general state of demoralization being produced. . ." – Weer to Moonlight, June 21, 1862, *ibid.*, 441-442.

V. THE MARCH TO TAHLEQUAH AND THE RETROGRADE MOVEMENT OF THE "WHITE AUXILIARY"

Towards the end of June, the various elements designed to comprise the First Indian Expedition had encamped at Baxter Springs[312] and two brigades formed. As finally organized, the First Brigade was put under the command of Colonel Salomon and the Second, of Colonel William R. Judson. To the former, was attached the Second Indian Regiment, incomplete, and, to the latter, the First. Brigaded with the Indian regiments was the white auxiliary that had been promised and that the Indians had almost pathetically counted upon to assist them in their straits. Colonel Weer's intention was not to have the white and red people responsible for the same duties nor immediately march together. The red were believed to be excellent for scouting and, as it would be necessary to scout far and wide all the way down into the Indian Territory, the country being full of bushwhackers, also, most likely, of the miscellaneous forces of General Rains, Colonel Coffee, and Colonel Stand Watie, they were to be reserved for that work.

The forward movement of the Indian Expedition began at daybreak on the twenty-eighth of June. It was then that the First Brigade started, its white contingent, "two sections Indiana Battery, one battalion of

[312] Baxter Springs was a government post, established on Spring River in the southwest corner of the Cherokee Neutral Lands, subsequent to the Battle of Pea Ridge [Kansas Historical Society, *Collections*, vol. vi, 150].

Second Ohio Volunteer Cavalry, and six companies of Ninth Wisconsin Volunteer Infantry,"[313] taking the military road across the Quapaw Strip and entering the Indian Territory, unmolested. A day's journey in the rear and travelling by the same route came the white contingent of the Second Brigade and so much of the First Indian as was unmounted.[314] Beyond the border, the cavalcade proceeded to Hudson's Crossing of the Neosho River, where it halted to await the coming of supply trains from Fort Scott. In the meantime, the Second Indian Regiment, under Colonel John Ritchie, followed, a day apart, by the mounted men of the First under Major William A. Phillips,[315] had also set out, its orders[316] being to leave the military road and to cross to the east bank of Spring River, from thence to march southward and scour the country thoroughly between Grand River and the Missouri state line.

The halt at Hudson's Crossing occupied the better part of two days and then the main body of the Indian Expedition resumed its forward march. It crossed the Neosho and moved on, down the west side of Grand River, to a fording place, Carey's Ford, at which point, it passed over to the east side of the river and camped, a short distance from the ford, at Round Grove, on Cowskin Prairie, Cherokee ground, and the scene of Doubleday's recent encounter with the enemy. At this

[313] Salomon to Weer, June 30, 1862, *Official Records*, vol. xiii, 458.

[314] James A. Phillips to Judson, June 28, 1862 [*Official Records*, vol. xiii, 456].

[315] William A. Phillips, a Scotsman by birth, went out to Kansas in the autumn of 1855 as regular staff correspondent of the New York *Tribune* [Kansas Historical Society *Collections*, vol. v, 100, 102]. He was a personal friend of Dana's [Britton, *Memoirs*, 89], became with Lane an active Free State man and later was appointed on Lane's staff [*Daily Conservative*, January 24, 31, 1862]. He served as correspondent of the *Daily Conservative* at the time when that newspaper was most guilty of incendiarism.

[316] James A. Phillips to Judson, June 28, 1862, *Official Records*, vol. xiii, 456.

place it anxiously awaited the return of Lieutenant-colonel Ratliff, who had been despatched to Neosho in response to an urgency call from General E. B. Brown in charge of the Southwestern Division of the District of Missouri.[317]

The Confederates were still in the vicinity, promiscuously wandering about, perhaps; but, none the less, determined to check, if possible, the Federal further progress; for they knew that only by holding the territorial vantage, which they had secured through gross Federal negligence months before, could they hope to maintain intact the Indian alliance with the Southern States. Stand Watie's home farm was in the neighborhood of Weer's camp and Stand Watie himself was even then scouting in the Spavinaw hills.[318]

In the latter part of May, under directions from General Beauregard[319] but apparently without the avowed knowledge of the Confederate War Department and certainly without its official[320] sanction, Thomas C.

[317] Weer to Moonlight, June 23, 1862, *Official Records*, vol. xiii, 445, and same to same, July 2, 1862, *ibid.*, 459-461.

[318] Anderson, *Life of General Stand Watie*, 18.

[319] *Official Records*, vol. xiii, 28.

[320] The emphasis should be upon the word, *official*, since the government must assuredly have acquiesced in Hindman's appointment. Hindman declared that the Secretary of War, in communicating on the subject to the House of Representatives, "ignored facts which had been officially communicated to him," in order to convey the impression that Hindman had undertaken to fill the post of commander in the Trans-Mississippi Department without rightful authority [Hindman to Holmes, February 8, 1863, *ibid.*, vol. xxii, part 2, p. 785]. The following telegram shows that President Davis had been apprised of Hindman's selection, and of its tentative character.

BALDWIN, June 5, 1862.
(Received 6th.)

THE PRESIDENT:

Do not send any one just now to command the Trans-Mississippi District. It will bring trouble to this army. Hindman has been sent there temporarily. Price will be on to see you soon.

EARL VAN DORN, Major-General.

[*Ibid.*, vol. lii, part 2, supplement, p. 320.]

Hindman had assumed the command of the Trans-Mississippi Department.[321]   As an Arkansan, deeply moved by the misfortunes and distress of his native state, he had stepped into Van Dorn's place with alacrity, intent upon forcing everything within his reach to subserve the interests of the Confederate cause in that particular part of the southern world. To the Indians and to their rights, natural or acquired, he was as utterly indifferent as were most other American men and all too soon that fact became obvious, most obvious, indeed, to General Pike, the one person who had, for reasons best known to himself, made the Indian cause his own.

General Hindman took formal command of the Trans-Mississippi Department at Little Rock, May 31. It was a critical moment and he was most critically placed; for he had not the sign of an army, Curtis's advance was only about thirty-five miles away, and Arkansas was yet, in the miserable plight in which Van Dorn had left her in charge of Brigadier-general J. S. Roane, it is true, but practically denuded of troops. Pike was at Fort McCulloch, and he had a force not wholly to be despised.[322]   It was to him, therefore, that Hindman

---

[321] *Department* seems to be the more proper word to use to designate Hindman's command, although *District* and *Department* are frequently used interchangeably in the records. In Hindman's time and in Holmes's, the Trans-Mississippi Department was not the same as the Trans-Mississippi District of Department No. 2 [See Thomas Jordan, Chief of Staff, to Hindman, July 17, 1862, *Official Records*, vol. xiii, 855]. On the very date of Hindman's assignment, the boundaries of his command were defined as follows:

"The boundary of the Trans-Mississippi Department will embrace the States of Missouri and Arkansas, including Indian Territory, the State of Louisiana west of the Mississippi, and the State of Texas." – *Ibid.*, 829.

[322] Yet Hindman did, in a sense, despise it and, from the start, he showed a tendency to disparage Pike's abilities and efforts. On the nineteenth of June, he reported to Adjutant-general Cooper, among other things, that he had ordered Pike to establish his headquarters at Fort Gibson and added, "His force does not amount to much, but there is no earthly need of its

made one of his first appeals for help and he ordered
him so to dispose of his men that some of the more efficient, the white, might be sent to Little Rock and the
less efficient, the red, moved upward "to prevent the
incursions of marauding parties," from Kansas.[323] The
orders were repeated about a fortnight later; but Pike
had already complied to the best of his ability, although
not without protest[324] for he had collected his brigade
and accoutered it by his own energies and his own contrivances solely. Moreover, he had done it for the defence of Indian Territory exclusively.

Included among the marauders, whose enterprises
General Hindman was bent upon checking, were Doubleday's men; for, as General Curtis shrewdly surmised,[325] some inkling of Doubleday's contemplated
maneuvers had most certainly reached Little Rock.
Subsequently, when the Indian Expedition was massing
at Baxter Springs, more vigorous measures than any
yet taken were prepared for and all with the view of
delaying or defeating it. June 23, Pike ordered
Colonel Douglas H. Cooper to repair to the country
north of the Canadian River and to take command of
all troops, except Jumper's Seminole battalion, that
should be there or placed there.[326] Similarly, June 26,
Hindman, in ignorance of Pike's action, assigned Colonel J. J. Clarkson[327] to the supreme command, under

remaining 150 miles south of the Kansas line throwing up intrenchments."
[*Official Records*, vol. xiii, 837].

[323] Hindman to Pike, May 31, 1862 [*ibid.*, 934].

[324] Pike to Hindman, June 8, 1862 [*ibid.*, 936-943].

[325] —*Ibid.*, 398, 401.

[326] General Orders, *ibid.*, 839, 844-845.

[327] Of Clarkson, Pike had this to say: "He applied to me while raising his
force for orders to go upon the Santa Fe' road and intercept trains. I wrote
him that he could have such orders if he chose to come here, and the next I
heard of him he wrote for ammunition, and, I learned, was going to make

Pike, "of all forces that now are or may hereafter be within the limits of the Cherokee, Creek, and Seminole countries." [328]   As fate would have it, Clarkson was the one of these two to whom the work in hand first fell.

The Indian Expedition was prepared to find its way contested; for its leaders believed Rains, [329] Coffey, and Stand Watie to be all in the immediate vicinity, awaiting the opportunity to attack either singly or with combined forces; but, except for a small affair between a reconnoitering party sent out by Salomon and the enemy's pickets, [330] the march was without incident worth recording until after Weer had broken camp at Cowskin Prairie. Behind him the ground seemed clear enough, thanks to the very thorough scouting that had been done by the Indians of the Home Guard regiments, some of whom, those of Colonel Phillips's command, had been able to penetrate Missouri. [331]   Of conditions ahead of him, Weer was not so sure and he was soon made aware of the near presence of the foe.

Colonel Watie, vigilant and redoubtable, had been on the watch for the Federals for some time and, learning of their approach down the east side of Grand River, sent two companies of his regiment to head off their advance guard.   This was attempted in a surprise movement at Spavinaw Creek and accomplished with some measure of success. [332]   Colonel Clarkson was at

forays into Missouri. I had no ammunition for that business. He seized 70 kegs that I had engaged of Sparks in Fort Smith, and soon lost the whole and Watie's also. Without any notice to me he somehow got in command of the northern part of the Indian country over two colonels with commissions nine months older than his." – Pike to Hindman, July 15, 1862, *Official Records,* vol. xiii, 858.

[328] *Official Records,* vol. xiii, 845-846.

[329] Rains had made Tahlequah the headquarters of the Eighth Division Missouri State Guards. – PIKE to Hindman, July 15, 1862, *ibid.,* 858.

[330] — *Ibid.,* vol. xiii, 458, 460.

[331] — *Ibid.,* 460.

[332] Anderson, *Life of General Stand Watie,* 18. This incident is most

Locust Grove and Weer, ascertaining that fact, prepared for an engagement. His supplies and camp equipage, also an unutilized part of his artillery he sent for safety to Cabin Creek, across Grand River and Lieutenant-colonel Lewis R. Jewell of the Sixth Kansas Cavalry he sent eastward, in the direction of Maysville, Arkansas, his expectation being – and it was realized – that Jewell would strike the trail of Watie and engage him while Weer himself sought out Clarkson.[333]

The looked-for engagement between the main part of the Indian Expedition and Clarkson's force, a battalion of Missourians that had been raised by Hindman's orders and sent to the Indian Territory "at the urgent request of Watie and Drew," [334] occurred at Locust Grove on the third of July. It was nothing but a skirmish, yet had very significant results. Only two detachments of Weer's men were actively engaged in it.[335] One of them was from the First Indian Home Guard and upon it the brunt of the fighting fell.[336]

likely the one that is referred to in Carruth and Martin's letter to Coffin, August 2, 1862, Commissioner of Indian Affairs, *Report*, 1862, p. 162.

[333] Britton, *Civil War on the Border*, vol. i, 300-301.

[334] Report of General Hindman, *Official Records*, vol. xiii, 40.

[335] Weer to Moonlight, July 6, 1862, *ibid.*, 137.

[336] Carruth and Martin reported to Coffin, August 2, 1862, that the Indians did practically all the fighting on the Federal side. In minor details, their account differed considerably from Weer's.

"When near Grand Saline, Colonel Weer detached parts of the 6th, 9th, and 10th Kansas regiments, and sent the 1st Indian regiment in advance. By a forced night march they came up to the camp of Colonel Clarkson, completely surprising him, capturing all his supplies, and taking one hundred prisoners; among them the colonel himself.

"The Creek Indians were first in the fight, led by Lieutenant Colonel Wattles and Major Ellithorpe. We do not hear that any white man fired a gun unless it was to kill the surgeon of the 1st Indian regiment. We were since informed that one white man was killed by the name of McClintock, of the 9th Kansas regiment. In reality, it was a victory gained by the 1st Indian regiment; and while the other forces would, no doubt, have acted well, it is the height of injustice to claim this victory for the whites. . ." – COMMISSIONER OF INDIAN AFFAIRS, *Report*, 1862, p. 162.

The Confederates were worsted and lost their train and many prisoners. Among the prisoners was Clarkson himself. His battalion was put to flight and in that circumstance lay the worst aspect of the whole engagement; for the routed men fled towards Tahlequah and spread consternation among the Indians gathered there, also among those who saw them by the way or heard of them. Thoroughly frightened the red men sought refuge within the Federal lines. Such conduct was to be expected of primitive people, who invariably incline towards the side of the victor; but, in this case, it was most disastrous to the Confederate Indian alliance. For the second time since the war began, Colonel John Drew's enlisted men defected from their own ranks [337] and, with the exception of a small body under Captain Pickens Benge, [338] went boldly over to the enemy. The result was, that the Second Indian Home Guard, Ritchie's regiment, which had not previously been filled up, had soon the requisite number of men [339] and there were more to spare. Indeed, during the days that followed, so many recruits came in, nearly all of them Cherokees, that lists were opened for starting a third regiment of Indian Home Guards. [340] It was not long before it was organized, accepted by Blunt, and W. A. Phillips commissioned as its colonel. [341] The regular mustering in of the new recruits had to be done at Fort Scott and thither Ritchie sent the men, intended for his regiment, immediately.

The Indian Expedition had started out with a very definite preliminary programme respecting the man-

---

[337] *Official Records,* vol. xiii, 138.

[338] Hindman's Report, *ibid.*, 40.

[339] Ritchie to Blunt, July 5, 1862, *ibid.*, 463-464.

[340] Weer to Moonlight, July 12, 1862, *ibid.*, 488.

[341] Blunt to Salomon, August 3, 1862, *ibid.*, 532; Britton, *Civil War on the Border*, vol. i, 304.

agement of Indian affairs, particularly as those affairs might be concerned with the future attitude of the Cherokee Nation. The programme comprised instructions that emanated from both civil and military sources. The special Indian agents, Carruth and Martin, had been given suitable tasks to perform and the instructions handed them have already been commented upon. Personally, these two men were very much disposed to magnify the importance of their own position and to resent anything that looked like interference on the part of the military. As a matter of fact, the military men treated them with scant courtesy and made little or no provision for their comfort and convenience.[342] Colonel Weer seems to have ignored, at times, their very existence. On more than one occasion, for instance, he deplored the absence of some official, accredited by the Indian Office, to take charge of what he contemptuously called "this Indian business," [343] which business, he felt, greatly complicated all military undertakings [344] and was decidedly beyond the bounds of his peculiar province.[345]

---

[342] Pretty good evidence of this appears in a letter, which Carruth and Martin jointly addressed to Coffin, September 4, 1862, in anticipation of the Second Indian Expedition, their idea being to guard against a repetition of some of the experiences of the first. "We wish to call your attention," wrote they, "to the necessity of our being allowed a wagon to haul our clothing, tents, etc. in the Southern expedition.

"In the last expedition we had much annoyance for the want of accommodations of our own. Unless we are always by at the moment of moving, our things are liable to be left behind, that room may be made for *army baggage* which sometimes accumulates amazingly. . .

"The cold nights of autumn and winter will overtake us in the next expedition and we ought to go prepared for them. We must carry many things, as clothing, blankets, etc." – General Files, *Southern Superintendency, 1859-1862.*

[343] *Official Records,* vol. xiii, 460.

[344] —*Ibid.,* 487.

[345] Weer, nevertheless, was not long in developing some very pronounced ideas on the subject of Indian relations. The earliest and best indication of

The military instructions for the management of Indian affairs outlined a policy exceedingly liberal, a policy that proceeded upon the assumption that stress of circumstances had conditioned the Indian alliance with the Confederacy. This idea was explicitly conveyed in a communication from Weer, through his acting assistant adjutant-general, to John Ross, and again in the orders issued to Salomon and Judson. Ross and his people were to be given an opportunity to return to their allegiance, confident that the United States government would henceforth protect them.[346] And the military commanders were invited to give their "careful attention to the delicate position" which the Indian Expedition would occupy

> In its relation to the Indians. The evident desire of the government is to restore friendly intercourse with the tribes and return the loyal Indians that are with us to their homes. Great care must be observed that no unusual degree of vindictiveness be tolerated between Indian and Indian. Our policy toward the rebel portion must be a subject of anxious consideration, and its character will to a great degree be shaped by yourself (Judson) in conjunction with Colonel Salomon. No settled policy can at present be marked out. Give all questions their full share of investigation. No spirit of private vengeance should be tolerated.[347]

After the skirmish at Locust Grove, Colonel Weer deemed that the appropriate moment had come for approaching John Ross with suggestions that the Cherokee Nation abandon its Confederate ally and return to its allegiance to the United States government. From

that is to be found in his letter of July twelfth, in which he gave his opinion of the negroes, whom he found very insolent. He proposed that the Cherokee Nation should abolish slavery by vote.

[346] J. A. Phillips to Ross, June 26, 1862, *Official Records,* vol. xiii, 450.

[347] Phillips to Judson, June 28, 1862, *ibid.,* 456. Orders, almost identically the same, were issued to Salomon. See Phillips to Salomon, June 27, 1862, *ibid.,* 452.

his camp on Wolf Creek, therefore, he addressed a conciliatory communication [348] to the Cherokee chief, begging the favor of an interview and offering to make full reparation for any outrages or reprisals that his men, in defiance of express orders to the contrary, might have made upon the Cherokee people through whose country they had passed.[349] Weer had known for several days, indeed, ever since he first crossed the line, that the natives were thoroughly alarmed at the coming of the Indian Expedition. They feared reprisals and Indian revenge and, whenever possible, had fled out of reach of danger, many of them across the Arkansas River, taking with them what of their property they could.[350] Weer had done his best to restrain his troops, especially the Indian, and had been very firm in insisting that no "outrages perpetrated after Indian fashion" should occur.[351]

Weer's message to Ross was sent, under a flag of truce, by Doctor Gillpatrick, a surgeon in the Indian Expedition, who had previously served under Lane.[352] Ross's reply,[353] although prompt, was scarcely satisfactory from Weer's standpoint. He refused pointblank the request for an interview and reminded Weer that the Cherokee Nation, "under the sanction and authority of the whole Cherokee people," had made a formal alliance with the Confederate government and pro-

[348] Weer to Ross, July 7, 1862, *Official Records*, vol. xiii, 464.

[349] That there had been outrages and reprisals, Carruth and Martin admitted but they claimed that they had been committed by white men and wrongfully charged against Indians [Commissioner of Indian Affairs, *Report*, 1862, 162-163].

[350] Weer to Moonlight, July 2, 1862, *Official Records*, vol. xiii, 460.

[351] — *Ibid.*, 452, 456, 461.

[352] *Daily Conservative*, December 27, 1861.

[353] Ross to Weer, July 8, 1862, *Official Records*, vol. xiii, 486-487; Moore, *Rebellion Record*, vol. v, 549.

posed to remain true, as had ever been its custom, to its treaty obligations. To fortify his position, he submitted documents justifying his own and tribal actions since the beginning of the war.[354] Weer was naturally much embarrassed. Apparently, he had had the notion that the Indians would rush into the arms of the Union with the first appearance of a Federal soldier; but he was grievously mistaken. None the less, verbal reports that reached his headquarters on Wolf Creek restored somewhat his equanimity and gave him the impression that Ross, thoroughly anti-secessionist at heart himself, was acting diplomatically and biding his time.[355] Weer referred[356] the matter to Blunt for instructions at the very moment when Blunt, ignorant that he had already had communication with Ross, was urging[357] him to be expeditious, since it was "desirable to return the refugee Indians now in Kansas to their homes as soon as practicable."

There were other reasons, more purely military, why a certain haste was rather necessary. Some of those reasons inspired Colonel Weer to have the country around about him well reconnoitered. On the fourteenth of July, he sent out two detachments. One, led by Major W. T. Campbell, was to examine "the alleged position of the enemy south of the Arkansas," and the other, led by Captain H. S. Greeno, to repair to Tahlequah and Park Hill.[358] Campbell, before he had advanced far, found out that there was a strong Confederate force at Fort Davis[359] so he halted at Fort Gibson and was

---

[354] Weer to Moonlight, July 12, 1862, *Official Records,* vol. xiii, 487. The documents are to be found accompanying Weer's letter, *ibid.,* 489-505.

[355] Blunt to Stanton, July 21, 1862, *ibid.,* 486.

[356] Weer to Moonlight, July 12, 1862, *ibid.,* 487-488.

[357] Blunt to Weer, July 12, 1862, *ibid.,* 488-489.

[358] Weer to Moonlight, July 16, 1862, *ibid.,* 160-161.

[359] Campbell to Weer, July 14, 1862, *ibid.,* 161.

there joined by Weer. Meanwhile, Greeno with his detachment of one company of whites and fifty Cherokee Indians had reached Tahlequah and had gone into camp two and one-half miles to the southward.[360] He was then not far from Park Hill, the residence of Chief Ross. All the way down he had been on the watch for news; but the only forces he could hear of were some Indian, who were believed to be friendly to the Union although ostensibly still serving the Confederacy. It was a time of crisis both with them and with him; for their leaders had just been summoned by Colonel Cooper, now in undisputed command north of the Canadian, to report immediately for duty at Fort Davis, his headquarters. Whatever was to be done would have to be done quickly. There was no time to lose and Greeno decided the matter for all concerned by resorting to what turned out to be a very clever expedient. He made the commissioned men all prisoners of war[361] and then turned his attention to the Principal Chief, who was likewise in a dilemma, he having received a despatch from Cooper ordering him, under authority of treaty provisions and "in the name of President Davis, Confederate States of America, to issue a proclamation calling on all Cherokee Indians over 18 and under 35 to come forward and assist in protecting the country from invasion."[362] Greeno thought the matter over and concluded there was nothing for him to do but to capture Ross also and to release him, subsequently, on parole. These things he did and there were many people who thought, both then and long after-

---

[360] Greeno to Weer, July 15, 1862, *Official Records*, vol. xiii, 473; Carruth and Martin to Coffin, July 19, 1862, Commissioner of Indian Affairs, *Report*, 1862, 158-160.

[361] Greeno to Weer, July 17, 1862, *Official Records*, vol. xiii, 161-162.

[362] *Official Records*, vol. xiii, 473.

wards, that the whole affair had been arranged for beforehand and that victor and victim had been in collusion with each other all the way through.

Up to this point the Indian Expedition can be said to have met with more than a fair measure of success; but its troubles were now to begin or rather to assert themselves; for most of them had been present since the very beginning. Fundamental to everything else was the fact that it was summer-time and summer-time, too, in a prairie region. Troops from the north, from Wisconsin and from Ohio, were not acclimated and they found the heat of June and July almost insufferable. There were times when they lacked good drinking water, which made bad matters worse. The Germans were particularly discontented and came to despise the miserable company in which they found themselves. It was miserable, not so much because it was largely Indian, but because it was so ill-equipped and so disorderly. At Cowskin Prairie, the scouts had to be called in, not because their work was finished, but because they and their ponies were no longer equal to it.[363] They had played out for the simple reason that they were not well fitted out. The country east of Grand River was "very broken and flinty and their ponies unshod." It has been claimed, although maybe with some exaggeration, that not "a single horse-shoe or nail" had been provided for Colonel Salomon's brigade.[364]

The supplies of the Indian Expedition were insufficient and, although at Spavinaw Creek Colonel Watie's entire commissary had been captured[365] and Clarkson's at Locust Grove, there was great scarcity. Weer had

---

[363] *Official Records*, vol. xiii, 460.
[364] Love, *Wisconsin in the War of Rebellion*, 580.
[365] Anderson, *Life of General Stand Watie*, 19.

been cautioned again and again not to cut himself off from easy communication with Fort Scott.[366] He had shown a disposition to wander widely from the straight road to Fort Gibson; but Blunt had insisted that he refrain altogether from making excursions into adjoining states.[367] He had himself realized the shortness of his provisions and had made a desperate effort to get to the Grand Saline so as to replenish his supply of salt at the place where the Confederates had been manufacturing that article for many months. He had known also that for some things, such as ordnance stores, he would have to look even as far as Fort Leavenworth.[368]

The climax of all these affairs was reached July 18, 1862. On that day, Frederick Salomon, colonel of the First Brigade, took matters into his own hands and arrested his superior officer. It was undoubtedly a clear case of mutiny[369] but there was much to be said in extenuation of Salomon's conduct. The reasons for his action, as stated in a *pronunciamento*[370] to his associates in command and as submitted to General Blunt[371] are here given. They speak for themselves.

> HEADQUARTERS INDIAN EXPEDITION,
> Camp on Grand River, July 18, 1862.
> To COMMANDERS OF THE DIFFERENT CORPS CONSTITUTING
> Indian Expedition:
> SIRS: In military as well as civil affairs great and violent wrongs need speedy and certain remedies. The time had arrived, in my judgment, in the history of this expedition when the greatest wrong ever perpetrated upon any troops was about

---

[366] Consider, for example, Blunt's orders of July 14 [*Official Records*, vol. xiii, 472].

[367] Blunt to Weer, July 3, 1862, *ibid.*, 461.

[368] Weer to Moonlight, July 2, 1862, *ibid.*

[369] As such the Indian agents regarded it. See their communication on the subject, July 19, 1862, *ibid.*, 478.

[370] *Ibid.*, 475-476.

[371] *Ibid.*, 484-485.

to fall with crushing weight upon the noble men composing the command. Some one must act, and that at once, or starvation and capture were the imminent hazards that looked us in the face.

As next in command to Colonel Weer, and upon his express refusal to move at all for the salvation of his troops, I felt the responsibility resting upon me.

I have arrested Colonel Weer and assumed command.

The causes leading to this arrest you all know. I need not reiterate them here. Suffice to say that we are 160 miles from the base of operations, almost entirely through an enemy's country, and without communication being left open behind us. We have been pushed forward thus far by forced and fatiguing marches under the violent southern sun without any adequate object. By Colonel Weer's orders we were forced to encamp where our famishing men were unable to obtain anything but putrid, stinking water. Our reports for disability and unfitness for duty were disregarded; our cries for help and complaints of unnecessary hardships and suffering were received with closed ears. Yesterday a council of war, convened by the order of Colonel Weer, decided that our only safety lay in falling back to some point from which we could reopen communication with our commissary depot. Colonel Weer overrides and annuls the decision of that council, and announces his determination not to move from this point. We have but three days' rations on hand and an order issued by him putting the command on half rations. For nearly two weeks we have no communication from our rear. We have no knowledge when supply trains will reach us, neither has Colonel Weer. Three sets of couriers, dispatched at different times to find these trains and report, have so far made no report. Reliable information has been received that large bodies of the enemy were moving to our rear, and yet we lay here idle. We are now and ever since our arrival here have been entirely without vegetables or healthy food for our troops. I have stood with arms folded and seen my men faint and fall away from me like the leaves of autumn because I thought myself powerless to save them.

I will look upon this scene no longer. I know the responsibility I have assumed. I have acted after careful thought

and deliberation. Give me your confidence for a few days, and all that man can do, and with a pure purpose and a firm faith that he is right, shall be done for the preservation of the troops.   F. SALOMON, *Colonel Ninth Wis. Vols.,*
Comdg. Indian Expedition.

HEADQUARTERS INDIAN EXPEDITION,
Camp on Wolf Creek, Cherokee Nation, July 20, 1862.
BRIG. GEN. JAMES G. BLUNT,
    Commanding Department of Kansas:

SIR: I have the honor to report that I have arrested Col. William Weer, commanding the Indian Expedition, and have assumed command. Among the numerous reasons for this step a few of the chief are as follows:

From the day of our first report to him we have found him a man abusive and violent in his intercourse with his fellow-officers, notoriously intemperate in habits, entirely disregarding military usages and discipline, always rash in speech, act, and orders, refusing to inferior officers and their reports that consideration which is due an officer of the U.S. Army.

Starting from Cowskin Prairie on the 1st instant, we were pushed rapidly forward to the vicinity of Fort Gibson, on the Arkansas River, a distance of 160 miles from Fort Scott. No effort was made by him to keep communication open behind us. It seemed he desired none. We had but twenty-three days' rations on hand. As soon as he reached a position on Grand River 14 miles from Fort Gibson his movements suddenly ceased. We could then have crossed the Arkansas River, but it seemed there was no object to be attained in his judgment by such a move. There we lay entirely idle from the 9th to the 19th. We had at last reached the point when we had but three days' rations on hand. Something must be done. We were in a barren country, with a large force of the enemy in front of us, a large and now impassable river between us, and no news from our train or from our base of operations for twelve days. What were we to do? Colonel Weer called a council of war, at which he stated that the Arkansas River was now impassable to our forces; that a train containing commissary stores had been expected for three days; that three different sets of couriers sent out some time previous had entirely failed to report; that he had been twelve days entirely without communication with or from the department, and that he had received reliable information that a large force of the enemy were moving to our rear via the Verdigris River for the purpose of cutting off our train.

Upon this and other information the council of war decided that our only safety lay in falling back to some point where we could reopen communication and learn the whereabouts of our train of subsistence. To this decision of the council he at the time assented, and said that he would arrange with the commanders of brigades the order of march. Subsequently he issued an order putting the command on half rations, declaring that he would not fall back, and refused utterly, upon my application, to take any steps for the safety or salvation of his command. I could but conclude that the man was either insane, premeditated treachery to his troops, or perhaps that his grossly intemperate habits long continued had produced idiocy or monomania. In either case the command was imperiled, and a military necessity demanded that something be done, and that without delay. I took the only step I believed available to save your troops. I arrested this man, have drawn charges against him, and now hold him subject to your orders.

On the morning of the 19th I commenced a retrograde march and have fallen back with my main force to this point.

You will see by General Orders, No. 1, herewith forwarded, that I have stationed the First and Second Regiments Indian Home Guards as a corps of observation along the Grand and Verdigris Rivers; also to guard the fords of the Arkansas. Yesterday evening a courier reached me at Prior Creek with dispatches saying that a commissary train was at Hudson's Crossing, 75 miles north of us, waiting for an additional force as an escort. Information also reaches me this morning that Colonel Watie, with a force of 1,200 men, passed up the east side of Grand River yesterday for the purpose of cutting off this train. I have sent out strong reconnoitering parties to the east of the river, and if the information proves reliable will take such further measures as I deem best for its security.

I design simply to hold the country we are now in, and will make no important moves except such as I may deem necessary for the preservation of this command until I receive specific

instructions from you. I send Major Burnett with a small
escort to make his way through to you. He will give you more
at length the position of this command, their condition, &c.

Very respectfully, your obedient servant,

F. SALOMON, *Colonel Ninth Wis. Vols.,*
Comdg. Indian Expedition.

Salomon's insubordination brought the Indian Expedition in its original form to an abrupt end, much
to the disgust and righteous indignation of the Indian
service. The arrest of Colonel Weer threw the whole
camp into confusion,[372] and it was some hours before
anything like order could be restored. A retrograde
movement of the white troops had evidently been earlier resolved upon and was at once undertaken. Of
such troops, Salomon assumed personal command and
ordered them to begin a march northward at two
o'clock on the morning of the nineteenth.[373] At the
same time, he established the troops, he was so brutally
abandoning, as a corps of observation on or near the
Verdigris and Grand Rivers. They were thus expected to cover his retreat, while he, unhampered, proceeded to Hudson's Crossing.[374]

With the departure of Salomon and subordinate commanders in sympathy with his retrograde movement,
Robert W. Furnas, colonel of the First Indian, became
the ranking officer in the field. Consequently it was
his duty to direct the movements of the troops that remained. The troops were those of the three Indian
regiments, the third of which had not yet been formally
recognized and accepted by the government. Not all
of these troops were in camp when the arrest of Weer
took place. One of the last official acts of Weer as

[372] Carruth and Martin to Blunt, July 19, 1862.
[373] Blocki, by order of Salomon, July 18, 1862, *Official Records,* vol. xiii,
477.
[374] Carruth and Martin to Coffin, August 2, 1862.

commander of the Indian Expedition had been to order the First Indian to proceed to the Verdigris River and to take position "in the vicinity of Vann's Ford." Only a detachment of about two hundred men had as yet gone there, however, and they were there in charge of Lieutenant A. C. Ellithorpe. A like detachment of the Third Indian, under John A. Foreman, major, had been posted at Fort Gibson.[375] Salomon's *pronunciamento* and his order, placing the Indian regiments as a corps of observation on the Verdigris and Grand Rivers, were not communicated to the regimental commanders of the Indian Home Guard until July 22;[376] but they had already met, had conferred among themselves, and had decided that it would be bad policy to take the Indians out of the Territory.[377] They, therefore agreed to consolidate the three regiments into a brigade, Furnas in command, and to establish camp and headquarters on the Verdigris, about twelve miles directly west of the old camp on the Grand.[378]

The brigading took place as agreed upon and Furnas, brigade commander, retained his colonelcy of the First Indian, while Lieutenant-colonel David B. Corwin took command of the Second and Colonel William A. Phillips of the Third. Colonel Ritchie had, prior to recent happenings, been detached from his command in order to conduct a party of prisoners to Fort Leavenworth, also to arrange for the mustering in of Indian recruits.[379] But two days' rations were on hand, so jerked beef was accepted as the chief article of diet until other supplies could be obtained.[380] There was likely to be plenty of

---

[375] Furnas to Blunt, July 25, 1862, *Official Records,* vol. xiii, 512.

[376] — *Ibid.,* 512.

[377] Britton, *Civil War on the Border,* vol. i, 309.

[378] *Official Records,* vol. xiii, 512; Commissioner of Indian Affairs, *Report,* 1862, 163.

[379] Commissioner of Indian Affairs, *Report,* 1862, 163-164.

[380] Carruth and Martin to Coffin, July 25, 1862, *ibid.,* 160.

that; for, as Weer had once reported, cattle were a drug on the market in the Cherokee country, the prairies "covered with thousands of them." [381] The encampment on the Verdigris was made forthwith; but it was a failure from the start.

The Indians of the First Regiment showed signs of serious demoralization and became unmanageable, while a large number of the Second deserted. [382] It was thought that deprivation in the midst of plenty, the lack of good water and of the restraining influence of white troops had had much to do with the upheaval, although there had been much less plundering since they left than when they were present. With much of truth back of possible hatred and malice, the special agents reported that such protection as the white men had recently given Indian Territory "would ruin any country on earth." [383]

With the hope that the morale of the men would be restored were they to be more widely distributed and their physical conditions improved, Colonel Furnas concluded to break camp on the Verdigris and return to the Grand. He accordingly marched the Third Indian to Pryor Creek [384] but had scarcely done so when orders came from Salomon, under cover of his usurped authority as commander of the Indian Expedition, for him to cross the Grand and advance northeastward to Horse Creek and vicinity, there to pitch his tents. The new camp was christened Camp Wattles. It extended from Horse to Wolf Creek and constituted a point from which the component parts of the Indian Brigade did

[381] Weer to Moonlight, July 12, 1862.

[382] Furnas to Blunt, July 25, 1862.

[383] Commissioner of Indian Affairs, *Report*, 1862, 160-161.

[384] Named in honor of Nathaniel Pryor of the Lewis and Clark expedition and of general frontier fame, and, therefore, incorrectly called Prior Creek in Furnas's report.

extensive scouting for another brief period. In reality, Furnas was endeavoring to hold the whole of the Indian country north of the Arkansas and south of the border.[385]

Meanwhile, Salomon had established himself in the neighborhood of Hudson's Crossing, at what he called, Camp Quapaw. The camp was on Quapaw land. His idea was, and he so communicated to Blunt, that he had selected "the most commanding point in this (the trans-Missouri) country not only from a military view as a key to the valleys of Spring River, Shoal Creek, Neosho, and Grand River, but also as the only point in this country now where an army could be sustained with a limited supply of forage and subsistence, offering ample grazing[386] and good water."[387] No regular investigation into his conduct touching the retrograde movement, such as justice to Weer would seem to have demanded, was made.[388] He submitted the facts to Blunt and Blunt, at first alarmed[389] lest a complete abandonment of Indian Territory would result, acquiesced[390] when he found that the Indian regiments were holding their own there.[391] Salomon, indeed, so far strengthened Furnas's hand as to supply him with ten days rations and a section of Allen's battery.

[385] For accounts of the movements of the Indian Expedition after the occurrence of Salomon's retrograde movement, see the *Daily Conservative,* August 16, 21, 26, 1862.

[386] On the subject of grazing, see Britton, *Civil War on the Border,* vol. i, 308.

[387] Salomon to Blunt, July 29, 1862, *Official Records,* vol. xiii, 521.

[388] H. S. Lane called Stanton's attention to the matter, however, *ibid.,* 485.

[389] Blunt to Salomon, August 3, 1862, *ibid.,* 531-532.

[390] He acquiesced as, perforce, he had to do but he was very far from approving.

[391] In November, Dole reported to Smith that Salomon's retrograde movement had caused about fifteen hundred or two thousand additional refugees to flee into Kansas. Dole urged that the Indian Expedition should be reënforced and strengthened [Indian Office *Report Book,* no. 12, 503-504].

VI. GENERAL PIKE IN CONTROVERSY WITH GENERAL HINDMAN

The retrograde movement of Colonel Salomon and the white auxiliary of the Indian Expedition was peculiarly unfortunate and ill-timed since, owing to circumstances now to be related in detail, the Confederates had really no forces at hand at all adequate to repel invasion. On the thirty-first of May, as earlier narrated in this work, General Hindman had written to General Pike instructing him to move his entire infantry force of whites and Woodruff's single six-gun battery to Little Rock without delay. In doing this, he admitted that, while it was regrettable that Pike's force in Indian Terriory should be reduced, it was imperative that Arkansas should be protected, her danger being imminent. He further ordered, that Pike should supply the command to be sent forward with subsistence for thirty days, should have the ammunition transported in wagons, and should issue orders that not a single cartridge be used on the journey.[392]

To one of Pike's proud spirit, such orders could be nothing short of galling. He had collected his force and everything he possessed appertaining to it at the cost of much patience, much labor, much expense. Untiring vigilance had alone made possible the formation of his brigade and an unselfish willingness to advance his own funds had alone furnished it with quartermaster and commissary stores. McCulloch and Van

[392] *Official Records,* vol. xiii, 934.

Dorn[393] each in turn had diverted his supplies from their destined course, yet he had borne with it all, uncomplainingly. He had even broken faith with the Indian nations at Van Dorn's instance; for, contrary to the express terms of the treaties that he had negotiated, he had taken the red men across the border, without their express consent, to fight in the Pea Ridge campaign. And with what result? Base ingratitude on the part of Van Dorn, who, in his official report of the three day engagement, ignored the help rendered[394] and left Pike to bear the stigma[395] of Indian atrocities alone.

With the thought of that ingratitude still rankling in his breast, Pike noted additional features of Hindman's first instructions to him, which were, that he should advance his Indian force to the northern border of Indian Territory and hold it there to resist invasion from Kansas. He was expected to do this unsupported

---

[393] Van Dorn would seem to have been a gross offender in this respect. Similar charges were made against him by other men and on other occasions [*Official Records*, vol. liii, supplement, 825].

[394] It was matter of common report that Van Dorn despised Pike's Indians [*ibid.*, vol. xiii, 814-816]. The entire Arkansas delegation in Congress, with the exception of A. H. Garland, testified to Van Dorn's aversion for the Indians [*ibid.*, 815].

[395] How great was that stigma can be best understood from the following:
"The horde of Indians scampered off to the mountains from whence they had come, having murdered and scalped many of the Union wounded. General Pike, their leader, led a feeble band to the heights of Big Mountain, near Elk Horn, where he was of no use to the battle of the succeeding day, and whence he fled, between roads, through the woods, disliked by the Confederates and detested by the Union men; to be known in history as a son of New Hampshire – a poet who sang of flowers and the beauties of the sunset skies, the joys of love and the hopes of the soul – and yet one who, in the middle of the 19th century, led a merciless, scalping, murdering, uncontrollable horde of half-tame savages in the defense of slavery – themselves slave-holders – against that Union his own native State was then supporting, and against the flag of liberty. He scarcely struck a blow in open fight. . . His service was servile and corrupt; his flight was abject, and his reward disgrace." – *War Papers and Personal Recollections of the Missouri Commandery*, 232.

by white troops, the need of which, for moral as well as for physical strength, he had always insisted upon.

It is quite believable that Van Dorn was the person most responsible for Hindman's interference with Pike, although, of course, the very seriousness and desperateness of Hindman's situation would have impelled him to turn to the only place where ready help was to be had. Three days prior to the time that Hindman had been assigned to the Trans-Mississippi Department, Roane, an old antagonist of Pike[396] and the commander to whose immediate care Van Dorn had confided Arkansas,[397] had asked of Pike at Van Dorn's suggestion[398] all the white forces he could spare, Roane having practically none of his own. Pike had refused the request, if request it was, and in refusing it, had represented how insufficient his forces actually were for purposes of his own department and how exceedingly difficult had been the task, which was his and his alone, of getting them together. At the time of writing he had not a single dollar of public money for his army and only a very limited amount of ammunition and other supplies.[399]

Pike received Hindman's communication of May 31 late in the afternoon of June 8 and he replied to it that same evening immediately after he had made arrangements[400] for complying in part with its requirements. The reply[401] as it stands in the records today is a strong indictment of the Confederate management of Indian

---

[396] Pike had fought a duel with Roane, Roane having challenged him because he had dared to criticize his conduct in the Mexican War [Hallum, *Biographical and Pictorial History of Arkansas,* vol. i, 229; *Confederate Military History,* vol. x, 99].

[397] Maury to Roane, May 11, 1862, *Official Records,* vol. xiii, 827.

[398] Maury to Pike, May 19, 1862, *ibid.*

[399] Pike to Roane, June 1, 1862, *ibid.,* 935-936.

[400] General Orders, June 8, 1862, *ibid.,* 943.

[401] Pike to Hindman, June 8, 1862, *ibid.,* 936-943.

affairs in the West and should be dealt with analytically, yet also as a whole; since no paraphrase, no mere synopsis of contents could ever do the subject justice. From the facts presented, it is only too evident that very little had been attempted or done by the Richmond authorities for the Indian regiments. Neither officers nor men had been regularly or fully paid. And not all the good intentions, few as they were, of the central government had been allowed realization. They had been checkmated by the men in control west of the Mississippi. In fact, the army men in Arkansas had virtually exploited Pike's command, had appropriated for their own use his money, his supplies, and had never permitted anything to pass on to Indian Territory, notwithstanding that it had been bought with Indian funds, "that was fit to be sent anywhere else." The Indian's portion was the "refuse," as Pike so truly, bitterly, and emphatically put it, or, in other words of his, the "crumbs" that fell from the white man's table.

Pike's compliance with Hindman's orders was only partial and he offered not the vestige of an apology that it was so. What he did send was Dawson's[402] infantry regiment and Woodruff's battery which went duly on to Little Rock with the requisite thirty days' subsistence and the caution that not a single cartridge was to be fired along the way. The caution Pike must have repeated in almost ironical vein; for the way to Little Rock lay through Indian Territory and cartridges like everything else under Pike's control had been collected solely for its defense.

Respecting the forward movement of the Indian troops, Pike made not the slightest observation in his

---

[402] C. L. Dawson of the Nineteenth Regiment of Arkansas Volunteers had joined Pike at Fort McCulloch in April [*Fort Smith Papers*].

reply. His silence was ominous. Perhaps it was intended as a warning to Hindman not to encroach too far upon his department; but that is mere conjecture; inasmuch as Pike had not yet seen fit to question outright Hindman's authority over himself. As if anticipating an echo from Little Rock of criticisms that were rife elsewhere, he ventured an explanation of his conduct in establishing himself in the extreme southern part of Indian Territory and towards the west and in fortifying on an open prairie, far from any recognized base.[403] He had gone down into the Red River country, he asserted, in order to be near Texas where supplies might be had in abundance and where, since he had no means of defence, he would be safe from attack. He deplored the seeming necessity of merging his department in another and larger one. His reasons were probably many but the one reason he stressed was, for present purposes, the best he could have offered. It was, that the Indians could not be expected to render to him as a subordinate the same obedience they had rendered to him as the chief officer in command. Were his authority to be superseded in any degree, the Indians would naturally infer that his influence at Richmond had declined, likewise his power to protect them and their interests.

During the night Pike must have pondered deeply

---

[403] His enemies were particularly scornful of his work in this regard. They poked fun at him on every possible occasion. Edwards, in *Shelby and His Men*, 63, but echoed the general criticism,

"Pike, also a Brigadier, had retreated with his Indian contingent out of North West Arkansas, unpursued, through the Cherokee country, the Chickasaw country, and the country of the Choctaws, two hundred and fifty miles to the southward, only halting on the 'Little Blue', an unknown thread of a stream, twenty miles from Red river, where he constructed fortifications on the open prairie, erected a saw-mill remote from any timber, and devoted himself to gastronomy and poetic meditation, with elegant accompaniments. . ."

over things omitted from his reply to Hindman and over all that was wanting to make his compliance with Hindman's instructions full and satisfactory. On the ninth, his assistant-adjutant, O. F. Russell, prepared a fairly comprehensive report[404] of the conditions in and surrounding his command. Pike's force,[405] so the report stated, was anything but complete. With Dawson gone, there would be in camp, of Arkansas troops, one company of cavalry and one of artillery and, of Texas, two companies of cavalry. When men, furloughed for the wheat harvest, should return, there would be "in addition two regiments and one company of cavalry, and one company of artillery, about 80 strong."[406] The withdrawal of white troops from the Territory would be interpreted by the Indians to mean its abandonment.

Of the Indian contingent, Russell had this to say:

The two Cherokee regiments are near the Kansas line, operating on that frontier. Col. Stand Watie has recently had a skirmish there, in which, as always, he and his men fought gallantly, and were successful. Col. D. N. McIntosh's Creek Regiment is under orders to advance up the Verdigris, toward the Santa Fé road. Lieut. Col. Chilly McIntosh's Creek Battalion, Lieut. Col. John Jumper's Seminole Battalion, and Lieut. Col. J. D. Harris' Chickasaw Battalion are under orders, and part of them now in motion toward the Salt Plains, to take Fort Larned, the post at Walnut Creek, and perhaps Fort Wise, and intercept trains going to New Mexico. The First Choctaw (new)[407] Regiment, of Col. Sampson Folsom, and the Choctaw Battalion (three companies), of Maj. Simpson (N.) Folsom, are at Middle Boggy, 23 miles northeast of this point. They were under orders to march northward to

---

[404] *Official Records,* vol. xiii, 943-945.

[405] For tabulated showing of Pike's brigade, see *ibid.,* 831.

[406] Compare Russell's statement with Hindman's [*ibid.,* 30]. See also Maury to Price, March 22, 1862 [*ibid.,* vol. viii, 798].

[407] The parentheses appear here as in the original.

the Salt Plains and Santa Fé road; but the withdrawal of Colonel Dawson's regiment prevents that, and the regiment is now ordered to take position here, and the battalion to march to and take position at Camp McIntosh, 17 miles this side of Fort Cobb, where, with Hart's Spies, 40 in number, it will send out parties to the Wichita Mountains and up the False Wichita, and prevent, if possible, depredations on the frontier of Texas.

The First Choctaw and Chickasaw Regiment, of Col. Douglas H. Cooper, goes out of service on the 25th and 26th of July. It is now encamped 11 miles east of here. . . The country to the westward is quiet, all the Comanches this side of the Staked Plains being friendly, and the Kiowas [408] having made peace, and selected a home to live at on Elk Creek, not far from the site of Camp Radziwintski, south of the Wichita Mountains.

The Indian troops have been instructed, if the enemy [409] invades the country, to harass him, and impede his progress by every possible means, and, falling back here as he advances, to assist in holding this position against him.

Included in Russell's report there might well have been much interesting data respecting the condition of the troops that Pike was parting with; for it can scarcely be said that he manifested any generosity in sending them forth. He obeyed the letter of his order and ignored its spirit. He permitted no guns to be taken out of the Territory that had been paid for with money that he had furnished. Dawson's regiment had not its full quota of men, but that was scarcely Pike's fault. Neither was it his fault that its equipment was so sadly below par that it could make but very slow progress on the nine hundred mile march between Fort McCulloch and Little Rock. Moreover, the health of the

[408] Pike had just received assurances of the friendly disposition of the Kiowas [Bickel to Pike, June 1, 1862, *Official Records,* vol. xiii, 936].

[409] The enemy in mind was the Indian Expedition. Pike had heard that Sturgis had been removed "on account of his tardiness in not invading the Indian country. . ." [*Ibid.,* 944].

men was impaired, their duties, especially the "fort duties, throwing up intrenchments, etc.," [410] had been very fatiguing. Pike had no wagons to spare them for the trip eastward. So many of his men had obtained furloughs for the harvest season and every company, in departing, had taken with it a wagon, [411] no one having any thought that there would come a call decreasing Pike's command.

So slowly and laboriously did Dawson's regiment progress that Hindman, not hearing either of it or of Woodruff's battery, which was slightly in advance, began to have misgivings as to the fate of his orders of May 31. He, therefore, repeated them in substance, on June 17, with the additional specific direction that Pike should "move at once to Fort Gibson." That order Pike received June 24, the day following his issuance of instructions to his next in command, Colonel D. H. Cooper, that he should hasten to the country north of the Canadian and there take command of all forces except Chief Jumper's.

The receipt of Hindman's order of June 17 was the signal for Pike to pen another lengthy letter [412] of description and protest. Interspersed through it were his grievances, the same that were recited in the letter of June 8, but now more elaborately dwelt upon. Pike was getting irritable. He declared that he had done all he could to expedite the movement of his troops. The odds were unquestionably against him. His Indians were doing duty in different places. Most of the men of his white cavalry force were off on furlough. Their furloughs would not expire until the

---

[410] Dawson to Hindman, June 20, 1862, *Official Records*, vol. xiii, 945-946.

[411] Dawson had allowed his wagons to go "of his own motion" [Pike to Hindman, June 24, 1862, *ibid.*, 947].

[412] — *Ibid.*, 947-950.

twenty-fifth and not until the twenty-seventh could they be proceeded against as deserters. Not until that date, too, would the reorganization, preliminary to marching, be possible. He was short of transportation and half of what he had was unserviceable.

Of his available Indian force, he had made what disposition to him seemed best. He had ordered the newly-organized First Choctaw Regiment, under Colonel Sampson Folsom, to Fort Gibson and had assigned Cooper to the command north of the Canadian, which meant, of course, the Cherokee country. Cooper's own regiment was the First Choctaw and Chickasaw, of which, two companies, proceeding from Scullyville, had already posted themselves in the upper part of the Indian Territory, where also were the two Cherokee regiments, Watie's and Drew's. The remaining eight companies of the First Choctaw and Chickasaw were encamped near Fort McCulloch and would have, before moving elsewhere, to await the reorganization of their regiment, now near at hand. However, Cooper was not without hope that he could effect reorganization promptly and take at least four companies to join those that had just come from Scullyville. There were six companies in the Chickasaw Battalion, two at Fort Cobb and four on the march to Fort McCulloch; but they would all have to be left within their own country for they were averse to moving out of it and were in no condition to move. The three companies of the Choctaw Battalion would also have to be left behind in the south for they had no transportation with which to effect a removal. The Creek commands, D. N. McIntosh's Creek Regiment, Chilly McIntosh's Creek Battalion, and John Jumper's Seminole Battalion, were operating in the west, along the Santa Fé Trail and towards Forts Larned and Wise.

June 17 might be said to mark the beginning of the real controversy between Pike and Hindman; for, on that day, not only did Hindman reiterate the order to hurry that aroused Pike's ire but he encroached upon Pike's prerogative in a financial particular that was bound, considering Pike's experiences in the past, to make for trouble. Interference with his commissary Pike was determined not to brook, yet, on June 17, Hindman put N. Bart Pearce in supreme control at Fort Smith as commissary, acting quartermaster, and acting ordnance officer.[413] His jurisdiction was to extend over northwestern Arkansas and over the Indian Territory. Now Pike had had dealings already with Pearce and thought that he knew too well the limits of his probity. Exactly when Pike heard of Pearce's promotion is not quite clear; but, on the twenty-third, Hindman sent him a conciliatory note explaining that his intention was "to stop the operations of the commissaries of wandering companies in the Cherokee Nation, who" were "destroying the credit of the Confederacy by the floods of certificates they" issued and not "to restrict officers acting under" Pike's orders.[414] All very well, but Pearce had other ideas as to the functions of his office and lost no time in apprising various people of them. His notes[415] to Pike's officers were most impertinently prompt. They were sent out on the twenty-fourth of June and on the twenty-sixth Pike reported[416] the whole history of his economic embarrassments to the Secretary of War.[417]

---

[413] *Official Records*, vol. xiii, 967.

[414] — *Ibid.*, 946.

[415] — *Ibid.*, 968, 968-969, 969.

[416] — *Ibid.*, 841-844.

[417] George W. Randolph.

His indignation must have been immense; but whether righteously so or not, it was for others higher up to decide. That Pike had some sort of a case against the men in Arkansas there can be no question. The tale he told Secretary Randolph was a revelation such as would have put ordinary men, if involved at all, to deepest shame. Hindman, perforce, was the victim of accumulated resentment; for he, personally, had done only a small part of that of which Pike complained. In the main, Pike's report simply furnished particulars in matters, such as the despoiling him of his hard-won supplies, of which mention has already been made; and his chief accusation was little more than hinted at, the gist of it being suggested in some of his concluding sentences:

. . . I struggled for a good while before I got rid of the curse of dependence for subsistence, transportation, and forage on officers at Fort Smith. I cannot even get from that place the supplies I provide myself and hardly my own private stores. My department quartermaster and commissary are fully competent to purchase what we need, and I mean they shall do it. I have set my face against all rascality and swindling and keep contractors in wholesome fear, and have made it publicly known by advertisement that I prefer to purchase of the farmer and producer and do not want any contractors interposed between me and them. My own officers will continue to purchase subsistence, transportation, forage, and whatever else I need until I am ordered to the contrary by you, and when that order comes it will be answered by my resignation. Mr. White's [418] contract will not be acted under here. I have beef enough on hand and engaged, and do not want any from him. I have had to buy bacon at 20 to 26 cents, and he ought to be made to pay every cent of the difference between that price and fifteen cents. I also strenuously object to receiving mules or anything else purchased at Fort Smith.

[418] "George E. White, formerly a partner, I believe, of Senator Oldham of Texas . . ." – *Official Records,* vol. xiii, 842.

I could get up a mule factory now with the skeletons I have, and there are a few miles from here 600 or 800 sent up by Major Clark [419] in even a worse plight.

I know nothing about Major Pearce as a quartermaster nor of any right Major-General Hindman has to make him one. He is an assistant commissary of subsistence, with the rank of major, and Major Quesenbury, my brigade or department quartermaster, is major by an older commission. . .

While I am here there will be no fine contracts for mules, hay, keeping of mules, beef on the hoof at long figures, or anything of the kind. Fort Smith is very indignant at this, and out of this grief grows the anxious desire of many patriots to see me resign the command of this country or be removed. . .[420]

Subsequent communications [421] from Pike to Randolph reported the continued despoiling of his command and the persistent infringement of Pearce upon his authority, in consequence of which, the Indians were suffering from lack of forage, medicines, clothing, and food.[422] Pearce, in his turn, reported [423] to Hindman Pike's obstinacy and intractability and he even cast insinuations against his honesty. Pike was openly defying the man who claimed to be his superior officer, Hindman. He was resisting his authority at every turn and had already boldly declared,[424] with special reference to Clarkson, of course, that

No officer of the Missouri State Guard, whatever his rank, unless he has a command adequate to his rank, can ever exercise or assume any military authority in the Indian country, and much less assume command of any Confederate troops or

---

[419] George W. Clark, *Official Records*, vol. xiii.

[420] For an equally vigorous statement on this score, see Pike to Randolph, June 30, 1862 [*ibid.*, 849].

[421] — *Ibid.*, 846-847, 848-849, 850-851, 852.

[422] Chilly McIntosh to Pike, June 9, 1862, *ibid.*, 853; Pike to Chilly McIntosh, July 6, 1862, *ibid.*, 853-854.

[423] July 5, 1862 [*ibid.*, 963-965]; July 8, 1862 [*ibid.*, 965-967].

[424] — *Ibid.*, 844-845.

compare rank with any officer in the Confederate service. The commissioned colonels of Indian regiments rank precisely as if they commanded regiments of white men, and will be respected and obeyed accordingly.

With the same confidence in the justness of his own cause, he called [425] Pearce's attention to an act of Congress which seemed "to have escaped his observation," and which Pike considered conclusively proved that the whole course of action of his enemies was absolutely illegal.

In some of his contentions, General Pike was most certainly on strong ground and never on stronger than when he argued that the Indians were organized, in a military way, for their own protection and for the defence of their own country. Since first they entered the Confederate service, many had been the times that that truth had been brought home to the authorities and not by Pike [426] alone but by several of his subordinates and most often by Colonel Cooper. [427] The Indians had many causes of dissatisfaction and sometimes they murmured pretty loudly. Not even Pike's arrangements satisfied them all and his inexplicable conduct in establishing his headquarters at Fort McCulloch was exasperating beyond measure to the Cherokees. [428] Why, if he were really sincere in saying that his supreme duty was the defence of Indian Territory, did he not place himself where he could do something, where, for instance, he could take precautions against invasions from

---

[425] Pike to Pearce, July 1, 1862, *Official Records*, vol. xiii, 967.

[426] One of the best statements of the case by Pike is to be found in a letter from him to Stand Watie, June 27, 1862 [*ibid.,* 952].

[427] For some of Cooper's statements, illustrative of his position, see his letter to Pike, February 10, 1862 [*ibid.,* 896] and that to Van Dorn, May 6, 1862 [*ibid.,* 824].

[428] It was at the express wish of Stand Watie and Drew that Hindman placed Clarkson in the Cherokee country [Carroll to Pike, June 27, 1862, *ibid.,* 952].

Kansas? And why, when the unionist Indian Expedition was threatening Fort Gibson, Tahlequah, and Cherokee integrity generally, did he not hasten northward to resist it? Chief Ross, greatly aggrieved because of Pike's delinquency in this respect, addressed[429] himself to Hindman and he did so in the fatal days of June.

In addressing General Hindman as Pike's superior officer, John Ross did something more than make representations as to the claims, which his nation in virtue of treaty guaranties had upon the South. He urged the advisability of allowing the Indians to fight strictly on the defensive and of placing them under the command of someone who would "enjoy their confidence." These two things he would like to have done if the protective force, which the Confederacy had promised, were not forthcoming. The present was an opportune time for the preferring of such a request. At least it was opportune from the standpoint of Pike's enemies and traducers.[430] It fitted into Hindman's scheme of things exactly; for he had quite lost patience, granting he had ever had any, with the Arkansas poet. It was not, however, within his province to remove him; but it was within his power so to tantalize him that he could render his position as brigade and department commander, intolerable. That he proceeded to do. Pike's quick sensibilities were not proof against such treatment and he soon lost his temper.

His provocations were very great. As was perfectly

---

[429] Ross to Hindman, June 25, 1862, *Official Records*, vol. xiii, 950-951. A little while before, Ross had complained, in a similar manner, to President Davis [*ibid.*, 824-825].

[430] Pike had his traducers. The Texans and Arkansans circulated infamous stories about him. See his reference to the same in a letter to Hindman, July 3, 1862 [*ibid.*, 955].

natural, the Confederate defeat at Locust Grove counted heavily against him.[431] On the seventh of July, Hindman began a new attack upon him by making requisition for his ten Parrott guns.[432] They were needed in Arkansas. On the eighth of July came another attack in the shape of peremptory orders, two sets of them, the very tone of which was both accusatory and condemnatory. What was apparently the first[433] set of orders reached Pike by wire on the eleventh of July and commanded him to hurry to Fort Smith, travelling night and day, there to take command of all troops in the Indian Territory and in Carroll's district.[434] Almost no organization, charged Hindman, was in evidence among the Confederate forces in the upper Indian country and a collision between the two Cherokee regiments was impending. Had he been better informed he might have said that there was only one of them now in existence.

The second[435] set of orders, dated July 8, was of a tenor much the same, just as insulting, just as peremptory. The only difference of note was the substitution of the upper Indian country for Fort Smith as a point for headquarters. In the sequel, however, the second set proved superfluous; for the first so aroused Pike's ire that, immediately upon its receipt, he prepared his resignation and sent it to Hindman for transmission to Richmond.[436]

Hindman's position throughout this affair was not

---

[431] July 3.

[432] *Official Records,* vol. xiii, 854.

[433] First, probably only in the sense that it was the first to be received.

[434] *Official Records,* vol. xiii, 857.

[435] — *Ibid.,* 856-857.

[436] Pike to Hindman, July 15, 1862 [*ibid.,* 858]; Pike to Secretary of War, July 20, 1862 [*ibid.,* 856].

destitute of justification.[437]   One has only to read his general reports to appreciate how heavy was the responsibility that rested upon him.   It was no wonder that he resorted to questionable expedients to accomplish his purposes, no wonder that he instituted martial law[438] in a seemingly refractory country, no wonder that he took desperate measures to force Pike to activity.   Pike's leisurely way of attending to business was in itself an annoyance and his leisurely way of moving over the country was a positive offence.   He had been ordered to proceed with dispatch to Fort Gibson.   The expiration of a month and a half found him still at Fort McCulloch.   He really did not move from thence until, having sent in his resignation, he made preparations for handing over his command to Colonel Cooper. That he intended to do at some point on the Canadian and thither he wended his way.[439]   By the twenty-first of July, "he had succeeded in getting as far as Boggy Depot, a distance of 25 miles;[440] but then he had not left Fort McCulloch until that very morning.[441]

Pike's definite break with Hindman was, perhaps, more truly a consummation of Hindman's wishes than of Pike's own.   On the third of July, as if regretting his previous show of temper, he wrote to Hindman a long letter,[442] conciliatory in tone throughout.   He discussed the issues between them in a calm and temperate spirit,

---

[437] In September, Hindman declared he had never had any knowledge of the order creating Pike's department [*Official Records*, vol. xiii, 978].

[438] He instituted martial law, June 30, 1862 and, although he believed he had precedent in Pike's own procedure, Pike criticized him severely. See Pike to J. S. Murrow, Seminole Agent, October 25, 1862, *ibid.*, 900-902.   Hindman had authorized Pearce, June 17, 1862, to exercise martial law in the cities of Fort Smith and Van Buren and their environs [*ibid.*, 835].

[439] Pike to Hindman, July 15, 1862.

[440] Hindman's Report [*Official Records*, vol. xiii, 40].

[441] Pike to the Secretary of War, July 20, 1862 [*ibid.*, 859].

[442] *Ibid.*, 954-962.

changing nothing as regarded the facts but showing a
willingness to let bygones be bygones. Considering
how great had been his chagrin, his indignation, and
his poignant sense of ingratitude and wrong, he rose
to heights really noble. He seemed desirous, even
anxious, that the great cause in which they were both
so vitally interested should be uppermost in both their
minds always and that their differences, which, after
all, were, comparatively speaking, so very petty, should
be forgotten forever. It was in the spirit of genuine
helpfulness that he wrote and also in the spirit of great
magnanimity. Pike was a man who studied the art of
war zealously, who knew the rules of European warfare, and a man, who, even in war times, could read
Napier's *Peninsular War* and succumb to its charm.
He was a classicist and a student very much more than
a man of action. Could those around him, far mean-
er souls many of them than he, have only known and
remembered that and, remembering it, have made due
allowances for his vagaries, all might have been well.
His generous letter of the third of July failed utterly
of its mission; but not so much, perhaps, because of
Hindman's inability to appreciate it or unwillingness
to meet its writer half-way, as because of the very seriousness of Hindman's own military situation, which
made all compromises impossible. The things he felt
it incumbent upon him to do must be done his way or
not at all. The letter of July 3 could scarcely have
been received before the objectionable orders of July
8 had been planned.

The last ten days of July were days of constant scouting on the part of both the Federal and Confederate
Indians but nothing of much account resulted. Colonel W. A. Phillips of the Third Indian Home Guard,

whose command had been left by Furnas to scout around Tahlequah and Fort Gibson, came into collision with Stand Watie's force on the twenty-seventh at Bayou Bernard, seven miles, approximately, from the latter place. The Confederate Cherokees lost considerably in dead and prisoners.[443] Phillips would have followed up his victory by pursuing the foe even to the Verdigris had not Cooper, fearing that his forces might be destroyed in detail, ordered them all south of the Arkansas and thereby circumvented his enemy's designs. Phillips then moved northward in the direction of Furnas's main camp on Wolf Creek.[444]

Pike had his own opinion of Cooper and Watie's daring methods of fighting and most decidedly disapproved of their attempting to meet the enemy in the neighborhood of Fort Gibson. That part of the Indian Territory, according to his view of things, was not capable of supporting an army. He discounted the ability of his men to conquer, their equipment being so meagre. He, therefore, persisted in advising that they should fight only on the defensive. He advised that, notwithstanding he had a depreciatory[445] regard for the Indian Expedition, and, both before and after the retrograde movement of Colonel Salomon, underestimated its size and strength. He was confident that Cooper would have inevitably to fall back to the Canadian, where, as he said, "the defensible country commences." Pike objected strenuously to the courting of an open battle and, could he have followed the bent of his own inclinations, "would have sent only

---

[443] Phillips to Furnas, July 27, 1862, *Official Records*, vol. xiii, 181-182.

[444] Same to same, August 6, 1862, *ibid.,* 183-184.

[445] Cooper reported that Pike regarded the Indian Expedition as only a "jayhawking party," and "no credit due" "for arresting its career" [Cooper to Davis, August 8, 1862, *ibid.,* vol liii, supplement, 821].

small bodies of mounted Indians and white troops to the Arkansas." [446]

No doubt it was in repudiation of all responsibility for what Cooper and Watie might eventually do that he chose soon to bring himself, through a mistaken notion of justice and honor, into very disagreeable prominence. Discretion was evidently not Pike's cardinal virtue. At any rate, he was quite devoid of it when he issued, July 31, his remarkable circular address [447] "to the Chiefs and People of the Cherokees, Creeks, Seminoles, Chickasaws, and Choctaws." In that address, he notified them that he had resigned his post as department commander and dilated upon the causes that had moved him to action. He shifted all blame for failure to keep faith with the Indian nations from himself and from the Confederate government to the men upon whom he steadfastly believed it ought to rest. He deprecated the plundering that would bring its own retribution and begged the red men to be patient and to keep themselves true to the noble cause they had espoused.

> Remain true, I earnestly advise you, to the Confederate States and yourselves. Do not listen to any men who tell you that the Southern States will abandon you. They will not do it. If the enemy has been able to come into the Cherokee country it has not been the fault of the President; and it is but the fortune of war, and what has happened in Maryland, Virginia, Kentucky, Tennessee, and even Arkansas. We have not been able to keep the enemy from our frontier anywhere; but in the interior of our country we can defeat them always.
>
> Be not discouraged, and remember, above all things, that you can have nothing to expect from the enemy. They will have no mercy on you, for they are more merciless than wolves and more rapacious. Defend your country with what help you

---

[446] Pike to the Secretary of War, July 20, 1862, *Official Records*, vol. xiii, 859-860.

[447] — *Ibid.*, 869-871.

can get until the President can send you troops. If the enemy ever comes to the Canadian he cannot go far beyond that river. The war must soon end since the recent victories near Richmond, and no treaty of peace will be made that will give up any part of your country to the Northern States. If I am not again placed in command of your country some other officer will be in whom you can confide. And whatever may be told you about me, you will soon learn that if I have not defended the whole country it was because I had not the troops with which to do it; that I have cared for your interest alone; that I have never made you a promise that I did not expect, and had not a right to expect, to be able to keep, and that I have never broken one intentionally nor except by the fault of others.

The only fair way to judge Pike's farewell address to his Indian charges is to consider it in the light of its effect upon them, intended and accomplished.[448] So little reason has the red man had, in the course of his long experience with his white brother, to trust him that his faith in that white brother rests upon a very slender foundation. Pike knew the Indian character amazingly well and knew that he must retain for the Confederacy the Indian's confidence at all cost. Were he to fail in that, his entire diplomatic work would have been done in vain. To stay the Cherokees in their desertion to the North was of prime necessity. They had already gone over in dangerously large numbers and must be checked before other tribes followed in their wake. Very possibly Pike had been made aware

---

[448] Pike gives this as the effect of his proclamation:

" . . . it effected what I desired. The Choctaw force was immediately increased to two full regiments; the Creek force to two regiments and two companies; the Seminole force was doubled; the Chickasaws reorganized five companies and a sixth is being made up. The Indians looked to me alone, and for me to vindicate myself was to vindicate the Government. We lost half the Cherokees solely because their moneys and supplies were intercepted . . ." – *Ibid.*, 904-905. See also Pike to Holmes, December 30, 1862. Another effect was, the creation of a prejudice self-confessed in General Holmes's mind against Pike.

of Chief Ross's complaint to Hindman. If so, it was all important that he should vindicate himself. So maligned had he been that his sensitiveness on the score of the discharge of his duties was very natural, very pardonable. After all he had done for the Confederacy and for the Indians, it seemed hardly right that he should be blamed for all that others had failed to do. His motives were pure and could not be honestly impugned by anybody. The address was an error of judgment but it was made with the best of intentions.

And so the authorities at Richmond seem to have regarded it; that is, if the reference in President Davis's letter[449] to Pike of August 9 is to this affair. Pike wrote to the president on the same day that he started his address upon its rounds, but that letter,[450] in which he rehearsed the wrongs he had been forced to endure, also those more recently inflicted upon him, did not reach Richmond until September 20. His address was transmitted by Colonel D. H. Cooper, who had taken great umbrage at it and who now charged the author with having violated an army regulation, which prohibited publications concerning Confederate troops.[451] Davis took the matter under advisement and wrote to Pike a mild reprimand. It was as follows:

RICHMOND, VA., August 9, 1862.
BRIG. GEN. ALBERT PIKE,
    Camp McCulloch, Choctaw Nation:
GENERAL: Your communication of July 3 is at hand. I regret the necessity of informing you that it is an impropriety for an officer of the Army to address the President through a printed circular.[452] Under the laws for the government of

---

[449] *Official Records,* vol. liii, supplement,, 822.

[450] — *Ibid.,* vol. xiii, 860-869.

[451] — *Ibid.,* vol. liii, supplement, 820-821.

[452] It is possible that the *printed circular* here referred to was some other one that was directly addressed to the president but none such has been found.

the Army the publication of this circular was a grave military offense, and if the purpose was to abate an evil, by making an appeal that would be heeded by me, the mode taken was one of the slowest and worst that could have been adopted.

Very respectfully, yours,   JEFFERSON DAVIS.

The sympathy of Secretary Randolph was conceivably with Pike; for, on the fourteenth of July, he wrote assuring him that certain general orders had been sent out by the Adjutant and Inspector General's Office which were "intended to prevent even the major-general commanding the Trans-Mississippi Department from diverting from their legitimate destination (the Department of Indian Territory) munitions of war and supplies procured by 'him' for that department." [453] That did not prevent Hindman's continuing his pernicious practices, however. On the seventeenth he demanded [454] that Pike deliver to him his best battery and Pike, discouraged and yet thoroughly beside himself with ill-suppressed rage, [455] sent it to him. [456] At the same time he insisted that he be immediately relieved of his command. [457] He could endure the indignities to which he was subjected no longer. The order for his relief arrived in due course and also directions for him to report in person at Hindman's headquarters. [458] He had not then issued his circular; but, as

---

[453] *Official Records*, vol. xiii, 903; Pike to Holmes, December 30, 1862, Pike *Papers*, Library of the Supreme Council, 33°. Pike did not receive Randolph's letter of July fourteenth until some time in August and not until after he had had an interview with Holmes. See Pike to Holmes, December 30, 1862.

[454] *Official Records*, vol. xiii, 970.

[455] This is inferred from the very peculiar *General Orders* that issued from Fort McCulloch that selfsame day. They were sarcastic in the extreme. No general in his right senses would have issued them. They are to be found, *ibid.*, 970-973.

[456] — *Ibid.*, 973, 974.

[457] — *Ibid.*, 973.

[458] Pike to Hindman, July 31, 1862, *ibid.*, 973.

soon as he had, the whole situation changed. He had
deliberately put himself in the wrong and into the hands
of his enemies. The address was, in some respects, the
last act of a desperate[459] man. And there is no doubt
that General Pike was desperate. Reports were
spreading in Texas that he was a defaulter to the government and, as he himself in great bitterness of spirit
said, "The incredible villainy of a slander so monstrous,
and so without even any ground for suspicion," was
"enough to warn every honest man not to endeavor to
serve his country."[460]

Not until August 6 did General Pike's circular address reach Colonel D. H. Cooper, who was then at
Cantonment Davis. Cooper wisely suppressed all the
copies he could procure and then, believing Pike to be
either insane or a traitor, ordered his arrest,[461] sending
out an armed force for its accomplishment. Hindman,
as soon as notified, "indorsed and approved" his action.[462] This is his own account of what he did:

> . . . I approved his action, and ordered General Pike
> sent to Little Rock in custody. I also forwarded Colonel
> Cooper's letter to Richmond, with an indorsement, asking to
> withdraw my approval of General Pike's resignation, that I
> might bring him before a court-martial on charges of false-
> hood, cowardice, and treason. He was also liable to the
> penalties prescribed by section 29 of the act of Congress regu-
> lating intercourse with the Indians and to preserve peace on
> the frontiers, approved April 8, 1862. . .
> But his resignation had been accepted. . .[463]

[459] And yet, August 1, 1862, Pike wrote to Davis one of the sanest papers
he ever prepared. It was full of sage advice as to the policy that ought
to be pursued in Indian Territory [*Official Records*, vol. xiii, 871-874].

[460] Pike to S. Cooper, August 3, 1862, *ibid.*, 975. See also Pike to Newton,
August 3, 1862, *ibid.*, 976.

[461] D. H. Cooper to Hindman, August 7, 1862, *ibid.*, 977.

[462] Pike to Anderson, October 26, 1862, *ibid.*, 903.

[463] Hindman's Report, *ibid.*, 41.

VII. ORGANIZATION OF THE ARKANSAS AND RED RIVER SUPERINTENDENCY

The mismanagement of southern Indian affairs of which General Pike so vociferously complained was not solely or even to any great degree attributable to indifference to Indian interests on the part of the Confederate government and certainly not at all to any lack of appreciation of the value of the Indian alliance or of the strategic importance of Indian Territory. The perplexities of the government were unavoidably great and its control over men and measures, removed from the seat of its immediate influence, correspondingly small. It was not to be expected that it would or could give the same earnestness of attention to events on the frontier as to those nearer the seaboard, since it was, after all, east of the Mississippi that the great fight for political separation from the North would have to be made.

The Confederate government had started out well. It had dealt with the Indian nations on a basis of dignity and lofty honor, a fact to be accounted for by the circumstance that Indian affairs were at first under the State Department with Toombs at its head; [464] and, in this connection, let it be recalled that it was under authority of the State Department that Pike had en-

---

[464] Toombs did not long hold the portfolio. Among the Pickett *Papers*, is a letter from Davis to Toombs, July 24, 1861, accepting with regret his resignation [Package 89].

tered upon his mission as diplomatic agent to the tribes west of Arkansas.[465]   Subsequently, and, indeed, before Pike had nearly completed his work, Indian affairs were transferred [466] to the direction of the Secretary of War and a bureau created in his department for the exclusive consideration of them, Hubbard receiving the post of commissioner.[467]

The Provisional Congress approached the task of dealing with Indian matters as if it already had a big grasp on the subject and intended, at the outset, to give them careful scrutiny and to establish, with regard to them, precedents of extreme good faith.   Among the

[465] In evidence of this, note, in addition to the material published in Abel, *The American Indian as Slaveholder and Secessionist,* the following letters, the first from Robert Toombs to L. P. Walker, Secretary of War, dated Richmond, August 7, 1861; and the second from William M. Browne, Acting Secretary of State, to Walker, September 4, 1861:

1. "I have the honor to inform you that under a resolution of Congress, authorizing the President to send a Commissioner to the Indian tribes west of Arkansas and south of Kansas, Mr. Albert Pike of Arkansas was appointed such Commissioner under an autograph letter of the President giving him very large discretion as to the expenses of his mission. Subsequent to the adoption of the resolution, above named, Congress passed a law placing the Indian Affairs under the control of your Department and consequently making the expenses of Mr. Pike and all other Indian Agents, properly payable out of the appropriation at your disposal for the service of the Indian Bureau." – Pickett *Papers,* Package 106, Domestic Letters, Department of State, vol. i, p. 86.

2. "The accompanying letters and reports from Commissioner Albert Pike addressed to your Department are respectfully referred to you, the affairs to which they relate being under your supervision and control." – *Ibid.,* p. 93.

[466] A re-transfer to the State Department was proposed as early as the next November [*Journal of the Congress of the Confederate States,* 489].

[467] President Davis recommended the creation of the bureau, March 12, 1861 [Richardson, *Messages and Papers of the Confederacy,* vol. i, p. 58: *Journal of the Congress of the Confederate States,* vol. i, p. 142]. On the sixteenth, he nominated David Hubbard of Alabama for commissioner [Pickett *Papers,* Package 88]. The bill for the creation of the bureau of Indian Affairs was signed the selfsame day [*Journal,* vol. i, 151]. S. S. Scott became Acting Commissioner of Indian Affairs before the year was out.

things [468] it considered and in some cases favorably disposed of were, the treaties of amity and alliance negotiated by Albert Pike, the transfer of Indian trust

[468] The preliminaries of the negotiations with the Indians have not been enumerated here, although they might well have been. On the twentieth of February, 1861, W. P. Chilton of Alabama offered a resolution to inquire into the expediency of opening negotiations [*Journal*, vol. i, 70]. March 4, Toombs urged that a special agent be sent and offered a resolution to that effect [*ibid.*, 105]. The day following, Congress passed the resolution [*ibid.*, 107]: but left the powers and duties of the special agent, or commissioner, undefined. Davis appointed Pike to the position and, after Congress had expressed its wishes regarding the mission in the act of May 21, 1861, had a copy of the act transmitted to him as his instructions [Richardson, vol. i, 149].

The act of May 21, 1861, carried a blanket appropriation of $100,000, which was undoubtedly used freely by Pike for purposes connected with the successful prosecution of his mission. In December, the Provisional Congress appropriated money for carrying into effect the Pike treaties. The following letter is of interest in connection therewith:

RICHMOND, VA., 9" December 1861.

SIR: On the 1st or 2nd of August 1861, after I had made Treaties with the Creeks and Seminoles, I authorized James M. C. Smith, a resident citizen of the Creek Nation, to raise and command a company of Creek Volunteers, to be stationed at the North Fork Village, in the Creek country, on the North Fork of the Canadian, where the great road from Missouri to Texas crosses that river, to act as a police force, watch and apprehend disaffected persons, intercept improper communications, and prevent the driving of cattle to Kansas.

The Company was soon after raised, and has remained in the service ever since. At my appointment George W. Stidham acted as Quartermaster and Commissary for it, and without funds from the Government, has supplied it.

By the Treaty with the Seminoles, made on the 1st of August, they agreed to furnish, and I agreed to receive, five companies of mounted volunteers of that Nation. Two companies, and perhaps more, were raised, and have since been received, I understand, by Col. Cooper, and with Captain Smith's company employed in putting down the disaffected party among the Creeks. Under my appointment, Hugh McDonald has acted as Quartermaster and Commissary for the Seminole companies, and made purchases without funds from the Government.

After I had made the Treaties with the Reserve Indians and Comanches, in August 1861, Fort Cobb being about to be abandoned by the Texan Volunteers who had held it, I authorized M. Leeper, the Wichita agent, to enlist a small force, of twenty or twenty-five men, under a Lieutenant, for the security of the Agency. He enlisted,

funds from the United to the Confederate States government,[469] the payment of Indian troops and their pensioning.[470] Its disposition to be grateful and generous came out in the honor which it conferred upon John Jumper, the Seminole chief.[471]

A piece of very fundamental work the Provisional Congress did not have time or opportunity to complete.

I learn, only some fifteen, and he has had them for some time in the service.

I also appointed a person named McKuska, formerly a soldier, to take charge of what further property remained at Fort Cobb, and employed another person to assist him, agreeing that the former should be paid as Ordnance Sergeant, and the latter as private; and directing the Contractor for the Indians to issue to the former two rations, and to the latter one.

In consequence of the collection of some force of disaffected Creeks and others, and an apprehended attack by them, Col. Douglas H. Cooper called for troops from all the Nations, and I understand that several companies were organized and marched to join his regiment. I think they are still in the service.

I am now empowered to receive all the Indians who offer to enter the service. To induce them to enlist, what is already owing them must be paid; and I earnestly hope that Congress will pass the bill introduced for that purpose. Respectfully your obedient servant

ALBERT PIKE, *Brig. Genl Comm^g Dept of Ind. Terr^y.*
Hon. W. Miles, Chairman Com. on Mil. Affs.
[War Department, Office of the Adjutant-General, Archives Division, *Confederate Records.*]

[469] *Journal*, vol. i, 650, 743, 761. The Confederate government took, in the main, a just, reasonable, and even charitable view on the subject of the assumption of United States obligations. Pike had exceeded his instructions in promising the Indians that monetary obligations would be so assumed. See his letter to Randolph, June 30, 1862.

[470] This matter went over into the regular Congress, which began its work, February 18, 1862. For details of the bill for pensions see *Journal*, vol. i, 43, 79.

[471] "*The Congress of the Confederate States of America do enact,* That the President of the Confederate States be authorized to present to Hemha Micco, or John Jumper, a commission, conferring upon him the honorary title of Lieutenant Colonel of the army of the Confederate States, but without creating or imposing the duties of actual service or command, or pay, as a complimentary mark of honor, and a token of good will and confidence in his friendship, good faith, and loyalty to this government . . ." – *Statutes at Large of the Provisional Government,* 284.

That work was, the establishment of a superintendency of Indian Affairs in the west that should be a counterpart, in all essentials, of the old southern superintendency, of which Elias Rector had been the incumbent. Elias Rector and the agents [472] under him, all of whom, with scarcely a single exception, had gone over to the Confederacy, had been retained, not under authority of law, but provisionally. The intention was to organize the superintendency as soon as convenient and give all employees their proper official status. Necessarily, a time came when it was most expedient for army men to exercise the ordinary functions of Indian agents; [473] but even that arrangement was to be only temporary. Without doubt, the enactment of a law for the establishment of a superintendency of Indian affairs was unduly delayed by the prolonged character of Pike's diplomatic mission. The Confederate government evidently did not anticipate that the tribes with which it sought alliance would be so slow [474] or so wary in accepting the protectorate it offered. Not until January 8, 1862, did the Provisional Congress have before it the proposition for superintendency organization. The measure was introduced by Robert W. Johnson of Arkansas and it

[472] Quite early a resolution was submitted that had in view "the appointment of agents to the different tribes of Indians occupying territory adjoining this Confederacy . . ." [*Journal*, vol. i, 81.]

[473] *Journal*, vol. i, 245.

[474] Pike was not prepared beforehand for so extended a mission. In November, he wrote to Benjamin, notifying him that he was enclosing "an account in blank for my services as commissioner to the Indian nations west of Arkansas.

"It was not my intention to accept any remuneration, but the great length of time during which I found it necessary to remain in the Indian Country caused me such losses and so interfered with my business that I am constrained unwillingly to present this account. I leave it to the President or to Congress to fix the sum that shall be paid me. . ."—PIKE to Benjamin, November 25, 1861, Pickett *Papers*, Package 118.

went in succession to the Judiciary and Indian Affairs committees; but never managed to get beyond the committee stage.[475]

February 18, 1862, saw the beginning of the first session of the first congress that met under the Confederate constitution. Six days thereafter, Johnson, now senator from Arkansas, again took the initiative in proposing the regular establishment of an Indian superintendency.[476] As Senate Bill No. 3, his measure was referred to the Committee[477] on Indian Affairs and, on March 11, reported back with amendments.[478] Meanwhile, the House was considering a bill of similar import, introduced on the third by Thomas B. Hanly, likewise from Arkansas.[479] On the eighteenth, it received Senate Bill No. 3 and substituted it for its own, passing the same on April Fool's day. The bill was signed by the president on April 8.[480]

The information conveyed by the journal entries is unusually meagre; nevertheless, from the little that is given, the course of debate on the measure can be inferred to a certain extent. The proposition as a whole carried, of course, its own recommendation, since the Confederacy was most anxious to retain the Indian friendship and it certainly could not be retained were not some system introduced into the service. In matters of detail, local interests, as always in American legislation, had full play. They asserted themselves most prominently, for example, in the endeavor made

---

[475] *Journal*, vol. i, 640, 672, 743.

[476] —*Ibid.*, vol. ii, 19.

[477] The Committee on Indian Affairs, at the time, consisted of Johnson, chairman, Clement C. Clay of Alabama, Williamson S. Oldham of Texas, R. L. Y. Payton of Missouri, and W. E. Simms of Kentucky.

[478] *Journal*, vol. ii, 51-52.

[479] *Journal*, vol. v, 47.

[480] —*Ibid.*, 210.

to make Fort Smith, although quite a distance from all parts of the Indian Territory except the Cherokee and Choctaw countries, the permanent headquarters, also in that to compel disbursing agents to make payments in no other funds than specie or treasury notes. The amendment of greatest importance among those that passed muster was the one attaching the superintendency temporarily to the western district of Arkansas for judicial purposes. It was a measure that could not fail to be exceedingly obnoxious to the Indians; for they had had a long and disagreeable experience, judicially, with Arkansas. They had their own opinion of the white man's justice, particularly as that justice was doled out to the red man on the white man's ground.[481]

Taken in connection with regulations[482] made by the War Department for the conduct of Indian affairs, the Act of April 8 most certainly exhibited an honest intention on the part of the Confederate government to carry out the provisions of the Pike treaties. The following constituted its principal features: With headquarters at either Fort Smith or Van Buren, as the president might see fit to direct, the superintendency was to embrace "all the Indian country annexed to the Confederate States, that lies west of Arkansas and Missouri, north of Texas, and east of Texas and New Mexico." A superintendent and six agents were immediately provided for, individually bonded and obligated to continue resident during the term of office, to engage in no mercantile pursuit or gainful occupation what-

---

[481] The Confederacy, as a matter of fact, never did keep its promise regarding the establishment of a judiciary in Indian Territory. Note Commissioner Scott's remarks in criticism, December 1, 1864 [*Official Records*, vol. xli, part iv, 1088-1089].

[482] The regulations referred to can be found in *Confederate Records*, chap. 7, no. 48.

soever, and to prosecute no Indian claims against the government. In the choice of interpreters, preference was to be given to applicants of Indian descent. Indian trade privileges were to be greatly circumscribed and, in the case of the larger nations, the complete control of the trade was to rest with the tribal authorities. In the case, also, of those same larger nations, the restrictions formerly placed upon land alienations were to be removed. Intruders and spirituous liquors were to be rigidly excluded and all payments to Indians were to be carefully safeguarded against fraud and graft. Indian customs of citizenship and adoption were to be respected. No foreign interference was to be permitted. Foreign emissaries were to be dealt with as spies and as such severely punished. The Confederate right of eminent domain over agency sites and buildings, forts, and arsenals was to be recognized, as also the operation of laws against counterfeiting and of the fugitive slave law. In default of regular troops, the Confederacy was to support an armed police for protection and the maintenance of order. The judicial rights of the Indians were to be very greatly extended but the Confederacy reserved to itself the right to apprehend criminals other than Indian.

The intentions of the Confederate government were one thing, its accomplishments another. The act of April 8 was not put into immediate execution, and might have been allowed to become obsolete had it not been for the controversy between Pike and Hindman. On the first of August, while the subject-matter of the address, which he had so imprudently issued to the Indians, was yet fresh in his mind, General Pike wrote a letter of advice, eminently sound advice, to President Davis.[483] Avoiding all captiousness, he set forth a pro-

---

[483] *Official Records,* vol. xiii, 871-874.

gramme of what ought to be done for Indian Territory and for the Indians, in order that their friendly alliance might be maintained. He urged many things and one thing very particularly. It was the crux of them all and it was that Indian Territory should be absolutely separated from Arkansas, in a military way, and that no troops from either Arkansas or Texas should be stationed within it. Other suggestions of Pike's were equally sound. Indeed, the entire letter of the first of August was sound and in no part of it more sound than in that which recommended the immediate appointment of a superintendent of Indian affairs for the Arkansas and Red River Superintendency, also the appointment of Indian agents for all places that had none.[484] It was high time that positions in connection with the conduct of Indian affairs should be something more than sinecures.

Aspirants for the office of superintendent had already made their wants known. Foremost among them was Douglas H. Cooper. It was not in his mind, however, to separate the military command from the civil and he therefore asked that he be made brigadier-general and *ex officio* superintendent of Indian affairs in the place of Pike removed.[485] His own representations of Pike's grievous offence had fully prepared him for the circumstance of Pike's removal and he anticipated it in making his own application for office. Subsequent knowledge of Pike's activities and of his standing at Richmond must have come to Cooper as a rude awakening.

Nevertheless, Cooper did get his appointment. It

---

[484] In his message of August 18, 1862 [Richardson, vol. i, 238], President Davis remarked upon the vacancies in these offices and said that, in consequence of them, delays had occurred in the payment of annuities and allowances to which the Indians were entitled.

[485] *Official Records,* vol. liii, supplement, 821.

came the twenty-ninth of September in the form of special orders from the adjutant-general's office.[486] Pike was still on the ground, as will be presently shown, and Cooper's moral unfitness for a position of so much responsibility was yet to be revealed. The moment was one when the Confederacy was taking active steps to keep its most significant promise to the Indian nations, give them a representation in Congress. The Cherokees had lost no time in availing themselves of the privilege of electing a delegate, neither had the Choctaws and Chickasaws. Elias C. Boudinot had proved to be the successful candidate of the former and Robert M. Jones[487] of the latter. Over the credentials of Boudinot, the House of Representatives made some demur; but, as there was no denying his constitutional right, under treaty guarantee, to be present, they were accepted and he was given his seat.[488] Provisions had, however, yet to be determined for regulating Indian elections and fixing the pay and mileage, likewise also, the duties and privileges of Indian delegates.[489] Perhaps it is unfair to intimate that the provisions would have been determined earlier, had congress not preferred to go upon the assumption that they would never be needed, since it was scarcely likely that the Indians would realize the importance of their rights and act upon them.[490]

---

[486] War Department, *Confederate Records, Special Orders of the Adjutant and Inspector General's Office*, C.S.A., 1862, p. 438; *Official Records*, vol. xiii, 885.

[487] See document of date, October 7, 1861, signed by Douglas H. Cooper, certifying that Robert M. Jones had received the "greatest number of votes cast" as delegate in Congress for the Choctaws and Chickasaws [Pickett *Papers*, Package 118].

[488] *Journal*, vol. v, 513, 514.

[489] — *Ibid.*, vol. ii, 452, 457, 480; vol. v, 514, 523, 561.

[490] Davis had thrown the responsibility of the whole matter upon Congress, when he insisted that the "delegate" clauses in the treaties should

While Congress was debating the question of Indian delegate credentials and their acceptance, a tragedy took place in Indian Territory that more than confirmed General Pike's worst prognostications and proved his main contention that Indian affairs should be considered primarily upon their own merits, as an end in themselves, and dealt with accordingly. Had the Arkansas and Red River Superintendency been regularly established, the tragedy referred to might never have occurred; but it was not yet established and for many reasons, one of them being that, although Douglas H. Cooper's appointment had been resolved upon, he had not yet been invested with the office of superintendent.[491] His commission was being withheld because charges of incapacity and drunkenness had been preferred against him.[492]

General Pike's disclosures had aroused suspicion and grave apprehension in Richmond, so much so, indeed, that the War Department, convinced that conditions in Indian Territory were very far from being what they should be, decided to undertake an investigation of its own through its Indian bureau. Promptly, therefore, S. S. Scott, acting commissioner, departed for the West. General Pike was in Texas.

Now one of the contingencies that Pike had most constantly dreaded was tribal disorder on the Leased

---

be so modified as to make the admission of the Indians dependent, not upon the treaty-making power, but upon the legislative. See his message of December 12, 1861, Richardson, vol. i, 149-151.

[491] Elias Rector, who had been retained as superintendent under the Confederate government, seems never to have exercised the functions of the office subsequent to the assumption by Pike of his duties as commander of the Department of Indian Territory. He was probably envious of Pike and resigned rather than serve in a subordinate capacity. He seems to have made some trouble for Pike [*Official Records*, vol. xiii, 964, 976].

[492] —*Ibid.*, 906, 908, 910-911, 927-928.

District,[493] a disorder that might at any moment extend itself to Texas and to other parts of the Indian Territory, imperiling the whole Confederate alliance. So long as there was a strong force at Fort McCulloch and at the frontier posts of longer establishment, particularly at Fort Cobb, the Reserve Indians could be held in check with comparative ease. Hindman, ignorant of or indifferent to the situation, no matter how serious it might be for others, had ordered the force to be scattered and most of it withdrawn from the Red River Valley.

The so-called Wichita, or Reserve, Indians, to call them by a collective term only very recently bestowed, had ever constituted a serious problem for the neighboring states as well as for the central government. It was with the Confederacy as with the old Union. The Reserve Indians were a motley horde, fragments of many tribes that had seen better days. They were all more or less related, either geographically or linguistically. Some of them, it is difficult to venture upon what proportion, had been induced to enter into negotiations with Pike and through him had formed an alliance with the Confederacy. Apparently, those who had done this were chiefly Tonkawas. Other Reserve Indians continued true to the North. As time went on hostile feelings, engendered by living in opposite camps, gained in intensity, the more especially because white men, both north and south, encouraged them to go upon the war-path, either against their own associates or others. Reprisals, frequently bloody, were regularly instituted. With Pike's departure from Fort McCulloch an opportunity for greater vindictiveness offered, notwithstanding the fact that the Choctaw and Chickasaw

[493] *Official Records*, vol. xiii, 868.

troops had been left behind and were guarding the near-by country, their own.

Sometime in the latter part of August or the early part of September, Matthew Leeper, the Wichita agent under the Confederate government, a left-over from Buchanan's days, went from the Leased District,[494] frightened away, some people thought, perhaps afraid of the inevitable results of the mischief his own hands had so largely wrought, and sojourned in Texas, his old home. The sutler left also and a man named Jones was then in sole charge of the agency. The northern sympathizers among the Indians thereupon aroused themselves. They had gained greatly of late in strength and influence and their numbers had been augmented by renegade Seminoles from Jumper's battalion and by outlawed Cherokees. They warned Jones that Leeper would be wise not to return. If he should return, it would be the worse for him; for they were determined to wreak revenge upon him for all the misery his machinations in favor of the Confederacy and for his own gain had cost them. Presumably, Jones scorned to transmit the warning and, in course of time, Leeper returned.

The twenty-third of October witnessed one of the bloodiest scenes ever enacted on the western plains. The northern Indians of the Reserve together with a lot of wandering Shawnees, Delawares, and Kickapoos, many of them good-for-nothing or vicious, some Seminoles and Cherokees attacked Leeper unawares, killed him,[495] as also three white male employees of the agency.

---

[494] *Official Records*, vol. liii, supplement, 828.

[495] On the murder of Agent Leeper, see Scott to Holmes, November 2, 1862, *Official Records*, vol. xiii, 919-921; Holmes to Secretary of War, November 15, 1862, *ibid.*, 919: F. Johnson to Dole, January 20, 1863, Abel, *American Indian as Slaveholder and Secessionist*, 329-330, *footnote*;

They then put "the bodies into the agency building and fired it." The next morning they made an equally brutal attack upon the Tonkawas and with most telling effect. More than half of them were butchered. The survivors, about one hundred fifty, fled to Fort Arbuckle.[496] Their condition was pitiable. The murderers, for they were nothing less than that, fled northward, they and their families, to swell the number of Indian refugees already living upon government bounty in Kansas.

Commissioner Scott then at Fort Washita hurried to the Leased District to examine into the affair. He had made many observations since leaving Richmond, had talked with Pike, now returned from Texas, and had come around pretty much to his way of thinking. His recommendations to the department commander that were intended to reach the Secretary of War as well were in every sense a corroboration of Pike's complaints in so far as the woeful neglect of the Indians was concerned. Better proof that Hindman's conduct had been highly reprehensible could scarcely be asked for.

Moore, *Rebellion Record,* vol. vi, 6; W. F. Cady to Cox, February 16, 1870, Indian Office *Report Book,* no. 19, 186-188; Coffin to Dole, September 24, 1863, Commissioner of Indian Affairs, *Report,* 1863, 177.

[496] S. S. Scott asked permission of Governor Winchester Colbert, November 10, 1862, to place the fugitive Tonkawas "temporarily on Rocky or Clear Creek, near the road leading from Fort Washita to Arbuckle." Colbert granted the permission, "provided they are subject to the laws of the Chickasaw Nation, and will furnish guides to the Home Guards and the Chickasaw Battalion, when called upon to do so."

VIII. THE RETIREMENT OF GENERAL PIKE

The tragedy at the Wichita agency brought General Pike again to the fore. His resignation had not been accepted at Richmond as Hindman supposed was the case at the time he released him from custody. In fact, as events turned out, it looked as though Hindman were decidedly more in disrepute there than was Pike. His arbitrary procedure in the Trans-Mississippi District had been complained of by many persons besides the one person whom he had so unmercifully badgered. Furthermore, the circumstances of his assignment to command were being inquired into and everything divulged was telling tremendously against him.

The irregularity of Hindman's assignment to command has been already commented upon in this narrative. Additional details may now be given. Van Dorn had hopes, on the occasion of his own summons to work farther east, that Sterling Price would be the one chosen eventually to succeed him or, at all events, the one to take the chief command of the Confederate forces in the West. He greatly wished that upon him and upon him alone his mantle should fall.[497] The filling of the position by Hindman was to be but tentative, to last only until Price,[498] perhaps also Van Dorn,

---

[497] Van Dorn to President Davis, June 9, 1862, *Official Records,* vol. xiii, 831-832.

[498] Price was preferred to H. M. Rector; because Van Dorn felt that Rector's influence with the people of Arkansas had greatly declined. The truth was, Governor Rector had become incensed at the disregard shown for Arkansas by Confederate commanders. In a recent proclamation, he had announced that the state would henceforth look out for herself.

could discuss matters personally with the president and remove the prejudice believed to be existing in his mind against Price; but the War Department had quite other plans developed, a rumor of which soon reached the ears of Van Dorn. It was then he telegraphed, begging Davis to make no appointment for the present to the command of the Trans-Mississippi District and informing him that Hindman had been sent there temporarily.[499] The request came to Richmond too late. An appointment had already been resolved upon and made. The man chosen was John Bankhead Magruder, a major-general in the Army of Northern Virginia. However, as he was not yet ready to take up his new duties, Hindman was suffered to assume the command in the West; but Magruder's rights held over. They were held in abeyance, so to speak, temporarily waived.[500]

The controversy between Pike and Hindman would seem to have impelled Secretary Randolph to wish to terminate early Magruder's delay; but Magruder was loath to depart. His lack of enthusiasm ought to have been enough to convince those sending him that he

---

[499] The orders for Hindman to repair west, issuing from Beauregard's headquarters, were explicit, not upon the point of the temporary character of his appointment, but upon that of its having been made "at the earnest solicitation of the people of Arkansas." [*Official Records,* vol. x, part ii, 547].

[500] Price, nothing daunted, continued to seek the position and submitted plans for operations in the West. His importunities finally forced the inquiry from Davis as to whether Magruder's appointment had ever been rescinded and whether, since he seemed in no hurry to avail himself of it, he really wanted the place. Randolph reported that Magruder had no objection to the service to which he had been ordered but desired to remain near Richmond until the expected battle in the neighborhood should have occurred. Randolph then suggested that Price be tendered the position of second in command [Randolph to Davis, June 23, 1862, *Official Records,* vol. xiii, 837], an arrangement that met with Magruder's hearty approval [Magruder to R. E. Lee, June 26, 1862, *Ibid.,* 845].

was hardly the man for the place. His acquaintance with Trans-Mississippi conditions was very superficial, yet even he found out that they were of a nature to admonish those concerned of their urgency, especially in the matter of lack of arms.[501] By the fourteenth of July his indecision was apparently overcome. At any rate, on that day Randolph wrote Pike that Magruder, the real commander of the Trans-Mississippi District, would soon arrive at Little Rock and that the offences of which Pike had had reason to complain would not be repeated.

Letters travelled slowly in those days and Randolph's comforting intelligence did not reach Pike in time to avert the catastrophe of his proclamation and consequent arrest. And it was just as well, all things considered, for Magruder never reached Little Rock. He was a man of intemperate habits and, while *en route*, was ordered back to Richmond to answer "charges of drunkenness and disobedience of orders."[502] His appointment was thereupon rescinded. The man selected in his place, to the total ignoring of Price's prior claims, was Theophilus H. Holmes, a native of North Carolina.[503] President Davis was still possessed of the notion that frontier affairs could be best conducted by men who had no local attachments there. Late events had all too surely lent weight to his theory. Nevertheless, in holding it, Davis was strictly inconsistent and illogical; for loyalty to the particular home state constituted the strongest asset that the Confederacy had. It was the lode-star that had drawn Lee and

---

[501] Magruder to Randolph, July 5, 1862, *Official Records*, vol. xiii, 851-852.

[502] Clark to Price, July 17, 1862, *Official Records,* vol. liii, supplement, 816-817.

[503] Wright, *General Officers of C.S.A.*, 15-16.

many another, who cared not a whit for political principles in and for themselves, from their allegiance to the Union. It was the great bulwark of the South.

Holmes was ordered west July 16;[504] but, as he had the necessary preparations to make and various private matters to attend to, August had almost begun before it proved possible for him to reach Little Rock.[505] The interval had given Hindman a new lease of official life and a further extension of opportunity for oppression, which he had used to good advantage. The new department commander, while yet in Richmond, had discussed the Pike-Hindman controversy with his superior officers and had arrived at a conclusion distinctly favorable to Pike. He frankly confessed as much weeks afterwards. Once in Little Rock, however, he learned from the Hindman coterie of Pike's Indian proclamation and immediately veered to Hindman's side.[506] Pike talked with him, recounted his grievances in a fashion that none could surpass, but made absolutely no impression upon him. So small a thing and so short a time had it taken to develop a hostile prejudice in Holmes's mind, previously unbiased, so deep-seated that it never, in all the months that followed, knew the slightest diminution. Conversely and most fortuitously, a friendliness grew up between Holmes and the man whom he had supplanted that made the former, either forget the orders given him in Richmond or put so new a construction upon them that they were rendered nugatory. It was a situation, exceedingly fortunate for

---

[504] *Official Records*, vol. xiii, 855.

[505] He had reached Vicksburg by the thirtieth of July and from that point he issued his orders assuming the command [*ibid.*, 860].

[506] Pike to Holmes, December 30, 1862 (Appendix); *Confederate Military History*, vol. x, 121-122.

the service as a whole, no doubt, but most unhappy for Indian Territory.

It finally dawned upon Pike that it was useless to argue any longer upon the matters in dispute between him and Hindman, for Holmes had pre-judged the case. Moreover, Holmes was beginning to appreciate the advantage of being in a position where he could, by ignoring Pike's authority and asserting his own, be much the gainer in a material way. How he could have reconciled such an attitude with the instructions he had received from Randolph it is impossible to surmise. The instructions, whether verbal or written, must have been in full accord with the secretary's letter to Pike of the fourteenth of July, which, although Pike was as yet ignorant of it, had explicitly said that no supplies for Indian Territory should be diverted from their course and that there should be no interference whatever with Pike's somewhat peculiar command.[507] All along the authorities in Richmond, their conflicting departmental regulations to the contrary notwithstanding, had insisted that the main object of the Indian alliance had been amply attained when the Indians were found posing as a Home Guard. Indians were not wanted for any service outside the limits of their own country. Service outside was to be deprecated, first, last, and always. Indeed, it was in response to a suggestion from Pike, made in the autumn of 1861, that the Indian Territory ought to be regarded as a thing apart, to be held for the Confederacy most certainly but not to be involved in the warfare outside, that Pike's department had been created and no subsequent ar-

---

[507] Pike to Holmes, December 30, 1862. The same assurance had apparently been given to Pike in May [*Official Records,* vol. xiii, 863].

rangements for the Trans-Mississippi Department or District, whichever it may have been at the period, were intended to militate against that fundamental fact.[508]

Despairing of accomplishing anything by lingering longer in Little Rock, Pike applied to Holmes for a leave of absence and was granted it for such time as might have to elapse before action upon his resignation could be secured.[509] The circumstance of Hindman's having relieved Pike from duty was thus ignored or passed over in silence. General Pike had come to Little Rock to see his family[510] but he now decided upon a visit to Texas. Exactly what he expected to do there nobody knows; but he undoubtedly had at heart the interests of his department. He went to Warren first and later to Grayson County. At the latter place, he made Sherman his private headquarters and it was from there that he subsequently found it convenient to pass over again into Indian Territory.

Pike was in Arkansas as late as the nineteenth of August and probably still there when Randolph's letter of the fourteenth of July, much delayed, arrived.[511] If angry before, he was now incensed; for he knew for a certainty at last that Hindman had been a sort of usurper in the Trans-Mississippi District and, with power emanating from no one higher than Beauregard, had never legally possessed a flicker of authority for doing the many insulting things that he had arrogantly done to him.[512] Next, from some source, came the

---

[508] *Official Records*, vol. xiii, 861, 864, 868.

[509] Holmes to the Secretary of War, November 15, 1862 [*ibid.*, 918].

[510] For an account of Pike's movements, see *Confederate Military History*, vol. x, 126.

[511] Abel, *American Indian as Slaveholder and Secessionist*, 356.

[512] Pike to Holmes, December 30, 1862, "Appendix."

news that President Davis had refused positively to accept Pike's resignation.[513] What better proof could anyone want that Pike was sustained at headquarters? What that view of the matter may have meant in emboldening him to his later excessively independent actions must be left to the reader's conjecture. It never occurred to Pike that if his resignation had been refused, it had probably been refused upon the supposition that, with Hindman out of the way, all would be well. One good reason for thinking that that was the Richmond attitude towards the affair is the fact that no record of anything like immediate and formal action upon the resignation is forthcoming. Pike heard that it had been refused and positively, which was very gratifying; but it is far more likely that it had been put to one side and purposely; in order that, since Pike was unquestionably the best man for Indian Territory, all difficulties might be left to adjust themselves, the less said about Hindman's autocracy the better it would be for all concerned.

But it was soon apparent that Hindman was not to be put out of the way. It was to be still possible for him to work mischief in Indian Territory. With some slight modifications, the Trans-Mississippi District had been converted into the Trans-Mississippi Department and, on the twentieth of August, orders[514] issued from

---

[513] There is something very peculiar about the acceptance or non-acceptance of Pike's resignation. Randolph wrote to Holmes, October 27, 1862, these words: ". . . General Pike's resignation having been accepted, you will be left without a commanding officer in the Indian Territory . . ." [*Official Records*, vol. xiii, 906]. A letter endorsement, made by Randolph, on or later than September 19th, was to this effect: "General Pike's resignation has not yet been accepted" [*ibid.*, liii, supplement, 821], and another, made by him, November 5th, to this: "Accept General Pike's resignation, and notify him of it" [*ibid.*, 822].

[514] *Official Records*, vol. xiii, 877.

Little Rock, arranging for an organization into three districts, the Texas, the Louisiana,[515] and the Arkansas. The last-named district was entrusted to General Hindman and made to embrace Arkansas, Missouri, and the Indian Territory.   Hindman took charge at Fort Smith, August twenty-fourth and straightway planned such disposition of his troops as would make for advancing the Confederate line northward of the Boston Mountains, Fort Smith, and the Arkansas River.   The Indian forces that were concentrated around Forts Smith and Gibson were shifted to Carey's Ferry that they might cover the military road southward from Fort Scott.   To hold the Cherokee country and to help maintain order there, a battalion of white cavalry was posted at Tahlequah and, in each of the nine townships, or districts, of the country, the formation of a company of home guard, authorized.[516]

The maintaining of order in the Cherokee Nation had come to be imperatively necessary.   John Ross, the Principal Chief, was now a prisoner within the Federal lines.[517]   His capture had been accomplished by strategy only a short time before and not without strong suspicion that he had been in collusion with his captors.   Early in August, General Blunt, determined that the country north of the Arkansas should not be abandoned, notwithstanding the retrograde movement of Colonel Salomon, had ordered Salomon, now a brigadier in command of the Indian Expedition, to send

---

[515] Not all of Louisiana was in Holmes's department and only that part of it west of the Mississippi constituted the District of Louisiana.   Governor Moore had vigorously protested against a previous division, one that "tacked" "all north of Red River" "onto Arkansas" [*Official Records*, vol. liii, supplement, 819].

[516] —*Ibid.*, vol. xiii, 46-47.

[517] Nominally, Ross was yet a prisoner, although, as a matter of fact, he had started upon a mission to Washington, his desire being to confer with President Lincoln in person regarding the condition of the Cherokees [Blunt to Lincoln, August 13, 1862, *ibid.*, 565-566].

back certain white troops in support of the Indian.[518]
Dr. Gillpatrick, who was the bearer of the orders, im-
parted verbal instructions that the expeditionary force
so sent should proceed to Tahlequah and complete what
Colonel Phillips had confessed he had not had sufficient
time for, the making of diplomatic overtures to the
Cherokee authorities.[519]

Blunt's expeditionary force had proceeded to Tahlequah and to Park Hill and there, under the direction
of Colonel William F. Cloud, had seized John Ross
and his family, their valuables, also official papers and
the treasury of the Cherokee Nation.[520] The departure
of the Principal Chief had had a demoralizing effect
upon the Cherokees; for, when his restraining influence
was removed, likewise the Federal support, political
factions, the Pins, or full-bloods, and the Secessionists,
mostly half-breeds, had been able to indulge their thirst
for vengeance uninterruptedly.[521] Chaos had well-
nigh resulted.

The departure of the expeditionary force had meant
more than mere demoralization among the Indians. It
had meant the abandonment of their country to the
Confederates and the Confederates, once realizing that,
delaying nothing, took possession. The secessionist
Cherokees then called a convention, formally deposed
John Ross, and elected Stand Watie as Principal Chief
in his stead.[522] Back of all such revolutionary work,
was General Hindman and it was not long before Hindman himself was in Tahlequah.[523] Once there, he proceeded to set his stamp upon things with customary

---

[518] *Official Records*, vol. xiii, 531-532.
[519] — *Ibid.*, 182.
[520] — *Ibid.*, 552.
[521] — *Ibid.*, 623, 648.
[522] *Confederate Military History*, vol. x, 129.
[523] *Official Records*, vol. xiii, 42.

vigor and order was shortly restored both north and south of the Arkansas. Guerrilla warfare was summarily suppressed, marauding stopped, and the perpetrators of atrocities so deservedly punished that all who would have imitated them lost their taste for such fiendish sport. As far north as the Moravian Mission, the Confederates were undeniably in possession; but, at that juncture, Holmes called Hindman to other scenes. A sort of apathy then settled like a cloud upon the Cherokee Nation.[524] Almost lifeless, it awaited the next invader.

One part of the programme, arranged for at the time of the re-districting of the Trans-Mississippi Department, had called for a scheme to reënter southwest Missouri. Hindman was to lead but Rains, Shelby, Cooper, and others were to constitute a sort of outpost and were to make a dash, first of all, to recover the lead mines at Granby. The Indians of both armies were drawn thitherward, the one group to help make the advance, the other to resist it. At Newtonia on September 30 the first collision of any moment came and it came and it ended with victory for the Confederates.[525] Cooper's Choctaws and Chickasaws fought valiantly but so also did Phillips's Cherokees. They lost heavily in horses,[526] their own poorly shod ponies; but they themselves stood fire well. To rally them after defeat proved, however, a difficult matter. Their disciplin-

---

[524] Report of M. W. Buster to Cooper, September 19, 1862, *Official Records*, vol. xiii, 273-277.

[525] For detailed accounts of the Battle of Newtonia, see *ibid.*, 296-307; Edwards, *Shelby and his Men*, 83-89; Britton, *Civil War on the Border*, vol. i, 355-363; Anderson, *Life of General Stand Watie*, 20; Crawford, *Kansas in the Sixties*, 54; *Confederate Military History*, vol. x, 132.

[526] Evan Jones to Dole, January 8, 1864, Indian Office General Files, *Cherokee*, 1859-1865, J 401.

ing had yet left much to be desired.[527]   Scalping[528] of the dead took place as on the battle-field of Pea Ridge; but, in other respects, the Indians of both armies acquitted themselves well and far better than might have been expected.

The participation of the Indians in the Battle of Newtonia was significant.   Federals and Confederates had alike resorted to it for purposes other than the red man's own.   The Indian Expedition had now for a surety definitely abandoned the intention for which it was originally organized and outfitted.   As a matter of fact, it had long since ceased to exist.   The military organ-

---

[527] "Since leaving the Fugitive Indians on Dry Wood Creek, nothing has occurred of material interest other than you will receive through official Dispatches from the Officers of our Army. The Indians under Col. Phillips fought well at the Battle Newtonia, they have at all times stood fire. The great difficulty of their officers is in keeping them together in a retreat, and should such be necessary on the field in presence of an enemy in their present state of discipline it would be almost impossible to again return them to the attack in good order – Another Battle was fought at this place in which the enemy were defeated with considerable loss, four of their guns being taken by a charge of the 2d Kansas.

"In this Contest the Indians behaved well, the officers and soldiers of our own regiments now freely acknowledge them to be valuable Allies and in no case have they as yet faltered, untill ordered to retire, the prejudice once existing against them is fast disappearing from our Army and it is now generaly conceded that they will do good service in our border warfare. This we have never doubted and confident as we have been of their fitness for border warfare we have been content to await, untill they had proven to the country not only their loyalty but their ability to fight. Since their organization they have been engaged in several battles and in every case successfully, one of us will start in a day or two for Tahlequah and may find something of interest on the march. We are now in the Cherokee Nation. An effort is now being made by Gen¹ Blunt to punish plundering in the country. Union People have suffered from this as much as rebels. We have before called the attention of our Army Officers to this fact; with our Fifteen Hundred Cherokee Warriors in the service of our government – we feel that every possible protection should be extended to them as a people" [Carruth to Coffin, October 25, 1862, enclosed in Coffin to Dole, November 16, 1862, Indian Office General Files, *Southern Superintendency 1859-1862*].

[528] *Official Records*, vol. xiii, 894.

ization, of which the Indian regiments in the Federal service now formed a part, was Blunt's division of the Army of the Frontier and it had other objects in view, other tasks to perform, than the simple recovery of Indian Territory.

It is true General Blunt had set his heart upon that particular accomplishment but he was scarcely a free agent in the matter. Men above him in rank had quite other aims and his, perforce, had to be subordinated to theirs. In August, Blunt had planned a kind of second Indian Expedition to go south to Fort Gibson and to restore the refugees to their homes.[529] It had started upon its way when the powers higher up interposed.

General Schofield, anticipating the renewed endeavor of the Confederates to push their line forward, had called upon Blunt for assistance and Blunt had responded with such alacrity as was possible, considering that many of the troops he summoned for Schofield's use were those that had been doing hard service within and on the border of the Indian country for full two months. During all that time their horses had been deprived entirely of grain feed and had been compelled to subsist upon prairie grass. They were in a bad way.[530] Once outside the Indian Territory, the Indian regiments, begrudging the service demanded of them, were kept more fully occupied than were the white; for there was al-

---

[529] "Orders have been given by General Blunt for the Indian Expedition to go South soon; he says the families of the Indians may go" – CARRUTH to Coffin, August 29, 1862, enclosed in Coffin to Mix, August 30, 1862, Indian Office General Files, *Southern Superintendency,* 1859-1862.

"Enclosed you will find an order from General James G. Blunt in regard to the removal of the Indian families to their homes. I start to-morrow for Fort Scott, Kansas, to overtake the second Indian expedition, commanded by General Blunt in person." – CARRUTH to Coffin, September 19, 1862, Commissioner of Indian Affairs, *Report,* 1862, p. 166.

[530] Britton, *Civil War on the Border,* vol. i, 337.

ways scouting[531] for them to do and frequently skirmishing. On Cowskin River, Phillips's Third Indian and, near Shirley's Ford on Spring River, Ritchie's Second had each engaged the Confederates with success, although not entirely with credit. Ritchie had allowed his men to run amuck even to the extent of attacking their comrades in Colonel Weer's brigade, which was the second in Blunt's reorganized army. On account of his lack of control over his troops, Ritchie was reported upon for dismissal from the service.[532]

The Battle of Newtonia was inconclusive. Subsequent to it, the Federals were greatly reënforced and, in the first days of October, Schofield and Blunt, who had both arrived recently upon the scene, coming to the aid of Salomon, who had been the vanquished one at Newtonia, were able, in combination with Totten, to deprive Cooper of all the substantial fruits of victory. He was obliged to fall back into Arkansas, whither a part of Blunt's division pursued him and encamped themselves on the old battle-field of Pea Ridge.[533]

Cooper was far from being defeated, however, and, under orders from Rains, soon made plans for attempting an invasion of Kansas; but Blunt, ably seconded by Crawford of the Second Kansas, was too quick for him. He followed him to Maysville and then a little beyond the Cherokee border to old Fort Wayne in the present Delaware District of the Nation. There, on the open prairie, a battle was fought,[534] on October 22, so dis-

---

[531] Phillips to Blunt, September 5, 1862, *Official Records*, vol. xiii, 614-615.

[532] Weer to Moonlight, September 12, 1862, *ibid.*, 627; Weer to Blunt, September 24, 1862, *ibid.*, 665-666; Britton, *Civil War on the Border*, vol. i, 352.

[533] Britton, *Civil War on the Border*, vol. i, 366; Crawford, *Kansas in the Sixties*, 54.

[534] Anderson, *Life of General Stand Watie*, 20; Crawford, *Kansas in the*

astrous to the Confederates, who, by the by, were greatly outnumbered, that they fled, a demoralized host, by way of Fort Gibson across the Arkansas River to Cantonment Davis,[535] Stand Watie and his doughty Cherokees covering their retreat. The Federals had then once again an undisputed possession of Indian Territory north of the Arkansas.[536]

Such was the condition of affairs when Pike emerged from his self-imposed retreat in Texas. The case for the Confederate cause among the Indians was becoming desperate. So many things that called for apprehension were occurring. Cooper and Rains were both in disgrace, the failure of the recent campaign having been attributed largely to their physical unfitness for duty. Both were now facing an investigation of charges for drunkenness. Moreover, the brutal attack upon and consequent murder of Agent Leeper had just shocked the community. Hearing of that murder and considering that he was still the most responsible party in Indian Territory, General Pike made preparations to proceed forthwith to the Leased District. His plans were frustrated by his own arrest at the command of General Holmes.

His unfriendliness to Pike was in part due to Holmes's own necessities. It was to his interest to assert authority over the man who could procure supplies for Indian Territory and when occasion offered, if that man should dare to prove obdurate, to ignore his position altogether. Nevertheless, Holmes had not seen fit in early October to deny Pike his title of com-

---

Sixties, 56-62; Edwards, *Shelby and his Men*, 90; *Official Records*, vol. xiii, 43, 324, 325, 325-328, 329-331, 331-332, 332-336, 336-337, 759; Britton, *Civil War on the Border*, vol. i, 364-375.

[535] *Official Records*, vol. xiii, 765.

[536] Blunt was ordered "to clean out the Indian country" [*ibid.*, 762].

mander and had personally addressed him by it.[537] Yet all the time he was encroaching upon that commander's prerogatives, was withholding his supplies, just as Hindman had done, and was exploiting Indian Territory, in various ways, for his own purposes. Rumors came that Pike was holding back munition trains in Texas and then that he was conspiring with Texan Unionists against the Confederacy. To further his own designs, Holmes chose to credit the rumors and made them subserve the one and the same end; for he needed Pike's ammunition and he wanted Pike himself out of the way. He affected to believe that Pike was a traitor and, when he reappeared as brigade commander, to consider that he had unlawfully reassumed his old functions. Accordingly, he issued an order to Roane,[538] to whom he had entrusted the Indians, for Pike's arrest; but he had already called Pike to account for holding back the munition trains and had ordered him, if the charge were really true, to report in person at Little Rock.[539]

The order for General Pike's arrest bore date of November 3. Roane, the man to whom the ungracious task was assigned, was well suited to it. He had been adjudged by Holmes himself as absolutely worthless as a commander and, being so, had been sent to take care of the Indians,[540] a severe commentary upon Holmes's own fitness for the supreme control of anything that had to do with them or their concerns. Others had an equally poor opinion of Roane's generalship and character. John S. Phelps, indeed, was writing at this very time, the autumn of 1862, to Secretary

---

[537] *Official Records*, vol. xiii, 924.

[538] — *Ibid.*, 923, 980, 981.

[539] — *Ibid.*, 904.

[540] — *Ibid.*, 899.

Stanton in testimony of Roane's unsavory reputation.[541]

The arrest of Pike took place November 14 at Tishomingo in the Chickasaw country and a detachment of Shelby's brigade was detailed to convey him to Little Rock.[542] Then, as once before, his reported resignation saved him from long confinement and from extreme ignominy. On the fifth of November, President Davis instructed the adjutant-general to accept Pike's resignation forthwith and five days thereafter,[543] before the arrest had actually taken place, Holmes advised Hindman that he had better let Pike go free so soon as he should leave the Indian country; inasmuch as his resignation was now an assured thing.[544] Holmes evidently feared to let the release take place within the limits of Pike's old command; for some of the Indians were still devotedly attached to him and were still pinning their faith upon his plighted word. John Jumper and his Seminole braves were among those most loyal to Pike; and Holmes was afraid that wholesale desertions from their ranks would follow inevitably Pike's degradation. Many desertions had already occurred, ostensibly because of lack of food and raiment. Commissioner Scott had complained to Holmes of the Indian privations[545] and Holmes had been forced to concede, although only at the eleventh hour, the Indian claim to some consideration. He had arbitrarily shared tribal quota of supplies, bought with tribal money, with white troops and had lamely excused himself by saying that he had done it to prevent grum-

[541] *Official Records*, vol. xiii, 752.
[542] — *Ibid.*, 921.
[543] — *Ibid.*, vol. liii, supplement, 821.
[544] — *Ibid.*, vol. xiii, 913.
[545] — *Ibid.*, 920.

bling[546] and the charge of favoritism. One other offence of which Holmes was guilty he did not attempt to palliate, the taking of the Indians out of their own country without their consent. To the very last Pike had expostulated[547] against such violation of treaty promises; but Holmes and Hindman were deaf alike to entreaty and to reprimand.

General Pike, poet and student, was now finally deprived of his command and the Indians left to their own devices or at the mercy of men, who could not be trusted or were not greatly needed elsewhere. No one attempted any longer to conceal the truth that alliance with the Indians was a supremely selfish consideration, and nothing more, on the part of those who coveted Indian Territory because of its geographical position, its strategic and economic importance. For a little while longer, Pike contended with his enemies by means of the best weapon he had, his facile pen. His acrimonious correspondence with the chief of those enemies, Hindman and Holmes, reached its highest point of criticism in a letter of December 30 to the latter. That letter summed up his grievances and was practically his last charge. Having made it, he retired from the scene, not to reappear until near the close of the war, when Kirby Smith found it advantageous to reëmploy him for service among the red men.

---

[546] *Official Records*, vol. xiii, 928.
[547] — *Ibid.*, 905, 963.

IX. THE REMOVAL OF THE REFUGEES TO THE SAC AND FOX AGENCY

General Blunt's decision to restore the Indian refugees in Kansas to their own country precipitated a word war of disagreeable significance between the civil and military authorities. The numbers of the refugees had been very greatly augmented in the course of the summer, notwithstanding the fact that so large a proportion of the men had joined the Indian Expedition. It is true they had not all stayed with it. The retrograde movement of Colonel Salomon and his failure later on to obey Blunt's order to the letter[548] that he should return to the support of the Indians had disheartened them and many of the enlisted braves had deserted the ranks, as chance offered, and had strayed back to their families in the refugee camps of southern Kansas.[549]

---

[548] Blunt to Caleb Smith, November 21, 1862 [Indian Office General Files, *Southern Superintendency, 1859-1862, I 860*].

[549] One of the first notices of their desertion was the following:

"We are getting along well, very well. The Indians seem happy and contented, and seemingly get enough to eat and wear. At least I hear no complaint. For the last two or three days the Indian soldiers have been stragling back, until now there are some three or four hundred in, and they are still coming. I held a council with them to-day to try and find out why they are here. But they don't seem to have any idea themselves. All I could learn was that Old George started and the rest followed. The Col. it seems told them to go some where else. I shall send an express to Col. Furness in the morning to find out if possible what it means. It seems to me it will not do to give the provisions purchased for the women and children to the soldiers. . .

"The soldiers look clean and hearty, and complain of being treated like dogs, starved etc, which I must say their looks belie. . ." – GEO. A. CUTLER to Wm. G. Coffin, August 13, 1862, *ibid.*

Then the numbers had been augmented in other ways. The Quapaws, who had been early driven from their homes and once restored,[550] had left them again when they found that their country had been denuded of all its portable resources. It was exposed to inroads of many sorts. Even the Federal army preyed upon it and, as all the able-bodied male Quapaws were gradually drawn into that army, there was no way of defending it. Its inhabitants, therefore, returned as exiles to the country around about Leroy.[551]

It was much the same with near neighbors of the Quapaws, with the Senecas and the Seneca-Shawnees. These Indians had been induced to accept one payment of their annuities from the Confederate agent[552] but had later repented their digression from the old allegiance to the United States and had solicited its protection in order that they might remain true. Some of them stayed with Agent Elder near Fort Scott,[553] others moved northward and lived upon the charity of the Shawnees near Lawrence.[554] But those Shawnees were doomed themselves to be depredated upon, especially that group of them known as Black Bob's Band, a band that had been assigned a settlement in Johnson

[550] Coffin to Elder, August 9, 1862; Coffin to Mix, August 16, 1862, Indian Office General Files, *Neosho*, C 1745 of 1862.

[551] Some of the Quapaws that went to Leroy were not *bona fide* refugees. Elder reported them as lured thither by the idea of getting fed [Elder to Dole, July 9, 1862, *ibid.*, E 114 of 1862].

[552] Coffin to Dole, May 31, 1862, Indian Office General Files, *Neosho*.

[553] Coffin to Mix, July 30, 1862, *ibid.*, C 1732 of 1862.

[554] J. J. Lawler to Mix, August 2, 1862, *ibid.*, *Shawnee*, 1855-1862; Abbott to Branch, July 26, 1862, *ibid.* Some of the Senecas, about one hundred twenty-three, went as far as Wyandot City. For them and their relief, the Senecas in New York interceded. See Chief John Melton to Commissioner of Indian Affairs, September 2, 1862, *ibid.*, *Neosho*, H 541; Mix to Coffin, September 11, 1862, Indian Office *Letter Book*, no. 69, 99.

County, adjoining the Missouri border.[555] In August[556] and again in the first week of September[557] guerrillas under Quantrill,[558] crossed over the line and raided the Black Bob lands, robbing the Indians of practically everything they possessed, their clothing, their household goods, their saddles, their ponies, their provisions, and driving the original owners quite away. They fired upon them as they fled and committed atrocities upon the helpless ones who lagged behind. They then raided Olathe.[559] Somewhat earlier, guerrillas had similarly devastated the Kansas Agency, although not to the same extent.[560] The Black Bob Shawnees found a refuge in the western part of the tribal reserve.[561]

[555] This group of Shawnee refugees must be distinguished from the so-called *Absentee Shawnees*, who also became refugees. The Shawnees had been very much molested and disturbed during the period of border strife following the passage of the Kansas-Nebraska Bill. Black Bob's Band was then exceedingly desirous of going south to dwell with the Seneca-Shawnees [Rector to Greenwood, January 6, 1860, enclosing Dorn to Greenwood, December 30, 1859, Indian Office General Files, *Neosho*, R 463 of 1860]. The Absentee Shawnees had taken refuge in Indian Territory prior to the war, but were expelled immediately after it began. They obtained supplies for a time from the Wichita Agent and lived as refugees on Walnut Creek [Paschal Fish and other Shawnee delegates to Cooley, December 5, 1865, Indian Office Land Files, *Shawnee*, 1860-1865]. Later on, they seem, at least some of them, to have gone up to the Shawnee Reserve [Dole to Coffin, July 27, 1863, Indian Office *Letter Book*, no. 71, 195; Dole to Usher, July 27, 1863, *ibid.*, *Report Book*, no. 13, 208-209].

[556] H. B. Branch to Dole, June 19, 1863, enclosing various letters from Agent Abbott, Indian Office General Files, *Shawnee*, 1863-1875, B 343.

[557] Branch to Dole, October 3, 1862, transmitting letter from Abbott to Branch, September 25, 1862, *ibid.*, *Shawnee*, 1855-1862, B 1583.

[558] Connelley, *Quantrill and the Border Wars*, 269, says that, from August 15, 1862, the Confederate government was directly responsible for the work of Quantrill. From that day, the guerrillas were regular Confederate soldiers. They were not generally regarded as such, however; for, in November, 1863, Price was trying to prevail upon Quantrill and his men to come into the regular army [*Official Records*, vol. liii, supplement, 907-908].

[559] Governor Robinson issued a proclamation, on the occasion of this emergency for volunteers against guerrillas.

[560] Farnsworth to Dole, July 23, 1862 [Indian Office General Files, *Kansas*, 1855-1862, F386].

[561] Letter of Agent Abbott, June 5, 1863, *ibid.*, *Shawnee*, 1863-1875, B 343.

Some Wyandot Indians, who before the war had sought and found homes among the Senecas,[562] were robbed of everything they possessed by secessionist Indians,[563] who would not, however, permit them to go in search of relief northward.[564] When all efforts to induce them to throw in their lot with the Confederacy proved unavailing, the strict watch over them was somewhat relaxed and they eventually managed to make their escape. They, too, fled into Kansas. And so did about one hundred Delawares, who had been making their homes in the Cherokee country. In the spring of 1862, they had begun to return destitute to the old reservation[565] but seem not to have been counted refugees until much later in the year.[566] The Delaware Reservation on the northern bank of the Kansas River and very near to Missouri was peculiarly exposed

---

[562] Indian Office General Files, *Neosho*, I 81 of 1860.

[563] Lawrence and others, Wyandots, to Dole, December 23, 1862, *ibid.*, Land Files, *Shawnee*, 1860-1865, L 12 of 1862. This letter was answered January 20, 1863, and, on the same day, Coffin was instructed to relieve their distress.

[564] "Being personally acquainted with the condition of the Wyandots . . . would here state, that a portion of them are living among the Senecas bordering on the Cherokee Country, and they are in a suffering condition. The rebel portion of the Senecas and Cherokees have robbed them of all of their ponies, and in fact all the property they had, and will not allow them to leave to come to Wyandott, which is about 2 hundred miles in distance, and their friends in Wyandott are unable to relieve them (on account of the rebel forces) without protection of our armies. The Wyandotts that are here are anxious to go and relieve their friends, and would respectfully request that they be allowed to form into a military company and be mustered into Gov^{nt} service and go with the expedition south to relieve their friends and assist in reclaiming the rebel Indians. A few of the Wyandotts are in service. . . They are all very anxious to be transferred into a company by themselves for the purpose above stated. . ."– CHARLES MOORE to Dole, February 9, 1862, Indian Office Special Files, no. 201, D 576.

[565] Johnson to Dole, April 2, 1862, Indian Office General Files, *Delaware*, 1862-1866.

[566] Johnson to Dole, November 5, 1862, *ibid., Southern Superintendency*, 1859-1862.

to ravages, horses and cattle being frequently stolen.[567] For that reason and because so much urged thereto by Agent Johnson,[568] who was himself anxious for service, the Delawares were unusually eager to enlist.

The Osages had been induced by Ritchie and others to join the Indian Expedition or to serve as independent scouts.[569] Their families, consequently, found it safe and convenient to become refugees.[570] In July, they formed much the larger part of some five hundred from Elder's agency, who sought succor at Leroy. That did not deter the Osages, however, from offering a temporary abiding-place, within their huge reserve, to the homeless Creeks under Opoeth-le-yo-ho-la.[571]

[567] Johnson to Dole, May 28, 1862, Indian Office General Files, *Delaware,* I 667 of 1862.

[568] Johnson wished to retain his agency and also hold a commission as colonel of volunteers, Department of the Interior, *Register of Letters Received,* no. 4, pp. 214, 357. James H. Lane endorsed his request and it was granted.

[569] The Osages rendered occasionally some good service. They and the Comanches plundered the Chickasaws very considerably [Holmes Colbert to N. G. Taylor, April 14, 1868, Indian Office Consolidated Files, *Chickasaw,* C 716 of 1868. See also Office letter to Osage treaty commissioners, May 4, 1868]. In October, the Osage force advanced as far as Iola and then retreated [Henning to Blunt, October 11, 1862, *Official Records,* vol. xiii, 726]. Soon after that they were mustered out and in a very disgruntled condition. They claimed that the government had used them very badly and had never paid them anything [Henning to Chipman, November 13, 1862, *ibid.,* 790]. They knew little of the discipline of war and left the army whenever they had a mind to.

[570] The Osages joined the Indian Expedition only upon condition that their families would be supported during their absence [Coffin to Dole, June 4, 1862, Indian Office Consolidated Files, *Neosho,* C 1662 of 1862]. The families were soon destitute. Coffin ordered Elder to minister to them at Leroy; but he seems to have distrusted the southern superintendent and to have preferred to keep aloof from him. Coffin then appointed a man named John Harris as special Osage agent [Coffin to Dole, July 7, 1862, *ibid.,* C 1710]. Elder tried to circumvent Coffin's plans for the distribution of cattle [Coffin to Elder, July 16, 1862, *ibid.,* C 1717] and Coffin lodged a general charge of neglect of duty against him [Coffin to Dole, July 19, 1862, *ibid.*].

[571] The invitation was extended by White Hair and Charles Mograin [Coffin to Dole, November 16, 1862, *ibid.,* C 1904]. Coffin was anxious for

During the summer the wretched condition of the Indian refugees had, thanks to fresh air, sunlight, and fair weather, been much ameliorated. Disease had obtained so vast a start that the medical service, had it been first-class, which it certainly was not, would otherwise have proved totally inadequate. The physicians in attendance claimed to have from five to eight thousand patients,[572] yet one of them, Dr. S. D. Coffin, found it possible to be often and for relatively long periods absent from his post. Of this the senior physician, Dr. William Kile, made complaint[573] and that circumstance marked the beginning of a serious estrangement between him and Superintendent Coffin.[574]

In August, General Blunt announced his intention of returning the Indian families to their homes.[575] He was convinced that some of the employees of the Indian Office and of the Interior Department were personally profiting by the distribution of supplies to the refugees and that they were conniving with citizens of Kansas in perpetrating a gigantic fraud against the government. The circumstances of the refugees had been well aired

Opoeth-le-yo-ho-la who had been rather obstreperous, to accept [Coffin to Dole, November 14, 1862, Indian Office General Files, *Southern Superintendency*, 1859-1862].

[572] Dr. S. D. Coffin, to Dole, July 5, 1862, *ibid.*, General Files, *Southern Superintendency*, 1859-1862; J. C. Carter to Dole July 22, 1862, *ibid.*

[573] Kile to Dole, *ibid.*

[574] The estrangement resulted in the retirement of Kile from the service. In September, Dr. Kile asked for a leave of absence. Shortly afterwards, Secretary Smith instructed Charles E. Mix, the acting commissioner, that the services of Kile were no longer needed, since the superintendent could attend to the purchasing and distributing of supplies [Smith to Mix, September 22, 1862, Indian Office General Files, *Southern Superintendency*, 1859-1862]. Mix promptly informed Kile that his resignation was accepted [Mix to Kile, September 22, 1862, *ibid.*, *Letter Book*, no. 69, p. 133].

[575] "Orders have been given by General Blunt for the Indian Expedition to go South soon; he says the families of the Indians may go. They wish to do so but no provision is made for their subsistence or conveyance. We wish immediate instructions in this particular." – CARRUTH to Coffin, August 29, 1862, *ibid.*, General Files, *Southern Superintendency*, 1859-1862.

in Congress, first in connection with a Senate resolution for their relief.[576]   On July fifth, Congress had passed an act suspending annuity appropriations to the tribes in hostility to the United States government and authorizing the president to expend, at discretion, those same annuities in behalf of the refugees.[577]   At once, the number[578] of refugees increased and white men rushed forward to obtain contracts for furnishing supplies.

There was a failure of the corn crop in southern Kansas that year and Dr. Kile, appreciating certain facts, that the Indian pony is dear, as is the Arabian horse, to his master, that the Indian ponies were pretty numerous in spite of the decimation of the past winter, and that they would have to be fed upon corn, advised a return to Indian Territory before the cold weather should set in.[579]   He communicated with Blunt[580] and found Blunt of the same opinion, so also Cutler[581] and Coleman.[582] Contrariwise was Superintendent Coffin,[583] whose view of the case was strengthened by E. H. Carruth, H. W. Martin,[584] and A. C. Ellithorpe.[585]

[576] *U. S. Congressional Globe*, 37th congress, second session, part i, 815, 849, 875, 891, 940.

[577] *U. S. Statutes at Large*, vol. xii, 528.

[578] In October, Coffin put the number of refugees, inclusive of the Cherokees on Drywood Creek, at almost seven thousand five hundred [Commissioner of Indian Affairs, *Report* 1862, p. 137] and asked for sixty-nine thousand dollars for their support during the third quarter of 1862 [Coffin to Mix, September 16, 1862, Indian Office General Files, *Southern Superintendency*, 1859-1862].

[579] Kile to Dole, July 25, 1862, *ibid.*

[580] Kile to Blunt, September 2, 1862, *ibid.*

[581] Cutler to Coffin, September 30, 1862, Commissioner of Indian Affairs, *Report*, 1862, 139.

[582] Coleman to Coffin, September 30, 1862, *ibid.*, 141.

[583] Coffin to Mix, August 30, 1862, Indian Office General Files, *Southern Superintendency*, 1859-1862: same to same, September 13, 1862, *ibid.*

[584] Carruth and Martin to Coffin, September 28, 1862, Commissioner of Indian Affairs, *Report, 1862*, 167.

[585] "In replying to the several interrogatorys contained in your letter of the 11th inst, I shall base my answer entirely upon my own observa-

In the contest that ensued between the military and
civil authorities or between Blunt and Coffin,[586] Coffin
triumphed, although Blunt made no concealment of his

tions and experience, obtained during a six months campaign with the
Indians, and in the Creek and Cherokee countries. Taking a deep interest
in the welfare of these loyal refugee Indians, who have sacrificed *all,*
rather than fight against our Flag, I shall be cautious and advise no
policy but that which will insure their safe restoration to their homes.

"The important question in your letter and that which embodies the
whole subject matter is the following – 'Would it be safe in the present
condition of the country to restore the southern refugee Indians now in
southern Kansas, the women and children, the old, feeble and infirm to
their homes in the Indian country?'

"I answer – It would not be safe to take the women and children to the
Creek or Cherokee countries this fall for the following reasons, 1st The
corn and vegetable crop north of the Arkansas River will not afford them
subsistence for a single month. The excessive drouth has almost completely destroyed it, and what little would have matured is laid waste
by the frequent foraging parties of our own Army, or those of the Rebels.

"The amount of Military force necessary to restore and safely protect
this people in their homes would far exceed what is at present at the disposal of the Department of Kansas; and should they be removed to the
Indian country, and our forces again be compelled to fall back for the
protection of Missouri or Kansas, it would again involve their precipitate
flight, or insure their total destruction.

"Again – the effectiveness of our troops would be materially embarased
by the presence of such a vast number of timid and helpless creatures – I
base my judgment upon the following facts – viz.:

"The expedition which I have been with during the summer, exploring
this country, consisted of three Brigades but containing actually only about
6 thousand men. We routed, captured, and pursued the fragments of several
Rebel commands, driving them south of the Arkansas River, opposite to,
and in the vicinity of Fort Gibson. This done, we found the whole of
Western Arkansas alive, and the numerous rebel squads were at once
reinforced from the guerila parties of Missouri, Arkansas, Texas, and the
various rebel Indian tribes, until they now number a force of from 30 to
4c thousand strong, under the command of Pike, Drew, McIntosh, Rains,
Stand Watie and others, ready to contest the passage of the Arkansas River
at any point and in fact capable of crossing to the north side of the river
and possessing the country we have twice passed over. Why did our
command fall back? Simply because we had not force sufficient to cross
the Arkansas River and maintain our position and because we were to
remote from our dipo of supplies.

"The Creek country west of the Verdigris River is almost destitute

[586] A dispute between Blunt and Coffin had been going on for some
time. In August, Coffin wrote to Mix that "The contrariness and interfer-

suspicions of graft and peculation[587] and the moment, following the defeat of the Confederates at old Fort Wayne, seemed rather auspicious for the return of the refugees.   In reality, it was not, however; for the Federals were far from possessing Indian Territory and they had no force that they could devote to it exclusively.

of forage for man or beast, owing to the drouth – Hence to remove these families would involve to the gov't great additional expense, not only to subsist but to protect them – Where they are they need no military protection and food is abundant.

"You will bear in mind that a large portion of the Indian country is south of the Arkansas River and is at present the stronghold of the Rebels. Many portions of it mountainous and rugged, affording secure retreats that will require a powerful army to dislodge." – A. C. ELLITHORPE to Coffin, September 12, 1862, Indian Office General Files, *Southern Superintendency, 1859-1862.*

ence manifested by the military authorities in the Indian Country towards those who are having charge of the Indians within the Cherokee Nation is so annoying and embarrassing that it has become unpleasant, difficult, and almost impossible for them to attend to the duties of their official capacities with success. If the Military would only make it their business to rid the Indian Territory of Rebels instead of intermeddling with the affairs of the Interior Department or those connected with or acting for the same, the Refugee Indians in Kansas might have long since been enabled to return to their homes   . . ." – Indian Office General Files, *Southern Superintendency,* 1863-1864, C 466.

[587] It was not long before the Indians were complaining of the very things that General Blunt suspected. For instance, in December, the Delawares begged President Lincoln to remove Agent Johnson because of his peculations and ungovernable temper. They also asked that the store of Thomas Carney and Co. be ordered away from their reservation. The latter request had been made before, the Delawares believing that Leavenworth and Lawrence were sufficiently near for them to trade independently [Indian Office General Files, *Delaware,* 1862-1866]. Coffin made a contract with Stettaner Bros. November 29, 1862, and Dole confirmed it by letter, December 13, 1862 [*ibid., Southern Superintendency,* 1863-1864]. Secretary Smith was not very well satisfied with the Stettaner bids. They were too indefinite [*ibid.,* 1859-1862, I 837]. Nevertheless, Dole, who was none too scrupulous himself, recommended their acceptance [Dole to Smith, December 11, 1862]. Number 201 of Indian Office *Special Files* is especially rich in matter relating to transactions of Stettaner Bros., Carney and Stevens, and Perry Fuller, so also are the files of the Indian Division of the Interior Department, and also, to some extent, the House Files in the Capitol Building at Washington, D.C.

Aside from pointing out the military inadequacy, Coffin had chiefly argued that provisions could easily be obtained where the refugees then were; but his opposition to Blunt's suggestion was considerably vitiated by recommendations of his own, soon given, for the removal of the refugees to the Sac and Fox Agency upon the plea that they could not be supported much longer to advantage in southern Kansas. The drouth was the main reason given; but, as Kile had very truly said, the settlers were getting pretty tired of the Indian exiles, whose habits were filthy and who were extremely prodigal in their use of timber. The Sac and Fox Agency was headquarters for the Sacs and Foxes of Mississippi, for the Ottawas, and for the confederated Chippewas and Munsees. C. C. Hutchinson was the agent there and there Perry Fuller, Robert S. Stevens, and other sharpers had their base of operations.

The removal northward was undertaken in October and consummated in a little less than two months; but at an expense that was enormous and in spite of great unwillingness on the part of most of the Indians, who naturally objected to so greatly lengthening the distance between them and their own homes.[588] The refugees were distributed in tribal groups rather generally over the reserves included within the Sac and Fox Agency. At the request of Agent Elder, the Ottawas consented to accommodate the Seneca-Shawnees and the Quapaws, although not without expressing their fears that the dances and carousals of the Quapaws would demoralize their young men[589] and, finally, not without insisting upon a mutual agreement that no

---

[588] Coffin to Dole, November 14, 1862, *ibid.*, Indian Office General Files, *Southern Superintendency*, 1859-1862.

[589] C. C. Hutchinson to Dole, August 21, 1863, Indian Office General Files, *Ottawa*, 1863-1872, D 236.

spirituous liquors should be brought within the limits of their Reserve under any circumstances whatsoever.[590] The Creeks, Choctaws, and Chickasaws found a lodgment on the Sac and Fox Reservation and the Seminoles fairly close at hand, at Neosho Falls. That was as far north as they could be induced to go.

Of the Cherokees, more needs to be said for they were not so easily disposed of. At various times during the past summer, Cherokees, opposed to, not identified with, or not enthusiastic in the Confederate cause, had escaped from Indian Territory and had collected on the Neutral Lands. Every Confederate reverse or Federal triumph, no matter how slight, had proved a signal for flight. By October, the Cherokee refugees on the Neutral Lands were reported to be nearly two thousand in number, which, allowing for some exaggeration for the sake of getting a larger portion of relief, was a goodly section of the tribal population.[591] At the end of October, Superintendent Coffin paid them a visit and urged them to remove to the Sac and Fox Agency, whither the majority of their comrades in distress were at that very moment going.[592] The Cherokees refused; for General Blunt had given them his word that, if he were successful in penetrating the Indian Territory, they should at once go home.[593] Not long after Coffin's departure, their camp on Drywood

---

[590] J. T. Jones to Dole, December 30, 1862, Indian Office General Files, *Sac and Fox*, 1862-1866. The precautions proved of little value. Whiskey was procured by both the hosts and their guests and great disorders resulted. Agent Hutchinson did his best to have the refugees removed, but, in his absence, the Ottawas were prevailed upon by Agent Elder to extend their hospitality for a while longer.

[591] Commissioner of Indian Affairs, *Report*, 1862, 137.

[592] —*Ibid.*, 1863, 175.

[593] Coffin to Dole, November 10, 1862, enclosing copies of a correspondence between him and a committee of the Cherokee refugees, October 31, 1862, Indian Office General Files, *Cherokee*, 1859-1865, C 1892.

Creek, about twelve miles south of Fort Scott, was raided by guerrillas;[594] but even that had no effect upon their determination to remain. The Neutral Lands, although greatly intruded upon by white people, were legally their own and they declined to budge from them at the instance of Superintendent Coffin.

Arrangements were undertaken for supplying the Cherokee refugees with material relief;[595] but scarcely had anything been done to that end when, to Coffin's utter surprise, as he said, the military authorities "took forcible possession of them" and had them all conveyed to Neosho, Missouri, presumably out of his reach. But Coffin would not release his hold and detailed the new Cherokee agent, James Harlan,[596] and Special Agent A. G. Proctor to follow them there.

John Ross, his family, and a few friends were, meanwhile, constituting another kind of refugee in the eastern part of the United States.[597] and were criticized by some

---

[594] Coffin to Dole, November 14, 1862, Indian Office General Files, *Southern Superintendency*, 1859-1862.

[595] Coffin to Mix, August 31, 1863, Indian Office General Files, *Southern Superintendency*, 1863-1864, C 466. A. M. Jordan, who acted as commissary to the Cherokees at Camp Drywood, reported to Dole, December 6, 1862, that he was feeding about a thousand who were then there [*ibid., Cherokee*, I 847 of 1862].

[596] Charles W. Chatterton, of Springfield, Illinois, who had been appointed Cherokee agent in the place of John Crawford, removed [Dole to Coffin, March 18, 1862, *ibid., Letter Book*, no. 67 pp. 492-493] had died, August 31, at the Sac and Fox Agency [Hutchinson to Mix September 1, 1862, *ibid.*, General Files, *Cherokee*, H 538 of 1862]; Coffin to Dole, September 13, 1862, *ibid.*, C 1827: W. H. Herndon to Dole, November 15, 1862, *ibid.*, H 605]. Harlan was not regularly commissioned as Cherokee agent until January, 1863 [Coffin to Dole, April 7, 1863, *ibid.*, C 143 of 1863; Harlan to Dole, January 26, 1863, *ibid.*, H 37 of 1863].

[597] John Ross asked help for his own family and for the families of various relations, thirty-four persons in all. He wanted five hundred dollars for each person [Ross to Dole, October 13, 1862, *ibid.*, R1857 of 1862]. Later, he asked for seventeen thousand dollars, likewise for maintenance [Ross to Dole, November 19, 1862, *ibid.*]. The beginning of the next year, he notified the department that some of his party were about to return home [*ibid.*, R 14 of

of their opponents for living in too sumptuous a manner.[598]

The removal, under military supervision, of the Cherokee refugees, had some justification in various facts, Blunt's firm conviction that Coffin and his instigators or abettors were exploiting the Indian service, that the refugees at Leroy were not being properly cared for, and that those on the Neutral Lands had put themselves directly under the protection of the army.[599] His then was the responsibility. When planning his second Indian Expedition, Blunt had discovered that the Indian men were not at all inclined to accompany it unless they could have some stronger guarantee than any yet given that their families would be well looked after in their absence. They had returned from the first expedition to find their women and children and aged men, sick, ill-fed, and unhappy.

It was with knowledge of such things and with the hope that they would soon be put a stop to and their repetition prevented by a return of the refugees to Indian Territory, that John Ross, in October, made a personal appeal to President Lincoln and interceded with him to send a military force down, sufficient to over-awe the Confederates and to take actual possession

---

1863] and requested that transportation from Leavenworth and supplies be furnished them [Indian Office General Files, *Cherokee*, R 13 of 1863]. Dole informed Coffin that the request should be granted [see Office letter of January 6, 1863] and continued forwarding to John Ross his share of the former remittance [Indian Office *Letter Book*, no. 69, 503]. To make the monetary allowance to John Ross, Cherokee chief, the Chickasaw funds were drawn upon [Second Auditor, E. B. Trench, to Dole, June 19, 1863, *ibid.*, General Files, *Cherokee*, A 202 of 1863; Office letter of June 20, 1863].

[598] Ross and others to Dole, July 29, 1864 [*ibid.*, General Files, *Cherokee*, 1859-1865, R 360]; Secretary of the Interior to Ross, August 25, 1864 [*ibid.*, I 651]; John Ross and Evan Jones to Dole, August 26, 1864 [*ibid.*, R 378]; Office letter of October 14, 1864; Coffin's letter of July 8, 1864.

[599] Blunt to Smith, November 21, 1862.

of the land. Lincoln's sympathies and sense of justice were immediately aroused and he inquired of General Curtis, in the field, as to the practicability of occupying "the Cherokee country consistently with the public service."[600] Curtis evaded the direct issue, which was the Federal obligation to protect its wards, by boasting that he had just driven the enemy into the Indian Territory "and beyond" and by doubting "the expediency of occupying ground so remote from supplies."[601]

General Blunt's force continued to hold the northeastern part of the Cherokee country until the end of October when it fell back, crossed the line, and moved along the Bentonville road in order to meet its supply train from Fort Scott.[602] Blunt's division finally took its stand on Prairie Creek[603] and, on the twelfth of November, made its main camp on Lindsay's prairie, near the Indian boundary.[604] The rout of Cooper at Fort Wayne had shaken the faith of many Indians in the invincibility of the Confederate arms. They had disbanded and gone home, declaring "their purpose to join the Federal troops the first opportunity" that presented itself.[605] To secure them and to reconnoitre once more, Colonel Phillips had started out near the beginning of November and, from the third to the fifth, had made his way down through the Cherokee Nation, by way of Tahlequah and Park Hill, to Webber's Falls on the Arkansas.[606] His return was by

---

[600] Lincoln to Curtis, October 10, 1862, *Official Records,* vol. xiii, 723.

[601] Curtis to Lincoln, October 10, 1862, *ibid.*

[602] Britton, *Civil War on the Border,* vol. i, 376-377.

[603] — *Ibid.,* 379.

[604] — *Ibid.,* 380; Bishop, *Loyalty on the Frontier,* 56.

[605] Blunt to Schofield, November 9, 1862, *Official Records,* vol. xiii, 785.

[606] H. W. Martin to Coffin, December 20, 1862, Indian Office General Files, *Southern Superintendency,* 1859-1862, C 1950.

Dwight's Mission. His view of the country through which he passed must have been discouraging.[607] There was little to subsist upon and the few Indians lingering there were in a deplorable state of deprivation, little food, little clothing[608] and it was winter-time.

So desolate and abandoned did the Cherokee country appear that General Blunt considered it would be easily possible to hold it with his Indian force alone, three regiments, yet he said no more about the immediate return of the refugees,[609] but issued an order for their removal to Neosho. The wisdom of his action might well be questioned since the expense of supporting them there would be immeasurably greater than in Kansas[610] unless, indeed, the military authorities intended to assume the entire charge of them.[611] Special Agent Martin regarded some talk that was rife of letting them forage upon the impoverished people of Missouri as

---

[607] It was not discouraging to Blunt, however. His letter referring to it was even sanguine [*Official Records*, vol. xiii, 785-786].

[608] Martin to Coffin, December 20, 1862.

[609] The Interior Department considered it, however, and consulted with the War Department as late as the twenty-sixth. See *Register of Letters Received*, vol. D., p. 155.

[610] Coffin to Henning, December 28, 1862, Indian Office Consolidated Files, *Cherokee*, C 17 of 1863.

[611] Coffin's letter to Dole of December 20 [Indian Office General Files, *Southern Superintendency*, 1859-1862, C 1950] would imply that the superintendent expected that to be the case. He said, having reference to Martin's report, " . . . The statement of facts which he makes, from all the information I have from other sources, I have no doubt are strictly true and will no doubt meet your serious consideration.

"If the Programme as fixed up by the Military Officers, and which I learn Dr. Gillpatrick is the bearer to your city and the solicitor general to procure its adoption is carried out, the Indian Department, superintendent, and agents may all be dispensed with. The proposition reminds me of the Fable of the Wolves and the Shepherds, the wolves represented to the shepherds that it was very expensive keeping dogs to guard the sheep, which was wholly unnecessary; that if they would kill off the dogs, they, the wolves, would protect the sheep without any compensation whatever."

sheer humbug. The army was not doing that and why should the defenceless Indians be expected to do it. As it was, they seem to have been reduced to plundering in Kansas.[612] On the whole, it is difficult to explain Blunt's plan for the concentration of the Cherokee refugees at Neosho, since there were, at the time, many indications that Hindman was considering another advance and an invasion of southwest Missouri.

The November operations of the Federals in northeastern Arkansas were directed toward arresting Hindman's progress, if progress were contemplated. Meanwhile, Phillips with detachments of his Indian brigade was continuing his reconnoissances and, when word came that Stand Watie had ventured north of the Arkansas, Blunt sent him to compel a recrossing.[613] Stand Watie's exploit was undoubtedly a preliminary to a general Confederate plan for the recovery of northwestern Arkansas and the Indian Territory, a plan, which Blunt, vigorous and aggressive, was determined to circumvent. In the action at Cane Hill,[614] the latter part of November, and in the Battle of Prairie Grove,[615] December seventh, the mettle of the Federals was put to a severe test which it stood successfully and Blunt's cardinal purpose was fully accomplished.[616] In both engagements, the Indians played a part and played it con-

---

[612] These Indians must have been the ones referred to in Richard C. Vaughn's letter to Colonel W. D. Wood, December 1, 1862 [*Official Records*, vol. xxii, part i, 796].

[613] Britton, *Civil War on the Border*, vol. i, p. 382.

[614] — *Ibid.*, vol. i, chapter xxix.

[615] — *Ibid.*, vol. i, chapter xxx; *Official Records*, vol. xxii, part i, 66-82, 82-158, vol. liii, supplement, 458-461, 866, 867; Livermore, *The Story of the Civil War*, part iii, bk. 1, 84-85.

[616] One opinion is to the effect that the result of the Battle of Prairie Grove, Fayetteville, or Illinois Creek, was virtually to end the war north of the Arkansas River [*ibid.*, p. 85; *Official Records*, vol. xxii, part i, 82].

spicuously and well, the northern regiments so well,[617] indeed, that shortly afterwards two additional ones, the Fourth and the Fifth, were projected.[618] Towards the end of the year, Phillips, whom Blunt had sent upon another excursion into Indian Territory,[619] could report

Bishop wrote, "After the battle of Prairie Grove, and the gradual retrogression of the Army of the Frontier into Missouri, Fayetteville was still held as a military post, and those of us who remained there were given to understand that the place would not be abandoned. . . The demoralized enemy had fallen back to Little Rock, with the exception of weak nomadic forces that, like Stygian ghosts, wandered up and down the Arkansas from Dardanelle to Fort Smith. . ." [*Loyalty on the Frontier*, 205]. Schofield was of the opinion, however, that the Battle of Prairie Grove was a hard-won victory. "Blunt and Herron were badly beaten in detail, and owed their escape to a false report of my arrival with re-enforcements." [*Official Records*, vol. xxii, part ii, p. 6].

[617] And yet it was only a short time previously that Major A. C. Ellithorpe, commanding the First Regiment Indian Home Guards, had had cause to complain seriously of the Creeks of that regiment. On November 7, he wrote from Camp Bowen that Opoeth-le-yo-ho-la was enticing the Indians away from the performance of their duties. "You will now perceive that we are on the border of the Indian country and a very large portion of the Indians are now scouting through their own Territory. What I now desire is that *every man* who was enlisted as a soldier shall at once return to his command by the way of Fort Scott unless otherwise ordered by competent authority. . ." [Indian Office Land Files, *Southern Superintendency*, 1855-1870, C 1933]. Coffin, as usual, appeared as an apologist for the Indians and attempted to exonerate Opoeth-le-yo-ho-la from all blame [Letter to Dole, December 3, 1862, *ibid.*]. He called the aged chief, "that noble old Roman of the Indians," and the chief himself protested against the injustice and untruth of Ellithrope's accusation [Opoeth-le-yo-ho-la to Coffin, November 24, 1862, *ibid.*].

[618] Officers for these two regiments were appointed by the president, December 26, 1862, and ordered to report to Blunt, who, in turn ordered them to report to Phillips. When the officers arrived in Indian Territory, they found no such regiments as the Fourth and Fifth Indian [*U. S. Senate Report*, 41st congress, third session, no. 359]. They never did materialize as a matter of fact; but the officers did duty, nevertheless, and were regularly mustered out of the service in 1863. In 1864, Congress passed an act for the adjudication of their claim for salary [*U. S. Statutes at Large*, vol. xiii, 413]. It is rather surprising that the regiments were not organized; inasmuch as many new recruits were constantly presenting themselves.

[619] Phillips to Blunt, December 25, 1862 [*Official Records*, vol. xxii, part i, 873-874].

that Stand Watie and Cooper had been pushed considerably below the Arkansas, that many of the buildings at Fort Davis had been demolished,[620] that one of the Creek regiments was about to retire from the Confederate service, and that the Choctaws, once so deeply committed, were wavering in their allegiance to the South.[621]

---

[620] The buildings at Fort Davis were burnt, and deliberately, by Phillips's orders. [See his own admission, *ibid.*, part ii, 56, 62].

[621] Blunt to Weed, December 30, 1862, *ibid.*, part i, 168.

X. NEGOTIATIONS WITH UNION INDIANS

As though the Indians had not afflictions enough to endure merely because of their proximity to the contending whites, life was made miserable for them, during the period of the Civil War, as much as before and after, by the insatiable land-hunger of politicians, speculators, and would-be captains of industry, who were more often than not, rogues in the disguise of public benefactors.   Nearly all of them were citizens of Kansas.   The cessions of 1854, negotiated by George W. Manypenny, Commissioner of Indian Affairs, were but a prelude to the many that followed.   For years and years there was in reality never a time when some sort of negotiation, *sub rosa* or official, was not going on. The order of procedure was pretty much what it had always been: a promise that the remaining land should be the Indian's, undisturbed by white men and protected by government guarantee, forever; encroachment by enterprising, covetous, and lawless whites; conflict between the two races, the outraged and the aggressive; the advent of the schemer, the man with political capital and undeveloped or perverted sense of honor, whose vision was such that he saw the Indian owner as the only obstacle in the way of vast material and national progress; political pressure upon the administration in Washington, lobbying in Congress; authorization of negotiations with the bewildered Indians; delimitation of the meaning of the solemn and grandly-sounding word, *forever.*

When the war broke out, negotiations, begun in the

border warfare days, were still going on. This was most true as regarded the Osages, whose immense holding in southern Kansas was something not to be tolerated, so the politicians reasoned, indefinitely. Petitions,[622] praying that the lands be opened to white settlement were constantly being sent in and intruders,[623] who intended to force action, becoming more and more numerous and more and more recalcitrant. One of the first official communications of Superintendent Coffin embodied a plea for getting a treaty of cession for which the signs had seemed favorable the previous year. Coffin, however, discredited[624] a certain Dr. J. B. Chapman, who, notwithstanding he represented white capitalists,[625] had yet found favor with the Osages. To their ever-

[622] For example, take the petitions forwarded by M. W. Delahay, surveyor-general of Kansas [Indian Office Consolidated Files, *Neosho,* D 455 of 1861]. One of the petitions contains this statement: " . . . The lands being largely settled upon and improved and those adjacent being all claimed and settled upon by residents – while a large emigration from Texas and other rebellious States are forced to seek homes in a more northern and uncongenial climate greatly against their interests and inclinations. . ."

[623] Intruders upon the Osage lands, as upon the Cherokee Neutral, were numerous for years before the war. Agent Dorn was continually complaining of them, chiefly because they were free-state in politics. He again and again asked for military assistance in removing them. See his letter to Greenwood, February 26, 1860, *Neosho,* 1833-1865, D 107. Buchanan's administration had conceived the idea of locating other Kansas Indians upon the huge Osage Reserve. See Dorn to Greenwood, March 26, 1860, *ibid.,* D 119. Apparently, the fragments of tribes in the northeastern corner of Indian Territory had been approached on the same subject, but they did not favor it and Agent Dorn was doubtful if the Osages would [Dorn to Greenwood, April 17, 1860, *ibid.,* D 129].

[624] He described him as a self-appointed guardian of the Osages, as a scamp and a nuisance [Coffin to Dole, June 17, 1861, *ibid.,* C 1223 of 1861].

[625] Chapman, August 26, 1860, inquired of Greenwood whether there was any prospect of a treaty being negotiated with the Osages and whether the capitalists he represented would be likely to secure railroad rights to the South by it. He asserted that the Delawares had been "humbugged" by their treaty, it having been negotiated "in the interests of the Democrats at Leavenworth" [*ibid.,* C 702 of 1860].

lasting sorrow and despoliation, the Indians have been fated to place a child-like trust in those least worthy.

The defection of portions of the southern tribes offered an undreamed of opportunity for Kansas politicians to accomplish their purposes. They had earlier thought of removing the Kansas tribes, one by one, to Indian Territory; but the tribes already there had a lien upon the land, titles, and other rights, that could not be ignored. Their possession was to continue so long as the grass should grow and the water should run. It was not for the government to say that they should open their doors to anybody. An early intimation that the Kansans saw their opportunity was a resolution[626] submitted by James H. Lane to the Senate, March 17, 1862, proposing an inquiry into "the propriety and expediency of extending the southern boundary of Kansas to the northern boundary of Texas, so as to include within the boundaries of Kansas the territory known as the Indian territory." Obviously, the proposition had a military object immediately in view; but Commissioner Dole, to whom it was referred, saw its ulterior meaning and reported[627] adversely upon it as he had upon an earlier proposition to erect a regular territorial form of government in the Indian country south of Kansas.[628] He was "unable to perceive any advantage to be derived from the adoption of such a measure, since the same military power that would be required to enforce the authority of territorial officers is all-sufficient to protect and enforce the authority of such officers as are required in the management of our present system

[626] *United State Congressional Globe,* 37th congress, second session, part ii, p. 1246.

[627] Dole to Smith, April 2, 1862, Indian Office *Report Book,* no. 12, 353-354.

[628] Dole to Smith, March 17, 1862, *ibid.,* 335-337.

of Indian relations."[629]   And he insisted that the whole
of the present Indian country should be left to the Indians.[630]   The honor of the government was pledged to
that end.   Almost coincidently he negatived[631] another
suggestion, one advocated by Pomeroy for the confiscation of the Cherokee Neutral Lands.[632]   For the time
being, Dole was strongly opposed to throwing either the
Neutral Lands or the Osage Reserve open to white settlers.

Behind Pomeroy's suggestion was the spirit of retaliation, of meting out punishment to the Indians, who, because they had been so basely deserted by the United
States government, had gone over to the Confederacy;
but the Kansas politicians saw a chance to kill two birds
with one stone, vindictively punish the southern Indians
for their defection and rid Kansas of the northern Indians, both emigrant and indigenous.   The intruders
upon Indian lands, the speculators and the politicians,
would get the spoils of victory.   Against the idea of
punishing the southern Indians for what after all was
far from being entirely their fault, the friends of justice
marshaled their forces.   Dole was not exactly of their
number; for he had other ends to serve in resisting measures advanced by the Kansans, yet, to his credit be it said
that he did always hold firmly to the notion that tribes
like the Cherokee were more sinned against than sin-
ning.   The government had been the first to shirk responsibility and to violate sacred obligations.   It had
failed to give the protection guaranteed by treaties and
it was not giving it yet adequately.

[629] Dole to Smith, March 17, 1862, Indian Office *Report Book*, no. 12, 335.
[630] Report of April 2, 1862.
[631] Dole to Smith, March 20, 1862, Indian Office *Report Book*, no. 12,
343-344.
[632] *Daily Conservative*, May 10, 1862.   Note the arguments in favor of
confiscation as quoted from the *Western Volunteer*.

The true friends of justice were men of the stamp of W. S. Robertson[633] and the Reverend Evan Jones,[634] who went out of their way to plead the Indian's cause and to detail the extenuating circumstances surrounding his lamentable failure to keep faith. Supporting the men of the opposite camp was even the Legislature of Kansas. In no other way can a memorial from the General Assembly, urging the extinguishment of the title of certain Indian lands in Kansas, be interpreted.[635]

It is not easy to determine always just what motives did actuate Commissioner Dole. They were not entirely above suspicion and his name is indissolubly connected with some very nefarious Indian transactions; but fortunately they have not to be recounted here. At the very time when he was offering unanswerable arguments against the propositions of Lane and Pomeroy, he was entertaining something similar to those propositions in his own mind. A special agent, Augustus Wattles, who had been sufficiently familiar and mixed-up with the free state and pro-slavery controversy to be called upon to give testimony before the Senate Har-

---

[633] Robertson wrote to the Secretary of the Interior, January 7, 1862, asking most earnestly "that decisive measures be not taken against the oppressed and betrayed people of the Creek and Cherokee tribes, until everything is heard about their struggle in the present crisis" [Department of the Interior, *Register of Letters Received*, "Indians," no. 4]. The letter was referred to the Indian Office and Mix replied to it, February 14, 1862 [Indian Office *Letter Book*, no. 67, p. 357]. The concluding paragraph of the letter is indicative of the government feeling, " . . . In reply I transmit herewith for your information the Annual Report of this Office, which will show . . . what policy has governed the Office as to this matter, and that it is in consonance with your wish . . ."

[634] Jones wrote frequently and at great length on the subject of justice to the Cherokees. One of his most heartfelt appeals was that of January 21, 1862 [Indian Office Consolidated Files, *Cherokee*, J 556 of 1862].

[635] Cyrus Aldrich, representative from Minnesota and chairman of the House Committee on Indian Affairs referred the memorial to the Indian Office [*Letters Registered,* vol. 58, *Southern Superintendency*, A. 484 of 1862].

per's Ferry Investigating Committee[636] and who had been on the editorial staff of the New York *Tribune*,[637] had, in 1861, been sent by the Indian Office to inspect the houses that Robert S. Stevens had contracted to build for the Sacs and Foxes of Mississippi and for the Kaws.[638]   The whole project of the house-building was a fraud upon the Indians, a scheme for using up their funds or for transferring them to the pockets of promoters like Stevens[639] and M. C. Dickey[640] without the trouble of giving value received.

From a letter[641] of protest, written by Stevens against Wattles's mission of inspection, it can be inferred that there was a movement on foot to induce the Indians to emigrate southward. Stevens, not wholly disinterested, thought it a poor time to attempt changes in tribal

---

[636] Robinson, *Kansas Conflict,* 358.

[637] — *Ibid.,* 370.   For other facts touching Wattles and his earlier career, see Villard, *John Brown,* index; Wilson, *John Brown: Soldier of Fortune,* index.

[638] On the entire subject of negotiations with the Indians of Kansas, see Abel, *Indian Reservations in Kansas and the Extinguishment of Their Titles.* The house-building project is fully narrated there.

[639] For additional information about Stevens, see *Daily Conservative,* February 11, 12, 13, 28, 1862.   Senator Lane denounced him as a defaulter to the government in the house-building project. See Lane to Dole, April 22, 1862; Smith to Dole, May 13 1862; Dole to Lane, May 5, 1862, *Daily Conservative,* May 21, 1862.   In July, Lane, hearing that certificates of indebtedness were about to be issued to Stevens on his building contract for the Sacs and Foxes, entered a "solemn protest against such action" and requested that the Department would let the matter lie over until the assembling of Congress [Interior Department, *Register of Letters Received,* January 2, 1862 to December 27, 1865, "Indians," no. 4].   Governor Robinson's enemies regarded him as the partner of Stevens [*Daily Conservative,* November 22, 1861] in the matter of some other affairs, and that fact may help to explain Senator Lane's bitter animosity.   The names of Robinson and Stevens were connected in the bond difficulty, which lay at the bottom of Robinson's impeachment.

[640] Dickey's interest in the house-building is seen in the following: Dickey to Greenwood, February 26, 1861, Indian Office General Files, *Kansas,* 1855-1862, D 250; same to same, March 1, 1861, *ibid.,* D 251.

[641] Stevens to Mix, August 24, 1861, Indian Office Special Files, no. 201, *Sac and Fox,* S 439 of 1861.

policy. His conclusions were right, his premises, necessarily unrevealed, were false. Wattles became involved in the emigration movement, if he did not initiate it, and, subsequent to making his report upon the house-building, received a private communication from Dole, asking his opinion "of a plan for confederating the various Indian tribes, in Kansas and Nebraska, into one, and giving them a Territory and a Territorial Government with political privileges." [642] This was in 1861, long before any scheme that Lane or Pomeroy had devised would have matured. Wattles started upon a tour of observation and inquiry among the Kansas tribes and discovered that, with few exceptions, they were all willing and even anxious to exchange their present homes for homes in Indian Territory. Some had already discussed the matter tentatively and on their own account with the Creeks and Cherokees. On his way east, after completing his investigations, Wattles stopped in New York and "consulted with our political friends" there "concerning this movement, and they not only gave it their approbation, but were anxious that this administration should have the credit of originating and carrying out so wise and so noble a scheme for civilizing and perpetuating the Indian race." Would Wattles and his friends have said the same had they been fully cognizant of the conditions under which the emigrant tribes had been placed in the West?

In February of 1862, the House of Representatives called [643] for the papers relating to the Wattles mission [644] and, in March, Wattles expatiated upon the

---

[642] Wattles to Dole, January 10, 1862, Indian Office Special Files, no. 201, *Central Superintendency*, W 528 of 1862.

[643] Department of the Interior, *Register of Letters Received*, "Indians," no. 4, p. 439.

[644] The papers relating to the mission are collected in Indian Office Special Files, no. 201.

emigration and consolidation scheme in a report to Secretary Smith.[645] Then, yet in advance of congressional authorization, began a systematic course of Indian negotiation, all having in view the relieving of Kansas from her aboriginal encumbrance. No means were too underhand, too far-fetched, too villainous to be resorted to. Every advantage was taken of the Indian's predicament, of his pitiful weakness, political and moral. The reputed treason of the southern tribes was made the most of. Reconstruction measures had begun for the Indians before the war was over and while its issue was very far from being determined in favor of the North.

As if urged thereto by some influence malign or fate sinister, the loyal portion of two of the southern tribes, the Creeks and the Seminoles, took in April, 1862, a certain action that, all unbeknown to them, expedited the northern schemes for Indian undoing. The action referred to was tribal reörganization. Each of the two groups of refugees elected chiefs and headmen and notified the United States government that it was prepared to do business as a nation.[646] The business in mind had to do with annuity payments[647] and other dues but the Indian Office soon extended it to include treaty-making.

---

[645] Indian Office Consolidated Files, *Central Superintendency*, W 528 of 1862; Department of the Interior, *Register of Letters Received*, "Indians," no. 4, p. 517.

[646] Ok-ta-ha-ras Harjo and others to Dole, April 5, 1862, Indian Office General Files, *Creek*, 1860-1869, O 45; Coffin to Dole, April 15, 1862, transmitting communication of Billy Bowlegs and others, April 14, 1862 *ibid.*, *Seminole*, 1858-1869, C 1594; *Letters Registered*, vol. 58.

[647] On the outside of the Seminole petition, the office instruction for its answer of May 7, 1862, reads as follows: "Say that by resolution of Congress the annuities were authorized to be used to prevent starvation and suffering amongst them and that being the only fund in our hands must not be diverted from that purpose at present."

Negotiations with the Osages had been going on intermittently all this time. No opportunity to press the point of a land cession had ever been neglected and much had been made, in connection with the project for territorial organization, of the fact that the Osages had memorialized Congress for a civil government, they thinking by means of it to prevent further frauds and impositions being practiced upon them.[648] Coffin and Elder, suspicious of each other, jealously watched every avenue of approach to Osage confidence. On the ninth of March, Elder inquired if Coffin had been regularly commissioned to open up negotiations anew and asked to be associated with him if he had.[649] A treaty was started but not finished for Elder received a private letter from Dole that seemed to confine the negotiations to a mere ascertaining of views.[650] Then the Indians grown weary of uncertainty took matters into their own hands and appointed several prominent tribesmen for the express purpose of negotiating a treaty that would end the "suspense as to their future destiny."[651] From the treaty of cession that Coffin drafted, he having taken a miserably unfair advantage of Osage isolation and destitution, the Osages turned away in disgust.[652] In November, some of their leading men journeyed up to Leroy to invite the dissatisfied Opoeth-le-yo-ho-la to winter with them.[653] Coffin seized the occasion to reopen the subject of a cession and the Indians manifested

---

[648] Indian Office Consolidated Files, *Neosho,* A 476 of 1862. See also Indian Office report to the Secretary of the Interior, May 6, 1862. The Commissioner's letter and the memorial were sent to Aldrich, May 9, 1862.

[649] Indian Office Consolidated Files, *Neosho,* E 94 of 1862.

[650] Coffin to Dole, April 5, 1862, *ibid.,* C 1583.

[651] Communication of April 10, 1862, transmitted by Chapman to Dole, *ibid.,* C 1640.

[652] Elder to Coffin, July 9, 1862, *ibid.,* E 114.

[653] Coffin to Dole, November 16, 1862, *ibid.,* C 1904.

a willingness to sell a part of their Reserve; but again Coffin was too grasping and another season of waiting intervened.

With slightly better success the Kickapoos were approached. Their lands were coveted by the Atchison and Pike's Peak Railway Company and Agent O. B. Keith used his good offices in the interest of that corporation.[654] Good offices they were, from the standpoint of benefit to the grantees, but most disreputable from that of the grantors. He bribed the chiefs outrageously and the lesser men among the Kickapoos indignantly protested.[655] Rival political and capitalistic concerns, emanating from St. Joseph, Missouri, and from the northern tier of counties in Kansas,[656] took up the quarrel and never rested until they had forced a hearing from the government. The treaty was arrested after it had reached the presidential proclamation stage and was in serious danger of complete invalidation.[657] It passed muster only when a Senate amendment had rendered it reasonably acceptable to the Kickapoos.

Not much headway was made with Indian treaty-making in 1862.[658] In March, 1863, an element con-

[654] Indian Office Consolidated Files, *Kickapoo*, I 655 of 1862 and I 361 of 1864.

[655] — *Ibid.*, B 355 of 1863 and I 361 of 1864.

[656] Albert W. Horton to Pomeroy, June 20, 1863 and O. B. Keith to Pomeroy, June 20, 1863, Indian Office Consolidated Files, *Kickapoo*, G 59 and P 64 of 1863.

[657] Lane and A. C. Wilder requested the Interior Department, September 1, 1863, "that no rights be permitted to attach to R. R. Co. until charges of fraud in connection with Kickapoo Treaty are settled." Their request was replied to, September 12, 1863 [Interior Department, *Register of Letters Received*, January 2, 1862 to December 27, 1865, "Indians," no. 4, 361].

[658] Dole, however, seems to have become thoroughly reconciled to the idea. He submitted his views upon the subject once more in connection with a memorial that Pomeroy referred to the Secretary of the Interior "for the concentration of the Indian tribes of the West and especially those of Kansas, in the Indian country . . ." [Dole to Smith, November 22, 1862, Indian Office *Report Book*, no. 12, pp. 505-506; Department of the

ditioning a greater degree of success was introduced into the government policy.[659] That was by the Indian appropriation act, which, in addition to continuing the practice of applying tribal annuities to the relief of refugees, authorized the president to negotiate with Kansas tribes for their removal from Kansas and with the loyal portion of Indian Territory tribes for cessions of land on which to accommodate them.[660] As Dole pertinently remarked to Secretary Usher, the measure was all very well as a policy in prospect but it was one that most certainly could not be carried out until Indian Territory was in Federal possession. Blunt was still striving after possession or re-possession but his force was not "sufficient to insure beyond peradventure his success."[661]

Scarcely had the law been enacted when John Ross and other Cherokees, living in exile and in affluence, offered to consider proposals for a retrocession to the United States public domain of their Neutral Lands. The Indian Office was not yet prepared to treat and not until November did Ross and his associates[662] get any

Interior, *Register of Letters Received,* vol. D, November 22, 1862]. December 26, 1862, Dole wrote to Smith thus: " . . . It being in contemplation to extinguish the Indian title to lands . . . in Kansas and provide them with homes in the Indian Territory . . . I would recommend that a commissioner should be appointed to negotiate . . . I would accordingly suggest that Robt. S. Corwin be appointed . . ." [Indian Office *Report Book, no.* 13, pp. 12-13]. Now Corwin's reputation was not such as would warrant his selection for the post. He was not a man of strict integrity. His name is connected with many shady transactions in the early history of Kansas.

[659] Presumably, Lane was the chief promoter of it. See Baptiste Peoria to Dole, February 9, 1863, Indian Office General Files, *Osage River,* 1863-1867.

[660] *U. S. Statutes at Large,* vol. xii, 793.

[661] Dole to Usher, July 29, 1863, Indian Office *Report Book, no.* 13, p. 211.

[662] His associates were then the three men, Lewis Downing, James McDaniel, and Evan Jones, who had been appointed delegates with him,

real encouragement[663] to renew their offer, yet the Cherokees had as early as February repudiated their alliance with the southern Confederacy. That the United States government was only awaiting a time most propitious for itself is evident from the fact that, when, in the spring following, refugees from the Neutral Lands were given an opportunity to begin their backward trek, they were told that they would not be permitted to linger at their old homes but would have to go on all the way to Fort Gibson, one hundred twenty miles farther south.[664]   That was one way of ridding Kansas of her Indians and a way not very creditable to a professed and powerful guardian.

Almost simultaneously with Ross's first application came an offer from the oppressed Delawares to look for a new home in the far west, in Washington Territory. The majority preferred to go to the Cherokee country.[665] Some of the tribe had already lived there and wanted to return.   Had the minority gained their point, the Delawares would have traversed the whole continent within the space of about two and a half centuries. They would have wandered from the Atlantic to the Pacific, from the Susquehanna River to the Willamette, in a desperate effort to escape the avaricious pioneer, and, to their own chagrin, they would have found him on the western coast also.   Never again would there be any place for them free from his influence.

In the summer of 1863, negotiations were undertaken

by the newly-constructed national council, for doing business with the United States government [Commissioner of Indian Affairs, *Report*, 1863, p. 23].

[663] See Office letter of November 19, 1863.

[664] David M. Harlan to Dole, December 20, 1864, Indian Office General Files, Cherokee 1859-1865, H 1033.

[665] Johnson to Dole, May 24, 1863, *ibid., Delaware*, 1862-1866.

in deadly earnest. A commencement was made with the Creeks in May, Agent Cutler calling the chiefs in council and laying before them the draft of a treaty that had been prepared, upon the advice of Coffin,[666] in Washington and that had been entrusted for transmission to the unscrupulous ex-agent, Perry Fuller.[667] The Creek chiefs consented to sell a tract of land for locating other Indians upon, but declared themselves opposed to any plan for "sectionizing" their country and asked that they might be consulted as to the Indians who were to share it with them. The month before they had prayed to be allowed to go back home. Well fed and clothed though they were, and quite satisfied with their agent, they were terribly homesick.[668] Might they not go down and clean out their country for themselves? It seemed impossible for the army to do it.[669]

Coffin next came forward with a suggestion that Indian colonization in Texas would be far preferable to colonization elsewhere, although if nothing better could be done, he would advocate the selection of the Osage land on the Arkansas and its tributaries.[670] Why he wanted to steer clear of the Indian Territory is not evi-

---

[666] " . . . I would most respectfully suggest that a Treaty be gotten up by you and the Sec^ty of the Interior, and sent to me and Gov. Carney and some other suitable com. to have ratified in due form and returned. And you will pardon me for saying that the Treaty should be a model for all that are to follow with the broken and greatly reduced, and fragmental tribes in the Indian Territory, and may be made greatly to promote the interests of the Indians and the Government especially in view of the removal of the Indians from Kansas and Nebraska as contemplated by recent Act of Congress." – COFFIN to Dole, March 22, 1863, *ibid.*, Land Files, *Southern Superintendency*, 1855-1870, C 117.

[667] Cutler to Dole, May, 1863, *ibid.*, General Files, *Creek*, 1860-1869, C 240.

[668] Ok-ta-ha-ras Harjo and others to "Our Father," April 1, 1863, (Indian Office General Files, *Creek*, 1860-1869).

[669] Same to same, May 16, 1863, *ibid.*, O 6.

[670] Coffin to Dole, May 23, 1863, *ibid.*, Land Files, *Southern Superintendency*, 1855-1870.

dent. The Pottawatomies[671] asked to be allowed to settle on the Creek land,[672] but the Creeks were letting their treaty hang fire. They wanted it made in Washington, D.C., and they wanted one of their great men, Mik-ko-hut-kah, then with the army, to assist in its negotiation.[673] Ópoeth-le-yo-ho-la had died in the spring[674] and they were seemingly feeling a little helpless and forlorn.

Thinking to make better progress with the treaties and better terms if he himself controlled the government end of the negotiations, Commissioner Dole undertook a trip west in the late summer.[675] By the third of September the Creek treaty was an accomplished fact.[676] Aside from the cession of land for the accommodation of Indian emigrants, its most important provision was a recognition of the binding force of Lincoln's Emancipation Proclamation. In due course, the treaty went to the Senate and, in March, was accepted by that body with amendments.[677] It went back to the

[671] A treaty had been made with the Pottawatomies by W. W. Ross, their agent, November 15, 1861 [*ibid., Pottawatomie,* I 547 of 1862]. Its negotiation was so permeated by fraud that the Indians refused to let it stand [Dole to Smith, January 15, 1862]. At this time, 1863, Superintendent Branch, against whom charges of gambling, drunkenness, licentiousness, and misuse of annuity funds had been preferred by Agent Ross [Indian Office General Files, *Pottawatomie,* R 21 and I 43 of 1863], was endeavoring to persuade Father De Smet to establish a Roman Catholic Mission on their Reserve. De Smet declined because of the exigencies of the war. His letter of January 5, 1863, has no file mark.

[672] Cutler to Dole, June 6, 1863, Indian Office General Files, *Creek,* 1860-1869.

[673] — *Ibid.*

[674] Coffin to Dole, March 22, 1863.

[675] Proctor's letter of July 31, 1863 would indicate that Dole went to the Cherokee Agency before the Sac and Fox. Proctor was writing from the former place and he said, "Mr. Dole leaves to-day for Kansas. . ." [Indian Office General Files, *Southern Superintendency,* 1863-1864, C 466].

[676] Indian Office Land Files, *Treaties,* Box 3, 1864-1866.

[677] Usher to Dole, March 23, 1864, *ibid.*

Indians but they rejected it altogether.[678]   The Senate amendments were not such as they could conscientiously and honorably submit to and maintain their dignity as a preëminently loyal and semi-independent people.[679] One of the amendments was particularly obnoxious.   It affected the provision that deprived the southern Creeks of all claims upon the old home.[680]   Dole's Creek treaty of 1863 was never ratified.

Other treaties negotiated by Dole were with the Sacs and Foxes of Mississippi,[681] the Osages, the Shawnees,[682]

[678] Its binding force upon them was, however, a subject of discussion afterwards and for many years [Superintendent Byers to Lewis V. Bogy, Commissioner of Indian Affairs, February 7, 1867, *ibid.*, General Files, *Creek*, 1860-1869, B 94].

[679] For an interpretation of the treaty relative to the claims of the loyal Creeks, see Dole to Lane, January 27, 1864 [*ibid., Report Book*, no. 13, pp. 287-291]. It is interesting to note that a certain Mundy Durant who had been sixty years in the Creek Nation, put in a claim, February 23, 1864, in behalf of the "loyal Africans." He asked "that they have guaranteed to them equal rights with the Indians. . ." "All of our boys," said he, "are in the army and I feel they should be remembered . . ." [*ibid.*, General Files, *Creek*, 1860-1869, D 362].

[680] Article IV. Both the Creeks and the Seminoles, in apprising the Indian Office of the fact that they had organized as a nation, had voiced the idea that the southern Indians had forfeited all their rights "to any part of the property or annuities. . ."

[681] The Sacs and Foxes brought forward a claim against the southern refugees, for the "rent of 204 buildings," amounting to $14,688.00 [Indian Office Land Files, *Southern Superintendency*, 1855-1870, Letter of May 14, 1864. See also Dole to Usher, March 25, 1865, *ibid.*, also I 952, C 1264, and C 1298, *ibid.*]. Coffin thought the best way to settle their claim was to give them a part of the Creek cession [Coffin to Martin, May 23, 1864, and Martin to Dole, May 26, 1864, *ibid.*, General Files, *Sac and Fox*, 1862-1866, M 284]. The Sac and Fox chiefs were willing to submit the case to the arbitrament of Judge James Steele. Martin was of the opinion that should their treaty, then pending, fail it would be some time before they would consent to make another. This treaty had been obtained with difficulty, only by Dole's "extraordinary exertions with the tribe" [Martin to Dole, May 2, 1864, *ibid.*, M 270].

[682] Negotiations with the Shawnees had been undertaken in 1862. In June, Black Bob, the chief of the Shawnees on the Big Blue Reserve in Johnson County, Kansas, protested against a treaty then before Congress. He claimed it was a fraud [Telegram, A. H. Baldwin to Dole, June 4,

and the New York Indians. He attempted one with the Kaws but failed.[683] The Osages, who had recent-

1862, *ibid., Shawnee,* 1855-1862, B 1340 of 1862], which was the red man's usual appraisement of the white man's dealings. A rough draft of another treaty seems to have been sent to Agent Abbott for the Shawnees on July 18 and another, substantially the same, December 29. One of the matters that called for adjustment was the Shawnee contract with the Methodist Episcopal Church South, Dole affirming that "as the principal members of that corporation, and those who control it are now in rebellion against the U. S. Government, the said contract is to be regarded as terminated. . ." [Indian Office Land Files, *Shawnee,* 1860-1865, I 865]. Usher's letter to Dole of December 27, 1862 was the basis of the instruction. Dole's negotiations of 1863 were impeached as were all the previous, Black Bob and Paschal Fish, the first and second chiefs of the Chillicothe Band of Shawnees, leading the opposition. Agent Abbott was charged with using questionable means for obtaining Indian approval [*ibid.,* General Files, *Shawnee,* 1863-1875]. Conditions at the Shawnee Agency had been in a bad state for a long time, since before the war. Guerrilla attacks and threatened attacks had greatly disturbed domestic politics. They had interfered with the regular tribal elections.

"Last fall [1862], owing to the constant disturbance on the border of Mo., the election was postponed from time to time, until the 12th of January. Olathe had been sacked, Shawnee had been burned, and the members of the Black Bob settlement had been robbed and driven from their homes, and it had not been considered safe for any considerable number to congregate together from the fact that the Shawnees usually all come on horseback, and the bushwhackers having ample means to know what was going on, would take the opportunity to make a dash among them, and secure their horses.

"De Soto was designated as the place to hold the election it being some twenty miles from the border. . ." – ABBOTT to Dole, April 6, 1863, *ibid.,* Land Files, *Shawnee,* 1860-1865, A 158. In the summer, the Shawnees made preparations for seeking a new home. Their confidence in Abbott must have been by that time somewhat restored, since the prospecting delegation invited him to join it [*ibid., Shawnee* A 755 of 1864]. A chief source of grievance against him and cause for distrust of him had reference to certain depredation claims of the Shawnees [*ibid.,* General Files, *Shawnee,* 1855-1862, I 801].

683 The Kaw lands had been greatly depredated upon and encroached upon [*ibid.,* Land Files, *Kansas,* 1862]. Dole anticipated that troubles were likely to ensue at any moment. He, therefore, desired to put the Kaws upon the Cherokee land just as soon as it was out of danger [Dole to H. W. Farnsworth, October 24, 1863, *ibid., Letter Book,* no. 72, p. 57]. Jeremiah Hadley, the agent for a contemplated Mission School among the Kaws, was much exercised as to how a removal might affect his contract and work. See his letter to Dole, November 17, 1863.

An abortive treaty was likewise made with the Wyandots, whom Dole

ly[684] so generously consented to receive the unwelcome

designed to place upon the Seneca-Shawnee lands. Both the Wyandots and the Seneca-Shawnees objected to the ratification of the treaty [Coffin to Dole, January 28, 1864, Indian Office Consolidated Files, *Neosho,* C 639 of 1864].

[684] They had recently done another thing that, at the time of occurrence, the Federals in Kansas deemed highly commendable. They had murderously attacked a group of Confederate recruiting officers, whom they had overtaken or waylaid on the plains. The following contemporary documents, when taken in connection with Britton's account [*Civil War on the Border,* vol. ii, 228], W. L. Bartles's address [Kansas Historical Society, *Collections,* vol. viii, 62-66], and Elder's letter to Blunt, May 17, 1863, *Official Records,* vol. xxii, part ii, 286, amply describe the affair:

(a) "I have just returned to this place from the Grand Council of the Great and Little Osage Indians. I found them feeling decidedly fine over their recent success in destroying a band of nineteen rebels attempting to pass through their country. A band of the Little Osages met them first and demanded their arms and that they should go with them to Humboldt (as we instructed them to do at the Council at Belmont). The rebels refused and shot one of the Osages dead. The Osages then fired on them. They ran and a running fight was kept up for some 15 miles. The rebel guide was killed early in the action. After crossing Lightning Creek, the rebels turned up the creek toward the camp of the Big Hill Camp. The Little Osages had sent a runner to aprise the Big Hills of the presence of the rebels and they were coming down the creek 400 strong, and met the rebels, drove them to the creek and surrounded them. The rebels displayed a white flag but the Indians disregarded it. They killed all of them as they supposed; but afterwards learned that two of them, badly wounded, got down a steep bank of the creek and made their escape down the creek. They scalped them all and cut their heads off. They killed 4 of their horses (which the Indians greatly regretted) and captured 13, about 50 revolvers, most of the rebels having 4 revolvers, a carbine and saber. There were 3 colonels, one lieutenant-colonel, one major and 4 captains. They had full authority to organise enroll and muster into rebel service all the rebels in Colorado and New Mexico where they were doubtless bound. Major Dowdney [Doudna] in command of troops at Humboldt went down with a detachment and buried them and secured the papers, letting the Indians keep all the horses, arms, etc. I have no doubt that this will afford more protection to the frontiers of Kansas than anything that has yet been done and from the frequency and boldness of the raids recently something of the kind was very much needed. The Indians are very much elated over it. I gave them all the encouragement I could, distributed between two and three hundred dollars worth of goods amongst them. There was a representative at the Council from the Osages that have gone South, many of them now in the army. He stated that they were all now very anxious to get back, and wished to know if they should meet the loyal Osages on the hunt on the Plains and come in with them if they could be suffered to stay. I gave him a letter to them promising them if they returned immediately and

refugees on the Ottawa Reserve,[685] were distinctly over-
reached by the government representatives, working in
the interest of corporate wealth. In August, the chief
men of the Osages had gone up to the Sac and Fox
Agency to confer with Dole,[686] but Dole was being un-

joined their loyal brethren in protecting the frontiers, running down Bushwhackers, and ridding the country of rebels, they should be protected. I
advised them to come immediately to Humboldt and report to Major Dowdney and he would furnish them powder and lead to go on the hunt. This
seemed to give great satisfaction to all the chiefs as they are exceedingly
desirous to have them back and the representative started immediately back
with the letter, and the Indians as well as the Fathers of the Mission have
no doubt but they will return. If so, it will very materially weaken the
rebel force now sorely pressing Col. Phillips' command at Fort Gibson.

"The Osages are now very desirous to make a treaty are willing to sell
25 miles in width by 50 off the east end of their reservation and 20 miles
wide off the north side, but I will write more fully of this in a day or two." –
COFFIN to Dole, June 10, 1863, Indian Office Consolidated Files, *Neosho*,
C 299 of 1863.

(b) "It will be remembered that sometime in the month of May last a
party consisting of nineteen rebel officers duly commissioned and authorised
to organise the Indians and what rebels they might find in Colorado and
New Mexico against the Government of the United States while passing
through the country of the Great and Little Osages were attacked and the
whole party slaughtered by these Indians. As an encouragement to those
Indians to continue their friendship and loyalty to our Government, I would
respectfully recommend that medals be given to the Head Chief of the combined tribes, White Hair, and the Head Chief of the Little Bear and the
chiefs of the Big Hill bands, Clarimore and Beaver, four in all who were
chiefly instrumental in the destruction of those emissaries.

"I believe the bestowal of the medals would be a well deserved acknowl-
edgment to those chiefs for an important service rendered and promotive
of good." – COFFIN to Dole, Indian Office Consolidated Files, *Neosho*, C 596.

[685] Coffin to Dole, July 13, 1863, *ibid.*, General Files, *Southern Superintendency*, 1863-1864. Coffin had been directed, by an office letter of June
24 to have the refugees removed. See also, Dole to Hutchinson, June 24,
1863, *ibid.*, *Letter Book*, no. 71, p. 69. Other primary sources bearing upon
this matter are, Hutchinson to ?, June 11, 1863, *ibid.*, *Ottawa*, 1863-1873,
H 230; Elder to Dole, August 10, 1863, *Neosho*, E 22 of 1863; Hutchinson
to Dole, August 21, 1863, *Ottawa*, D 236 of 1863; Mix to Elder, September
11, 1863, *ibid.*, *Letter Book*, no. 71, p. 383.

[686] "About 100 of the Osages with their Chiefs and headmen visited the
Sac and Fox agency to meet me on the 20th to Council and probably make
a treaty to dispose of a part of their reserve. I was detained with the Delawares and Quantrels raid upon Lawrence and did not reach the reserve

avoidably detained by the Delawares and by Quantrill's raid upon Lawrence,[687] so, becoming impatient, they left. The commissioner followed them to Leroy and before the month was out, he was able to report a treaty as made.[688]   It was apparently done over-night and yet

untill the 25th and found the Osages had left that day for their homes. I followed them to this place [Leroy] 40 miles south of the Sac and Fox agency and have been in Council with them for two days. I have some doubt about succeeding in a treaty as the Indians do not understand parting with their lands in trust. I could purchase all we want at present for not exceeding 25 cts pr acre but doubt whether the Senate would ratify such a purchase – as they have adopted the Homestead policy with the Gov^t lands and would not wish to purchase of the Indians to give to the whites. I propose to purchase 25 miles by 40 in the S. E. corner of their reserve @ 5 pr. ct making a dividend of 10,000 annually. I have two reasons for this purchase. 1st I want the land for other Kansas tribes and 2nd The Indians are paupers now and must have this much money any way or starve. Then I propose to take in trust the north half of their reserve – to be sold for their benefit as the Sac and Fox and other tribes dispose of their lands. To this last the Indians object they want to sell outright and I may fail in consequence. We shall not differ much about the details – if we can agree on the main points – I shall know to-day –

"From here I return to the Sac and Fox agency where I have some hopes of making a treaty with them or at least agree upon the main points so soon as they can be provided with another home – The fact that we have failed to drive the traitors out of the Indian Country interfers very much with my operations here – from the Sac and Fox Reserve I may go to the Pottawatamies but rather expect that I will return to Leavenworth where I shall again council with the Delawares and from there go to the Kickapoos – Senator Pomeroy is here with me and will probably remain with me – Judge Johnston is also with me and assisting me as Clerk since Mr. Whiting left. This is not considered as a very safe country as Bush Whackers are plenty and bold – You may show this to Sec Usher –" — Indian Office Consolidated Files, *Neosho*, D 195 of 1863.

[687] Connelley, *Quantrill and the Border Wars*, 335-420.

[688] "I arrived here last night from Leroy, after having succeeded in effecting a treaty with the Osage Indians by which the Govt. obtain of them *by purchase* thirty miles in extent off the East end of their reserve (at a cost of 300,000$ to remain on interest *forever* at 5 pr ct – which gives them an annuity of 15000$ annually) – They also cede to the U. S. *in trust* twenty miles off the North side of the Bal. of their reserve the full extent east and west – to be disposed of as the Sec. Int. shall direct for their benefit – with the usual reserves to half breeds – provision for schools etc. – I have been all this afternoon in Council with the Delewares who have to the No. of 30 or 40 followed me out here for the purpose of again talking over

it was not a conclusive thing; for, in October, the
Osage chiefs were still making propositions [689] and mak-

the proposed treaty with them. They had trouble after I left them at Leavenworth. but our council today has done good and they have just left for
home with the agreement to call a council and send a delegation to the
Cherokees to look up a new home – When will Jno. Ross leave for his
people. I wish he could be there when the Delaware delegation goes
down – as I am exceedingly anxious that they get a home of the Cherokees.

"I think there is but little doubt but I shall make a treaty with the Sac
and Foxes as they say they are *satisfied* to remove to a part of the Land I
have purchased of the Osages – on the line next the Cherokees – I can make
a treaty with the Creeks and may do so but I think I will make it *conditional* upon the signatures of some of the Chiefs now in the army – Those
here are very anxious to treat and sell us a large tract of the country / The
trouble with the Southern Indians is their claims for losses by the war I will
have to put in a clause of some kind to satisfy them on that subject – That
they are entitled to it I have no doubt – but what view Congress will take
of it – or the Senate in ratifying the treaty of course I cannot tell – Some
of the Wyandots are here–

"I have just closed a Council with the Sac and Foxes and have heard
many fine speeches. We meet again day after tomorrow – as tomorrow
must be appropriated to the Creeks – I think I shall have a success here –
The Sack and Foxes to the No of say two hundred have a dance out on the
green They are dressed and painted for the occasion and as it is in honor
of my visit I must go out and witness it * * * Well we have had an
extensive dance which cost me a beef and while waiting for a Chipaway
Chief who comes as I learn to complain of his agent I go on with my Letter – The New York Indians are tolerably well represented and I shall talk
with them tonight – This is a grand jubilee amongst the Indians here. So
many tribes and parts of tribes or their Chiefs gathered here to see the
Comr. Paint and feathers are in great demand and singing, whooping –
and the Drum is constantly ringing in my ears. I am satisfied that it is a
good arrangement to have them here together it is cheaper and better and
saves much time

"I made a great mistake that I did not bring maps of the reserves and
especially of the Indian Territory – I do the best I can from the Treaties.

"I have had no mail for Eight Days as my mail is at Leavenworth. I
expect my letters day after tomorrow when I hope to have a late letter
from you as well as one from the Sec. – Will you please send Hutchinson
some money he must have funds to pay for surveying and alloting the Ottawa
reserve The survey is finished and pay demanded."

[Indian Office Consolidated Files, *Neosho*, D 198 of 1863].

[689] The propositions were in the form of a memorandum, drawn up by
White Hair, principal chief of the Great and Little Osages, and Little Bear,
principal chief of the Little Osages, who, in conjunction with Charles Mograin, assistant head chief of the Great and Little Osages, had been so-

ing them after the fashion of the Creeks long before at Indian Springs.[690]   Dole had finally to be told that the rank and file of the Osages would not allow their chiefs to confer with him except in general council.[691] As a matter of fact, not one of the Dole treaties could run the gauntlet of criticism and, consequently, the whole project of treaty-making in 1862 and 1863 accomplished nothing beneficial.   It only served to complicate a situation already serious and to forecast that when the great test should come, as come it surely would, the government would be found wanting, lacking in magnanimity, lacking in justice, and all too willing to sacrifice its honor for big interests and transient causes.

---

licited by their people, when in council at Humboldt, July 4, to proceed to Washington and interview their Great Father [Coffin to Dole, July 16, 1863, Indian Office Consolidated Files, *Neosho*, C 365 of 1863]. The propositions were to the effect that the Osages would gladly sell thirty miles by twenty miles off the southeast corner of their Reserve and one-half of the Reserve on the north for $1,350,000, which should draw six per cent interest until paid [*ibid.*, D 239 of 1863]. John Schoenmaker of the Osage Mission was apprehensive that the Roman Catholic interests would be disregarded as in the Potawatomi Treaty. See letter to Coffin, June 25th.

[690] Abel, *Indian Consolidation West of the Mississippi.*

[691] Charles Mograin warned Dole of this.

XI. INDIAN TERRITORY IN 1863, JANUARY TO JUNE INCLUSIVE

As with the war as a whole, so with that part of it waged on the Arkansas frontier, the year 1863 proved critical. Its midsummer season saw the turning-point in the respective fortunes of the North and the South, both in the east and in the west. The beginning of 1863 was a time for recording great depletion of resources in Indian Territory, as elsewhere, great disorganization within Southern Indian ranks, and much privation, suffering, and resultant dissatisfaction among the tribes generally. The moment called for more or less sweeping changes in western commands. Those most nearly affecting the Arkansas frontier were the establishment of Indian Territory as a separate military entity [692] and the detachment of western Louisiana

---

[692] The establishment of a separate command for Indian Territory was not accomplished all at once. In December, 1862, Steele had been ordered to report to Holmes for duty and, in the first week of January, he was given the Indian Territory post, subject to Hindman. On or about the eighth, he assumed command [*Official Records*, vol. xxii, part i, 28] at Fort Smith. In less than a week thereafter, his command was separated from that of Hindman [*ibid.*, part ii, 771]. The following document shows exactly what had been the previous relation between the two:

HEAD QRS DEPT INDN TERRY

Ft. Smith, Jany 31st, 1863.

COLONEL: Your special No. 22, par. viii has been recd. I would respectfully suggest that when assigned to this command by Maj. Genl Hindman the command was styled in orders, "1st Divn 1st Corps Trans. Miss. Army." The special order referred to, it is respectfully suggested, may be susceptible of misconstruction as there are under my command two separate Brigades, one under the command

and Texas from the Trans-Mississippi Department.[693] Both were accomplished in January and both were directly due to a somewhat tardy realization of the vast strategic importance of the Indian country. Unwieldy, geographically, the Trans-Mississippi Department had long since shown itself to be. Moreover, it was no longer even passably safe to leave the interests of Indian Territory subordinated to those of Arkansas.[694]

The man chosen, after others, his seniors in rank, had declined the dubious honor,[695] for the command of Indian Territory was William Steele, brigadier-general, northern born, of southern sympathies. Thus was ignored whatever claim Douglas H. Cooper might have been thought to have by reason of his intimate and long acquaintance with Indian affairs and his influence, surpassingly great, with certain of the tribes. Cooper's unfortunate weakness, addiction to intemperance, had stood more or less in the way of his promotion right along just as it had decreased his military efficiency on at least one memorable occasion and had hindered the confirmation of his appointment as superintendent of Indian affairs in the Arkansas and Red River constituency. In this narrative, as events are divulged, it will be seen that the preference for Steele exasperated Cooper, who was not a big enough man to put love of country before the gratification of his own

of Gen¹ D. H. Cooper and one under command of Col. J. W. Speight.

I am, Col., Very Res^py   W. STEELE, *Brig. Gen¹.*

Col. S. S. Anderson, A.A.G.

P.S. Please find enclosed printed Gen. Order, no. 4, which I have assumed the responsibility of issuing on receipt of Lt. Gen¹ Holmes' order declaring my command in the Ind^n country independent.

(Sd) W. STEELE, *Brig. Gen¹.*

[A.G.O., *Confederate Records*, chap. 2, no. 270, p. 65].

[693] *Official Records*, vol. xxii, part ii, 771-772.

[694] —*Ibid.*, 771.

[695] —*Ibid.*, 843; *Confederate Records*, chap. 2, no. 270, pp. 25-27.

Monthly Inspection of the 2d Creek Regiment of Mounted Volunteers, commanded by Col Chilly McIntosh

Colonel   Chilly McIntosh   Capacity, diligence and attention to duties — good
L. Colonel   Pink Hawkins   Capacity, diligence and attention to duties — Good   Good
Major   Timothy Barnett   Capacity, diligence &c   Good
Adjutant   Geo. W. Grayson   Capacity, diligence &c &c   Good
            Condition of Papers, Books and files in good order

F.M. Sauqer   Quarter Master   Capacity, Condition of Books Papers and files Good

        Fidelity and economy —   Good

        Public Property
            Mules — Good Condition. Wagons, Running gear good
            Beds in bad Condition — No wagon sheets
            Regularity of issues and Payments good
            Finds a portion of Pay for this Regt during the month
        of December 1862 not yet paid for on account of the men
            not appearing in Camps —

Dr. M. Alexander Surgeon
        Capacity, and Condition Hospital good

Company	Com. Offices Present	Non Com. Offices Present	Privates Present	Total Present	Agregate Pres. Absent & com'md	No. of men on sick report with Name	Remarks
Company a	2	7	23	30	89	32	Zeal and ability of Officers of the entire Command
Company b	4	8	14	17	63	21	and discipline of the Men — is very good
Company c	2	3	9	12	74	14	Instruction of all military exercises — bad
Company d	3	3	7	11	83	13	Condition of arms is very bad. Consisting of
Company e	1	2	17	19	82	21	Flint & Percussion Rifles
Company f	3	1	7	27	38	11	with a few Muskets and Shot Guns — all of which
Company g	3	4	11	15	98	18	have been in use for many Years —
Company h	1	#	4	4	74	5	Clothing and equipments very poor — Men in manner destitute —
Company i	1	2	2	4	68	8	Ammunition — in good order on hand not over 24.00
Company K	1	1	2	3	93	3	Kitchens and messes show attention from officers to
Company L	2	3	6	9	58	11	their men very good —
Total	23	29	121	150	831	153	

The Drill and Instruction in military exercises of the Regiment is bad — General appearance
is good — guard duties attended to strictly — No Prisoners — Mode
of enforcing discipline by court martial — Encampments clean and
in order — order of Marches on the march good — Conduct in battle
desperate — Bloody.

The large number of the Regiment absent are so distant from — about
one half of the Regt. is armed — balance no arms — Clothing in manner
destitute — If there are arms furnished and clothing sufficient the great
portion of the absentees would be in Camps —

I certify that the above is substantially in accordance with a careful inspection made
by me
                October 31 1863

ambition, consequently friction developed between him and his rival highly detrimental to the service to which each owed his best thought, his best endeavor.[696]

Conditions in Indian Territory, at the time Steele took command, were conceivably the worst that could by any possibility be imagined. The land had been stripped of its supplies, the troops were scarcely worthy of the name.[697] Around Fort Smith, in Arkansas, things were equally bad.[698] People were clamoring for protection against marauders, some were wanting only the opportunity to move themselves and their effects far away out of the reach of danger, others were demanding that the unionists be cleaned out just as secessionists had, in some cases, been. Confusion worse confounded prevailed. Hindman had resorted to a system of almost wholesale furloughing to save expense.[699] Most of the Indians had taken advantage of it and were off duty when Steele arrived. Many had preferred to subsist at government cost.[700] There was so little in their own homes for them to get. Forage was practically non-existent and Steele soon had it impressed[701] upon him that troops in the Indian Territory ought, as Hindman had come to think months before,[702] to be all unmounted.

Although fully realizing that it was incumbent upon him to hold Fort Smith as a sort of key to his entire command, Steele knew it would be impossible to main-

---

[696] It might as well be said, at the outset, that Cooper was not the ranking officer of Steele. He claimed that he was [*Official Records*, vol. xxii, part ii, 1037-1038]; but the government disallowed the contention [*ibid.*, 1038].

[697] — *Ibid.*, part i, 28; part ii, 862, 883, 909.

[698] *Confederate Records*, chap. 2, no. 270, pp. 29-30.

[699] *Official Records*, vol. xxii, part ii, 895, 909.

[700] — *Ibid*, part i, 30.

[701] *Confederate Records*, chap. 2, no. 270, p. 31.

[702] *Official Records*, vol. xiii, 51.

tain any considerable force there. He, therefore, resolved to take big chances and to attempt to hold it with as few men as his commissary justified, trusting that he would be shielded from attack "by the inclemency of the season and the waters of the Arkansas." [703] The larger portion of his army [704] was sent southward, in the direction of Red River. [705] But lack of food and forage was, by no manner of means, the only difficulty that confronted Steele. He was short of guns, particularly of good guns, [706] and distressingly short of money. [707] The soldiers had not been paid for months.

The opening of 1863 saw changes, equally momentous, in Federal commands. Somewhat captiously, General Schofield discounted recent achievements of Blunt and advised that Blunt's District of Kansas should be completely disassociated from the Division of the Army of the Frontier, [708] which he had, at Schofield's own earlier request, been commanding. It was another instance of personal jealousy, interstate rivalry, and local

[703] *Official Records*, vol. xxii, part i, 30.

[704] Perhaps the word, *army*, is inapplicable here. Steele himself was in doubt as to whether he was in command of an army or of a department [*Confederate Records*, chap. 2, no. 270, p. 54].

[705] *Confederate Records*, chap. 2, no. 270, p. 36. See also, Steele to Anderson, January 22, 1863 [*ibid.*, 50-51], which besides detailing the movements of Steele's men furnishes, on the authority of "Mr. Thomas J. Parks of the Cherokee Nation," evidence of brutal murders and atrocities committed by Blunt's army "whilst on their march through the northwestern portion of this State in the direction of Kansas."

[706] Crosby's telegram, February first, to the Chief of Ordnance is sufficient attestation,

"Many of Cooper's men have inferior guns and many none at all. Can you supply?" [*Ibid.*, 65-66].

[707] The detention and the misapplication of funds by William Quesenbury seem to have been largely responsible for Steele's monetary embarrassment [*ibid.*, 28, 63-64, 75, 76, 77, 79-81, 101, 147]. Cotton speculation in Texas was alluring men with ready money southward [*ibid.*, 94, 104].

[708] *Official Records*, vol. xxii, part ii, 6.

conflict of interests.[709]   So petty was Schofield and so
much in a mood for disparagement that he went the
length of condemning the work of Blunt and Herron [710]
in checking Hindman's advance as but a series of blun-
ders and their success at Prairie Grove as but due to an
accident.[711]   General Curtis, without, perhaps, having
any particular regard for the aggrieved parties himself,
resented Schofield's insinuations against their military
capacity, all the more so, no doubt, because he was not
above making the same kind of criticisms himself and
was not impervious to them.   In the sequel, Schofield
reorganized the divisions of his command, relieved
Blunt altogether, and personally resumed the direction
of the Army of the Frontier.[712]   Blunt went back to his
District of Kansas and made his headquarters at Fort
Leavenworth.

In some respects, the reorganization decided upon by
Schofield proved a consummation devoutly to be
wished; for, within the reconstituted First Division
was placed an Indian Brigade, which was consigned
to the charge of a man the best fitted of all around to
have it, Colonel William A. Phillips.[713]   And that
was not all; inasmuch as the Indian Brigade, consisting of the three regiments of Indian Home Guards, a
battalion of the Sixth Kansas Cavalry, and a four-gun
battery that had been captured at the Battle of Old

---

[709] It seems unnecessary and inappropriate to drag into the present nar-
rative the political squabbles that disgraced Missouri, Kansas, Arkansas, and
Colorado during the war. Lane was against Schofield, Gamble against
Curtis.

[710] Yet both Blunt and Herron were, at this very time, in line for promotion, as was Schofield, to the rank of major-general [*Official Records*, vol
xxii, part ii, 11, 95].

[711] — *Ibid.*, 6, 12, 95; *Confederate Military History*, vol. x, 195.

[712] — *Ibid.*, 22.

[713] Britton, *Civil War on the Border*, vol. ii, 18-19.

Fort Wayne,[714] was almost immediately detached from the rest of Schofield's First Division and assigned to discretionary "service in the Indian Nation and on the western border of Arkansas."[715] It continued so detached even after Schofield's command had been deprived by Curtis of the two districts over which the brigade was to range, the eighth and the ninth.[716] Thus, at the beginning of 1863, had the Indian Territory in a sense come into its own. Both the Confederates and the Federals had given it a certain measure of military autonomy or, at all events, a certain opportunity to be considered in and for itself.

Indian Territory as a separate military entity came altogether too late into the reckonings of the North and the South. It was now a devastated land, in large areas, desolate. General Curtis and many another like him might well express regret that the red man had to be offered up in the white man's slaughter.[717] It was unavailing regret and would ever be. Just as with the aborigines who lay athwart the path of empire and had to yield or be crushed so with the civilized Indian of 1860. The contending forces of a fratricidal war had little mercy for each other and none at all for him. Words of sympathy were empty indeed. His fate was inevitable. He was between the upper and the nether mill-stones and, for him, there was no escape.

Indian Territory was really in a terrible condition. Late in 1862, it had been advertised even by southern men as lost to the Confederate cause and had been prac-

---

[714] It is not very clear whether or not the constituents of the Indian Brigade were all at once decided upon. They are here listed as they appear in Britton, *Civil War on the Border*, vol. ii, 3. Schofield seems to have hesitated in the matter [*Official Records*, vol. xxii, part ii, 26].

[715] — *Ibid.*, 33.

[716] On the subject of the reduction of Schofield's command, see *ibid.*, 40.

[717] Curtis to Phillips, February 17, 1863, *ibid.*, 113-114.

tically abandoned to the jayhawker. Scouting parties of both armies, as well as guerrillas, had preyed upon it like vultures. Indians, outside of the ranks, were tragic figures in their utter helplessness. They dared trust nobody. It was time the Home Guard was being made to justify its name. Indeed, as Ellithorpe reported, "to divert them to any other operations" than those within their own gates "will tend to demoralize them to dissolution." [718]

The winter of 1862-1863 was a severe one. Its coming had been long deferred; but, by the middle of January, the cold weather had set in in real earnest. Sleet and snow and a constantly descending thermometer made campaigning quite out of the question. Colonel Phillips, no more than did his adversary, General Steele, gave any thought to an immediate offensive. Like Steele his one idea was to replenish resources and to secure an outfit for his men. They had been provided with the half worn-out baggage train of Blunt's old division. It was their all and would be so until their commander could supplement it by contrivances and careful management. Incidentally, Phillips expected to hold the line of the Arkansas River; but not to attempt to cross it until spring should come. It behooved him to look out for Marmaduke whose expeditions into Missouri [719] were cause for anxiety, especially as their range might at any moment be extended.

The Indian regiments of Phillips's brigade were soon reported [720] upon by him and declared to be in a sad state. The first regiment was still, to all intents and purposes, a Creek force, notwithstanding that its fortunes had been varied, its desertions, incomparable.

---

[718] *Official Records*, vol. xxii, part ii, 49.

[719] *Confederate Military History*, vol. x, 161, 162.

[720] *Official Records*, vol. xxii, part ii, 56-58.

The second regiment, after many vicissitudes, and after having gotten rid of its unmanageable elements, notably, the Osages and the Quapaws, had become a Cherokee and the third was largely so. That third regiment was Phillips's own and was the only one that could claim the distinction of being disciplined and even it was exposed occasionally to the chronic weakness of all Indian soldiers, absence without leave. The Indian, on his own business bent, was disposed to depart whenever he pleased, often, too, at times most inopportune, sometimes, when he had been given a special and particular task. He knew not the usages of army life and really meant no offence; but, all the same, his utter disregard of army discipline made for great disorder.

It was not the chief cause of disorder, however, for that was the unreliability of the regimental officers. The custom, from the first, had been to have the field officers white men, a saving grace; but the company officers, with few exceptions, had been Indians and totally incompetent. Strange as it may seem, drilling was almost an unknown experience to the two regiments that had been mustered in for the First Indian Expedition. To obviate some of the difficulties already encountered, Phillips had seen to it that the third regiment had profited by the mistakes of its forerunners. It had, therefore, been supplied with white first lieutenants and white sergeants, secured from among the non-commissioned men of other commands. The result had fully justified the innovation. After long and careful observation, Phillips's conclusion was that it was likely to be productive of irretrievable disaster and consequently an unpardonable error of judgment "to put men of poor ability in an Indian regiment." Primitive man has an inordinate respect for a strong character. He appreciates integrity, though he may not have it among his own gifts of nature. "An Indian company improperly officered" will inevitably become, to somebody's discomfiture, "a frightful mess."

If any one there was so foolish as to surmise that the independent commands, northern and southern, would be given free scope to solve the problems of Indian Territory, unhampered by contingent circumstances, he was foreordained to grevious disappointment. Indian Territory had still to subserve the interests of localities, relatively more important. It would be so to the very end. In and for herself, she would never be allowed to do anything and her commanders, no matter how much they might wish it otherwise – and to their lasting honor, be it said, many of them did – would always have to subordinate her affairs to those of the sovereign states around her; for even northern states were sovereign in practice where Indians were concerned. General Steele was one of the men who endeavored nobly to take a large view of his responsibilities to Indian Territory. Colonel Phillips, his contemporary in the opposite camp, was another; but both met with insuperable obstacles. The attainment of their objects was impossible from the start. Both men were predestined to failure.

Foraging or an occasional scouting when the weather permitted was the only order of the winter days for Federals and Confederates. With the advent of spring, however, Phillips became impatient for more aggressive action. He had been given a large programme, no insignificant part of which was, the restoration of refugees to their impoverished homes; but his first business would necessarily have to be, the occupancy of the country. Not far was he allowed to venture within it during the winter; because his superior officers wished him to protect, before anything else, western Arkansas. Schofield and, after Schofield's withdrawal from the command of southwestern Missouri, Curtis had insisted upon that, while Blunt, to whom Phillips, after a time, was made immediately accountable, was guardedly of another way of thinking and, although not very explicit, seemed to encourage Phillips in planning an advance.

Phillips's inability to progress far in the matter of occupancy of Indian Territory did not preclude his keeping a close tab on Indian affairs therein, such a tab, in fact, as amounted to fomenting an intrigue. It will be recalled that on the occasion of his making the excursion into the Cherokee Nation, which had resulted in his incendiary destruction of Fort Davis, he had gained intimations of a rather wide-spread Indian willingness to desert the Confederate service. He had sounded Creeks and Choctaws and had found them surprisingly responsive to his machinations. They were nothing loath to confess that they were thoroughly disgusted with the southern alliance. It had netted them nothing but unutterable woe. Among those that Phillips approached, although not personally, was Colonel McIntosh, who communicated with Phillips through two intimate friends. McIntosh was persuaded to attempt no immediate demonstration in favor of the North; for that would be premature, foolhardy; but to bide the time, which could not be far distant, when the Federal troops would be in a position to support him.[721] The psychological moment was not yet. Blunt called Phillips back for operations outside of Indian Terri-

[721] *Official Records*, vol. xxii, part ii, 61-62.

tory; but the seed of treason had been sown and sown in fertile soil, in the heart of a McIntosh.[722]

In January, 1863, Phillips took up again the self-imposed task of emissary.[723] The unionist Cherokees, inclusive of those in the Indian Brigade, were contemplating holding a national council on Cowskin Prairie, which was virtually within the Federal lines. Secessionist Cherokees, headed by Stand Watie, were determined that such a council should not meet if they could possibly prevent it and prevent it they would if they could only get a footing north of the Arkansas River. Their suspicion was, that the council, if assembled, would declare the treaty with the Confederate States abrogated. To circumvent Stand Watie, to conciliate some of the Cherokees by making reparation for past outrages, and to sow discord among others, Phillips despatched Lieutenant-colonel Lewis Downing on a scout southward. He was just in time; for the Confederates were on the brink of hazarding a crossing at two places, Webber's Falls and Fort Gibson.[724] Upon the return of Downing, Phillips himself moved across the border with the avowed intention of rendering military support, if needed, to the Cherokee Council, which convened on the fourth of February.[725] From Camp Ross, he continued to send out scouting parties, secret agents,[726] and agents of distribution.

The Cherokee Council assembled without the preliminary formality of a new election. War conditions

---

[722] This remark would be especially applicable if the Colonel McIntosh, mentioned by Phillips, was Chilly, the son of William McIntosh of Indian Springs Treaty notoriety.

[723] *Official Records*, vol. xxii, part ii, 100.

[724] — *Ibid.*, 85.

[725] — *Ibid.*, 96-97.

[726] — *Ibid.*, 100, 108.

had made regular pollings impossible. Consequently, the council that convened in February, 1863 was, to all intents and purposes, the selfsame body that, in October, 1861, had confirmed the alliance with the Confederate States. It was Phillips's intention to stand by, with military arm upraised, until the earlier action had been rescinded. While he waited, word came that the harvest of defection among the Creeks had begun; for "a long line of persons" [727] was toiling through the snow, each wearing the white badge on his hat that Phillips and McIntosh had agreed should be their sign of fellowship. Then came an order for Phillips to draw back within supporting distance of Fayetteville, which, it was believed, the Confederates were again threatening.[728] Phillips obeyed, as perforce, he had to; but he left a detachment behind to continue guarding the Cherokee Council.[729]

The legislative work of the Cherokee Council, partisan body that it was, with Lewis Downing as its presiding officer and Thomas Pegg as acting Principal Chief, was reactionary, yet epochal. It comprised several measures and three of transcendant importance, passed between the eighteenth and the twenty-first:

1. An act revoking the alliance with the Confederate States and re-asserting allegiance to the United States.

2. An act deposing all officers of any rank or character whatsoever, inclusive of legislative, executive, judicial, who were serving in capacities disloyal to the United States and to the Cherokee Nation.

---

[727] *Official Records*, vol. xxii, part ii, 101.
[728] — *Ibid.*, 111-112.
[729] — *Ibid.*, 115.

3. An act emancipating slaves throughout the Cherokee country.[730]

His detention in Arkansas was not at all to Phillips's liking.   It tried his patience sorely; for he felt the crying need of Indian Territory for just such services as his and, try as he would, he could not visualize that of Arkansas.   Eagerly he watched for a chance to return to the Cherokee country.   One offered for the fifth of March but had to be given up.   Again and yet again in letters [731] to Curtis and Blunt he expostulated against delay but delay could not well be avoided.   The pressure from Arkansas for assistance was too great.   Blunt sympathized with Phillips more than he dared openly admit and tacitly sanctioned his advance.   Never at any time could there have been the slightest doubt as to the singleness of the virile Scotchman's purpose.   In imagination he saw his adopted country repossessed of Indian Territory and of all the overland approaches to Texas and Mexico from whence, as he supposed, the Confederacy expected to draw her grain and other supplies.   Some regard for the Indian himself he doubtless had; but he used it as a means to the greater end.   His sense of justice was truly British in its keenness.

---

[730] Ross to Dole, April 2, 1863 [Indian Office General Files, *Cherokee*, 1859-1865, R 87]; Commissioner of Indian Affairs, *Report*, 1863, p. 23; Britton, *Civil War on the Border*, vol. ii, 24-25; Moore, *Rebellion Record*, vol. vi, 50; Eaton, *John Ross and the Cherokee Indians*, 196.

[731] Britton [*Civil War on the Border*, vol. ii, 27] conveys the idea that, while Phillips, truly enough, wished to enter the Indian country at the earliest day practicable, he did not care to go there before the Indian ponies could "live on the range." He knew that the refugees at Neosho would insist upon following in his wake. It would be heartless to expose them to starvation and to the ravages of diseases like the small-pox. Nevertheless, the correspondence of Phillips, scattered through the *Official Records*, vol. xxii, part ii, 121-367, shows conclusively that the weeks of waiting were weary ones.

His Indian soldiers loved him. They believed in him. He was able to accomplish wonders in training them. He looked after their welfare and he did his best to make the government and its agents of the Indian Office keep faith with the refugees. Quite strenuously, too, he advocated further enlistments from among the Indians, especially from among those yet in Indian Territory. If the United States did not take care, the Confederates would successfully conscript where the Federals might easily recruit. In this matter as in many another, he had Blunt's unwavering support; for Blunt wanted the officers of the embryo fourth and fifth regiments to secure their commands. Blunt's military district was none too full of men.

March was then as now the planting season in the Arkansas Valley and, as Phillips rightly argued, if the indigent Indians were not to be completely pauperized, they ought to be given an opportunity to be thrown once more upon their own resources, to be returned home in time to put in crops. When the high waters subsided and the rivers became fordable, he grew more insistent. There was grass in the valley of the Arkansas and soon the Confederates would be seizing the stock that it was supporting. He had held the line of the Arkansas by means of scouts all winter, but scouting would not be adequate much longer. The Confederates were beginning, in imitation of the Federals, to attach indigents to their cause by means of relief distribution and the "cropping season was wearing on."

At the end of March, some rather unimportant changes were made by Curtis in the district limits of his department and coincidently Phillips moved over the border. The first of April his camp was at Park Hill. His great desire was to seize Fort Smith; for he realized that not much recruiting could be done among the Choctaws while that post remained in Confederate hands. Blunt advised caution. It would not even do to attempt as yet any permanent occupation south of the Arkansas. Dashes at the enemy might be made, of course, but nothing more; for at any moment those higher up might order a retrograde movement and anyhow no additional support could be counted upon. Halleck was still calling for men to go to Grant's assistance and accusing Curtis of keeping too many needlessly in the West. The Vicksburg campaign was on.

The order that Blunt anticipated finally came and Curtis called for Phillips to return. La Rue Harrison, foraging in Arkansas,[732] was whining for assistance. Phillips temporized, having no intention whatsoever of abandoning his appointed goal. His arguments were unanswerable but Curtis like Halleck could never be made to appreciate the plighted faith that lay back of Indian participation in the war and the strategic importance of Indian Territory. The northern Indian regiments, pleaded Phillips, were never intended for use in Arkansas. Why should they go there? It was doubtful if they could ever be induced to go there again. They had been recruited to recover the Indian Territory and now that they were within it they were going to stay until the object had been attained. Phillips solicited Blunt's backing and got it, to the extent, indeed, that Blunt informed Curtis that if he wanted Indian Territory given up he must order it himself and take the consequences. It was not given up but Phillips suffered great embarrassments in holding it. The only support Blunt could render him was to send a negro regiment to Baxter Springs to protect supply

---

[732] *Confederate Military History*, vol. x, 166-168.

trains. Guerrillas and bushwhackers were everywhere and Phillips's command was half-starved. Smallpox[733] broke out and, as the men became more and more emaciated, gained ground. Phillips continued to make occasional dashes at the enemy and in a few engagements he was more than reasonably successful. Webber's Falls was a case in point.

As May advanced, the political situation in Missouri seemed to call loudly for a change in department commanders and President Lincoln, quite on his own initiative apparently, selected Schofield to succeed Curtis,[734] Curtis having identified himself with a faction opposed to Governor Gamble. The selection was obnoxious to many and to none more than to Herron and to Blunt, whose military exploits Schofield had belittled. The former threatened resignation if Schofield were appointed but the latter restrained himself and for a brief space all went well, Schofield even manifesting some sympathy for Phillips at Fort Gibson, or Fort Blunt, as the post, newly fortified, was now called. He declared that the Arkansas River must be secured its entire length; but the Vicksburg campaign was still demanding men and Phillips had to struggle on, unaided. Indeed, he was finally told that if he could not hold on by himself he must fall back and let the Indian Territory take care of itself until Vicksburg should have fallen.

---

[733] Britton, *Civil War on the Border*, vol. ii, 26.

[734] A change had been resolved upon in March, E. V. Sumner being the man chosen; but he died on the way out [Livermore, *Story of the Civil War*, part iii, book i, 256]. Sumner had had a wide experience with frontier conditions, first, in the marches of the dragoons [Pelzer, *Marches of the Dragoons in the Mississippi Valley*] later, in New Mexico [Abel, *Official Correspondence of James S. Calhoun*], and, still later, in ante-bellum Kansas. His experience had been far from uniformly fortunate but he had learned a few very necessary lessons, lessons that Schofield had yet to con.

The inevitable clash between Schofield and Blunt was not long deferred. It came over a trifling matter but was fraught with larger meanings.[735] It was probably as much to get away from Schofield's near presence as to see to things himself in Indian Territory that led Blunt to go down in person to Fort Gibson. He arrived there on the eleventh of July, taking Phillips entirely by surprise. Vicksburg had fallen about a week before.

The difficulties besetting Colonel Phillips were more than matched by those besetting General Steele. He, too, struggled on unaided, nay, more, he was handicapped at every turn. Scarcely had he taken command at Fort Smith when he was apprised of the fact that the chief armorer there had been ordered to remove all the tools to Arkadelphia.[736] Steele was hard put to it to obtain any supplies at all.[737] Many that he did get the promise of were diverted from their course,[738] just as were General Pike's. This was true even in the case of shoes.[739] He tried to fit his regiments out one by one with the things the men required in readiness for a spring campaign[740] but it was up-hill work. And what was perfectly incomprehensible to him was, that when his need was so great there was yet corn available for private parties to speculate in and to realize enormous profits on.[741] In April, the Indian regiments, assembling and reforming in expectation of a call to action, made special demands upon his granaries but they were

---

[735] June 9, orders issued redistricting Schofield's Department of Missouri [*Official Records*, vol. xxii, part ii, 315].

[736] *Confederate Records*, chap. 2, no. 270, p. 34.

[737] Steele to Blair, February 10, 1863, *ibid.*, 87-88.

[738] Steele to Anderson, February 8, 1863, *ibid.*, 81-82.

[739] Duval to Cabell, May 15, 1863, *ibid.*, 244-245.

[740] Steele to Cabell, March 19, 1863, *ibid.*, 148.

[741] Steele to Anderson, March 22, 1863, *ibid.*, 158.

nearly empty.[742]   It was not possible for him to furnish corn for seed or, finally, the necessaries of life to indigent Indians.   Indian affairs complicated his situation tremendously.[743]   He could get no funds and no

---

[742] Steele to Anderson, April 3, 1863, *Confederate Records*, 179-180.

[743] For instance the officers of the First Cherokee regiment had a serious dispute as to the ranking authority among them [*ibid.*, Letter from Steele, March 14, 1863, p. 143]. The following letters indicate that there were other troubles and other tribes in trouble also:

(a) "Your communication of 13 Inst. is to hand. I am directed by the Commanding Gen¹ to express to you his warmest sympathy in behalf of your oppressed people, and his desire and determination to do all that may be in his power to correct existing evils and ameliorate the condition of the loyal Cherokees. The Gen¹ feels proud to know that a large portion of your people, actuated by a high spirit of patriotism, have shown themselves steadfast and unyielding in their allegiance to our Government notwithstanding the bitter hardships and cruel ruthless outrages to which they have been subjected.

"It is hoped that the time is not very far distant, when yʳ people may again proudly walk their own soil, exalted in the feeling, perhaps with the consciousness that our cruel and cowardly foe has been adequately punished and humiliated.

"Your communication has been forᵈ to Lt Gen¹ Holmes with the urgent request that immediate steps be taken to bring your people fully within the pale of civilized warfare.

"It is hoped that there may be no delay in a matter so vitally important.

"We are looking daily for the arrival of Boats from below with corn, tis the wish of the Gen¹ that the necessitous Indians shᵈ be supplied from this place. Boats wᵈ be sent farther up the river, were we otherwise circumstanced. As it is the Boats have necessarily to run the gauntlet of the enemy – The Gen¹ however hopes to be able to keep the River free to navigation until a sufficient supply of corn to carry us through the winter can be accumulated at this place.

"You will receive notice of the arrival of corn so that it may be conveyed to the Indians needing it." – Crosby to Stand Watie, commanding First Cherokee Regiment, February 16, 1863, *ibid.*, pp. 91-93.

(b) "I am directed by Gen¹ Steele to say that a delegation from the Creeks have visited him since your departure and a full discussion has been had of such matters as they are interested in.

"They brought with them a letter from the Principal Chief Moty Kennard asking that the Cattle taken from the refugee Creeks be turned over to the use of the loyal people of the nation. The Gen. Comᵈᵍ has ordered a disposition of these Cattle to be made in accordance with the wishes of the chief. If necessary please give such instructions as will attain this object.

instructions from Richmond so he dealt with the natives as best he could.[744] Small-pox became epidemic

No Boats yet. Will endeavor to send one up the river should more than one arrive." – CROSBY to D. H. Cooper, February 19, 1863, *ibid.*, p. 97.

(c) "I enclose, herewith, a letter from the agent of the Seminoles. You will see from that letter the danger we are in from neglecting the wants of the Indians. I have never had one cent of money pertaining to the Indian superintendency, nor have I received any copies of treaties, nor anything else that would give me an insight into the affairs of that Department. I wrote, soon after my arrival at this place, to the Commissioner of Indian Affairs but have received no reply. If you have any knowledge of the whereabouts of the superintendent who has been lately appointed I hope you will urge upon him the necessity of coming at once and attending to these matters." – STEELE to Anderson, April 6, 1863, *ibid.*, 180.

(d) "I have today received a long letter from the Chief of the Osages, which I enclose for your perusal. Maj. Dorn came in from Texas a few days since, and has, I understand, gone down to Little Rock on the steamer 'Tahlequah.' It is certainly represented that a portion of the funds in his hands is in specie. Please have the latter surely delivered. Please return Black Dog's letter unless you wish to forward it." – STEELE to Holmes, May 16, 1863, *ibid.*, 249.

(e) "Letters, received today, indicate a great necessity for your presence with the tribe for whom you are Agent. I wish you, therefore, to visit them, and relieve the discontent, as far as the means in your hands will permit. The Osage Chief, 'Black Dog,' now acting as 1st Chief, claims that certain money has been turned over to you for certain purposes, for which they have received nothing." – STEELE to A. J. Dorn, May 16, 1863, *ibid.*, 249.

[744] "Your letter of May 6th, with letter of Black Dog enclosed, has been received and the enclosure forwarded to Lieut. Gen. Holmes for his information. The General Com^{dg} desires me to express his regrets that the affairs of the Osage and Seminole tribes should be in such a deplorable condition, but he is almost powerless, at present, to remedy the evils you so justly complain of. He has written again and again to the Commissioner of Indian Affairs at Richmond requesting instructions in the discharge of his duties as ex-officio Superintendent of Indian Affairs, but not a word has ever been received in reply to his reiterated requests, owing probably to the difficulty of communication between this point and the Capital. He has also requested that funds be sent him to liquidate the just demands of our Indian Allies, but from the same cause his requests have met with no response. You must readily appreciate the difficulties under which Gen. Steele necessarily labors. In fact his action is completely paralized by the want of instructions and funds. In connection with this he has been compelled to exert every faculty in defending the line of the Arkansas River against an enemy, vastly his superior in arms, numbers, artillery and everything that adds to the efficiency of an army, and consequently has not been able to pay

among his men,[745] as among Phillips's – and from like causes.

Then General Steele had difficulty in getting his men and the right kind of men together. Lawless Arkansans were unduly desirous of joining the Indian regiments, thinking that discipline there would be lax enough to suit their requirements.[746] Miscellaneous conscripting by ex-officers of Arkansan troops gave much cause for annoyance[747] as did also Cooper's unauthorized commissioning of officers to a regiment made

that attention to the business of the superintendency that he would under other circumstances.

"It was stated, some time ago, in the newspapers, that a superintendent had been appointed in Richmond, and the General Com^{dg} has been anxiously expecting his arrival for several weeks. He earnestly hopes that the superintendent may soon reach the field of his labors, provided with instructions, funds and everything necessary to the discharge of his important duties.

"Major Dorn, the Agent for the Osages, was here, a few days ago, but he is now in Little Rock. The General has written to him, requiring him to come up immediately, visit the tribe for which he is the Agent and relieve their necessities as far as the means in his hands will permit.

"The General has been offically informed that Major D. has in his possession, for the use of the Osages twenty odd thousand dollars.

"I have to apologize, on the part of Genl Steele, for the various letters which have been received from you, and which still remain unanswered, but his excuse must be that, in the absence of proper instructions etc. he was really unable to answer your questions or comply with your requests, and he cannot make promises that there is not, at least, a *very strong probability* of his being able to fulfil. Too much harm has already been occasioned in the Indian Country by reckless promises, and he considers it better, in every point of view, to deal openly and frankly with the Indians than to hold out expectations that are certain not to be realized.

"It is not possible, however, to say in a letter what could be so much better said in a personal interview, and the Genl therefore, desires me to say that as soon as your duties will admit of your absence, he will be happy to see and converse with you fully and freely at his Head Quarters" [*ibid.*, no. 268, pp. 27-29].

On this same subject, see also Steele to Wigfall, April 15, 1863, *Official Records*, vol. xxii, part ii, 819-821.

[745] *Confederate Records*, chap. 2, no. 270, p. 220.
[746] Steele to Anderson, May 9, 1863, *ibid.*, 233-234.
[747] Same to same, March 1, and 3, 1863, *ibid.*, 112-113, 113-114.

out of odd battalions and independent companies.[748]
Cooper, in fact, seemed bent upon tantalizing Steele
and many of the Indians were behind him.[749] Colonel
Tandy Walker was especially his supporter. Cooper
had been Walker's choice for department commander[750]
and continued so, in spite of all Steele's honest attempts
to propitiate him and in spite of his promise to use
every exertion to satisfy Choctaw needs generally.[751]
To Tandy Walker Steele entrusted the business of recruiting anew among the Choctaws.[752]

---

[748] Steele to Anderson, February 13, 1863, *Confederate Records*, chap 2,
no. 270, p. 89.

[749] It was not true, apparently, that the Chickasaws were dissatisfied with
Cooper. See the evidence furnished by themselves, *Official Records*, vol. xxii,
part ii, 1116-1117.

[750] *Confederate Military History*, vol. x, 134, *footnote*

[751] Steele to Tandy Walker, February 25, 1863, *Confederate Records*, chap.
2, no. 270, p. 109.

[752] Crosby to Walker, March 11, 1863, *ibid.*, p. 136. Steele thought that
the Indians might as well be employed in a military way since they were
more than likely to be a public charge. To Colonel Anderson he wrote, March
22, 1863 [*ibid.*, p. 155], "I forward the above copy of a letter from Gen¹
Cooper for Gen¹ Holmes' information. I purpose if not otherwise directed
to call out all the available force of the Nations within the conscript age. . .
They have to be fed and might as well be organized and put into a position
to be useful." From the correspondence of Steele, it would seem that there
was some trouble over Walker's promotion. April 10, Steele wrote again
to Anderson on the subject of Indian enrollment in the ranks and referred
to the other matter.

"The enclosed copy of some articles in the Treaty between the C. S. Govt
and the Choctaws with remarks by Gen¹ Cooper are submitted for the consideration of the Lt. Gen¹.

"It appears that Col. Walker was recommended to fill the vacancy made
by the promotion of Col. Cooper, the right being given by the treaty to
appoint to the office of Col., the other offices being filled by election, and that
at the time, the enemy were at Van Buren Col. Walker being at the convenient point was put upon duty by Col. Cooper and has since been recognized by several acts of my own, not however with a full knowledge of the
circumstances. That under instructions from Gen¹ Hindman a Regt was
being organized which it was expected would be commanded by Col. Folsom,
the whole of which appears to be a very good arrangement. The necessity
that exists of feeding nearly all the Indians would seem to present an addi-

Furloughs and desertions were the bane of Steele's existence.[753]   In these respects Alexander's brigade,

tional reason for having them in service. Companies are also being organized from the Reserve Indians, with the view to replace white troops with them who are now engaged protecting the frontier from the incursions of the wild tribes. Moreover the enemy's forces being composed partially of Indians, the troops would be effective against them, when they might not be against other troops. . ." [*ibid.*, pp. 186-187]. Appointments, as well as promotions, within the Indian service caused Steele much perplexity. See Steele to Anderson, April 13, 1863, *ibid.*, pp. 190-191.

[753] Steele thought it desirable to arrest all men, at large, who were subject to military duty under the conscript act, unless they could produce evidence "of a right to remain off duty" [Crosby to Colonel Newton, January 12, 1863, *ibid.*, p. 32]. Presumably whole companies were deserting their posts [Crosby to Cooper, February 1, 1863, *ibid.*, pp. 66-67]. It was suggested that some deserters should be permitted to organize against jayhawkers as, under sanction from Holmes, had been the case with deserters in the Magazine Mountains [Steele to Anderson, February 1, 1863, *ibid.*, p. 67]. When word came that the Federals were about to organize militia in northwestern Arkansas, Steele ordered that all persons, subject to military duty, who should fail to enroll themselves before February 6, should be treated as bushwhackers [same to same, February 3, 1863, *ibid.*, pp. 69-70]. Colonel Charles DeMorse, whose Texas regiment had been ordered, February 15, to report to Cooper [Crosby to DeMorse, February 15, 1863, *ibid.*], asked to be allowed to make an expedition against the wild tribes. Some two hundred fifty citizens would be more than glad to accompany it. Steele was indignant and Duval, at his direction, wrote thus to Cooper, April 19: ". . . Now if these men were so anxious to march three or four hundred miles to *find* the enemy, they could certainly be induced to take up arms *temporarily* in defence of their immediate homes" [*ibid.*, p. 203]. It was not that Steele objected to expeditions against the wild tribes but he was disgusted with the lack of patriotism and military enthusiasm among the Texans and Arkansans. Colonel W. P. Lane's regiment of Texas Partizan Rangers was another that had to be chided for its dilatoriness [*ibid.*, pp. 168-169, 199, 234]. Deficient means of transportation was oftentimes the excuse given for failure to appear but Steele's complaint to Anderson, April 10 [*ibid.*, 185-186], was very much more to the point. He wrote,

". . . I find that men are kept back upon every pretext; that QrMasters and Govt Agents or persons calling themselves such have detailed them to drive teams hauling cotton to Mexico, and employed them about the Gov't agencies. This cotton speculating mania is thus doing us great injury besides taking away all the transportation in the country. . ." Public feeling in Texas was on the side of deserters to a very great extent and in one instance, at least, Steele was forced to defer to it, "You will desist from the attempt to take the deserters from Hart's Company or any other in northern Texas if the state of public feeling is such that it cannot be done without

within which Colonel Phillips had detected traitors to the Confederate cause,[754] was, perhaps, the most incorrigible.[755] From department headquarters came impassioned appeals[756] for activity and for loyalty but

danger of producing a collision with the people. The men are no doubt deserters, but we have no men to spare, to enforce the arrest at the present time" [Steele to Captain Randolph, July 1, 1863, *ibid.*, p. 116. See also Steele to Borland, July 1, 1863, *ibid.*, no. 268, p. 117]. When West's Battery was ordered to report at Fort Smith it was discovered going in the opposite direction [Steele to J. E. Harrison, April 25, 1863, *ibid.*, no. 270, p. 213; Duval to Harrison, May 1, 1863, *ibid.*, p. 221; Steele to Anderson, May 9, 1863, *ibid.*, p. 233; Steele to Cooper, May 11 1863, *ibid.*, pp. 237-238].

One expedition to the plains that Steele distinctly encouraged was that organized by Captain Wells [Steele to Cooper, March 16, 1863, *ibid.*, pp. 145-146]. It was designed that Wells's command should operate on the western frontier of Kansas and intercept trains on the Santa Fé trail [Steele to Anderson, April 17, 1863, *ibid.*, p. 197].

[754] *Official Records*, vol. xxii, part ii, p. 62.

[755] For correspondence with Alexander objecting to further furloughing and urging the need of promptness, see *Confederate Records*, chap. 2, no. 270, pp. 121-122, 163-164, 170, 178-179, 210-211.

[756] The following are illustrations:

". . . Every exertion is being made and the Gen¹ feels confident that the means will be attained of embarking in an early spring campaign. It only remains for the officers and men to come forward to duty in a spirit of willingness and cheerfulness to render the result of operations in the Dept (or beyond it as the case may be) not only successful but to add fresh renown to the soldiers whom he has the honor to command. . ." – CROSBY to Talliaferro, February 24, 1863, *Confederate Records*, chap. 2, no. 270, pp. 105-106.

"The Commanding Gen¹ would be gratified to grant the within petition were it compatible with the interests of the service and the cause which petitioners 'Hold dearer than life.' He is fully aware of the many urgent reasons which a number of officers and men have for visiting their homes, providing for their families, etc., etc.

"The Enemy conscious of his superior strength is constantly threatening the small force that now holds him in check on the line of the Arkansas river. Speight's Brigade was sent to their present position – not because they were not needed here – but for the reason that it was an utter impossibility to subsist it in this region.

"Every consideration of patriotism and duty imperiously demands the presence of every officer and soldier belonging to this command. The season of active operations is at hand. The enemy in our front is actively employed in accumulating supplies and transportation and in massing, drilling, and disciplining his troops. His advance cannot be expected to be long de-

without telling or lasting effect. The Confederate service in Indian Territory was honeycombed with fraud and corruption.[757] Wastrels, desperadoes, scamps of every sort luxuriated at Indian expense. It was no wonder that false muster rolls had to be guarded against.[758] The Texans showed throughout so great an aversion to the giving of themselves or of their worldly goods[759] to the salvation of the country that

layed. This enemy is made up of Kansas Jayhawkers, 'Pin Indians,' and Traitors from Missouri, Arkansas and Texas. The ruin, devastation, oppression, and tyranny that has marked his progress has no parallel in history. The last official Report from your Brigade shews a sad state of weakness. Were the enemy informed on this point *our line of defence would soon be transferred from the Arkansas to Red river*. In the name of God, our country and all that is near and dear to us, let us discard from our minds every other consideration than that of a firm, fixed, and manly determination to do our duty and our whole duty to our country in her hour of peril and need. The season is propitious for an *advance*. Let not supineness, indifference and a lack of enthusiasm in a just and holy cause, compel a retreat. Texas is the great Commissary Depot west of the Mississippi. The enemy must be kept as far from her rich fields and countless herds, as possible. Let us cheerfully, harmoniously, and in a spirit of manly sacrifice bend every energy mental and physical to preparations for a forward movement. The foregoing reasons for a refusal to grant leave of absence will serve as an answer in all similar cases and will be disseminated among the officers and men of the Brigade by the Commanders thereof." – CROSBY, by command of Steele, March 20, 1863, *Confederate Records*, chap. 2, no. 270, pp. 151-152.

[757] J. A. Scales to Adair, April 12, 1863, *Official Records*, vol. xxii, part ii, 821-822.

[758] *Confederate Records*, chap. 2, no. 270, p. 224.

[759] Holmes, as early as March, warned Steele that he would have to get his supplies soon from Texas. It would not be possible to draw them much longer from the Arkansas River. He was told to prepare to get them in Texas "at all hazard," which instruction was construed by Steele to mean, "take it, if you cant buy it" [*ibid.*, 145-146]. It was probably the prospect of having to use force or compulsion that made Steele so interested, late in May, in finding out definitely whether Hindman's acts in Arkansas had really been legalized [Steele to Blair, May 22, 1863, *ibid.*, 34]. Appreciating that it was matter of vital concern that the grain crop in northern Texas should be harvested, Steele was at a loss to know how to deal with petitions that solicited furloughs for the purpose [Steele to Anderson, May 4, 1863, *ibid.*, 227; Duval to Cabell, May 7, 1863, *ibid.*, 230-231]. Perhaps, it was a concession to some such need that induced him, in June, to permit seven day furloughs [Duval to Cooper, June 27, 1863, *ibid.*, no. 268, p. 100].

Steele in despair cried out, ". . . it does appear as if the Texas troops on this frontier were determined to tarnish the proud fame that Texans have won in other fields."[760] The Arkansans were no better and no worse. The most fitting employment for many, the whole length and breadth of Steele's department, was the mere "ferreting out of jayhawkers and deserters."[761]

The Trans-Mississippi departmental change, effected in January, was of short duration, so short that it could never surely have been intended to be anything but transitional. In February the parts were re-united and Kirby Smith put in command of the whole,[762] President Davis explaining, not very candidly, that no dissatisfaction with Holmes was thereby implied.[763] Smith was the ranking officer and entitled to the first consideration. Moreover, Holmes had once implored that a substitute for himself be sent out. As a matter of fact, Holmes had become too much entangled with Hindman, too much identified with all that Arkansans objected to in Hindman,[764] his intolerance, his arrogance, his illegalities, for him to be retained longer, with complacency, in chief command. Hindman and he were largely to blame for the necessity[765] of suspending the privilege of the writ of *habeas corpus* in Arkansas and the adjacent Indian country, which had just been done. Strong

---

[760] Steele to Alexander, April 23, 1863, *Confederate Records*, no. 270, pp. 210-211.

[761] Duval to Colonel John King, June 30, 1863, *ibid.*, no. 268, p. 110.

[762] Livermore, *Story of the Civil War*, part iii, book i, p. 255.

[763] Davis to Holmes, February 26, 1863, *Official Records*, vol. liii, supplement, 849-850.

[764] Davis to Holmes, January 28, 1863, *ibid.*, 846-847.

[765] The necessity was exceedingly great. Take, for instance, the situation at Fort Smith, where the citizens themselves asked for the establishment of martial law in order that lives and property might be reasonably secure [Crosby to Mayor Joseph Bennett, January 10, 1863, *Confederate Records*, chap. 2, no. 270, pp. 33-34].

political pressure was exerted in Richmond[766] and the Arkansas delegation in Congress demanded Hindman's recall,[767] Holmes's displacement, and Kirby Smith's appointment. The loss of that historic fort, Arkansas Post,[768] also a tardy appreciation of the economic value of the Arkansas Valley and, incidentally, of the entire Trans-Mississippi Department,[769] had really determined matters; but, fortunately, the supersedure of Holmes by Smith did not affect the position of Steele.

Steele divined that the Federals would naturally make an early attempt to occupy in force the country north of the Arkansas River and beyond it to the southward in what had hitherto been a strictly Confederate stronghold. It was his intention to forestall them. The two Cherokee regiments constituted, for some little time, his best available troops and them he kept in almost constant motion.[770] His great reliance, and well it might be, was upon Stand Watie, whom he had

---

[766] Davis to Garland, March 28, 1863, *Official Records*, vol. liii, supplement, 861-863; Davis to the Arkansas delegation, March 30, 1863, *ibid.*, 863-865.

[767] Hindman was not immediately recalled; but he soon manifested an unwillingness to continue under Holmes [*ibid.*, 848]. He had very pronounced opinions about some of his associates. Price he thought of as a breeder of factions and Holmes as an honest man but unsystematic. In the summer, he actually asked for an assignment to Indian Territory [*ibid.*, vol. xxii, part ii, 895].

[768] Livermore, *Story of the Civil War*, part iii, book i, 85. Davis would fain have believed that so great a disaster had not befallen the Confederate arms [Letter to Holmes, January 28, 1863, *Official Records*, vol. liii, supplement, 847].

[769] Perhaps, it is scarcely fair to intimate that the Trans-Mississippi Department was regarded as unimportant at this stage. It was only relatively so. In proof of that, see Davis to Governor Flanagin, April 3, 1863, *ibid.*, 865-866; Davis to Johnson, July 14, 1863, *ibid.*, 879-880. When Kirby Smith tarried late in the assumption of his enlarged duties, Secretary Seddon pointed out the increasingly great significance of them [Letter to Smith, March 18, 1863, *ibid.*, vol. xxii, part ii, pp. 802-803].

[770] Steele to Cabell, April 18, 1863, *Confederate Records*, no. 270, p. 199.

brought up betimes within convenient distance of Fort Smith [771] and with whom, in April, Phillips's men had two successful encounters, on the fourteenth [772] and the twenty-fifth. The one of the twenty-fifth was at Webber's Falls and especially noteworthy, since, as a Federal victory, it prevented a convening of the secessionist Cherokee Council, [773] for which, so important did he deem it, Steele had planned an extra protection. [774] The completeness of the Federal victory was marred by the loss of Dr. Gillpatrick, [775] who had so excellently served the ends of diplomacy between the Indian Expedition and John Ross.

Through May and June, engagements, petty in themselves but contributing each its mite to ultimate success or failure, occupied detachments of the opposing Indian forces with considerable frequency. [776] Two, devised by Cooper, those of the fourteenth [777] and twentieth [778] of May may be said to characterize the entire

---

[771] "You will order Colonel Stand Watie to move his command down the Ark. River to some point in the vicinity of Fort Smith." – CROSBY to Cooper, February 14, 1863, *ibid.*, p. 90.

[772] Britton, *Civil War on the Border*, vol. ii, 37.

[773] Phillips to Curtis, April 26, 1863, *Official Records*, vol. xxii, part i, 314-315; Britton, *Civil War on the Border*, vol. ii, 40-41. Mrs. Anderson, in her *Life of General Stand Watie*, denies categorically that the meeting of the council was interrupted on this occasion [p. 22] and cites the recollections of "living veterans" in proof.

[774] "I am directed by the General Com^dg to say that he deems it advisable that you should move your Hd. Qrs. higher up the river, say in the vicinity of Webber's Falls or Pheasant Bluff. He is desirous that you should be somewhere near the Council when that body meets, so that any attempt of the enemy to interfere with their deliberations may be thwarted by you." – DUVAL to Cooper, April 22, 1863, *Confederate Records*, chap. 2, no. 270, p. 209.

[775] Britton, *Civil War on the Border*, vol. ii, 42.

[776] — *Ibid.*, vol. ii, chapters vi and vii.

[777] *Official Records*, vol. liii, supplement, 469.

[778] — *Ibid.*, vol. xxii, part i, 337-338; *Confederate Records*, chap. 2, no. 268, p. 34.

series and were nothing but fruitless demonstrations to seize the Federal grazing herds. A brilliant cavalry raid, undertaken by Stand Watie and for the same purpose, a little later, was slightly more successful;[779] but even its fair showing was reversed in the subsequent skirmish at Greenleaf Prairie, June 16.[780] To the northward, something more serious was happening, since actions, having their impetus in Arkansas,[781] were endangering Phillips's line of communication with Fort Scott, his base and his depot of supplies. In reality, Phillips was hard pressed and no one knew better than he how precarious his situation was. Among his minor troubles was the refusal of his Creeks to charge in the engagement of May 20.

The refusal of the Creeks to charge was not, however, indicative of any widespread disaffection.[782] So

[779] Anderson, 20-21. Interestingly enough, about this time Cooper reported that he could get plenty of beef where he was and at a comparatively low price, *Confederate Records*, chap. 2, no. 268, pp. 60-61.

[780] *Official Records*, vol. xxii, part i, 348-352.

[781] Not all got their impetus there. The following letter although not sent, contains internal evidence that Cooper was concocting some of them:

"I learn unofficially that Gen¹ Cooper, having received notice of the approach of a train of supplies for Gibson, was about crossing the Arkansas with the largest part of his force, to intercept it. It is reported that the train would have been in 15 miles of Gibson last night. If Gen¹ Cooper succeeds Phillips will leave soon, if not he will probably remain some time longer. Be prepared to move in case he leaves." – STEELE to Cabell, June 24, 1863, *Confederate Records*, chap. 2, no. 268, p. 96.

[782] The following letter shows the nature of the Creek disaffection:

DEAR GREAT FATHER: Sir, The wicked rebellion in the United States has caused a division in the Nation. Some of our many loving leaders have joined the rebels merely for speculation and consequently divided our people and that brought ruin in our Nation. They had help near and ours was far so that our ruin was sure. We saw this plain beforehand. Therefore we concluded to go to you our great father, remembering the treaty that you have made with us long ago in which you promised us protection. This was the cause that made us to go and meet you in your white house about eighteen months ago and there laid our complaint before you, as a weaker brother wronged of his rights by a stronger brother and you promised us your protection; but before we got back to our people they were

honorably had Phillips been conducting himself with reference to Indian affairs, so promptly and generously had he discharged his obligations to the refugees who had been harbored at Neosho—they had all returned now from exile [783] — so successfully had he everywhere encountered the foe that the Indians, far and wide, were beginning to look to him for succor,[784] many of them to

made to leave their humble and peaceful home and also all their property and traveled towards north in the woods without roads not only that but they were followed, so that they had to fight three battles so as to keep their families from being taken away from them. In the last fight they were overpowered by a superior force so they had to get away the best way they can and most every thing they had was taken away from them. . . Now this was the way we left our country and this was the condition of our people when we entered within the bounds of the State of Kansas. . .

Now Great Father you have promised to help us in clearing out our country so that we could bring back our families to their homes and moreover we have enlisted as home guards to defend our country and it will be twelve months in a few weeks . . . but there is nothing done as yet in our country. We have spent our time in the states of Mo. and Arks. and in the Cherokee Nation. We are here in Ft. Gibson over a month. Our enemies are just across the river and our pickets and theirs are fighting most every day. . .

There is only three regts. of Indians and a few whites are here. Our enemy are gathering fast from all sides . . .

A soldier's rights we know but little but it seems to us that our rations are getting shorter all the time but that may be on account of the teams for it have to be hauled a great ways. – CREEKS to the President of the United States, May 16, 1863, Office of Indian Affairs, General Files, *Creek,* 1860-1869, O 6 of 1863.

[783] Britton's account of the return of the Cherokee exiles is recommended for perusal. It could scarcely be excelled. See, *Civil War on the Border,* vol. ii, 34-37.

[784] Certain proceedings of Carruth and Martin would seem to suggest that they were endeavoring to reap the reward of Phillips's labors, by negotiating, somewhat prematurely, for an inter-tribal council. Coffin may have endorsed it, but Dole had not [Dole to Coffin, July 8, 1863, Indian Office *Letter Book,* no. 71, p. 116]. The pretext for calling such a council lay in fairly recent doings of the wild tribes. The subjoined letters and extracts of letters will elucidate the subject: February 7, Coffin reported to Dole [General Files, *Southern Superintendency,* 1863-1864] that the wild Indians had been raiding on the Verdigris and Fall Rivers into the Creek and Cherokee countries, "jayhawking property," and bringing it into Kansas and selling it to the settlers. Some of the cattle obtained in this way had been

wonder, whether in joining the Confederacy, they had not made a terrible mistake, a miscalculation beyond all remedying.

To the Confederates, tragically enough, the Indian's tale of woe and of regret had a different meaning. The

---

sold by a settler to the contractor and fed to the Indians. Jim Ned's band of wild Delawares, returning from such a jayhawking expedition, had stolen some Osage ponies and had become involved in a fight in which two Delawares had been killed [Coffin to Dole, February 12, 1863, *ibid., Neosho,* C 73 of 1863]. Coffin prevailed upon Jim Ned to stop the jayhawking excursions; inasmuch as "Considerable bad feeling exists on the part of the Cherokees in consequence of the bringing up . . . a great many cattle, ponies, and mules, which they allege belong to the Cherokee refugees. . ." [Coffin to Dole, February 24, 1863, Indian Office General Files, *Southern Superintendency*, 1863-1864].

Feelings of hostility continued to exist, notwithstanding, between the civilized and uncivilized red men and "aided materially the emissaries of the Rebellion in fomenting discords and warlike raids upon whites as well as Indians. . ." [Coffin to Dole, June 25, 1863, *ibid.*, C 325]. It was under such circumstances that Carruth took it upon himself to arrange an intertribal council. This is his report [Carruth to Coffin, June 17, 1863, *ibid.*]. His action was seconded by Martin [Martin to Coffin, June 18, 1863, *ibid.*]:

"I left Belmont (the temporary Wichita agency) May 26th to hold a Council with the Indians of the Wichita Agency, who have not as yet reached Kansas . . . I found . . . upon reaching Fall River . . . that the Wichitas alone had sent over 100 men. We reached the Ark. River May 31st. After having been compelled to purchase some provisions for the number of people, who have come, that were not provided for. The next day we were joined by the Kickapoos and Sacs, and here I was informed by the Kickapoos, that no runner had gone through to the Cadoes and Comanches from them, as we had heard at Belmont, yet I learned, that these tribes were then camped at the Big Bend, some sixty miles above and waiting at this point: I sent three Wichitas – among them the Chief – some Ionies, Wacoes, and Tawa Kuwus through to them calling on their Chiefs to come and have a 'talk.'

"They reached us on the 8th of June, and after furnishing the presents I had taken to them all the different tribes were called to Council. Present were, Arapahoes, Lipans, Comanches, Kioways, Sac and Foxes, Kickapoos and Cadoes besides the Indians who went out with me.

"All of them are true to the Government of the United States, but some are at war with each other. I proposed to them to make peace with all the tribes friendly to our Government, so that their 'Great Father' might view all of them alike.

"To this they agreed, and a Council was called to which the Osages, Potawatomies, Shians, Sac and Foxes, in fact all the tribes at variance, are

tale had been told many times of late and every time
with a new emphasis upon that part of it that recounted
delusion and betrayal. For quite a while now the Indians had been feeling themselves neglected. Steele
was aware of the fact but helpless. When told of
treaty rights he had to plead ignorance; for he had
never seen the treaties and had no official knowledge of
their contents. He was exercising the functions of
superintendent *ex officio*, not because the post had ever
been specifically conferred upon him or instructions
sent, but because he had come to his command to find
it, in nearly every aspect, Indian and no agent or superintendent at hand to take charge⁷⁸⁵ of affairs that were

to be invited, to hold a grand peace Council near the mouth of the Little
Arkansas River within six weeks. Meanwhile they are to send runners to
notify these tribes to gather on the Arkansas, sixty miles above, that they
may be within reach of our call when we get to the Council ground. Subsistence will have to be provided for at least 10000 Indians at that time.
They will expect something from the Government to convince them of its
power to carry through its promises. Some of the Cadoes and Comanches
connected with this Agency, after coming to the Arkansas, returned to Fort
Cobb. These will all come back to this Council. Their desire is to be subsisted on the Little Arkansas, some 70 miles from Emporia until the war
closes.

"They argue like this, 'The Government once sent us our provisions to
Fort Cobb over 300 miles from Fort Smith. We do not want to live near
the whites, because of troubles between them and us in regard to ponies,
timber, fields, green corn, etc. Our subsistence can be hauled to the mouth
of the Little Arkansas, easier by far, than it was formerly from Fort Smith,
and by being at this point we shall be removed from the abodes of the
whites, so they cannot steal our ponies, nor can our people trouble them.'

"I believe they are right. I have had more trouble the past winter in
settling difficulties between the Indians and whites on account of trades,
stolen horses, broken fences, etc. than from all other causes combined.

"I cannot get all the Indians of this Agency together this side of the
Little Arkansas. That point will be near enough the Texan frontier for the
Indians to go home easily when the war closes. It is on the direct route
to Fort Cobb. They are opposed to going via Fort Gibson . . ."

⁷⁸⁵ Without legislating on the subject, and without intending it, the
Confederacy had virtually put into effect, a recommendation of Hindman's
that "The superintendencies, agencies, etc., should be abolished, and a purely
military establishment substituted . . ." [*Official Records*, vol. xiii, p. 51.].

ordinarily not strictly within the range of military cognizance.

General Steele, like many another, was inclined to think that the red men greatly over-estimated their own importance; for they failed to "see and understand how small a portion of the field" [786] they really occupied. To Steele, it was not Indian Territory that was valuable but Texas. For him the Indian country, barren by reason of the drouth, denuded of its live stock, a prey to jayhawker, famine, and pestilence, did nothing more than measure the distance between the Federals and the rich Texan grain-fields, from whence he fondly hoped an inexhaustible supply of flour [787] for the Confederates was to come. In short, the great and wonderful expanse that had been given to the Indian for a perpetual home was a mere buffer.

But it was a buffer, throbbing with life, and that was something Steele dared not ignore and could not if he would. With such a consciousness, when the secessionist Cherokees were making arrangements for their council at Webber's Falls in April, he hastened to propitiate them ahead of time by addressing them "through the medium of their wants" for he feared what might be their action [788] should they assemble with a griev-

---

[786] Steele to Wigfall, April 15, 1863, *Official Records*, vol. xxii, part ii, 820.

[787] Steele's letter books furnish much evidence on this score. A large portion has been published in the *Official Records*. During the period covered by this chapter, he was drawing his supply of flour from Riddle's Station, "on the Fort Smith and Boggy Road" [*Confederate Records*, chap. 2, no. 270, p. 252] in charge of which was Captain Hardin of Bass's Texas Cavalry. He expected to draw from Arkansas likewise [Steele to Major S. J. Lee, June 9, 1863, *Confederate Records*, chap. 2, no. 268, pp. 70-71; Duval to Hardin, June 16, 1863, *ibid.*, p. 81; Steele to Lee, June 17, 1863, *ibid.* pp. 87-88].

[788] "Enclosed please find a letter to Col. Adair, and a note from him forwarding it. I send it for the consideration of General Holmes. The

ance[789] against the Confederacy in their hearts. Protection against the oncoming enemy and relief from want were the things the Indians craved, so, short though his own supplies were, Steele had to make provision for the helpless and indigent natives, the feeding of whom became a fruitful and constantly increasing source of embarrassment.[790]

Just and generous as General Steele endeavored to

subject is one of grave importance. If a regiment of infantry could be spared to take post at this place and General Cabell could be permitted to include it in his command, I would go more into the nation and would be able soon to give the required protection. The troops from Red River have been ordered up and should be some distance on the way before this. I fear the meeting of the Cherokee Council which takes place on the 20th . . . unless more troops arrive before they act."—STEELE to Anderson, April 15, 1863, *Confederate Records*, no. 270, p. 194.

This was not the first time Steele had expressed a wish to go into the Nation. March 20th, when writing to Anderson [*ibid.*, p. 150], he had thought it of "paramount importance" that he visit all parts of his command. Concerning his apprehension about the prospective work of the Cherokee Council, he wrote quite candidly to Wigfall [*Official Records*, vol. xxii, part ii, 821].

[789] The letter to Colonel W. P. Adair, written by one of his adjutants, J A. Scales, April 12, 1863 [*ibid.*, 821-822], is a creditable presentation of the Cherokee grievance.

[790] Steele here presents certain phases of the embarrassment,

" . . . The matter of feeding destitute Indians has been all through a vexatious one, the greatest trouble being to find in each neighborhood a reliable person to receive the quota for that neighborhood. These people seem more indifferent to the wants of others than any I have seen; they are not willing to do the least thing to assist in helping their own people who are destitute. I have, in many instances, been unable to get wagons to haul the flour given them. I have incurred a great responsibility in using army rations in this way and to the extent that I have. I have endeavored to give to all destitute and to sell at cost to those who are able to purchase. In this matter the Nation has been more favored than the adjacent States. I am told by Mr. Boudinot that a bill was passed by the Cherokee Council, taking the matter into their own hands. I hope it is so. In which case I shall cease issuing to others who have not, like them, been driven from their homes. Dr. Walker was appointed to superintend this matter, some system being necessary to prevent the same persons from drawing from different commissaries . . ."—STEELE to D. H. Cooper, June 15, 1863, *Confederate Records*, chap. 2, no. 268, pp. 80-81.

be in the matter of attention to Indian necessities, his efforts were unappreciated largely because of evil influences at work to undermine him and to advance Douglas H. Cooper. Steele had his points of vulnerability, his inability to check the Federal advance and his remoteness from the scene of action, his headquarters being at Fort Smith. Connected with the second point and charged against him were all the bad practices of those men who, in their political or military control of Indian Territory, had allowed Arkansas to be their chief concern. Such practices became the foundation stone of a general Indian dissatisfaction and, concomitantly, Douglas H. Cooper, of insatiable ambition, posed as the exponent of the idea that the safety of Indian Territory was an end in itself.

The kind of separate military organization that constituted Steele's command was not enough for the Indians. Seemingly, they desired the restoration of the old Pike department, but not such as it had been in the days of the controversy with Hindman but such as it always was in Pike's imagination. The Creeks were among the first to declare that this was their desire. They addressed[791] themselves to President Davis[792] and

---

[791] Moty Kanard and Echo Harjo to President Davis, May 18, 1863, *Official Records*, vol. xxii, part ii, 1118-1119.

[792] Davis, in his message of January 12, 1863 [Richardson, *Messages and Papers of the Confederacy*, vol. i, 295] had revealed an acquaintance with some Indian dissatisfaction but intimated that it had been dispelled, it having arisen "from a misapprehension of the intentions of the Government . . ." It was undoubtedly to allay apprehension on the part of the Indians that Miles, in the house of Representatives, offered the following resolution, February 17, 1863:

"*Resolved,* That the Government of the Confederate States has witnessed with feelings of no ordinary gratification the loyalty and good faith of the larger portion of its Indian allies west of the State of Arkansas.

"*Resolved further,* That no effort of the Confederate Government shall be spared to protect them fully in all their rights and to assist them in defending their country against the encroachments of all enemies."

[*Journal of the Congress of the Confederate States,* vol. vi, 113].

boldly said that their country had "been treated as a mere appendage of Arkansas, where needy politicians and *protégés* of Arkansas members of Congress must be quartered." The Seminoles followed suit,[793] although in a congratulatory way, after a rumor had reached them that the Creek request for a separate department of Indian Territory was about to be granted. The rumor was false and in June Tandy Walker, on behalf of the Choctaws, reopened the whole subject.[794] A few days earlier, the Cherokees had filed their complaint but it was of a different character, more fundamental, more gravely portentous.

The Cherokee complaint took the form of a deliberate charge of contemplated bad faith on the part of the Confederate government. E. C. Boudinot, the Cherokee delegate in the Southern Congress, had recently returned from Richmond, empowered to submit a certain proposal to his constituents. The text of the proposal does not appear in the records but its nature,[795] after account be taken of some exaggeration attributable to the extreme of indignation, can be inferred from the formal protest[796] against it, which was drawn up at Prairie Springs in the Cherokee Nation about fifteen miles from Fort Gibson on the twenty-first of June and signed by Samuel M. Taylor, acting assistant chief, John Spears of the Executive Council, and Alexander Foreman, president of the convention. To all intents and purposes the Cherokees were asked, in return for some paltry offices chiefly military, to institute a sort of system of military land grants. White people were to be induced to enlist in their behalf and were then to

---

[793] June 6, 1863, *Official Records*, vol. xxii, part ii, 1120.

[794] June 24, 1863, *ibid.*, 1122-1123.

[795] Steele's letter to Kirby Smith, June 24, 1863 [*ibid.*, 883-884], gives some hint of its nature also.

[796] — *Ibid.*, 1120-1122.

be allowed to settle, on equal terms with the Cherokees, within the Cherokee country. The proposal, as construed by Taylor and his party, was nothing more or less than a suggestion that the Cherokees surrender their nationality, their political integrity, the one thing above everything else that they had sought to preserve when they entered into an active alliance with the Confederate States. So sordid was the bargain proposed, so unequal, that the thought obtrudes itself that a base advantage was about to be taken of the Cherokee necessities and that the objectors were justified in insinuating that Boudinot and his political friends were to be the chief beneficiaries. The Cherokee country was already practically lost to the Confederacy. Might it not be advisable to distribute the tribal lands, secure individual holdings, while vested rights might still accrue; for, should bad come to worse, private parties could with more chance of success prosecute a claim than could a commonalty, which in its national or corporate capacity had committed treason and thereby forfeited its rights. One part of the Cherokee protest merits quotation here. Its noble indignation ought to have been proof enough for anybody.

> . . . We were present when the treaty was made, were a party to it, and rejoiced when it was done. In that treaty our rights to our country as a Nation were guaranteed to us forever, and the Confederate States promised to protect us in them. We enlisted under the banner of those States, and have fought in defense of our country under that treaty and for the rights of the South for nearly two years. We have been driven from our homes, and suffered severe hardships, privations, and losses, and now we are informed, when brighter prospects are before us, that you think it best for us to give part of our lands to our white friends; that, to defend our country and keep troops for our protection, we must raise and enlist them from

our own territory, and that it is actually necessary that they are citizens of our country to enable us to keep them with us. To do this would be the end of our national existence and the ruin of our people. Two things above all others we hold most dear, our nationality and the welfare of our people. Had the war been our own, there would have been justice in the proposition, but it is that of another nation. We are allies, assisting in establishing the rights and independence of another nation. We, therefore, in justice to ourselves and our people, cannot agree to give a part of our domain as an inducement to citizens of another Government to fight their own battles and for their own country; besides, it would open a door to admit as citizens of our Nation the worst class of citizens of the Confederate States. . .

XII. INDIAN TERRITORY IN 1863, JULY TO DECEMBER INCLUSIVE

Independence Day, 1863, witnessed climacteric scenes in the war dramas, east and west. The Federal victories of Gettysburg and Vicksburg, all-decisive in the history of the great American conflict, when considered in its entirety, had each its measure of immediate and local importance. The loss of all control of the Mississippi navigation meant for the Confederacy its practical splitting in twain and the isolation of its western part. For the Arkansas frontier and for the Missouri border generally, it promised, since western commands would now recover their men and resume their normal size, increased Federal aggressiveness or the end of suspended. Initial preparation for such renewed aggressiveness was contemporary with the fall of Vicksburg and lay in the failure of the Confederate attack upon Helena, an attack that had been projected for the making of a diversion only. The failure compelled Holmes to draw his forces back to Little Rock.

Confederate operations in Indian Territory through May and June had been, as already described, confined to sporadic demonstrations against Federal herds and Federal supply trains, all having for their main object the dislodgment of Phillips from Fort Gibson. What proved to be their culmination and the demonstration most energetically conducted occurred at Cabin Creek,[797] while far away Vicksburg was falling and

---

[797] For an official report of the action at Cabin Creek, see *Official Records*, vol. xxii, part i, 378-382. While, as things eventuated, it was an endeavor

Gettysburg was being fought. A commissary train from Fort Scott was expected. It was to come down, escorted by Colonel Williams who was in command of the negro troops that Blunt had stationed at Baxter Springs. To meet the train and to reinforce Williams, Phillips despatched Major Foreman from Fort Gibson. Cooper had learned of the coming of the train and had made his plans to seize it in a fashion now customary.[798] The plans were quite elaborate and involved the coöperation[799] of Cabell's Arkansas brigade,[800] which was to come from across the line and proceed down the east side of the Grand River. Thither also, Cooper sent a

---

to cut off the supply train, there was throughout the possibility that it might also result in heading off Blunt, who was known to be on his way to Fort Gibson [Steele to Cooper, June 29, 1863; Duval to Cooper, June 29, 1863; Duval to Cabell, June 29, 1863].

[798] Steele to Cabell, June 25, 1863 [*Confederate Records*, chap. 2, no. 268, p. 97; *Official Records*, vol. xxii, part ii, 885].

[799] Steele to Cabell, June 29, 1863 [*Confederate Records*, chap. 2, no. 268, p. 105; *Official Records*, vol. xxii, part ii, 893-894].

[800] Of W. L. Cabell, the *Confederate Military History*, vol. x, has this to say: "Maj. W. L. Cabell, who had been sent to inspect the accounts of quartermasters in the department, having well acquitted himself of this duty, was, in March 1863, commissioned brigadier-general and requested to collect absentees from the service in northwestern Arkansas. Given Carroll's and Monroe's regiments, he was directed to perfect such organizations as he could . . ." He collected his brigade with great rapidity and it soon numbered about four thousand men. Even, in April, Steele was placing much reliance upon it, although he wished to keep its relation to him a secret. He wrote to Cooper to that effect.

"Who will be in command of the Choctaws when you leave? Will they be sufficient to picket and scout on the other side of the river far enough to give notice of any advance of the enemy down the river? I do not wish it to be generally known that Cabell's forces are under my command, but prefer the enemy should think them a separate command; for this reason I do not send these troops west until there is a necessity for it; in the meantime the other troops can be brought into position, where if we can get sufficient ammunition all can be concentrated. I cannot direct positively, not having the intimate knowledge of the country, but you should be in a position which would enable you to move either down the Ark. River or on to the road leading from Boggy Depot to Gibson as circumstances may indicate. Let me hear from you frequently." — STEELE to Cooper, April 28, 1863, *Confederate Records*, chap. 2, no. 270, pp. 217-218.

part of his own brigade and at the same time ordered another part under Stand Watie to go to Cabin Creek and to take such position on its south bank as to command the crossing. It was a time when the rivers were all in flood, a circumstance that greatly affected the outcome since it prevented the forces on the east side of the Grand from coming to Stand Watie's support. As Foreman proceeded northward to effect a junction with Williams, he detached some Cherokees from the Third Indian, under Lieutenant Luke F. Parsons, to reconnoitre. In that way he became apprised of Watie's whereabouts and enabled to put himself on his guard. The commissary train, in due time, reached Cabin Creek and, after some slight delay caused, not by Stand Watie's interposition, but by the high waters, crossed. Federals and Confederates then collided in a somewhat disjointed but lengthy engagement with the result that Stand Watie retired and the train, nothing the worse for the hold-up, moved on without further molestation to Fort Gibson.[801]

The action at Cabin Creek, July 1 to 3, was the last attempt of any size for the time being to capture Federal supplies en route. The tables were thenceforth turned and the Confederates compelled to keep a close

---

[801] In describing what appears to be the action at Cabin Creek, Steele refers to "bad conduct of the Creeks," and holds it partly responsible for the failure [*Official Records*, vol. xxii, part ii, 910]. It is possible that he had in mind, however, a slightly earlier encounter, the same that he described, adversely to D. N. McIntosh's abilities as a commander, in his general report [*ibid.*, part i, 32]. Steele had little faith in the Indian brigade and frankly admitted that he expected it in large measure, to "dissolve," if the Confederates were to be forced to fall back at Cabin Creek [Steele to Blair, July 1, 1863, *Official Records*, vol. xxii, part ii, 902]. Nevertheless, he anticipated a victory for his arms there [Steele to Blair, July 3, 1863, *ibid.*, 903]. From his general report, it might be thought that Stand Watie disappointed him at this time, as later; but the Confederate failure was most certainly mainly attributable to the high waters, which prevented the union of their expeditionary forces [Steele to Blair, July 5, 1863, *ibid.*, 905].

watch on their own depots and trains. Up to date, since his first arrival at Fort Gibson, Colonel Phillips had been necessarily on the defensive because of the fewness of his men. Subsequent to the Cabin Creek affair came a change, incident to events and conditions farther east. The eleventh of July brought General Blunt, commander of the District of the Frontier, to Fort Gibson. His coming was a surprise, as has already been casually remarked, but it was most timely. There was no longer any reason whatsoever why offensive action should not be the main thing on the Federal docket in Indian Territory, as elsewhere.

To protect its own supplies and to recuperate, the strength of the Confederate Indian brigade was directed toward Red River, notwithstanding that Steele had still the hope of dislodging the Federals north of the Arkansas.[802] His difficulties[803] were no less legion than before, but he thought it might be possible to accomplish the end desired by invading Kansas,[804] a plan that seemed very feasible after S. P. Bankhead assumed command of the Northern Sub-District of Texas.[805] Steele himself had "neither the artillery nor the kind of force necessary to take a place" fortified as was Gibson; but to the westward of the Federal stronghold Bankhead might move. He might attack Fort Scott, Blunt's headquarters but greatly weakened now, and possibly also some small posts in southwest Missouri, replenishing his resources from time to time in the fertile and well settled Neosho River Valley. Again

---

[802] Steele took umbrage at a published statement of Pike that seemed to doubt this and to intimate that the line of the Arkansas had been definitely abandoned [Steele to Pike, July 13, 1863, *Official Records*, vol. xxii, part ii, 925].

[803] For new aspects of his difficulties, see Steele to Boggs, chief of staff, July 7, 1863, *ibid.*, 909-911.

[804] —*Ibid.*, p. 910.

[805] Steele to Bankhead, July 11, 1863, *ibid.*, 921-922.

local selfishness rose to the surface[806] and Bankhead, surmising Steele's weakness and that he would almost inevitably have to fall back, perhaps vacating Indian Territory altogether, became alarmed for the safety of Texas.[807]

Steele's recognition and admission of material incapacity for taking Fort Gibson in no wise deterred him from attempting it. The idea was, that Cooper should encamp at a point within the Creek Nation, fronting Fort Gibson, and that Cabell should join him there with a view to their making a combined attack.[808] As entertained, the idea neglected to give due weight to the fact that Cabell's men were in no trim for immediate action,[809] notwithstanding that concerted action was the only thing likely to induce success. Blunt, with

---

[806] Arkansas betrayed similar selfishness. President Davis's rejoinder to a protest from Flanagin against a tendency to ignore the claims of the West struck a singularly high note. Admitting certain errors of the past, he prayed for the generous coöperation of the future; for "it is to the future, not to the past, that we must address ourselves, and I wish to assure you, though I hope it is unnecessary, that no effort shall be spared to promote the defense of the Trans-Mississippi Department, and to develop its resources so as to meet the exigencies of the present struggle" [*Official Records*, vol. xxii, part ii, 932]. Five days afterwards, Governor Reynolds, in commending Secretary Seddon for a very able ministry, expressed confidence that his gubernatorial colleagues in Arkansas, Texas, and Louisiana would, with himself, "act in no sectional or separatist spirit." It was saying a good deal, considering how strong the drift of popular opinion had been and was to be in the contrary direction. However, in August, the four governors appealed collectively to their constituents and to "the Allied Indian Nations," proving, if proof were needed, that they personally were sincere [*ibid.*, vol. liii, supplement, 892-894; Moore's *Rebellion Record*, vol. vii, 406-407].

[807] *Official Records*, vol. xxii, part ii, 922.

[808] The plans for such concerted action were made as early as July 8 [Steele to Cooper, July 8, 1863, *Official Records*, vol. xxii, part ii, 911-912]. Cabell was instructed to take position between Webber's Falls and Fort Gibson [Duval to Cabell, July 10, 1863, *ibid.*, 916-917] and more specifically, two days before the battle, "within 15 or 20 miles of Gibson and this side of where Gen. Cooper is now encamped on Elk Creek" [Steele to Cabell, July 15, 1863, *Confederate Records*, chap. 2, no. 268, p. 145].

[809] Steele knew of the deficiencies in their equipment, however, and of their exhausted state [Duval to W. H. Scott, Commanding Post at Clarks-

scouts out in all directions and with spies in the very camps of his foes, soon obtained an inkling of the Confederate plan and resolved to dispose of Cooper before Cabell could arrive from Arkansas.[810] Cooper's position was on Elk Creek, not far from present Muskogee,[811] and near Honey Springs on the seventeenth of July the two armies met, Blunt forcing the engagement, having made a night march in order to do it. The Indians of both sides[812] were on hand, in force, the First and Second Home Guards, being dismounted as infantry and thus fighting for once as they had been mustered in. Of the Confederate, or Cooper, brigade Stand Watie, the ever reliable, commanded the First and Second Cherokee, D. N. McIntosh, the First and Second Creek, and Tandy Walker, the regiment of Choctaws and Chickasaws. The odds were all against Cooper from the start and, in ways that Steele had not specified, the material equipment proved itself inadequate indeed. Much of the ammunition was worthless.[813] Nevertheless, Cooper stubbornly contested every inch of the ground and finally gave way only when large numbers of his Indians, knowing their guns to be absolutely useless to them, became disheartened and then demoralized. In confusion, they led the van in

ville, Ark., July 8, 1863, *Confederate Records*, p. 133; Steele to Blair, July 10, 1863, *Official Records*, vol. xxii, part ii, 917; same to same, July 13, 1863, *ibid.*, 925].

[810] See Blunt's official report, dated July 26, 1863 [*ibid.*, part i, 447-448].

[811] Anderson, *Life of General Stand Watie*, 21.

[812] With respect to the number of white troops engaged on the Federal side there seems some discrepancy between Blunt's report [*Official Records*, vol. xxii, part i, 448] and Phisterer's statistics [*Statistical Record*, 145].

[813] See Cooper's report, dated August 12, 1863 [*Official Records*, vol. xxii, part i, 457-461]. The following references are to letters that substantiate, in whole or in part, what Cooper said in condemnation of the ammunition: Duval to Du Bose, dated Camp Prairie Springs, C. N., July 27, 1863 [*Confederate Records*, chap. 2, no. 268, p. 159]; Steele to Blair, dated Camp Imochiah, August 9, 1863 [*ibid.*, 185-187; *Official Records*, vol. xxii, part ii, 961].

flight across the Canadian; but enough of those more self-contained went thither in an easterly or southeasterly direction so as to create the impression among their enemies that they were retiring to meet the expected reinforcements from Fort Smith.[814]

But the reinforcements were yet far away. Indeed, it was not until all was over and a day too late that Cabell came up. A tragic sight confronted him; but his own march had been so dismal, so inauspicious that everything unfortunate that had happened seemed but a part of one huge catastrophe. He had come by the "old Pacific mail route, the bridges of which, in some places, were still standing in the uninhabited prairies."[815] The forsaken land broke the morale of his men — they had never been enthusiastic in the cause, some of them were conscripted unionists, forsooth, and they deserted his ranks by the score, by whole companies. The remnant pushed on and, in the far distance, heard the roaring of the cannon. Then, coming nearer, they caught a first glimpse of Blunt's victorious columns; but those columns were already retiring, it being their intention to recross to the Fort Gibson side of the Arkansas. "Moving over the open, rolling prairies,"[816] Nature's vast meadows, their numbers seemed great indeed and Cabell made no attempt to pursue or to court further conflict. The near view of the battle-field dismayed[817] him; for its gruesome records all too surely told him of another Confederate defeat.

---

[814] Cooper intended to create such an impression [*Official Records*, vol. xxii, part i, 460] and he did [Schofield to McNeil, July 26, 1863, *ibid.*, part ii, 399-400].

[815] *Confederate Military History*, vol. x, 199.

[816] — *Ibid.*, 200.

[817] Cabell might well be dismayed. Steele had done his best to hurry him up. A letter of July 15 was particularly urgent [*Official Records*, vol. xxii, part ii, 933].

In the fortunes of the Southern Indians, the Battle of Honey Springs was a decisive event. Fought and lost in the country of the Creeks, it was bound to have upon them a psychological effect disastrous to the steady maintenance of their alliance with the Confederacy, so also with the other great tribes; but more of that anon. In a military way, it was no less significant than in a political; for it was the beginning of a vigorously offensive campaign, conducted by General Blunt, that never ended until the Federals were in occupation of Fort Smith and Fort Smith was at the very door of the Choctaw country. No Indian tribe, at the outset of the war, had more completely gone over to the South than had the Choctaw. It had influenced the others but had already come to rue the day that had seen its own first defection. Furthermore, the date of the Confederate rout at Honey Springs marked the beginning of a period during which dissatisfaction with General Steele steadily crystallized.

Within six weeks after the Battle of Honey Springs, the Federals were in possession of Fort Smith, which was not surprising considering the happenings of the intervening days. The miscalculations that had eventuated in the routing of Cooper had brought Steele to the decision of taking the field in person; for there was just a chance that he might succeed where his subordinates, with less at stake than he, had failed. Especially might he take his chances on winning if he could count upon help from Bankhead to whom he had again made application, nothing deterred by his previous ill-fortune.

It was not, by any means, Steele's intention to attempt the reduction of Fort Gibson;[818] for, with such artillery

---

[818] Steele to Blair, July 22, 1863 [*Official Records*, vol. xxii, part ii, 940-941].

as he had, the mere idea of such an undertaking would be preposterous. The defensive would have to be, for some time to come, his leading role; but he did hope to be able to harry his enemy, somewhat, to entice him away from his fortifications and to make those fortifications of little worth by cutting off his supplies. Another commissary train would be coming down from Fort Scott via Baxter Springs about the first of August.[819] For it, then, Steele would lie in wait.

When all was in readiness, Fort Smith was vacated, not abandoned; inasmuch as a regiment under Morgan of Cabell's brigade was left in charge, but it was relinquished as department headquarters. Steele then took up his march for Cooper's old battle-ground on Elk Creek. There he planned to mass his forces and to challenge an attack. He went by way of Prairie Springs[820] and lingered there a little while, then moved on to Honey Springs, where was better grazing.[821] He felt obliged thus to make his stand in the Creek country; for the Creeks were getting fractious and it was essential for his purposes that they be mollified and held in check. Furthermore, it was incumbent upon him not to expose his "depots in the direction of Texas."[822]

As the summer days passed, Cabell and Cooper drew into his vicinity but no Bankhead, notwithstanding that Magruder had ordered him to hurry to Steele's

---

[819] Steele to Bankhead, July 22, 1863 [*Official Records*, vol. xxii, part ii, 940].

[820] Duval to A. S. Morgan, July 18, 1863 [*ibid.*, 933]; Steele to Blair, July 22, 1863 [*ibid.*, 940-941].

[821] Steele arrived at Prairie Springs on the twenty-fourth [Steele to Blair, July 26, 1863, *ibid.*, 948] and moved to Honey Springs two days later [same to same, July 29, 1863, *ibid.*, 950-951]. On August 7, his camp was at Soda Springs, whither he had gone "for convenience of water and grass" [same to same, August 7, 1863, *ibid.*, 956].

[822] — *Ibid.*, 951.

support.[823]   Bankhead had not the slightest idea of doing anything that would put Texas in jeopardy.   In northern Texas sympathy for the Federal cause, or "rottenness" as the Confederates described it, was rife.[824]   It would be suicidal to take the home force too far away.   Moreover, it was Bankhead's firm conviction that Steele would never be able to maintain himself so near to Fort Gibson, so he would continue where he was and decide what to do when time for real action came.[825]   It would be hazarding a good deal to amalgamate his command,[826] half of which would soon be well disciplined, with Steele's, which, in some of its parts, was known not to be.

As a matter of fact, Steele's command was worse than undisciplined.   It was permeated through and through with defection in its most virulent form, a predicament not wholly unforeseen.   The Choctaws had pretty well dispersed, the Creeks were sullen, and Cabell's brigade of Arkansans was actually disintegrating.   The prospect of fighting indefinitely in the Indian country had no attractions for men who were not in the Confederate service for pure love of the cause.   Day by day desertions[827] took place until the number became alarming and, what was worse, in some cases, the officers were in collusion with the men in delinquency.   Cabell himself was not above suspicion.[828]   To prevent the spread of

[823] By August third, Bankhead had not been heard from at all [Steele to Blair, August 3, 1863, *Official Records*, vol. xxii, part ii, 953]. The following communications throw some light upon Bankhead's movements [*ibid.*, 948, 956, 963].

[824] Crosby to G. M. Bryan, August 30, 1863, *ibid.*, 984.

[825] Bankhead to E. P. Turner, August 13, 1863, *ibid.*, 965-966.

[826] Bankhead to Boggs, August 10, 1863, *ibid.*, 966.

[827] There is an abundance of material in the *Confederate Records* on the subject of desertions in the West. Note particularly pp. 167, 168, 173-174, 192-193, 198, 204-205 of chap. 2, no. 268. Note, also, *Official Records*, vol. xxii, part ii, 956.

[828] Duval to Cabell, August 17, 1863, *Official Records*, vol. xxii, part ii, 969-970.

contagion among the Indians, his troops were moved to more and more isolated camps[829] across the Canadian[830] and, finally, back in the direction of Fort Smith. Ostensibly they were moved to the Arkansas line to protect Fort Smith; for Steele knew well that his present hold upon that place was of the frailest. It might be threatened at any moment from the direction of Cassville and Morgan had been instructed, in the event of an attack in prospect, to cross the boundary line and proceed along the Boggy road towards Riddle's station.[831] Steele was evidently not going to make any desperate effort to hold the place that for so long had been the seat of the Confederate control over the Southern Indians.

All this time, General Blunt had been patrolling the Arkansas for some thirty miles or so of its course[832] and had been thoroughly well aware of the assembling of Steele's forces, likewise of the disaffection of the Indians, with which, by the way, he had had quite a little to do. Not knowing exactly what Steele's intentions might be but surmising that he was meditating an attack, he resolved to assume the offensive himself.[833] The full significance of his resolution can be fully appreciated only by the noting of the fact that, subsequent to the Battle of Honey Springs, he had been instructed by General Schofield, his superior officer, not only not to advance but to fall back. To obey the order was inconceivable and Blunt had deliberately disobeyed it.[834] It was now his determination to do more. Fortunately, Schofield had recently changed his mind; for word had

---

[829] *Confederate Military History,* vol. x, 202.

[830] Steele to Scott, August 7, 1863, *Official Records,* vol. xxii, part ii, 957.

[831] Steele to Morgan, August, 1863, *ibid.,* 951; August 8, 1863, *ibid.,* 957.

[832] Steele to Blair, August 7, 1863, *ibid.,* 956.

[833] Blunt to Schofield, July 30, 1863, *ibid.,* 411.

[834] Blunt to Lincoln, September 24, 1863, *ibid.,* vol. liii, supplement, 572.

come to him that Congress had decided to relieve Kansas of her Indian encumbrance by compassing the removal of all her tribes, indigenous and immigrant, to Indian Territory.   It mattered not that the former had a title to their present holdings by ancient occupation and long continued possession and the latter a title in perpetuity, guaranteed by the treaty-making power under the United States constitution.   All the tribes were to be ousted from the soil of the state that had been saved to freedom; but it would be first necessary to secure the Indian Territory and the men of the Kansas tribes were to be organized as soldiers to secure it.   It is difficult to imagine a more ironical proceeding.   The Indians were to be induced to fight for the recovery of a section of the country that would make possible their own banishment.   Blunt strenuously objected, not because he was averse to ridding Kansas of the Indians, but because he had no faith in an Indian soldiery.   Said he,

There are several reasons why I do not think such a policy practicable or advisable. It would take several months under the most favorable circumstances to organize and put into the field the Indians referred to, even were they ready and willing to enlist, of which fact I am not advised, but presume they would be very slow to enlist; besides my experience thus far with Indian soldiers has convinced me that they are of little service to the Government compared with other soldiers. The Cherokees, who are far superior in every respect to the Kansas Indians, did very good service while they had a specific object in view – the possession and occupation of their own country; having accomplished that, they have become greatly demoralized and nearly worthless as troops. I would earnestly recommend that (as the best policy the Government can pursue with these Indian regiments) they be mustered out of service some time during the coming winter, and put to work raising their subsistence, with a few white troops stationed among them for their protection.

I would not exchange one regiment of negro troops for ten
regiments of Indians, and they can be obtained in abundance
whenever Texas is reached.

In ten days from this date, if I have the success I expect,
the Indian Territory south of the Arkansas River will be in
our possession. . .[835]

Blunt's mind was made up. He was determined to
go forward with the force he already had. Ill-health[836]
retarded his movements a trifle; but on the twenty-second of August, two days after the massacre by guerrillas
had occurred at Lawrence, he crossed the Arkansas.
He was at length accepting General Steele's challenge
but poor Steele was quite unprepared for a duel of any
sort. If Blunt distrusted the Indians, how very much
more did he and with greater reason! With insufficient
guns and ammunition, with no troops, white or red, upon whom he could confidently rely, and with no certainty of help from any quarter, he was compelled to
adopt a Fabian policy, and he moved slowly backward,
inviting yet never stopping to accept a full and regular
engagement. Out of the Creek country he went and
into the Choctaw.[837] At Perryville, on the road[838] to

---

[835] Blunt to Schofield, August 22, 1863, *Official Records*, vol. xxii, part ii,
465.

[836] — *Ibid.*, 466. There seems to have been a good deal of sickness at
Fort Gibson and some mortality, of which report was duly made to Steele
[*ibid.*, 956; *Confederate Records*, chap. 2, no. 268, pp. 192-193].

[837] Steele had crossed the line between the Creeks and Choctaws, however, before Blunt crossed the Arkansas. On August sixteenth, he had his
camp on Longtown Creek and was sending a detachment out as far south
as within about ten miles of Boggy Depot [*Official Records*, vol. xxii, part
ii, 968]. A few days later, he made his camp on Brooken Creek, a little
to the eastward [*ibid.*, 972]. By that time, Steele was evidently quite reconciled to the thought that Fort Smith might at any moment be attacked and,
perhaps, in such force that it would be needless to attempt to defend it.
Cabell was to move to a safe distance, in the neighborhood of Scullyville,
from whence, should there be reasonable prospect of success, he might send
out reënforcements. In the event of almost certain failure, he was to draw
off betimes in the direction of Riddle's station, where flour was stored
[*ibid.*].

[838] On the subject of roads and highways in Indian Territory, see *ibid.*,

Texas, his men did have a small skirmish with Blunt's and at both Perryville and North Fork, Blunt destroyed some of his stores.[839]   At North Fork, Steele had established a general hospital, which now passed from his control.

Following the unsuccessful skirmish at Perryville, the evening of August 25, Steele was "pushed rapidly down the country,"[840] so observed the wary Bankhead to whom fresh orders to assist Steele had been communicated.[841]   Boggy Depot to the Texan commander seemed the proper place to defend[842] and near there he now waited; but Steele on East Boggy, full sixty miles from Red River and from comparative safety, begged him to come forward to Middle Boggy, a battle was surely impending.[843]   No battle occurred, notwithstanding; for Blunt had given up the pursuit. He had come to know that not all of Steele's command was ahead of him,[844] that McIntosh with the Creeks had gone west within the Creek country, the Creeks having refused to leave it,[845] and that Cabell had gone east,

vol. xxxiv, part ii, 859; vol. xli, part ii, 997; Sheridan, *Memoirs*, vol. ii, 340.

[839] Blunt to Schofield, August 27, 1863, *Official Records*, vol. xxii, part i, 597-598; Steele to Snead, September 8, 1863, *Confederate Records*, chap. 2, no. 268, p. 223.

[840] *Official Records*, vol. xxii, part ii, 983.

[841] W. T. Carrington to Bankhead, August 22, 1863, *ibid.*, 975.

[842] Bankhead to Turner, August 23, 1863, *ibid.*, 977. Near Boggy Depot, "the Fort Gibson and Fort Smith roads" forked. At Boggy Depot, moreover, were "all the stores of the Indian Department." With Boggy Depot in the hands of the enemy, Bankhead's whole front would be uncovered [Bankhead to Turner August 20, 1863, *ibid.*, 972].

[843] Duval to Bankhead and other commanders, August 27, 1863, *ibid.*, 981.

[844] Blunt to Schofield, August 27, 1863, *ibid.*, part i, 597. He thought, however, that Stand Watie was with Steele but he was not. He was absent on a scout [Steele to Boggs, August 30, 1863, *ibid.*, part ii, 984].

[845] Steele to Snead, September 11, 1863, *ibid.*, part ii, 1012.

towards Fort Smith.⁸⁴⁶　It was Fort Smith that now engaged Blunt's attention and thither he directed his steps, Colonel W. F. Cloud⁸⁴⁷ of the Second Kansas Cavalry, who, acting under orders from General Mc-Neil,⁸⁴⁸ had coöperated with him at Perryville, being sent on in advance. Fort Smith surrendered with ease, not a blow being struck in her defence;⁸⁴⁹ but there was Cabell yet to be dealt with.

Steele's conduct, his adoption of the Fabian policy, severely criticized in some quarters, in Indian Territory, in Arkansas, in Texas, had yet been condoned and, indeed, approved⁸⁵⁰ by General Kirby Smith, the per-

---

⁸⁴⁶ Cabell's brigade, as already indicated, had had to be sent back "to avoid the contagion of demoralization" [*Official Records*, vol. xxii, part ii, 983; Steele to Snead, September 11, 1863, *ibid.*, 1012].

⁸⁴⁷ Cloud had arrived at Fort Gibson, August 21 [Cloud to McNeil, August 22, 1863, *ibid.*, 466].

⁸⁴⁸ John McNeil was commanding the District of Southwestern Missouri. The orders originated with Schofield [*ibid.*, part i, 15].

⁸⁴⁹ Cabell had taken a position on the Poteau. Steele had been much averse to his running the risk of having himself shut up in Fort Smith [Steele to Cabell, September 1, 1863, *ibid.*, part ii, 987].

⁸⁵⁰ "The general commanding is satisfied that the Fabian policy is the true one to adopt when not well satisfied that circumstances warrant a different course. . ." [G. M. Bryan to Steele, September 8, 1863, *ibid.*, 999]. Smith believed in "abandoning a part to save the whole" [Letter to General R. Taylor, September 3, 1863, *ibid.*, 989]; but President Davis and men of the states interested had impressed it upon him that that would never do. It must have been with some idea of justifying Steele's procedure in mind that Smith wrote to Stand Watie, September 8th [*ibid.*, 999-1000]. Watie had lodged a complaint with him, August 9th, against the Confederate subordination of the Indian interests. To that Smith replied in words that must have made a powerful appeal to the Cherokee chief, who had already, in fact on the selfsame day that he wrote to Smith, made an equally powerful one to his own tribe and to other tribes. Watie's appeal will be taken up later, the noble sounding part of Smith's may as well find a place for quotation here.

"I know that your people have cause for complaint. Their sufferings and the apparent ill-faith of our Government would naturally produce dissatisfaction. That your patriotic band of followers deserve the thanks of our Government I know. They have won the respect and esteem of our people

son most competent to judge fairly; because he possessed a full comprehension of the situation in Steele's
command. Smith knew and others might have known
that the situation had been largely created by envy,
hatred, and malice, by corruption in high places, by
peculation in low, by desertions in white regiments and
by defection in Indian.

The Confederate government was not unaware of
the increasing dissatisfaction among its Indian allies.
It had innumerable sources of information, the chief
of which and, perhaps, not the most reliable or the least
factional, were the tribal delegates [851] in Congress. Late

by their steadfast loyalty and heroic bravery. Tell them to remain true;
encourage them in their despondency; bid them struggle on through the dark
gloom which now envelops our affairs, and bid them remember the insur-
mountable difficulties with which our Government has been surrounded; that
she has never been untrue to her engagements, though some of her agents
may have been remiss and even criminally negligent. Our cause is the
same – a just and holy one; we must stand and struggle on together, till
that just and good Providence, who always supports the right, crowns our
efforts with success. I can make you no definite promises. I have your
interest at heart, and will endeavor faithfully and honestly to support you
in your efforts and in those of your people to redeem their homes from an
oppressor's rule. . .

"What might have been done and has not is with the past; it is
needless to comment upon it, and I can only assure you that I feel the importance of your country to our cause. . ."

That Smith was no more sincere than other white men had been, when
addressing Indians, goes almost without saying. It was necessary to pacify
Stand Watie and promises would no longer suffice. Candor was a better means
to the end sought. Had Smith only not so very recently had his interview
with the governors of the southwestern states, his tone might not have been
so conciliatory. In anticipation of that interview and in advance of it, for
it might come too late, some Arkansans, with R. W. Johnson among them,
had impressed it upon Governor Flanagin that both Arkansas and Indian
Territory were necessary to the Confederacy. In their communication, appeared these fatal admissions, fatal to any claim of disinterestedness:

"Negro slavery exists in the Indian Territory, and is profitable and
desirable there, affording a practical issue of the right of expansion, for
which the war began . . ." [July 25, 1863, *Official Records*, vol. xxii,
part ii, 945].

[851] Only two of the tribes, entitled to a delegate in the Confederate
Congress, seem to have availed themselves of the privilege in 1863, the

in May, Commissioner Scott[852] set out upon a tour of inspection, similar to the one he had made during the days of the Pike régime. On his way through Arkansas, he stopped at Little Rock to consult with General Holmes and to get his bearings before venturing again among the tribes; but Holmes was ill, too ill to attend to business,[853] and no interview with him was likely to be deemed advisable for some time to come. Scott had, therefore, to resume his journey without instructions or advice from the district commander, not regrettable from some points of view since it enabled

Cherokee and the Choctaw, which may account for the persistence with which, in one form or another, a measure for filling vacancies in the Indian representation came up for discussion or for reference [See *Journal*, vols. iii, vi]. It became law in January, 1864 [*ibid.*, vol. iii, 521]. A companion measure, for the regulation of Indian elections, had a like bearing. It became law earlier, in May, 1863 [*ibid.*, 420, vi, 459]. In the *Official Records*, fourth ser. vol. iii, 1189, *footnote o*, the statement is made that the name of Elias C. Boudinot appeared first on the roll, January 8, 1864; but it must be erroneous, since Boudinot, as the delegate from the Cherokee Nation, was very active in Congress all through the year 1863. His colleague from the Choctaw Nation was Robert M. Jones. On December 10, when Indian affairs had become exceedingly critical, Representative Hanly moved that one of the Indian delegates should be requested to attend the sessions of the Committee on Indian Affairs (*Journal*, vol. vi, 520). This proposition eventually developed into something very much more important,
"*Resolved*, First, That each Delegate from the several Indian nations with whom treaties have been made and concluded by the Confederate States of America shall have and be entitled to a seat upon the floor of this House, may propose and introduce measures being for the benefit of his particular nation, and be heard in respect and regard thereto, or other matters in which his nation may be particularly interested.
"Second. That, furthermore, it shall be the duty of the Speaker of this House to appoint one Delegate from one of the Indian nations upon the Committee on Indian Affairs, and the Delegate so appointed shall have and possess all the rights and privileges of other members of such committee, except the right to vote on questions pending before such committee" – *Journal*, vol. vi, 529. The Speaker appointed Boudinot to the position thus created.

[852] In February, upon the nomination of President Davis and the recommendation of Secretary Seddon, Scott had been appointed to the position of full commissioner [*ibid.*, vol. iii, 69].

[853] During the illness of Holmes, which was protracted, Price commanded in the District of Arkansas.

him to approach his difficult and delicate task with an open mind and with no preconceived notions derived from Holmes's prejudices.

Scott entered the Indian Territory in July and was at once beset with complaints and solicitations, individual and tribal. On his own account, he made not a few discoveries. On the eighth of August he reported[854] to Holmes upon things that have already been considered here, defective powder, deficient artillery, and the like; but not a word did he say about the Cooper[855] and Boudinot intrigues. It was too early to commit himself on matters so personal and yet so fundamental. The Indians were not so reticent. The evil influence that Cooper had over them, due largely to the fact that he professed himself to be interested in Indian Territory to the exclusion of all other parts of the country, was beginning to find expression in various communications to President Davis and others in authority. Just how far Stand Watie was privy to Cooper's schemes and in sympathy with them, it is impossible to say. Boudinot was Cooper's able coadjutor, fellow conspirator, while Boudinot and Watie were relatives and friends.

Watie's energies, especially his intellectual, were apparently being exerted in directions far removed from the realm of selfish and petty intrigue. He was a man of vision, of deep penetration likewise, and he was a patriot. Personal ambition was not his besetting sin. If he had only had real military ability and the qualities that make for discipline and for genuine leadership

---

[854] *Official Records*, vol. xxii, part ii, 1097.

[855] On August 14, Cooper complained to Smith that Steele had been given the place that rightfully should have been his [*ibid.*, 987]. Smith looked into the matter and made his reply, strictly non-partisan, September 1st [*ibid.*, 1037]. The authorities at Richmond declared against Cooper's claims and pretensions, yet, in no wise, did he abandon them.

among men, he might have accomplished great things for Indian Territory and for the Confederacy. Almost simultaneously with the forwarding of Scott's first report to Holmes, he personally made reports[856] and issued appeals,[857] some of which, because of their grasp, because of their earnestness, and because of their spirit of noble self-reliance, call for very special mention. Watie's purpose in making and in issuing them was evidently nothing more and nothing less than to dispel despondency and to arouse to action.

Watie's appeal may have had the effect designed but it was an effect doomed to be counteracted almost at once. Blunt's offensive had more of menace to the Creeks and their southern neighbors than had Steele's defensive of hope. The amnesty to deserters,[858] that issued under authority from Richmond on the twenty-sixth of August, even though conditional upon a return to duty, was a confession of weakness and it availed little when the Choctaws protested against the failure to supply them with arms and ammunition, proper in quality and quantity, for Smith to tell them that such things, intended to meet treaty requirements but diverted, had been lost in the fall of Vicksburg.[859] Had not white men been always singularly adept at making excuses for breaking their promises to red?

In September, when everything seemed very dark for the Confederacy on the southwestern front, desperate efforts were made to rally anew the Indians. Pro-

---

[856] Watie's report to Scott, August 8, 1863 [*Official Records*, vol. xxii, part ii, 1104-1105] was full of very just criticism, but not at all factional.

[857] The appeal to the Creeks, through their governor, is to be found in *Official Records*, vol. xxii, part ii, 1105-1106, and that to the Choctaws and Chickasaws, *ibid.*, 1106-1107.

[858] — *Ibid.*, 980.

[859] Smith to Principal Chief, Choctaw Nation, August 13, 1863, *ibid.*, 967; Bryan to Hon. R. M. Jones, September 19, 1863, *ibid.*, 1021.

posals[860] from Blunt were known to have reached both the Creeks and the Choctaws and were being considered, by the one, more or less secretly and, by the other, in open council. Israel G. Vore,[861] who had become the agent of the Creeks and whose influence was considerable, was called upon to neutralize the Federal advances. In a more official way, Commissioner Scott worked with the Choctaws, among whom there was still a strong element loyal to the Confederacy, loyal enough, at all events, to recruit for a new regiment to fight in its cause.

Nothing was more likely to bring reassurance to the Indians than military activity; but military activity of any account was obviously out of the question unless some combination of commands could be devised, such a combination, for example, as Magruder had in mind when he proposed that the forces of Steele, Cooper, Bankhead, and Cabell should coöperate to recover Forts Smith and Gibson, something more easily said than done. It was no sooner said than brigade transfers rendered it quite impracticable, Cabell and Bankhead both being needed to give support to Price. In charge now of the Northern Sub-district of Texas was Henry E. McCulloch. From him Steele felt he had a right to expect coöperation, since their commands were

---

[860] Steele to Snead, September 11, 1863, *Official Records*, vol. xxii, part ii, 1013; Bankhead to Steele, September 15, 1863, *ibid.*, 1016.

[861] In the spring of 1863, Vore was engaged in disbursing funds, more particularly, in paying the Indian troops [Steele to Anderson, April 17, 1863, *Confederate Records*, chap. 2, no. 270, pp. 197-198]. In November, 1862, the Creeks had requested that Vore be made their agent and the appointment was conferred upon him the following May [Scott to Seddon, December 12, 1863, *Official Records*, vol. xxii, part ii, 1095]. The Creeks were inclined to be displeased at the delay, especially as they later had no reason to regret their choice [Moty Kanard to Davis, August 17, 1863. *ibid.*, 1107]. It was Cooper, apparently, who suggested sending up Vore to have him work upon the Creeks [*ibid.*, 1000].

territorially in conjunction, and to consult with him he
journeyed to Bonham.[862]

Viewed in the light of subsequent events, the journey
was productive of more evil than good. With Steele
absent, the command in Indian Territory devolved upon Cooper[863] and Cooper employed the occasion to in-
gratiate himself with the Indians, to increase his influence with them, and to undermine the man who he still
insisted had supplanted him. When Steele returned
from Texas he noticed very evident signs of insubordination. There were times when he found it almost
impossible to locate Cooper within the limits of the
command or to keep in touch with him. Cooper was
displaying great activity, was making plans to recover
Fort Smith, and conducting himself generally in a very
independent way. October had, however, brought a
change in the status of Fort Smith; for General Smith
had completely detached the commands of Indian Territory and Arkansas from each other.[864] It was not to
Holmes that Steele reported thenceforth but to Smith
direct. Taken in connection with the need that soon
arose, on account of the chaos in northern Texas, for
McCulloch[865] to become absorbed in home affairs, the

---

[862] His destination was apparently to be Shreveport, the department headquarters [Crosby to Bankhead, September 23, 1863. *Confederate Records*,
chap. 2, no. 268. p. 251].

[863] Cooper's headquarters, in the interval, were to be at Fort Washita
[*ibid.*], where a company of Bass's regiment had been placed in garrison
[Duval to Cooper, July 15, 1863, *ibid.*. p. 145].

[864] *Official Records*, vol. xxii, part ii, 1045.

[865] McCulloch was being greatly embarrassed by the rapid spread of
unionist sentiment and by desertions from his army. The expedient of furloughing was restorted to. To his credit, be it said. that no embarrassments.
no dawning of the idea that he was fighting in a failing cause, could make
him forget the ordinary dictates of humanity. His scornful repudiation of
Quantrill and his methods was characteristic of the man. For that repudiation, see, particularly, McCulloch to Turner, October 22, 1863, *ibid.*, vol.
xxvi. part ii, 348.

separation from Arkansas left Indian Territory stranded.

Fort Smith, moreover, was about to become Blunt's headquarters and it was while he was engaged in transferring his effects from Fort Scott to that place that the massacre of Baxter Springs occurred, Blunt arriving upon the scene too late to prevent the murderous surprise having its full effect. The Baxter Springs massacre was another guerrilla outrage, perpetrated by Quantrill and his band[866] who, their bloody work accomplished at the Federal outpost, passed on down through the Cherokee Nation, killing outright whatever Indians or negroes they fell in with. It was their boast that they never burdened themselves with prisoners. The gang crossed the Arkansas about eighteen miles above Fort Gibson[867] and arrived at Cooper's camp on the Canadian, October twelfth.[868]

Scarcely had Blunt established his headquarters at Fort Smith, when political influences long hostile to him, Schofield at their head,[869] had accumulated force

---

[866] Quantrill's bold dash from the Missouri to the Canadian had been projected in a spirit of bravado, deviltry, and downright savagery, and had undoubtedly been incited by the execution of Ewing's notorious order, *Number Eleven* [*Official Records*, vol. xxii, part ii, 473]. That order, as modified by Schofield, had authorized the depopulating of those counties of Missouri, Jackson, Cass, Bates, and a part of Vernon, where the guerrillas were believed to have their chief recruiting stations and where secessionist feeling had always been dominant. It was at once retaliatory and precautionary and on a par with the instructions for the removal of the Acadians on the eve of the breaking out of the French and Indian War. The banished Missourians have, however, as yet found no Longfellow to sentimentalize over them or to idealize, in a story of *Evangeline*, their misfortunes and their character. History has been spared the consequent and inevitable distortion.

[867] Britton, *Civil War on the Border*, vol. ii, 224.

[868] Quantrill to Price, October 13, 1863, *Official Records*, vol. xxii, part i, 700-701.

[869] In the matter of domestic politics in Kansas, particularly as they were shaped by the excitement over the guerrilla outrages, Schofield belonged to the party of *Moderates*, "Paw Paws" as its members were called in derision,

sufficient to effect his removal. He was relieved, under Schofield's orders of October 19, and Brigadier-general John McNeil then assumed command of the District of the Frontier.[870] Colonel Phillips continued in charge at Fort Gibson,[871] his presence being somewhat of a reassurance to the Cherokees, who, appreciating Blunt's energetic administration, regretted his recall.[872]

Had the Federal Cherokees been authoritatively apprised of the real situation in the Indian Territory farther south, they need never have been anxious as to the safety of Fort Gibson. Steele's situation was peculiarly complex. As private personage and as commander he elicits commiseration. Small and incapable was his force,[873] intriguing and intractable were his subordi-

and Blunt, like Lane, Wilder, and others, to that of the *Extremists*, or *Radicals*. Of the Extremists the "Red Legs" were the active wing, those who indulged in retaliatory and provocative outrages. Schofield's animosity against Blunt, to some extent richly deserved, amounted almost to a persecution. He instituted an investigation of the District of the Frontier and it was upon the basis of the findings of the committee of investigation that he ordered Blunt's retirement [Schofield to Townsend, October 3, 1863, *Official Records*, vol. xxii, part ii, 595-597; Blunt to Curtis, November 30, 1864, *ibid.*, vol. xli, part iv, 727-729]. For evidence of continued animosity see the correspondence of Champion Vaughan, *ibid.*, vol. xxii, part ii, 738, 742.

[870] *Official Records*, vol. xxii, part ii, 666.

[871] For the condition and movements of the Indian Brigade from November 20, 1863, to December 20, 1863, see *Daily Conservative*, January 3, 1864.

[872] The resolutions, commendatory of his work, to which Blunt refers in his letter to Curtis of November 30, were passed by the Cherokee National Council, October 20, 1863. The text of them is to be found, as also Chief Christie's letter of transmittal, in *Official Records*, vol. xxxiv, part ii, 790-791.

[873] Steele reported that on October first he had "Seminoles, 106; Chickasaws, 208; Creeks, 305; Choctaws, 1,024; Choctaw militia, 200, and whites, 999" [*Official Records*, vol. xxii, part i, 34]. Concerning the condition of his entire command, the best understanding can be obtained from the inspection report of Smith's assistant inspector-general, W. C. Schaumburg, [*ibid.*, part ii, 1049-1053], October 26, 1863. Schaumburg exhibits conditions as simply deplorable, Indians poorly mounted, ignorant of drill, destitute of suitable

nates. Of the white force Magruder[874] was doing his utmost to deprive him, and of the Indian Steele found it next to impossible to keep account. Insignificant as it was, it was yet scattered here, there, and everywhere,[875] Cooper conniving at its desultory dispersion. Instead of strengthening his superior's hands, Cooper was, in fact, steadily weakening them and all for his own advancement. He disparaged Steele's work, discredited it with the Indians,[876] and, whenever possible, allowed a false construction to be put upon his acts. In connection with the movements of the white troops, is a case in point to be found. Rumor had it that Bankhead's brigade, now Gano's,[877] was to be called away for coast defence. Cooper knew perfectly well that such was not Steele's intention and yet he suffered

---

arms; posts dilapidated; and prominent tribesmen, like Colonel Tandy Walker, indulging in petty graft, drawing government rations for members of their families and for their negro slaves. McCulloch was also of the opinion that conditions in Indian Territory were pretty bad [*Official Records*, vol. xxii, part i, 1065], and that the red men were absolutely unreliable [*ibid.*, vol. xxvi, part ii, 378].

[874] For Magruder's insolent and overbearing attitude towards Steele, see his correspondence in *ibid.*, part ii. Magruder wanted Indian Territory attached to the District of Texas [p. 295] and was much disgusted that Gano's brigade was beyond his reach; inasmuch as Smith himself had placed it in Indian Territory and Steele could retain it there if he so pleased [pp. 349, 369, 371].

[875] *Official Records*, vol. xxii, part ii, 1063, 1065, 1076, 1109.

[876] Cooper's influence was greatest with the Choctaws and Chickasaws. The Choctaw wavering of which there were numerous signs [*ibid.*, 1019, 1024], the disposition of the Choctaw Council towards neutrality [*ibid.*, 1042, 1046], which Scott was called upon to check [*ibid.*, 1030-1031], and the Choctaw complaint about the absence or inadequacy of arms [*ibid.*, 1021] were all made the most of, in order to accentuate Steele's incapacity for his task. October 7, the Chickasaw Legislature petitioned for the elevation of Cooper to the full command in Indian Territory [*ibid.*, 1123-1124]. It was, of course, a covert attack upon Steele.

[877] Dissatisfaction with Bankhead on the part of his men had been the chief cause of the transfer to Richard M. Gano. Steele had a good deal of trouble with Gano's brigade as also with Bass's regiment [See *Confederate Records*, chap. 2, nos. 267, 268].

the Indians to believe that it was; in order that they might with impunity charge Steele with having violated their treaty pledges.[878]   To nothing did they hold so rigidly as to the promise that white troops were always to support Indian.

In the role of Indian superintendent ex officio, Steele had no fewer difficulties and perplexities than in that of military chief.   The feeding of indigents was a problem not easily solved, if solvable.   In the absence of legislative provision, Hindman had instituted the questionable practice of furnishing relief to civilians at the cost of the army commissary and no other course had ever been deemed expedient by his successors.   In July, 1863, Steele had ordered[879] practically all distribution agencies to be abolished, his reason being that only refugees,[880] Indians out of their own country, ought, in the season of ripened and ripening crops, to need subsistence and such subsistence, being limited in amount and derived altogether from the army supply, could be most economically handled by the regular commissaries.   As winter approached and the necessity for feeding on a large scale became again pronounced,

---

[878] *Official Records*, vol. xxii, part ii, 1063-1064, 1064-1065.

[879] "I am instructed by the Gen. Com^dg to direct that you issue an order abolishing all agencies in the Indian country for feeding 'Indigents.'

"It is thought that the crops now coming in will be sufficient to support these people without any further drain upon Govt supplies.

"What little issues are absolutely necessary will be made by post commissaries." – DUVAL to Lee, July 1, 1863, *Confederate Records*, chap. 2, no. 268, p. 119.

[880] "I beg leave to recommend to your favorable consideration the accompanying letter from the Hon. E. C. Boudinot.   The necessity of feeding not only the refugees, but to some extent during the winter the other Indians, has been recognized by all commanders, the drouth of last year having cut the crops very short.   As the crops are now maturing I have in a great measure discontinued the issue except to refugee Cherokees and Osages, both of whom are out of their own country. . ." – STEELE to Smith, July 13, 1863, *ibid.*, pp. 142-143.

he was disposed to keep the whole matter still under army regulations so as to "avoid increasing competition." [881] The army exchequer could be subsequently reimbursed when specific appropriations for Indians should be made. Supplies of clothing had naturally to be otherwise provided for and for those he contracted [882] in northern Texas. Steele's whole policy with regard to the indigents was subjected to the severest criticism; [883] for it was based upon the idea that to be forewarned is to be forearmed. Disappointed speculators and grafters were chief among his critics and, in spite of all his precautions, they outwitted him. Peculation appeared on every hand, white sharpers abounded, and Indians, relatively affluent, subsisted at government expense.

Another source of embarrassment was developed by the application of war measures, primarily intended for the states only, to the Indian country. Indian property was impressed [884] as occasion arose. Very

---

[881] Steele to Scott, August 7, 1863, *Confederate Records*, pp. 179-180.

[882] Steele to Bryan, November 9, 1863, *Confederate Records*, chap. 2, no. 267, p. 31. The Reserve Indians had all along been fed by contract [Steele to Scott, August 7, 1863, *ibid.*, no. 268, pp. 179-180]. In the fall, Steele renewed the contract with Johnson and Grimes [Steele to S. A. Roberts, November 15, 1863, *ibid.*, no. 267, p. 37] and detailed men from his command, from Martin's regiment, to assist in its execution [Steele to McCulloch, November 22, 1863, *ibid.*, p. 41].

[883] The Creeks were particularly dissatisfied. They claimed that food and raiment had been promised them, but the source of the promises Steele was powerless to determine [Steele to Vore, November 20, 1863, *ibid.*, p. 39]. Indian soldiers on leave seemed to expect their usual allowances and Cooper, although disclaiming that he had any desire to "pander to the prejudices" of the natives, was always to be found on their side in any contention with Steele. To all appearances, the Indians had Cooper's support, in demanding all the privileges and profits of regular troops and "all the latitude of irregular, or partisan" [Steele to Cooper, November 24, 1863, *ibid.*, pp. 44-45].

[884] Concerning the request of Steele that cotton and teams be ordered exempt from impressment, see Steele to Bryan, November 9, 1863. *Confederate Records*, chap. 2, no. 267, p. 31. The Choctaws had considerable cotton and the question was what was to be done with it in case of an advance of

frequently was this the case in the matter of transportation facilities, in that also of negro labor. It was Steele's opinion that the impressment law and the grain tithe law were not operative as against the Indians[885] but his necessities forced the practice, and execution by the army, under his orders, only intensified Indian opposition to him.

Indian opposition to Steele in tangible form took two directions, one of which, the advancement of Douglas H. Cooper, has already been frequently referred to. The other was the advancement of Stand Watie. During the summer, Stand Watie, as chief of the Confederate Cherokees, had authorized the formation of a Cherokee brigade,[886] the object being, the dislodgment of the Federals from Fort Gibson and their consequent retirement from the Cherokee country. The brigade had not materialized; but all Stand Watie's subsequent efforts were directed towards the accomplishment of its patriotic object. Love of country best explains his whole military endeavor. The enemy in the Cherokee country he harassed, the enemy elsewhere, he left for others to deal with. Generally speaking, in consequence, the autumn months of 1863 found Watie hovering around the Arkansas, the Cherokees and their neighbors with him, while Cooper, almost equally particularistic because the Choctaws and Chickasaws were his main support, concerned himself with plans for the recovery of Fort Smith.

the enemy. Was it to be burnt and the owners were they to be indemnified [Steele to Anderson, December 9, 1863, *Confederate Records*, p. 68]? Steele peremptorily forbade confiscation of Indian property and discouraged any interference "with the duties of agents, or with the National Council or government of the tribes" [Steele to Captain J. L. Randolph, enrolling officer, July 7, 1863, *ibid.*, no. 268, p. 132].

[885] Crosby to A. S. Cabell, October 6, 1863, *ibid.*, no. 267, p. 2.

[886] *Official Records*, vol. xxii, part ii, 1103.

The fervid patriotism of one leader and the over-weening personal ambition of the other divided the Indians, then, into two camps and it was but natural that the idea should soon evolve that Indian interests could be best subserved by the formation of two distinct Indian brigades. To this idea General Smith, when appealed to, subscribed;[887] but General Steele was dubious about the propriety of putting Stand Watie in charge of one of the brigades. "He appears to exercise," said Steele, "no restraint over his men in keeping them together, and his requisitions upon the depots seem to be made with utter disregard of the numbers present or even on his rolls."[888] General Smith conceived it would be possible, by organizing the Indians into their own brigades and satisfying them that way, to draw off the white contingent and make of it a separate brigade, still operating, however, within the Indian country. To Cooper, the thought of a separate white brigade was most unwelcome. The Indians could be an effective force only in close conjunction with white troops. The separation of whites and Indians would inevitably mean, although not at present intended, the isolation of the latter and, perhaps, their ultimate abandonment.

The various proposals and counter-proposals all converged in an opposition to Steele. His presence in the Indian country seemed to block the advancement of everybody. Cooper resented his authority over himself and Stand Watie interpreted his waiting policy as due to inertness and ineptitude. So small a hold did the Federals really have on the Indian country that if Steele would only exert himself it could easily be

---

[887] *Official Records*, vol. 22, part ii, 1055-1056.
[888] —*Ibid.*, 1065.

broken. But Steele was neither aggressive nor venturesome. His task was truly beyond him. Discouraged, he asked to be relieved and he was relieved, Brigadier-general Samuel B. Maxey being chosen as his successor.[889] Again Cooper had been passed over, notwithstanding that his Indian friends had done everything they could for him. They had made allegations against Steele; in order that a major-generalship might be secured for Cooper and brigadier-generalships for some of themselves.[890] Boudinot was believed by Steele to be at the bottom of the whole scheme; but it had been in process of concoction for a long time and Steele had few friends. General Smith was the stanchest of that few and even Holmes[891] was not among them.

Obviously, with things in such a chaotic state, military operations in the Indian country, during the autumn and early winter were almost negligible.[892] Steele expected that the Federals would attempt a drive from Fort Smith to the Red River and he collected what forces he could for that contingency. Little reliance was to be placed upon the Cherokees since they were intent upon recovering Fort Gibson; but the Choctaws through whose country the hostile force would proceed, were the drive made, aroused themselves as in the first days of the war. They recruited their regiments anew

---

[889] Special Orders, no. 214, December 11, 1863, *Official Records*, vol. xxii, part ii, 1094.

[890] Steele to S. Cooper December 19, 1863, *ibid.*, 1100-1101.

[891] Boudinot to Davis, December 21, 1863, *ibid.*, 1103.

[892] Steele contended that between the very natural fear that the Indians entertained that the white troops were going to be withdrawn from their country and Magruder's determination to get those same white troops, it was impossible to make any move upon military principles [Steele to Anderson, November 9, 1863, *ibid.*, 1064-1065]. Steele refused to recognize Magruder's right to interfere with his command [Steele to Cooper, November 8, 1863, *ibid.*, 1063-1064].

and they organized a militia; but the drive was never made.[893]

The only military activity anywhere was in the Cherokee country and it was almost too insignificant for mention. Towards the end of November, the Federal force there was greatly reduced in numbers, the white and negro contingents being called away to Fort Smith.[894] The Indian Home Guards under Phillips were alone in occupation. With a detachment of the Third Indian, Watie had one lone skirmish, although about one half of Phillips's brigade was out scouting. The skirmish occurred on Barren Fork, a tributary of the Illinois, on the eighteenth of December.[895] Late in November, Watie had planned a daring cavalry raid into the Neosho Valley.[896] The skirmish on Barren Fork arrested him in his course somewhat; but, as the Federals, satisfied with a rather petty success, did not pursue him, he went on and succeeded in entering southwest Missouri. The raid did little damage and was only another of the disjointed individual undertakings that Steele deplored but that the Confederates were being more and more compelled to make.

---

[893] Steele to Gov. Samuel Garland, Nov. 30, 1863, *Official Records*, vol. xxii, part ii, 1082. Col. McCurtain of the Choctaw militia reported to Cooper that he expected to have fifteen hundred Choctaws assembled by December first [Steele to Gano, December 2, 1863, *ibid.*, 1085]. The Second Choctaw regiment continued scattered and out of ammunition [Steele to Cooper, December 22, 1863, *ibid.*, 1109]. The Seminole battalion was ordered to report to Bourland for frontier defence [Duval to Cooper, December 20, 1863, *ibid.*, 1102].

[894] Britton, *Civil War on the Border*, vol. ii, 236.

[895] *Official Records*, vol. xxii, part i, 781-782.

[896] — *Ibid.*, part ii, 722, 746, 752.

XIII. ASPECTS, CHIEFLY MILITARY, 1864-1865

The assignment of General Maxey to the command of Indian Territory invigorated Confederate administration north of the Red River, the only part of the country in undisputed occupancy. Close upon the assumption of his new duties, came a project[897] for sweeping reforms, involving army reorganization, camps of instruction for the Indian soldiery, a more general enlistment, virtually conscription, of Indians — this upon the theory that "Whosoever is not for us is against us" — the selection of more competent and reliable staff officers, and the adoption of such a plan of offensive operations as would mean the retaking of Forts Smith and Gibson.[898] To Maxey, thoroughly familiar with the geography of the region, the surrender of those two places appeared as a gross error in military technique; for the Arkansas River was a natural line of defence, the Red was not. "If the Indian Territory gives way," argued he, "the granary of the Trans-Mississippi Department, the breadstuffs, and beef of this and the Arkansas army are gone, the left flank of Holmes' army is turned, and with it not only the meat and bread, but the salt and iron of what is left of the Trans-Mississippi Department."[899]

---

[897] Maxey to Anderson, January 12, 1864, *Official Records*, vol. xxxiv, part ii, 856-858.

[898] To this list might be added the proper fitting out of the troops, which was one of the first things that Maxey called to Smith's attention [*ibid.*, vol. xxii, part ii, 1112-1113].

[899] This idea met with Smith's full approval [*ibid.*, vol. xxxiv, part ii, 918].

Army reorganization was an immense proposition and was bound to be a difficult undertaking under the most favorable of auspices, yet it stood as fundamental to everything else. Upon what lines ought it to proceed? One possibility was, the formation of the two brigades, with Stand Watie and Cooper individually in command, which had already been suggested to General Smith and favored by him; but which had recently been found incompatible with his latest recommendation that all the Indian troops should be commanded, *in toto*, by Cooper.[900] One feature of great importance in its favor it had in that it did not ostensibly run counter to the Indian understanding of their treaties that white troops should be always associated with Indian in the guaranteed protection of the Indian country, which was all very well but scarcely enough to balance an insuperable objection, which Cooper, when consulted, pointed out.[901] The Indians had a strong aversion to any military consolidation that involved the elimination of their separate tribal characters. They had allied themselves with the Confederacy as nations and as nations they wished to fight. Moreover, due regard ought always to be given, argued Cooper, to their tribal prejudices, their preferences, call them what one will, and to their historical neighborhood alliances. Choctaws and Chickasaws might well stay together and Creeks and Seminoles; but woe betide the contrivance that should attempt the amalgamation of Choctaws and Cherokees.

---

[900] This is given upon the authority of Maxey [*Official Records*, vol. xxxiv, part ii, 857]. It seems slightly at variance with Smith's own official statements. Smith would appear to have entertained a deep distrust of Cooper, whose promotion he did not regard as either "wise or necessary" [*ibid.*, vol. xxii, part ii, 1102].

[901] Cooper to T. M. Scott, January, 1864 [*Ibid.*, vol. xxxiv, part ii, 859-862].

Monthly

Inspection Report of the 1st Creek Regt Mtd Vol   C S A

Colonel   D. N. McIntosh   Their Capacity, diligence and attention to duties and orders, zeal and activity, sobriety
Lt Col   Wm. R. McIntosh
Majr   Jas McHenry
Adjt   Wm Percival   Capacity, Condition of Books, papers and files,
a.q.m   Jno Barnwell   "   "   "   "   "
a c s   I A Clarke   "   "   "   "   "
Surgeon   O. Alexander   Capacity Condition of Hospital Attention to duties &c
           Co A   zeal and ability of officers discipline of   instruction in all military
                          condition of Arms Clothing equipments & accoutrements ammunition Kitchens
Capt Hakmak firin Candy and Messes & & the attention paid by the officers to the wants of the men, and the
           Co B   cooking
  "   F. B. Sivers   "
           Co C
  "   Cully Micco   "
           Co D
  "   Yahasly   "
           Co E
  "   Sulpotta Micco   "
           Co F
  "   Sam Miller   "
           Co G
  "   Wm Jacobs   "
           Co H
  "   Washy Kennard   "
           Co I
  "   Young Hardage   "
           Co K
  "   G B Callahan   "
   1st Creek Reg
Col D. N. McIntosh
        Comdg

Drill and instruction in all military   discipline of Troops General appearance Guard. Guard duty &
Missions, Mode of enforcing discipline &c & Court Martial or otherwise. Condition of encampment as
to cleanliness. and order of propriety and order of Troops. on the March, Conduct in Battle and
all other information which may be of interest or tutility in promoting the efecacy of the Service.

   I certify that the above is strictly in accordance with a careful inspection made by me at

   Station
   Date

FACSIMILE OF MONTHLY INSPECTION REPORT OF THE FIRST CREEK REGIMENT OF MOUNTED VOLUNTEERS

It seems a little strange that the Indians should so emphasize their national individualism at this particular time, inasmuch as six of them, the Choctaw, Chickasaw, Cherokee, Creek, Seminole, and Caddo, professing to be still in strict alliance with the Southern States, had formed an Indian confederacy, had collectively re-asserted their allegiance, pledged their continued support, and made reciprocal demands. All these things they had done in a joint, or general, council, which had been held at Armstrong Academy the previous November. Resolutions of the council, embodying the collective pledges and demands, were even at this very moment under consideration by President Davis and were having not a little to do with his attitude toward the whole Maxey programme.

In the matter of army reorganization, Smith was prepared to concede to Maxey a large discretion.[902] The brigading that would most comfortably fit in with the nationalistic feelings of the Indians and, at the same time, accord, in spirit, with treaty obligations and also make it possible for Cooper to have a supreme command of the Indian forces in the field was that which Cooper himself advocated, the same that Boudinot took occasion, at this juncture, to urge upon President Davis.[903] It was a plan for three distinct Indian brigades, a Cherokee, a Creek-Seminole, and a Choctaw-Chickasaw. Maxey thought "it would be a fine recruiting order,"[904] yet, notwithstanding, he gave his

---

[902] *Official Records*, vol. xxxiv, part ii, 917.

[903] Boudinot to Davis, January 4, 1864 [*ibid.*, vol. liii, supplement, 920-921]. Boudinot also suggested other things, some good, some bad. He suggested, for instance, that Indian Territory be attached to Missouri and Price put in command. Seddon doubted if Price would care for the place [*ibid.*, 921].

[904] —*Ibid.*, vol. xxxiv, part ii, 858.

preference for the two brigade plan.[905] The promotion
of Cooper, implicit in the three brigade plan, was not at
all pleasing to General Smith; for he thought of it as reflecting upon Steele, whom he loyally described as
having "labored conscientiously and faithfully in the
discharge of his duties."[906] With Steele removed from
the scene[907] – and he was soon removed for he had been
retained in the Indian country only that Maxey might
have for a brief season the benefit of his experience[908] –
the case was altered and Boudinot again pressed his
point,[909] obtaining, finally, the assurance of the War Department that so soon as the number of Indian regiments justified the organization of three brigades they
should be formed.[910]

The formation of brigades was only one of the Indian demands that had emanated from the general
council. Another was, the establishment of Indian
Territory as a military department, an arrangement
altogether inadvisable and for better reasons than the
one reason that Davis offered when he addressed the
united nations through their principal chiefs on the
twenty-second of February.[911] Davis's reason was that

---

[905] Maxey to Smith, January 15, 1864, *Official Records*, vol. xxxiv, part
ii, 875.

[906] — *Ibid.*, vol. xxii, part ii, 1101-1102.

[907] — *Ibid.*, vol. xxxiv, part ii, 845, 848.

[908] So Smith explained [*ibid.*, 845], when Steele objected to staying in the
Indian Territory in a subordinate capacity [*ibid.*, vol. xxii, part ii, 1108].
Steele was transferred to the District of Texas [*ibid.*, vol. xxxiv, part ii,
961]. The withdrawal of Steele left Cooper the ranking officer and the person on whom such a command, if created, would fall [*ibid.*, vol. liii, supplement, 968-969].

[909] Boudinot to Davis, February 11, 1864, *ibid.*, 968.

[910] Seddon to Davis, February 22, 1864, *ibid.*, 968-969.

[911] Richardson, *Messages and Papers of the Confederacy*, vol. i, 477-479;
Official Records, vol. xxxiv, part iii, 824-825. Davis addressed the chiefs
and not the delegation that had brought the resolutions [*ibid.*, vol. liii, supplement, 1030-1031]. John Jumper, Seminole principal chief, was a member of
the delegation.

as a separate department Indian Territory could not count upon the protection of the forces belonging to the Trans-Mississippi Department that was assured to her while she remained one of its integral parts. A distinct military district she should certainly be.

When Davis wrote, the ambition of Cooper had, in a measure, been satisfied; for he had been put in command of all "the Indian troops in the Trans-Mississippi Department on the borders of Arkansas."[912]   It was by no means all he wanted or all that he felt himself entitled to and he soon let it be known that such was the state of affairs. He tried to presume upon the fact that his commission as superintendent of Indian affairs had issued from the government, although never actually delivered to him, and, in virtue of it, he was in military command.[913]   The quietus came from General Smith, who informed Cooper that his new command and he himself were under Maxey.[914]

It was hoped that prospective Indian brigades would be a powerful incentive to Indian enlistment and so they proved. Moreover, much was expected in that direction from the reassembling of the general council at Armstrong Academy, and much had to be; for the times were critical. Maxey's position was not likely to be a sinecure. As a friend wrote him,

> Northern Texas and the Indian Department have been neglected so long that they have become the most difficult and the most responsible commands in the Trans-Mississippi Department. I tremble for you. A great name is in store for you or you fall into the rank of failures; the latter may be your

---

[912] *Official Records*, vol. xxxiv, part ii, 848; Special Orders of the Adjutant and Inspector General's Office, 1864, *Confederate Records*, no. 7, p. 15.

[913] Cooper to Davis, February 29, 1864, *Official Records*, vol. xxxiv, part ii, 1007.

[914] — *Ibid.*, 1008.

fate, and might be the fate of any man, even after an entire and perfect devotion of all one's time and talent, for want of the proper means. In military matters these things are never considered. Success is the only criterion – a good rule, upon the whole, though in many instances it works great injustice. Good and deserving men fall, and accidental heroes rise in the scale, kicking their less fortunate brothers from the platform.[915]

With a view to strengthening the Indian alliance and accomplishing all that was necessary to make it effective, Commissioner Scott was ordered by Seddon to attend the meeting of the general council.[916]   Unfortunately, he did not arrive at Armstrong Academy in time, most unfortunately, in fact, since he was expected to bring funds with him and funds were sadly needed. Maxey attended and delivered an address[917] that rallied the Indians in spite of themselves. In council meeting they had many things to consider, whether or no they should insist upon confining their operations henceforth to their own country. Some were for making a raid into Kansas, some for forming an alliance with the Indians of the Plains,[918] who, during this year of 1864, were to prove a veritable thorn in the flesh to Kansas and Colorado.[919] As regarded some of the work of the general council, Samuel Garland, the principal chief of the Choctaws, proved a huge stumbling block,

---

[915] S. A. Roberts to Maxey, February 1, 1864, *Official Records*, vol. xxxiv, part ii, 936-937.

[916] Seddon to Scott, January 6, 1864, *ibid.*, 828-829.

[917] Moty Kanard, late principal chief of the Creek Nation, spoke of it as a *noble* address and begged for a copy [*ibid.*, 960].

[918] Vore to Maxey, January 29, 1864, *ibid.*, 928; Maxey to Anderson, February 9, 1864, *ibid.*, 958; same to same, February 7, 1864, *ibid.*, vol. liii, supplement, 963-966.

[919] Inasmuch as the alliance with the Indians of the Plains was never fully consummated and inasmuch as these Indians harassed and devastated the frontier states for reasons quite foreign to the causes of the Civil War, the subject of their depredations and outrages is not considered as within the scope of the present volume.

and Cooper was forced, so he said, to "put the members of the grand council to work on" him.[920]   It was Cooper's wish, evidently, that the council would "insist under the Indian compact that all Choctaw troops shall be put at once in the field as regular Confederate troops for the redemption and defense of the whole Indian Territory." The obstinacy of the Choctaw principal chief had to be overcome in order "to bring out the Third Choctaw Regiment speedily and on the proper basis." In general, the council reiterated its recommendations of November previous and so Boudinot informed President Davis,[921] it being with him the opportunity he coveted of urging, as already noted, the promotion of Cooper to a major-generalship.

In January and so anterior to most of the foregoing incidents, the shaking of the political dice in Washington, D.C., had brought again into existence the old Department of Kansas, Curtis in command.[922]   Its limits were peculiar for they included Indian Territory[923] and the military post of Fort Smith as well as Kansas and the territories of Nebraska and Colorado. The status of Fort Smith was a question for the future to decide; but, in the meantime, it was to be a bone of contention between Curtis and his colleague, Frederick Steele, in command of the sister Department of Ar-

---

[920] Cooper to Maxey, February, 1864, *Official Records*, vol. xxxiv, part ii, 959. The report reached Phillips that the Choctaws wanted a confederacy quite independent of the southern [*ibid.*, part i, 107].

[921] Although Davis's address of February 22 could well, in point of chronology, have been an answer to the applications and recommendations of the second session of the general council, it has been dealt with in connection with those of the first session, notwithstanding that Boudinot made his appeal less than a fortnight before Davis wrote. In his address, Davis specifically mentioned the work of the first session and made no reference whatsoever to that of the second.

[922] *Official Records*, vol. xxxiv, part ii, 10.

[923] Ewing wanted the command of Indian Territory, *ibid.*, 89.

kansas; for Steele had control over all Federal forces within the political and geographical boundaries of the state that gave the name to his department except the Fort Smith garrison.[924] The termination of Schofield's career in Missouri[925] was another result of political dice-throwing, so also was the call for Blunt to repair to the national capital for a conference.[926]

But politics had nothing whatever to do with an event more notable still. With the first of February began one of the most remarkable expeditions that had yet been undertaken in the Indian country. It was an expedition conducted by Colonel William A. Phillips and it was remarkable because, while it professed to have for its object the cleaning out of Indian Territory,[927] its incidents were as much diplomatic and pacific as military. Its course was only feebly obstructed and might have been extended into northern Texas had Moonlight of the Fourteenth Kansas Cavalry chosen to coöperate.[928] As it was, the course was southward almost to Fort Washita. Phillips carried with him copies of President Lincoln's Amnesty Proclamation[929] and he distributed them freely. His interpretation of the proclamation was his own and perhaps not strictly warranted by the phraseology but justice and generosity debarred his seeing why magnanimity and forgiveness should not be extended betimes to the poor deluded red man as much as to the deliberately rebellious white. To various prominent chiefs

---

[924] *Official Records*, vol. xxxiv, part ii, 167, 187.

[925] — *Ibid.*, 188.

[926] Lane, Wilder, and Dole, requested that Blunt be summoned to Washington [*ibid.*, 52].

[927] See Phillips's address to his soldiers, January 30, 1864, *ibid.*, 190.

[928] Phillips to Curtis, February 16, 1864, *ibid.*, part i, 106-108.

[929] Richardson, *Messages and Papers of the Presidents*, vol. vi, 213-215.

of secessionist persuasion he sent messages of encouragement and good-will.[930]   More sanguine than circumstances really justified, he returned to report that,
for some of the tribes at least, the war was virtually
over.[931]   What his peace mission may have accomplished, the future would reveal; but there was no
doubting what his raid had done.   It had produced
consternation among the weaker elements.   The Creeks,
the Seminoles, and the Chickasaws had widely dispersed, some into the fastnesses of the mountains.   Only
the Choctaws continued obdurate and defiant.   It was
strange that Phillips should have arrived at conclusions
so sweeping; for his course [932] had led him within hearing range of the general council in session at Armstrong
Academy and there the division of sentiment was not
so much along tribal lines as along individual.   Strong
personalities triumphed; for, as Maxey so truly divined, the Indian nations were after all aristocracies.
The minority really ruled.   At Armstrong Academy,
in spite of tendencies toward an isolation that, in effect, would have been neutrality and, on the part of a
few, toward a definite retracing of steps, the southern
Indians renewed their pledges of loyalty to the Confederacy.   Phillips's olive branch was in their hands
and they threw it aside.   Months before they might
have been secured for the North but not now.   For
them the hour of wavering was past.   Maxey's vigor
was stimulating.

---

[930] To Governor Colbert of the Chickasaw Nation [*Official Records*, vol.
xxxiv, part i, 109-110], to the Council of the Choctaw Nation [*ibid.*, 110], to
John Jumper of the Seminole Nation [*ibid.*, 111], to McIntosh, possibly D. N.
[*ibid.*, part ii, 997].   For Maxey's comments upon Phillips and his letters,
see Maxey to Smith, February 26, 1864, *ibid.*, 994-997.

[931] Phillips to Curtis, February 24, 1864, *ibid.*, part i, 108-109.

[932] For the itinerary of the course, see *ibid.*, 111-112.

The explanation of Phillips's whole proceeding during the month of February is to be found in his genuine friendship for the Indian, which eventually profited him much, it is true, but, from this time henceforth, was lifelong. He stood in somewhat of a contrast to Blunt, whom General Steele thought unprincipled[933] and who in Southern parlance was "an old land speculator,"[934] and to Curtis, who was soon to show himself, as far as the Indians were concerned, in his true colors. While Phillips was absent from Fort Gibson, Curtis arrived there. He was making a reconnoissance of his command and, as he passed over one reservation after another, he doubtless coveted the Indian land for white settlement and justified to himself a scheme of forfeiture as a way of penalizing the red men for their defection.[935] Phillips was not encouraged to repeat his peace mission.

Blunt's journey to Washington had results, complimentary and gratifying to his vanity because publicly vindicatory. On the twenty-seventh of February he was restored to his old command or, to be exact, ordered "to resume command of so much of the District of the Frontier as is included within the boundaries of the Department of Kansas."[936] His headquarters were at Fort Smith and immediately began the controversy between him and Thayer, although scornfully unacknowledged by Thayer, as to the status of Fort Smith. Thayer refused to admit that there could be any issue[937] between them for the law in the case was clear. What Blunt and Curtis really wanted was to get hold of the

[933] F. Steele to S. Breck, March 27, 1864, *Official Records*, vol. xxxiv, part ii, 751.

[934] T. M. Scott to Maxey, April 12, 1864, *ibid.*, part iii, 762.

[935] This matter is very much generalized here for the reason that it properly belongs in the volume on reconstruction that is yet to come.

[936] February 23, 1864, *Official Records*, vol. xxxiv, part ii, 408.

[937] John M. Thayer to Charles A. Dana, March 15, 1864, *ibid.*, 617.

western counties of Arkansas[938] so as to round out the
Department of Kansas. To them it was absurd that
Fort Smith should be within their jurisdiction and its
environs within Steele and Thayer's. The upshot of
the quarrel was, the reorganization of the frontier departments on the seventeenth of April which gave Fort
Smith and Indian Territory to the Department of Arkansas[939] and sent Blunt back to Leavenworth. His
removal from Fort Smith, especially as Curtis had intended, had no change in department limits been made,
to transfer Blunt's headquarters to Fort Gibson,[940] was
an immense relief to Phillips. Blunt and Phillips
had long since ceased to have harmonious views with
respect to Indian Territory. During his short term
of power, Blunt had managed so to deplete Phillips's
forces that two of the three Indian regiments were practically all that now remained to him since one, the Second Indian Home Guards, had been permanently
stationed at Mackey's Salt Works on the plea that its
colonel, John Ritchie, was Phillips's ranking officer
and it was not expedient that he and Phillips "should
operate together."[941] Blunt had detached also a part
of the Third Indian and had placed it at Scullyville
as an outpost to Fort Smith. There were to be no more
advances southward for Phillips.[942] Instead of making
them he was to occupy himself with the completion of
the fortifications at Fort Gibson.[943]

[938] Thayer to Grant, March 11, 1864, *Official Records*, vol. xxxiv, part
ii, 566.

[939] — *Ibid.*, part iii, 192, 196.

[940] — *Ibid.*, part ii, 651. Blunt would have preferred Scullyville [*ibid.*,
part iii, 13].

[941] Blunt to Curtis, March 30, 1864, *ibid.*, part ii, 791.

[942] Blunt to Phillips, April 3, 1864, *ibid.*, part iii, 32; Phillips to Curtis,
April 5, 1864, *ibid.*, 52-53.

[943] Curtis had ordered the completion of the fortifications which might be
taken to imply that he too was not favoring a forward policy.

Among the southern Indians, Maxey's reconstruction policy was all this time having its effect. It was revitalizing the Indian alliance with the Confederacy, but army conditions were yet a long way from being satisfactory. In March Price relieved Holmes in command of the District of Arkansas.[944] A vigorous campaign was in prospect and Price asked for all the help the department commander could afford him. The District of Indian Territory had forces and of all the disposable Price asked the loan. Maxey, unlike his predecessors, was more than willing to coöperate but one difficulty, which he would fain have ignored himself – for he was not an Albert Pike – he was compelled to report. The Indians had to be free, absolutely free, to go or to stay.[945] The choice of coöperating was theirs but theirs also the power to refuse to coöperate, if they so desired, and no questions asked. The day had passed when Arkansans or Texans could decide the matter arbitrarily. Watie was expected to prefer to continue the irregular warfare that he and Adair, his colonel of scouts, had so successfully been waging for a goodly time now. Formerly, they had waged it to Steele's great annoyance;[946] but Maxey felt no repugnance to the services of Quantrill, so, of course, had nothing to say in disparagement of the work of Watie. It was the kind of work, he frankly admitted he thought the Indians best adapted to. The Choctaws under Tandy Walker were found quite willing to cross the line and they did excellent service in the Camden campaign, which, both in the cannonade near Prairie d'Ane on the thirteenth of April and in the Battle of Poison Spring on the

---

[944] *Official Records*, vol. xxxiv, part ii, 1034, 1036.

[945] Maxey to Smith, April 3, 1864, *ibid.*, part iii, 728-729.

[946] For Steele's opposition to Adair's predatory movements, see *Confederate Records*, chap. 2, nos. 267, 268.

eighteenth of April, offered a thorough test of what Indians could do when well disciplined, well officered, and well considered. The Indian reinforcement of Marmaduke was ungrudgingly given and ungrudgingly commended.[947] The Camden campaign was short and, when about over, Maxey was released from duty with Price's army. His own district demanded attention[948] and the Indians recrossed the line.

Price's call for help had come before Maxey had taken more than the most preliminary of steps towards the reorganization of his forces and not much was he able to do until near the end of June. Two brigades had been formed without difficulty and Cooper had secured his division; but after that had come protracted delay. The nature of the delay made it a not altogether bad thing since the days that passed were days of stirring events. In the case of Stand Watie's First Brigade no less than of Tandy Walker's Second were the events distinguished by measurable success. The Indians were generally in high good humor; for even small successes, when coupled with appreciation of effort expended, will produce that. One adventure of Watie's, most timely and a little out of the ordinary, had been very exhilarating. It was the seizure of a supply boat on the Arkansas at Pheasant Bluff, not far from the mouth of the Canadian up which the boat was towed until its commissary stores had been extracted. The boat was the Williams, bound for Fort Gibson.[949]

---

[947] Williamson to Maxey, April 28, 1864, *Official Records*, vol. xxxiv, part i, 845.

[948] It had not been Smith's intention that he should go out of his own district, where his services were indispensable, until Price's need should be found to be really urgent [Boggs to Maxey, April 12, 1864, *ibid.*, part iii, 760-761].

[949] — *Ibid.*, part i, 1011-1013; part iv, 686-687.

It was under the inspiration of such recent victories that the southern Indians took up for consideration the matter of reënlistment, the expiration "of the present term of service" being near at hand. Parts of the Second Brigade took action first and, on the twenty-third of June, the First Choctaw Regiment unanimously reenlisted for the war. Cooper was present at the meeting "by previous request." [950] Resolutions [951] were drawn up and adopted that reflected the new enthusiasm. Other Choctaw regiments were to be prevailed upon to follow suit and the leading men of the tribe, inclusive of Chief Garland who was not present, were to be informed that the First Choctaw demanded of them, in their legislative and administrative capacities "such co-operation as will force all able-bodied free citizens of the Choctaw Nation, between the ages of eighteen and forty-five years, and fitted for military service, to at once join the army and aid in the common defense of the Choctaw Nation, and give such other coöperation to the Confederate military authorities as will effectually relieve our country from Federal rule and ruin."

The First Brigade was not behindhand except in point of time by a few days. All Cherokee military units were summoned to Watie's camp on Limestone Prairie. [952] The assemblage began its work on the twenty-seventh of June, made it short and decisive and indicated it in a single resolution:

> Whereas, the final issue of the present struggle between the North and South involves the destiny of the Indian Territory alike with that of the Confederate States: Therefore,
> *Resolved*, That we, the Cherokee Troops, C. S. Army, do

---

[950] *Official Records*, vol. xxxiv, part iv, 694.

[951] — *Ibid.*, 695.

[952] Stand Watie to Cooper, June 27, 1864, *ibid.*, part i, 1013.

unanimously re-enlist as soldiers for the war, be it long or short.[953]

No action was taken on the policy of conscription; but, in July, the Cherokee National Council met and, to it, Chief Watie proposed the enactment of a conscription law.[954]

As a corollary to reorganization, the three brigade plan was now put tentatively into operation. It was, in truth, "a fine recruiting order," and Commissioner Scott, when making his annual rounds in August, was able to report to Secretary Seddon,

> It is proposed to organize them into three brigades, to be called the Cherokee, Choctaw, and Creek Brigades; the Cherokee Brigade, composed of Cherokees, Chickasaws, and Osages, has already been organized; the Creek Brigade, composed of Creeks and Seminoles, is about being so, and the Choctaws anticipate no difficulty in being able to raise the number of men required to complete the organization of the Choctaw Brigade.[955]

Behind all this virility was General Maxey. Without him, it is safe to say, the war for the Indians would have ended in the preceding winter. In military achievements, others might equal or excel him but in rulings[956] that endeared him to the Indians and in prop-

---

[953] *Official Records*, vol. xli, part ii, 1013.

[954] —*Ibid.*, 1046-1047. The general council of the confederated tribes had recommended an increase in the armed force of Indian Territory and that it was felt could best be obtained, in these days of wavering faith, only by conscription. The general council was expected to meet again, July 20, at Chouteau's Trading House [*ibid.*, 1047]. In October, the Chickasaws resorted to conscription. For the text of the conscription act, see *ibid.*, vol. liii, supplement, 1024-1025.

[955] —*Ibid.*, vol. xli, part ii, 1078. For additional facts concerning the progress of reorganization, see Portlock to Marston, August 5, 1864, *Confederate Records*, chap. 2, no. 259, p. 37; Portlock to Captain E. Walworth, August 27, 1864, *ibid.*, pp. 42-43.

[956] The most significant of Maxey's rulings was that on official precedence. His position was that no race or color line should be drawn in determining

aganda work he had no peer. At Fort Towson, his headquarters, he had set up a printing press, from which issued many and many a document, the purpose of each and every one the same. The following quotation from one of Maxey's letters illustrates the purpose and, at the same time, exhibits the methods and the temper of the man behind it. The matter he was discussing when writing was the Camden campaign, in connection with which, he said,

> . . . In the address of General Smith the soldiers of Arkansas, Missouri, Texas, and Louisiana are specially named. The soldiers from this Territory bore an humbler part in the campaign, and although they did not do a great deal, yet a fair share of the killed, wounded, captured, and captured property and cannon can be credite .o them. I had a number of General Smith's address struck off for circulation here, and knowing the omission would be noticed and felt, I inserted after Louisiana, "and of the Indian Territory," which I hope will not meet General Smith's disapproval.
>
> I would suggest that want of transportation in this Territory will cripple movements very much. . .
>
> During my absence General Cooper urged General McCulloch to help him in this particular; General M. replies he can do "absolutely nothing." I am not disposed to complain about anything, but I do think this thing ought to be understood and regulated. Supplies of breadstuffs and forage, as well as clothing, sugar, etc., all having to be drawn from beyond the limits of this Territory, a more than ordinary supply of transportation is necessary. To that for the troops must be added that made necessary by the destitute thrown on the hands of the Government and who must be taken care of. I do not expect General Smith to investigate and study the peculiar char-

---

the relative rank of officers [Maxey to Cooper, June 29, 1864, *Official Records*, vol. xxxiv, part iv, 698-699] and he held that Confederate law recognized no distinction between Indian and white officers of the same rank. Charles de Morse, a Texan, with whom General Steele had had several differences, took great exception to Maxey's decision. Race prejudice was strong in him. Had there been many like him, the Indians, with any sense of dignity, could never have continued long identified with the Confederate cause. For De Morse's letter of protest, see *ibid.*, 699-700.

acteristics of command here so closely as I have. He hasn't the time, nor is it necessary. In my opinion no effort should be spared to hold this country. Its loss would work a more permanent injury than the loss of any State in the Confederacy. States can be recovered – the Indian Territory, once gone, never. Whites, when exiled by a cruel foe, find friends amongst their race; Indians have nowhere to go. Let the enemy once occupy the country to Red River and the Indians give way to despair. I doubt whether many of the highest officials in our Government have ever closely studied this subject. It is the great barrier to the empire State of the South from her foe now and in peace. Let Federalism reach the Red River, the effects will not stop there. The doctrine of *uti possidetis* may yet play an important part.

I believe from what I have heard that Mr. Davis has a fair knowledge of this subject, and I think from conversations with General Smith he has, but his whole time being occupied with his immense department – an empire – I trust he will pardon me when I say that no effort of commissaries, quartermasters, or anybody else should be spared to hold this country, and I only regret that it has not fallen into abler hands than mine. . .[957]

Military reorganization[958] for the Indian troops had, in reality, come too late. Confederate warfare all along the frontier, in the summer and autumn of 1864, was little more than a series of raids, of which Price's Missouri was the greatest. For raiding, the best of organization was never needed. Watie, Shelby, Price were all men of the same stamp. Watie was the greatest of Indian raiders and his mere name became almost as much of a terror as Quantrill's with which it was frequently found associated, rightly or wrongly. Around Fort Smith in July and farther north in August the Indian raided to good effect. Usually, when he raided in the upper part of his own country, Federal

---

[957] Maxey to Boggs, May 11, 1864, *Official Records*, vol. xxxiv, part iii, 820.

[958] For progress reached in reorganization by October, see orders issued by direction of Maxey, *ibid.*, vol. liii, supplement, 1023.

supply trains were his objective, but not always. The refugees were coming back from Kansas and their new home beginnings were mercilessly preyed upon by their Confederate fellow tribesmen, who felt for the owners a vindictive hatred that knew no relenting.

Watie's last great raid was another Cabin Creek affair that reversed the failure of two years before. It occurred in September and was undertaken by Watie and Gano together, the former waiving rank in favor of the latter for the time being.[959] A brilliant thing, it was, so Maxey, and Smith's adjutant after him, reported.[960] The booty taken was great in amount and as much as possible of it utilized on the spot. Maxey regretted that the Choctaws were not on hand also to be fitted out with much-needed clothing.[961] It was in contemplation that Watie should make a raid into Kansas to serve as a diversion, while Price was raiding Missouri.[962] The Kansans had probably much to be thankful for that circumstances hindered his penetrating far, since, at Cabin Creek, some of his men, becoming intoxicated, committed horrible excesses and "slaughtered indiscriminately."[963]

Had the force at Fort Gibson been at all adequate to the needs of the country it was supposed to defend, such raids as Watie's would have been an utter impossibility. Thanks to Federal indifference and mismanagement, however, the safety of Indian Territory was

[959] Cooper to T. M. Scott, October 1, 1864, *Official Records*, vol. xli, part i, 783; Watie to T. B. Heiston, October 3, 1864, *ibid.*, 785.

[960] —*Ibid.*, 793, 794. Cooper described it "as brilliant as any one of the war [*ibid.*, 783] and Maxey confessed that he had long thought that movements of the raiding kind were the most valuable for his district [*ibid.*, 777].

[961] Maxey to Boggs, October 9, 1864, *ibid.*, part iii, 990.

[962] Cooper to Bell, October 6, 1864, *ibid.*, 982-984.

[963] Curtis Johnson to W. H. Morris, September 20, 1864 [*ibid.*, part i, 774].

of less consequence now than it had been before. The incorporation with the Department of Arkansas and the consequent separation from that of Kansas had been anything but a wise move. The relations of the Indian country with the state in which its exiles had found refuge were necessarily of the closest and particularly so at this time when their return from exile was under way and almost over. For reasons not exactly creditable to the government, when all was known, Colonel Phillips had been removed from command at Fort Gibson. At the time of Watie's raid, Colonel C. W. Adams was the incumbent of the post; but, following it, came Colonel S. H. Wattles[964] and things went rapidly from bad to worse. The grossest corruption prevailed and, in the midst of plenty, there was positive want. Throughout the winter, cattle-driving was indulged in, army men, government agents, and civilians all participating. It was only the ex-refugee that faced starvation. All other folk grew rich. Exploitation had succeeded neglect and Indian Territory presented the spectacle of one of the greatest scandals of the time; but its full story is not for recital here.

Great as Maxey's services to Indian Territory had been and yet were, he was not without his traducers and Cooper was chief among them, his overweening ambi-

---

[964] *Official Records*, vol. xli, part iii, 301. Wattles was not at Fort Gibson a month before he was told to be prepared to move even his Indian Brigade to Fort Smith [*ibid.*, part iv, 130]. The necessity for executing the order never arose, although all the winter there was talk off and on of abandoning Fort Gibson entirely, sometimes also there was talk of abandoning Fort Smith. So weak had the two places been for a long time that Cooper insisted there was no good reason why the Confederates should not attempt to seize them. It is interesting that Thayer notified Wattles to be prepared to move just when there was the greatest prospect of a Confederate Indian raid into Kansas.

tion being still unsatisfied. In November, at a meeting of the general council for the confederated tribes, Maxey spoke[965] in his own defence and spoke eloquently; for his cause was righteous. General Smith was his friend[966] in the sense that he had been Steele's; but there soon came a time when even the department commander was powerless to defend him further. Early in 1865, Cooper journeyed to Richmond.[967] What he did there can be inferred from the fact that orders were soon issued for him to relieve Maxey.[968] He assumed command of the district he had so long coveted and had sacrificed honor to get, March first,[969] General Smith disapproving of the whole procedure. "The change," said he, "has not the concurrence of my judgment, and I believe will not result beneficially."[970]

But Smith was mistaken in his prognostications. The change was not just but it did work beneficially. Cooper knew how to manage the Indians, none better, and the time was fast approaching when they would need managing, if ever. As the absolute certainty of Confederate defeat gradually dawned upon them, they became almost desperate. They had to be handled very carefully lest they break out beyond all restraint.[971]

---

[965] *Official Records*, vol. xli, part iv, 1035-1037; vol. liii, supplement, 1027.

[966] In July, 1864, orders issued from Richmond for the retirement of Maxey and the elevation of Cooper [*ibid.*, part ii, 1019]; but Smith held them in abeyance [*ibid.*, part iii, 971]; for he believed that Maxey's "removal, besides being an injustice to him, would be a misfortune to the department." The suppression of the orders failed to meet the approval of the authorities at Richmond and some time subsequent to the first of October Smith was informed that the orders were "imperative and must be carried into effect" [*ibid.*].

[967] *Official Records*, vol. xlviii, part i, 1382.

[968] — *Ibid.*, 1403.

[969] — *Ibid.*, 1408.

[970] — *Ibid.*

[971] The evidence for this is chiefly in Cooper's own letter book. One published letter is especially valuable in this connection. It is from Cooper

Phillips was again in charge of their northern com-
patriots [972] and, at Fort Gibson, he, too, was handling
Indians carefully.   It was in a final desperate sort of a
way that a league with the Indians of the Plains was
again considered advisable and held for debate at the
coming meeting of the general council.   To effect it,
when decided upon, the services of Albert Pike were
solicited.[973]   No other could be trusted as he.   Apparently he never served or agreed to serve [974] and no
alliance was needed; for the war was at an end.   On
the twenty-sixth of May, General E. Kirby Smith entered into a convention with Major-general E. R. S.
Canby, commanding the Military Division of West
Mississippi, by which he agreed to surrender the Trans-
Mississippi Department and everything appertaining
to it.[975]   The Indians had made an alliance with the
Southern Confederacy in vain.   The promises of Pike,
of Cooper, and of many another government agent had
all come to naught.

confidentially to Anderson, May 15, 1865. *Official Records*, vol. xlviii, part
ii, 1306.

[972] For Phillips's own account of his reinstallment, see his letter to Herron,
January 16, 1865, *ibid.*, part i, 542-543.

[973] Smith to Pike, April 8, 1864, *ibid.*, part ii, 1266-1269. It was necessary to have someone else beside Throckmorton, who was a Texan, serve;
because the Indians of the Plains had a deep distrust of Texas and of all
Texans [Smith to Cooper, April 8, 1864, *ibid.*, 1270-1271; and Smith to
Throckmorton, April 8, 1864, *ibid.*, 1271-1272].

[974] Smith issued him a commission however. See *ibid.*, 1266.

[975] — *Ibid.*, 604-606.

APPENDIX

LITTLE ROCK, ARKANSAS,[976]
December 30, 1862.

SIR: My letters, in respectful terms, addressed to your Adjutant General, when I re-assumed command of the Indian Country, late in October, have not been fortunate enough to be honored with a reply. This will reach you through another medium, and so that others besides yourself shall know its contents. I am no longer an officer under you, but a private citizen, and *free*, so far as any citizen of Arkansas can call himself free while he lives in this State; and I will see whether you are as impervious to *all* other considerations, as you are to all sense of courtesy and justice.

You were sent out to Arkansas with certain *positive* orders, which you were *immediately* to enforce. You *knew* that "Gen Hindman never was the commanding General of the Trans. Mississippi Department," and was not sent there by the War Department; and that, *therefore* and *of course*, all his orders were illegal, for want of power. You *knew* that he never had any right to interfere with my command in the Department of Indian Territory, to take away my troops and ordnance, or to send me *any* orders whatever; and that *therefore* I was *wholly* in the right, in all my controversy with him. You *knew*, also, that in stripping the Indian Country of troops, artillery, arms and ammunition, he had been guilty of multiplied outrages, contrary to the will and policy of the President, forbidden by the Secretary of War for the future, and hostile to the interests of the Confederacy.

I had been advised by the Secretary of War, on the 14th of July, before *you* were unfortunately thought of [in] connection with the Trans. Mississippi Department, that Gen. Magruder was assigned to the command of it; and that although I would be under his command, it was not doubted that my relations with him would be pleasant and harmonious, and that I would have such latitude in command of the Indian country, as might be necessary for me to

---

[976] Scottish Rite Temple, Pike *Papers.*

act to the best advantage in its defence. And by the same letter I was advised, that it was regretted I had met with so many embarrassments in procuring supplies; and that an order had been issued from the Adjutant and Inspector General's Office, to prevent the pursuing of such courses as I had complained of, in the seizure of what I had procured; and the Secretary said it was to be hoped that neither I nor any other officer would hereafter have cause to complain of supplies being diverted from their legitimate destination. And that Gen. Magruder might fully understand my position, &c., a copy of my letter of 8th June, to General Hindman, stating in detail the plundering process to which the Indian Service had before then been subjected, was furnished to the former officer. Three several copies of this letter were sent me, that it might be certain to reach me.

I do not repeat the substance of that letter, for *your* benefit. You have known it, no doubt, ever since you left Richmond. You told me in August, that the War Department was fully informed in regard to the matters between myself and Generals Van Dorn and Hindman. You spoke it in the way of a taunt, and as if the Department justified them and condemned me. You *meant* me so to understand it. You are a *very* ingenious person; inasmuch as you *knew* the exact contrary to be true. When I afterwards received the Secretary's letter, I remembered your remark, and did not doubt, and do not now doubt, that when you were substituted for Gen. Magruder, you received the same instructions that had been given *him* and were yourself furnished with a copy of the same letter, for the same purpose.

At all events, you were sent out to put an end to his outrages, and to avert, if you could, the mischiefs about to spring from them. But when you reached Little Rock, you found him there, and you found that the troops, artillery, ammunition and stores that had reached and were on their way there from the Indian Country, under his unrighteous orders, *and which it was your duty to restore to me*, were too valuable to be parted with, if that could be in any way avoided. Probably you foresaw that you might, by and by need to seize money and supplies procured by me. Twenty-six pieces of artillery, a supply of fixed ammunition and other trifles, on hand, with $1,350,000 in money, and over 6,000 suits of clothing in prospect, were the bait Hindman had to tempt you withal; and for it you

sold your soul, as Faust sold his to Mephistopheles. Your Lieutenant became your master; you found it convenient to believe his
version of every thing, and to justify him in every thing, and you
ended in making all his devilments your own, and adopting the
whole infernal spawn and brood, with additions of your own to the
family.

You told me in August, that you had been prepared to judge me
favorably, until you read my address to the Indians on resigning my
command, but after that, you could not judge me fairly. I did not
in the least doubt the *fact*; but I did *not* believe the *reason*. What,
moreover, had *you* to *judge* in regard to *me*? You were not sent
to *judge* any body. Hindman was the criminal you *were* to operate
upon.

And, if you were sent, or had otherwise any right, to judge *me*,
you administered the sort of justice that is in vogue in hell. Before
you *saw me, you heard him*. You adopted all his views, and never
asked me a question in regard to our controversy, or as to my own
action, or the condition of things in the Indian Country. I had
been infamously and assiduously slandered, from the moment when
I began to resist his illegal, impolitic and outrageous attempts to
deprive the Indian Department of every thing, to make it a mere
appanage of, and appendix to, North-Western Arkansas, to take the
Indians again out of their own country, and to compel me to unite
in that insane and miserable "expedition into Missouri," which was
projected and planned by Folly, mis-managed and misconducted by
Imbecility and ended, as I knew it would, in disaster and disgrace.
Lies of all varieties were ingeniously and laboriously invented at and
about Head Quarters, and despatches, by special and *fit* agents, to
be industriously circulated throughout the Indian Country and
Texas, as well as Arkansas. The Indians were told that I had
carried away into Texas the gold and silver belonging to *them*;
while the Texans were made to believe that I was paying *their*
moneys to the Indians. It was reported, in Bonham, Texas, by
officers sent from Hindman's Head Quarters, that I was defaulter
to the amount of $125,000 and at last there crawled out from the
sewer under the throne, and sneaked about the Indian Country and
Texas, the damnable lie, that an Indian had been taken, bearing
letters from me to the Northern Indians, or, to the enemy in Kansas;
or, as another version had it, from Gen. James H. Lane to me; and

three months ago it was whispered about that I was a member of the secret disloyal organization in Northern Texas. Such lies could have been counted by scores. Most of them are dead and rotten; but some still live, by means of assiduous nursing. And all these lies, and more either you or Hindman sent to the President at Richmond.

I say, sir, you never *inquired* into *any* thing. You never wished to *hear* any thing, whatever from *me*. You disobeyed the orders with which you were sent as a public curse and calamity into Arkansas, as if the State were not already sufficiently infested by Hindman. Is it true that he has lately, upon his single order, and without the ceremony of even a *mock* trial, caused three men "suspected of disloyalty" to be shot; and that, two of them being proven to him to be true Southern men, he sent a reprieve, which, either setting out too late, or lagging on the way, reached the scene of murder after their blood had bathed the desecrated soil of Arkansas? It has come to me so, from officers direct from Fort Smith. At any rate, he has put to death nine or ten persons, without any legal trial. Who is *he*, that he should do these things in this nineteenth century? And who are *you*, sir, that you should suffer, and by suffering, *approve* and adopt them? How many *more* murders will suffice to awaken public vengeance?

Was the Star Chamber any worse than Hindman's Military Commissions, that are ordered to preserve no records? Were the *Lettres de Cachet* of Louis xv, any greater outrage on the personal liberty of *French subjects,* than Hindman's arrests and committal to the Penitentiary of *suspected* persons? Was Tristan l'Hermite any more the minister of tyranny, than his Provost Marshals? or Caligula, Caesar Borgia or Colonel Kirke any more cruel and remorseless than he, that you have sustained all his acts, and made all his atrocities your own? Take care, sir! You are not so high, that you may not be reached by the arm of justice. The President is above you both, and God is above him, and *sometimes* interferes in human affairs.

Unless the late Secretary of War, through the President, sent an official falsehood to the Congress of the Confederate States, you were sent to Arkansas with *positive* and *unconditional* instructions, that, if Gen. Hindman *had* declared Martial Law in Arkansas, and adopted oppressive police regulations under it, *you should rescind the declarations of Martial Law, and the Regulations adopted to carry it into effect.* You have not done so. You have not only *not* rescinded *any* thing; but you have, by a General Order, long ago, continued in force all orders of General Hindman, not specially revoked by you. That order could have no retroactive effect, to make *his* orders *to have been valid* in the *past.* It could only put them in force for the *future;* and you thereby made them *your* orders, as fully as if you had re-issued them. In so doing, you became the enemy of your country, if not of the Human race, and outlawed yourself.

You have *yourself* established a tariff of prices exclusively on articles produced by the farmers, including the sweet potatoes raised by old women and superannuated negroes. You leave the Jews and extortioners, some of the former of whom go about in uniforms, claiming to be *officers* and your agents to charge these same venders of produce, whatever infamous prices they please for wares they need to purchase with the pittances received according to your scale of prices, for the vegetables that supply your and other tables.

You pretend, I learn, that the President gave you discretionary power, in regard to Martial Law, and the Regulations in question. I do not believe it; for, if he did, then he and the Secretary intentionally deceived Congress by the equivalent of a lie. Do you pretend that the President paltered with Congress in a double sense? I put you face to face. Is it *your* act, in *defiance* of orders, that continues Martial Law in force in Arkansas, stifles freedom of speech, muzzles the Press, tramples on all the rights at once of the People of that State, and makes the State itself only a congregation of Helots, incompetent to be represented in Congress? Is it merely a contest between you and Phelps, *which* of the two shall be Military Governor? If it *is* your act, then justice ought at once to be done upon you, lest the President, winking at the outrage, and not stripping from your back your uniform of Lieutenant General, should deserve to be impeached, as your accomplice.

Or, do you dare assert that it is *his* act, because he gave you discretionary power on the subject, after informing Congress that Hindman never was Commanding General of the Department, and that you had been ordered to rescind his declaration of Martial Law,—nay, after publicly proclaiming that *no* General had any power to declare Martial Law? All the Confederacy thanked and applauded him for so striking at the root of an immense outrage and abuse and an unexpected public course; but if he has authorized or sanctions *your* course, he is unworthy longer to be President. If he has not, you have defied his orders and justified men in judging yourself authorized and him guilty; and so you are unworthy longer to be General.

When I saw you in August, you were greatly exercised on the subject of my printed address to the Indians, publication of which in Little Rock you had suppressed, *as if it could do any harm in Arkansas.* You suppressed it, because it exposed those whose acts were losing the Indian Country. You wanted to keep what had been taken from *me*, and to escape damnation for the probable *consequences* of the acts, the *profit* of which you were reluctant to part with. I do not wonder the letter troubled you; for it told *the truth,* and condemned and denounced in advance *more* unjustifiable courses of conduct that you were about to pursue.

You pretended that it had produced a great "ferment" among the Indians; and that even many of the Chickasaws had in consequence of it, left the service. It had produced *no* ferment, and *none* of the Chickasaws had left us. On the contrary, the Indians were quieted by it, the Creeks re-organized, in numbers, two regiments, and the Chickasaws five companies. That was its purpose, and such was its effect.

But to *you,* its enormity consisted in its exposure of the conduct of two Major Generals. I told the Indians *plainly,* that it was not *my* fault or the fault of the Government, but of these two Generals, that moneys, clothing, arms and ammunition, procured for them, had not reached them; that troops raised for service among them had never entered their country; and that, finally, troops, artillery and ammunition were carried out of it. This censure of my *superiors,* in vindication of the President and Government, shocked your tender sensibilities. You were ready to follow in their footsteps, and already *had* the plunder; and you told me that "the act of the officer was the act of the Government." Did you really *mean,* that the Indians should have been led or left to suppose that these acts were the acts of the Government? That would have been *almost* as great an infamy, as it was to *take* the supplies, and so give them cause and reason to believe the robbery the act of the Government, *and thus excite them to revolt.* Moreover, when I told you that the act of the officer was *not,* in the case in question, the act of the Government; that, if I had permitted the Indians to suppose so, they would long have left us; and that, to quiet them, I had been compelled, for three months and more than a hundred times, to explain to them what had become of their supplies, and how and by whom they have been seized, you admitted that "that was right for local explanation." As there could be no objection to telling all, what I had often told part, that *they* might tell the rest; and as it was no more a crime to *print* than to *say* it; I have the right to believe and I *do* believe that your *real* objection to its publication was that it exposed *to our own people the actual* conduct of other Generals, and the *intended* conduct of yourself. Have *you* left the Indians to believe that the late seizure and appropriation, by *yourself,* of their clothing and moneys, is the act of the Government? If you have, you ought to be shot as a Traitor, for provoking them to revolt, and giving aid and comfort to the enemy.

But you told me, that when you first read my letter, you held up your hands, and exclaimed, "What! is the man a Traitor?" And you said that not one of my friends in Little Rock, and I had, you said, a great many, pretended to justify the letter. You have never found a friend of mine, or an indifferent person, silly enough to think, like you, that it savored of treason. It is only rarely one meets a man so scantily furnished with sense as to misunderstand and pervert what is written in plain English. I was vindicating myself, and still more the Government, and persuading the Indians to remain loyal, notwithstanding the wrongs they had endured. I, too, was an officer; and *my* acts *had* been the acts of the Government. *My* promises to them were *its* promises. The procuring of supplies by *me,* was *its* act; and when, reaching or not reaching the frontier, the supplies were like the unlucky traveler, who journeyed from Jerusalem to Jericho, *then* the Government *ceased* to act, and unlicensed outrage took its place. And, further, *my* act was the act of the Government, when I told the Indians *why* they had not received their supplies and money, and vindicated that Government at the expense of those who were guilty of the act; and who having done it and reaped the profit, should not be heard to object that all the world should know what they did, nor be allowed to escape the responsibility of *all* the consequences.

If to tell the Indians that other Generals had wrongfully stopped their supplies, in any degree *resembled* Treason, that could only be so, because it *was* treason to *do* the act. It cannot be wrong to make known what it was right and proper to do. The truth is, that the acts done were outrages, which it was desirable for the doers to conceal from the Indians. I refused to become a party to those outrages, by concealing them. I would not agree in advance to be *silent,* when *you* should repeat and improve on those outrages, and consummate what had been so felicitously begun.

I do not doubt that there are assassins wearing uniforms, who are knaves enough to *pretend* to read my letter as you do, and to see in it the desire of a disappointed man to be revenged, even by the ruin of his country. Power always has its pimps and catamites. These would no doubt gladly have made my letter the means of murdering me by that devilish engine of Military despotism, a Military commission, that is *ordered* to preserve no records. You, I think really look upon it with alarm. It is, no doubt, *very* desirable to *you,* that the blame of losing the Indian Country, which, if not already a fact accomplished, is a fact inevitable, should be made to fall upon me. You, as the pliant and useful implement of Gen. Hindman, are the cause of this loss; and you know I can prove it. You and he have left nothing *undone,* that *could* be done, to lose it. And you may rest assured, that whether I live or die, you shall not escape one jot or tittle of the deep damnation to which you are richly entitled for causing a loss so irretrievable, so astounding, so unnecessary and so *fatal,* and one which it will be impossible to excuse as owing to ignorance and stupidity. No degree of *these* misfortunes, can be pleaded in bar of judgment. *You* will have *forced* the Indians to go to the North for protection. *You* will have *given away* their country to the enemy. *You* will have turned their arms against us. You will have done this by disobeying the orders of your Government, continuing the courses it condemned, and to put an end to which it sent you out here; by falsifying its pledges and promises, taking for others' uses the moneys which it sent out to pay the Indians, robbing them of the clothing sent by it to cover their nakedness, and thus thrusting aside all the considerations of common honesty, of justice, of humanity, and even of policy, expediency and common sense.

When Mr. C. B. Johnson agreed, in September to loan your Quartermaster at Little Rock, $350,000 of the money he was conveying to Major Quesenbury, the Quartermaster of the Department of Indian Territory, *you promised* him that it should be repaid to Major Quesenbury as soon as you should receive funds, and before he would have disposed of the remaining million. *You got the money by means of that promise; and you did not keep the promise.* On the contrary, by an order that reached Fort Smith three hours before Mr. Johnson did, you compelled Major Quesenbury, the moment he received the money, to turn every dollar of it, over to a *Commissary* at Fort Smith; *and it was used to supply the needs of Gen. Hindman's troops;* when the Seminoles, fourteen months in the service have never been paid a dollar; and the Chickasaw and Choctaw Battalion, and Chilly McIntosh's Creeks, each corps a year and more in the service, have received only $45,000 each, and no clothing. Was this violation of your promise, the act of the Government?

To replace the clothing I had procured for the Indians in December, 1861, and which, with near 1,000 tents, fell into the hands of the troops of Generals Price and Van Dorn, I sent an agent, in June, to Richmond, who went to Georgia, and there procured some 6,500 suits, with about 3,000 shirts and 3,000 pairs of drawers, and some two or three hundred tents. These supplies were at Monroe early in September; and the Indians were informed that they and the moneys had been procured and were on the way. The good news went all over their country, as if on the wings of the wind; and universal content and rejoicing were the consequences.

The clothing reached Fort Smith; and its issue to Gen. Hindman's people commenced immediately. I sent a Quartermaster for it and he was retained there. If *any* of it has ever reached the Indians, it has been only recently, and but a small portion of it.

You pretend to believe that the Indians were in a "ferment" and discontented; and you took this very opportune occasion to stop all the moneys due their troops and for debts in their country and take and appropriate to the use of other troops the clothing promised to and procured for *them*. The clothing and the money were *theirs;* and you were in possession of an order from the War Department, forbidding you to divert any supplies from their legitimate destination; an order which was issued, *as you knew,* in consequence of *my* complaints, and to prevent moneys and supplies for the *Indians* being stopped: *and yet you stopped all.*

You borrow part of the money, and then seize the rest, like a *genteel* highwayman, who first borrows all he can of a traveler, on promise of punctual re-payment; and then claps a pistol to his head, and orders him to "stand and deliver" the rest. And you did even more than this.

For you promised the Acting Commissioner of Indian Affairs, when he was at Little Rock, about the 1st of October, on his way to the Indian Country, to give the Indians assurances of the good faith of the Government — *you promised him,* I say, *that the clothing in question should go to the Indians.* He told the Chickasaws and Seminoles, at least, of this promise. You broke it. You did *not* send them the clothing. You placed the Commissioner and the Government in an admirable attitude before the Indians; and the consequence has been, I understand, the disbanding of the Chickasaws, and the failure of the Seminole troops to re-organize. The consequence will be far more serious yet. Indians cannot be deceived, and promises made them shamelessly broken, with impunity.

While *you* were thus stopping their clothing, and robbing the half-naked Indians to clothe other troops, the Federals were sending home the Choctaws whom they had taken prisoners, after clothing them comfortably and putting money in their pockets. No one need be astonished, when *all* the Indians shall have turned their arms against us.

Why did you and Gen. Hindman not procure by your own exertions what you need for your troops? He reached Little Rock on the 31st of May. You came here in August. I sent my agents to Richmond, for money and clothing, in June and July. I never asked either of *you* for *any* thing. I could procure for *my* command all I wanted. You and he were Major Generals; I, only a Brigadier; and Brigadiers are plenty as blackberries in season. It is to be supposed that if I could procure money, clothing and supplies for *Indians,* you and he could do so for white troops. Both of you come blundering out to Arkansas with nothing, and supply yourselves with what *I* procure. Some officers would be ashamed *so* to supply deficiencies caused by their own want of foresight, energy or sense.

You do not even know you need an Engineer, until one of mine comes by, with $20,000 in his hands for Engineer Service in the

Indian Territory, some of which belongs to *me* for advances made, and with stationery and instruments procured by *me,* for *my* Department, in Richmond, a year ago; and *then* you find out that there are such things as Engineers, and that you need one; and you seize on Engineer, money, and stationery. You even take, notwithstanding Paragraph VI, of General Orders No. 50, the stationery procured by me for the Adjutant General's Office of my Department, by purchase in Richmond in December, 1861; for the want of which I had been compelled to permit my own private stock to be used for months.

I no longer wonder that you do these things. When you told me that you could not judge me fairly, because I told the Indians that others had done them injustice, you confessed much more than you intended. It was a pregnant sentence you uttered. By it you judged and convicted yourself, and pronounced *your own sentence,* when you uttered *it.*

The Federal authorities were proposing to the Indians *at the very time when you stopped their clothing and money,* that, if they would return to the old Union, they should not be asked to take up arms, their annuities should be paid them in money, the negroes taken from them be restored, all losses and damage sustained by them be paid for, and they be allowed to retain, as so much clear profit, what had been paid them by the Confederate States. It was a liberal offer and a great temptation, to come at the moment when you and Hindman were felicitously completing your operations, and when there were no breadstuffs in their country, and they and their women and children were starving and half-naked. You chose an admirable opportunity to rob, to disappoint, to outrage and exasperate them, and make your own Government fraudulent and contemptible in their eyes. If any human action *can* deserve it, the hounds of hell ought to hunt your soul and Hindman's for it through all eternity.

Instead of co-operating with the Federal authorities, and doing all that he and you *could* do to induce the Indians to listen to and accept their propositions, *he* had better have expelled the enemy from Arkansas or "have perished in the attempt;" and you had better have marched on Helena, before its fortifications were finished, and purged the eastern part of the State of the enemy's presence. If you had succeeded as admirably in that, as you have in losing the Indian Country, you would have merited the eternal gratitude of Arkansas, instead of its execrations; and the laurel, instead of a halter. I said that you and your Lieutenant had left *nothing* undone. I repeat it. Take another *small* example. Until I left the command, at the end of July, the Indian troops had regularly had their half rations of coffee. As soon as I was got rid of, an order from Gen. Hindman took all the remaining coffee, some 3,000 lbs., to Fort Smith. Even in this small matter, he could not forego an opportunity of injuring and disappointing them.

You asked me, in August, what was the need of any white troops at all, in the Indian Country; and you said that the few mounted troops, I had, if kept in the Northern part of the Cherokee Country, would have been enough to repel any Federal force that ever would have entered it. As you and Hindman never allowed any ammunition procured by me, to reach the Indian Country, if you could prevent it, whether I obtained it at Richmond or Corinth, or in Texas, and as you approve of his course in taking out of that country all that was to be found in it, I am entitled to suppose that you regarded ammunition for the Indians as little necessary, as troops to protect them in conformity to the pledge of honor of the Government. One thing, however, is to be said to the credit of your next in command. When he has ordered anything to be seized, he has never denied having done so, or tried to cast responsibility on an inferior. After you had written to me that you had ordered Col. Darnell to seize, at Dallas, Texas, ammunition furnished by me, you denied to him, I understand, that you had given the order. Is it so? and *did* he refuse to trust the order in your hands, or even to let you see it, but would show it to Gen. McCulloch?

Probably you know by this time, if you are capable of learning *any* thing, whether any white troops are needed in the Indian Country. The brilliant result of Gen. Hindman's profound calculations and masterly strategy, and of his long-contemplated invasion of Missouri, is before the country; and the disgraceful rout at Fort Wayne, with the manoeuvres and results on the Arkansas, are pregnant commentaries on the abuse lavished on me, for not taking "the line of the Arkansas," or making Head Quarters on Spring River, with a force too small to effect any thing any where.

I have not spoken of your Martial Law and Provost Marshals

in the Indian Country, and your seizure of salt-works there, or, in detail, of your seizure of ammunition procured by me in Texas, and on its way to the Indian troops, of the withdrawal of all white troops and artillery from their country, of the retention for other troops of the mountain howitzers procured by me for Col. Waitie, and the ammunition sent me, for them and for small arms, from Richmond. This letter is but a part of the indictment I will prefer bye and bye, when the laws are no longer silent, and the constitution and even public opinion no longer lie paralyzed under the brutal heel of Military Power; and when the results of your *im*policy and *mis*management shall have been fully developed.

But I have a word or two to say as to myself. From the time when I entered the Indian Country, in May, 1861, to make Treaties, until the beginning of June, 1862, when Gen. Hindman, in the plentitude of his self-conceit and folly, assumed absolute control of the Military and other affairs of the Department of Indian Territory, and commenced plundering it of troops, artillery and ammunition, dictating Military operations, and making the Indian country an appanage of Northwestern Arkansas, there was profound peace throughout its whole extent. Even with the wild Camanches and Kiowas, I had secured friendly relations. An unarmed man could travel in safety and alone, from Kansas to Red River, and from the Arkansas line to the Wichita Mountains. The Texan frontier had not been as perfectly undisturbed for years. We had fifty-five hundred Indians in service, under arms, and they were as loyal as our own people, little as had been done by any one save myself to keep them so, and much as had been done by others to alienate them. They referred all their difficulties to me for decision, and looked to me alone to see justice done them and the faith of Treaties preserved.

Most of the time without moneys (those sent out to that Department generally failing to reach it) I had managed to keep the white and Indian troops better fed than any other portion of the troops of the Confederacy any where. I had 26 pieces of artillery, two of the batteries as perfectly equipped and well manned as any, any where. I had on hand and on the way, an ample supply of ammunition, after being once plundered. While in command, *I had procured, first and last,* 36,000 pounds of rifle and cannon powder. If you would like to know, sir, how I effected this, in the face of all manner of discouragements and difficulties, it is no secret. My disbursing officers can tell you who supplied them with funds for many weeks, and whose means purchased horses for the artillery. Ask the Chickasaws and Seminoles who purchased the only shoes they had received — four hundred pairs, at five dollars each, procured and paid for by *me*, in Bonham, and which I sent up to them after I was taken "in personal custody" in November.

You dare pretend, sir, that *I* might be disloyal, or even in thought couple the word Treason with *my* name. What *peculiar* merit is it in *you* to serve on our side in this war? You were bred a soldier, and your only chance for distinction lay in obtaining promotion in the army, and in the army of the Confederacy. You *were* Major, or something of the sort, in the old army, and you *are* a Lieutenant General. Your reward I think, for what you have done or not done, is sufficient.

I was a private citizen, over fifty years of age, and neither needing nor desiring military rank or civil honors. I accepted the office of Commissioner, at the President's *solicitation*. I took that of Brigadier General, with all the odium that I knew would follow it, and fall on me as the Leader of a force of Indians, knowing there would be little glory to be reaped, and wanting no promotion, simply and solely to see *my* pledges to the Indians carried out, to keep them loyal to us, to save their country to the Confederacy, and to preserve the Western frontier of Arkansas and the Northern frontier of Texas from devastation and desolation.

What has been my *reward?* All my efforts have been rendered nugatory, and my attempts even to *collect* and *form* an army frustrated, by the continual plundering of my supplies and means by other Generals, and your and their deliberate efforts to disgust and alienate the Indians. Once before this, an armed force was sent to arrest me. You all disobeyed the President's orders, and treated me as a criminal for endeavoring to have them carried out. The whole country swarms with slanders against me; and at last, because I felt constrained reluctantly to re-assume command, after learning that the President would not accept my resignation, I am taken from Tishomingo to Washington, a prisoner, under an armed guard, it having been deemed necessary, for the sake of effect, to send two hundred and fifty men into the Indian Country to arrest me. *The Senatorial election was at hand.*

I had, unaided and alone, *secured* to the Confederacy a magnificent country, equal in extent, fertility, beauty and resources to any of our States – nay, superior to any. I had secured the means, in men and arms, of keeping it. I knew how only it could be defended. I asked no aid of any of you. I only asked to be let alone. Verily, I have my reward also, as Hastings had his, for winning India for the British Empire.

It is *your* day *now*. You sit above the laws and domineer over the constitution. "Order reigns in Warsaw." But bye and bye, there will be a *just* jury empannelled, who will hear *all* the testimony and decide impartially — no less a jury than the People of the Confederate States; and for their verdict as to myself, I and my children will be content to wait; as also for the sure and stern sentence and universal malediction, that will fall like a great wave of God's just anger on you and the murderous miscreant by whose malign promptings you are making yourself accursed.

Whether I am respectfully yours, you will be able to determine from the contents of this letter.

ALBERT PIKE, *Citizen of Arkansas.*

THEOPHILUS H. HOLMES, Major General &c.

SELECTED BIBLIOGRAPHY

I. ALPHABETICAL LIST OF SOURCES.

ABEL, ANNIE HELOISE, editor.   The official correspondence of
James S. Calhoun (Washington, D.C., 1915).

AMERICAN ANNUAL CYCLOPEDIA, 1861 – 1865 (New York).

BISHOP, ALBERT WEBB.   Loyalty on the frontier, or sketches of
union men of the southwest (St. Louis, 1863).

CENTRAL SUPERINTENDENCY RECORDS.

The Central Superintendency, embracing much of the territory included
in the old St. Louis Superintendency, was established in 1851 under an
act of congress, approved February 27 of that year.[977] Its headquarters
were at St. Louis from the date of its founding to 1859,[978] at St. Joseph
from that time to July, 1865,[979] at Atchison, from July, 1865 to 1869,[980]
and at Lawrence, from 1869 to 1878.

In February of 1878, J. H. Hammond, who was then in charge of the
superintendency, reported upon its records to the Commissioner of Indian
Affairs.[981] He spoke of the existence of "eight cases containing *Books,
Records, Papers,*" and he enclosed with his report schedules of the contents of certain boxes labelled A,B,C,D,E,F,H,L. Of Box A, the schedule
appertaining gave this information: "Old Records, Files, Memoranda,
etc., Miscellaneous Papers accumulated prior to 1869, when Enoch Hoag
became Sup^{t}Cent.Sup^{tcy}." More particularly, Box A contained "One
Bundle Old Treaties of various years, three (bundles) of Agency Accounts," and, for the period of 1830-1833, it contained "One Bundle
Ancient Maps," and one of "Old Bills and Papers."

The collection as a whole, undoubtedly sent into the United States
Indian Office as Hammond reported upon it, has long since been irre-
trievably broken up and its parts distributed. Knowing this the in-

---

[977] 9 *United States Statutes at Large,* p. 586, sec. 2; Indian Office *Letter
Book,* no. 44, p. 259.

[978] Greenwood to Robinson, November 21, 1859, *ibid.,* no. 62, p. 272.

[979] Dole to Murphy, June 23, 1865, *ibid.,* no. 77, p. 341.

[980] Parker to Hoag, May 26, 1869, *ibid.,* no. 90, p. 202.

[981] Dr. William Nicholson, who succeeded Enoch Hoag as superintendent,
was ordered to deliver the records to Hammond [Hoyt to Nicholson, telegram, January 15, 1878, Office of Indian Affairs, *Correspondence of the
Civilization Division*]. Hammond forwarded the records to Washington,
D.C., February 11, 1878.

vestigator is fain to deplore the advent of "efficiency" methods into the government service. Such efficiency, when interpreted by the ordinary clerk, has ever meant confusion where once was order and a dislocation that can never be made good. From the break-up, in the instance under consideration, the following books have been recovered:

Letter Book, July 25, 1853 to May 10, 1861.

" November 1, 1859 to February 5, 1863.

" February, 1863.

" "Letters to Commissioner of Indian Affairs," May 23, 1855 to October 31, 1859.

" "Letters to Commissioner," "Records," February 14, 1863 to June 6, 1868.

" "District of Nebraska, Letters to Commissioner," June 6, 1868 to April 10, 1871.

" April 12, 1871 to February 21, 1874.

" "Letters to Commissioner," February 21, 1874 to October 22, 1875.

" "Letters to Commissioner," October 25, 1875 to January 31, 1876.

" "Letters to Agents," October 4, 1858 to December 12, 1867.

" "Letters Sent to Agents, District of Nebraska," December 12, 1867 to August 22, 1871.

Account Book of Central Superintendency, being Abstract of Disbursements, 1853 to 1865.

CONFEDERATE STATES OF AMERICA. "Jefferson Davis Papers."

These papers, miscellaneous in character and now located in the Archives Division of the Adjutant General's Office of the United States War Department, seem to have belonged personally to President Davis or to have been retained by him. Among them is Albert Pike's Report of the Indian negotiations conducted by him in 1861.

—— Journal of the Congress, 1861-1865.

United States Senate *Executive Documents*, 58th congress, second session, no. 234.

Private Laws of the Confederate States of America, First Congress (Richmond, 1862).

Private Laws of the Confederate States of America, Second Congress (Richmond, 1864).

Provisional and Permanent Constitutions of the Confederate States and Acts and Resolutions of the First Session of the Provisional Congress (Richmond, 1861).

Public Laws of the Confederate States of America, 1863-1864 (Richmond, 1864).

Statutes at Large of the Confederate States of America, First Congress, edited by J. M. Matthews (Richmond, 1862).

Statutes at Large of the Provisional Government of the Confederate States of America from February 8, 1861 to February 18, 1862, together with the Constitution for the Provisional Government and the Permanent Constitution of the Confederate States, and the

Treaties Concluded by the Confederate States with the Indian Tribes, edited by J. M. Matthews (Richmond, 1864).

Statutes at Large of the Confederate States, commencing First Session of the First Congress and including First Session of the Second Congress, edited by J. M. Matthews (Richmond, 1864).

Statutes at Large of the Confederate States of America, Second Congress (Richmond, 1864).

CONFEDERATE STATES OF AMERICA. Papers of the Adjutant and Inspector General's Office.

Special Orders (Richmond, 1862).

General Orders, January, 1862 to December, 1863 (Columbia, 1863).

General Orders for 1863 (Richmond, 1864).

Special Orders (Richmond, 1864).

General Orders, January 1, to June 30, 1864, compiled by R. C. Gilchrist (Columbia, 1864).

—— "Pickett Papers."

State papers of the Southern Confederacy now lodged in the Library of Congress. Had Pike continued to prosecute his mission under the auspices of the State Department, these papers would undoubtedly have contained much of value for the present work, but as it is they yield only an occasional document and that of very incidental importance. The papers used were found in packages 81, 86, 88, 93, 95, 106, 107, 109, 113, 118. The "Pickett Papers" were originally in the hands of Secretary Benjamin. After coming into the possession of the United States government, they were at first confided to the care of the Treasury Department and were handed over later, by direction of the president, to the Library of Congress. The fact of their being in the charge of the Treasury Department explains the circumstance of its possession of the original treaty made by Pike with the Comanches, and the fact that that manuscript turned up long after the main body of "Pickett Papers" had been transferred to the Congressional Library suggests the possibility that detached Confederate records may yet repose in the recesses of the Treasury archives. Between the dates of their consignment and their transfer, they must have become to some degree disintegrated. The War Department borrowed some of the Pickett Papers for inclusion in the *Official Records of the War of the Rebellion.*

—— Records, or Archives.

Among these, which are to-day in the War Department in charge of the Chief Clerk of the Adjutant-general's Office, are the following:

Chap. 2, no. 258, Letter Book, Brig. Gen. D. H. Cooper, C.S.A., Ex officio Indian Agent, etc., May 10-27, 1865 (File Mark, W. 236).

It is a mere fragment. Its wrapper bears the following endorsement: War Department, Archive Office, Chap. 2, No. 258.

Chap. 2, no. 270, Letter Book, Col. and Brig. Gen. Wm. Steele's command.

The contents are,

a. A few letters dealing with Texas, Arizona, and New Mexico, March to July, 1862, pp. 7-22. These letters emanated from the authority of William Steele, Colonel of the Seventh Regiment of Texas Mounted Volunteers.

b. Letters dealing with matters in the Department of Indian Territory, January 8, 1863 to May 18, 1863, pp. 27-254. Pages 1-6, 23-26, and 47 and 48 are missing.

The list of the whole, as given, is,

Letters Sent – Col. and Brig. Gen. Wm. Steele's command – Mch. 7, 1862 to May 18, 1863, viz.,

1. 7th Regt Texas M. Vols. Mch. 7 to June 20/62
2. Dept. New Mexico, June 24/62
3. Forces of Arizona, July 12, 1862.
4. Dept. of Indian Territory, Jan. 8-12, 1863
5. 1st Div. 1st. Corps Trans-Miss. Dept., Jan. 13-20, 1863.
6. Dept. of Indian Territory, Jan. 21 to May 18, 1863.

Chap. 2, no. 268, Letters Sent, Department of Indian Territory, from May 19, 1863 to September 27, 1863.

This is another William Steele letter book, but is not quite complete. In point of time covered, it succeeds no. 270 and is itself succeeded by no. 267.

Chap. 2, no. 267, Letters Sent, September 28, 1863 to June 17, 1864.

Pages 3 to 6, inclusive, are missing and there are no letters after page 119.

Chap. 2, no. 259, Inspector General's Letters and Reports, from April 23, 1864, to May 15, 1865.

The cover has this as title: Letter Book A: Insp^t Genl's Office – Dis^t of Indian Ter^y From April 23rd, 1864 to May 15, 1865. On the inside of the front cover, appears this in pencil: "Received from Genl M. J. Wright, Oct. 16/79." Some pages at the beginning of the book have been cut out. Between pages 145 and 196, are reports, variously signed, some by E. E. Portlock, some by N. W. Battle, and some by James Patteson.

Chap. 2, no. 260, District of the Indian Territory, Inspector General's Letter Book, April 23, 1864 to January 7, 1865.

"Received from Genl M. J. Wright, Oct. 16/79." From a comparison of nos. 259 and 260, it is seen that no. 259 is a rough letter and report book and that no. 260 is a finished product. The 1864 material in no. 259 is duplicated by that in no. 260.

Chap. 7, no. 36. Indian Treaties.

Chap. 7, no. 48. Regulations adopted by the War Department, on the 15th of April 1862, for carrying into effect the Acts of Congress of the Confederate States, Relating to Indian Affairs, etc. (Richmond, 1862).

On page 1, is to be found, "Regulations for Carrying into effect, the Act of Congress of the Confederate States, approved May 21, 1861, entitled An Act for the protection of certain Indian Tribes, and of other Acts relating to Indian Affairs."

FORT SMITH PAPERS.

> See Abel, *The American Indian as Slaveholder and Secessionist*, p. 361.

GREELEY, HORACE. The American conflict (Hartford, 1864-1867), 2 vols.

INDIAN BRIGADE, Inspection Reports of, for 1864 and 1865.

> These were loaned for perusal by Luke F. Parsons, who was brigade inspector under Colonel William A. Phillips.

KAPPLER, CHARLES J., compiler and editor. Indian Affairs: Laws and Treaties.

> United States Senate Documents, 58th congress, second session, no. 319, 2 vols.
>
> Supplementary volume, United States Senate Documents, 62nd congress, second session, no. 719.

LEEPER PAPERS.

> See Abel, *The American Indian as Slaveholder and Secessionist*, pp. 360, 362.

LINCOLN, ABRAHAM. Complete Works, edited by John G. Nicolay and John Hay (New York, 1890), 10 vols.

McPHERSON, EDWARD. Political History of the United States of America during the Great Rebellion (Washington, D.C., 1864).

MISSIONARY HERALD, containing the proceeding of the American Board for Foreign Missions (Boston), vols. 56, 57, 60.

MOORE, FRANK, editor. Rebellion Record: Diary of American Events (New York, 1868), 11 vols. and a supplementary volume for 1861-1864.

PHILLIPS, WILLIAM ADDISON. Conquest of Kansas by Missouri and her allies (Boston, 1856).

"PIKE PAPERS."

> On subjects other than Indian, extant manuscripts written and received by Albert Pike are exceedingly numerous. One collection of his personal papers is in the possession of Mr. Fred Allsopp of Little Rock; but the largest proportion of those of more general interest, as also of more special, is in the Scottish Rite Temple, Washington, D.C., under the care of Mr. W. L. Boyden. Three things only deserve particular mention; viz.,
>
> a. Autobiography of General Albert Pike.
>
> A bound typewritten manuscript, "from stenographic notes, furnished by himself."
>
> b. Confederate States, a/c's with.
>
> These papers are in a small file-box and are chiefly receipts from John Crawford, Matthew Leefer, Douglas H. Cooper, John Jumper, and

others for money advanced to them and vouchers for purchases made
by Pike. There are three personal letters in the box: D. H. Cooper
to Pike, July 28, 1873; William Quesenbury to Pike, August 10, 1873;
William Quesenbury to Pike, August 11, 1873. All three letters have
to do with a certain $5000 seemingly unaccounted for, a subject in
controversy between Pike and Cooper, reflecting upon the latter's integrity. One of the papers is an itemized account of the money Pike
expended for the Indians, money "placed in his hands to be dis-
bursed among the Indian Tribes under Treaty stipulations in January,
A.D. 1862." It contains an enclosure, the receipt signed by Edward
Cross, depositary, showing that Pike restored to the Confederate Treasury the unexpended balance, $19,263 10/100 specie, $49,980 55/100, treasury notes. The receipt is dated Little Rock, March 13, 1863.

   c. Choctaw Case.

   Two packages of papers come under this heading. One is of manuscript matter mainly, the other of printed matter solely. In the latter
is the *Memorial of P. P. Pitchlynn*, House Miscellaneous Documents, no.
89, 43d congress, first session, and on it Pike has inscribed, "Written by
me, Albert Pike."

RICHARDSON, JAMES D., editor. Compilation of the messages and
papers of the Confederacy, including the diplomatic correspondence (Nashville, 1905), 2 vols.

—— Compilation of the messages and papers of the presidents,
1789-1897 (Washington, 1896-1899), 10 vols.

UNITED STATES OF AMERICA. Commissioner of Indian Affairs,
Reports, 1861, 1862, 1863, 1864, 1865.

—— Congressional Globe, 37th and 38th congresses, 1861-1865.

—— Department of the Interior, Files.

   The files run in two distinct series. One series has its material arranged in boxes, the other, in bundles. The former comprises letters
from the Commissioner of Indian Affairs only, and has been examined
to the extent here given,

        No. 9, January 1, 1861 to December 1, 1861.
        " 10, December 1, 1861 to November 1, 1862.
        " 11, November 1, 1862 to July 1, 1863.
        " 12, July 1, 1863 to June 15, 1864.
        " 13, June 15, 1864 to April 1, 1865.

   The latter were difficult of discovery. After an exhausting search,
however, they were located on a top-most shelf, under the roof, in the
file-room off from the gallery in the Patent Office building. The bundles
are small and each is bandaged as were the Indian Office files, originally.
The bandage, or wrapper, is labelled according to the contents. For
example, one bundle is labelled, "No. 1, 1849-1864, War;" another, "No.
24, 1852-1868, Exec." In the first are letters from the War Department,
in the second, from the White House. Some of the letters are from a

given department by reference only. A great number of the bundles have nothing but a number to distinguish them,

No. 53, January to June, 1865.
" 54, July to August, 1865.
" 55, September to December, 1865.
" 56, January to December, 1866.

UNITED STATES OF AMERICA. Department of the Interior, Letter Books, "Records of Letters Sent."

No. 3, July 22, 1857 to January 3, 1862.
" 4, January 3, 1862 to June 30, 1864.
" 5, July 1, 1864 to December 12, 1865.
" 6, December 14, 1865 to September 22, 1865.

—— Department of the Interior, Letter Press Books, "Letters, Indian Affairs."

No. 3, August 20, 1858 to March 5, 1862.
" 4, March 5, 1862 to July 1, 1863.
" 5, July 1, 1863 to June 22, 1864.
" 6, June 22, 1864 to April 11, 1865.

—— Department of the Interior, Register Books, "Register of Letters Received,"

Corresponding to the two series of files, are two series of registers. One series is a register of letters received from the Indian Office and each volume is labelled "Commissioner of Indian Affairs." The particular volume used for the present work covers the period from December 5, 1860 to January 6, 1866. It will be found cited as "D," that being a designation given to it by Mr. Rapp, the person at present in charge of the records. The second series is a register of letters received from persons other than the Commissioner of Indian Affairs. Each volume is labelled, "Indians."

"Indians," No. 3, January 8, 1856 to October 27, 1861.
"   " 4, January 2, 1862 to December 27, 1865.

—— Office of Indian Affairs, Consolidated Files.

During the last few years and since the time when most of this investigation was made, the various files of the Indian Office have been consolidated and, in many cases, hopelessly muddled. It has been thought best to refer in the text, wherever possible, to the old separate files, inasmuch as all letter books and registers were kept with the separate filing in view.

—— Office of Indian Affairs, General Files.

Central Superintendency, boxes 1860-1862, 1863-1868; Southern Superintendency, boxes 1859-1862, 1863-1864, 1865, 1866; Cherokee, 1859-1865, 1865-1867, 1867-1869, 1869-1870; Chickasaw, 1854-1868; Choctaw, 1859-1866; Creek, 1860-1869; Delaware, 1855-1861, 1862-1866; Kansas, 1855-1862, 1863-1868; Kickapoo, 1855-1865; Kiowa, 1864-1868; Miscellaneous, 1858-1863, 1864-1867, 1868-1869; Osage River, 1855-1862, 1863-

1867; Otoe, 1856-1862, 1863-1869; Ottawa, 1863-1872; Pottawatomie, 1855-1861, 1862-1865; Sac and Fox, 1862-1866; Seminole, 1858-1869; Wichita, 1860-1861, 1862-1871.

UNITED STATES OF AMERICA. Office of Indian Affairs, Irregularly-Shaped Papers.

This was a collection made for the convenience of the Indian Office. The name itself is a sufficient explanation.

—— Office of Indian Affairs, John Ross Papers.

These were evidently part of the evidence furnished at the Fort Smith Council, 1865.

—— Office of Indian Affairs, Land Files.

Central Superintendency, box 10, 1852-1869; Southern Superintendency, 1855-1870; Cherokee, box 21, 1850-1869; Choctaw, box 38, 1846-1873; Creek, box 45, 1846-1873; Dead Letters, box 51; Freedmen in Indian Territory, 2 boxes; Indian Talks, Councils, &c., box 3, 1856-1864, box 4, 1865-1866; Kansas, box 80, 1863-1865; Kickapoo, box 86, 1857-1868; Miscellaneous, box 103, 1860-1870; Neosho, box 117, 1833-1865; New York, box 130, 1860-1874; Osage, box 143, 1831-1873; Osage River, box 146, 1860-1866; Shawnee, box 190, 1860-1865; Special Cases, box 111, "Invasion of Indian Territory by White Settlers;" Treaties, box 2, 1853-1863, box 3, 1864-1866.

—— Office of Indian Affairs, Special Files.

No. 87, "Claims of Loyal Seminoles."
" 106, "Claims of Delawares for Depredations, 1863."
" 134, "Claims of Choctaws and Chickasaws."
" 142, " " " " "
" 201, "Southern Refugees."
" 284, "Claims of Creeks."

Kansas, box 78, 1860-1861, box 79, 1862; Otoe, box 153, 1856-1876; Ottawa, box 155, 1863-1873; Pawnee, box 156, 1859-1877; Pottawatomie, box 163, 1855-1865; Sac and Fox, box 177, 1860-1864, box 178, 1865-1868; Shawnee Deeds and Papers, box 195; Subsistence Indian Prisoners, one box; Wyandott, box 242, 1836-1863, and many other file boxes, with dates of the period under investigation, have been examined but have yielded practically nothing of interest for the subject.

Special Cases are quite distinct from Special Files. There are in all two hundred three of the former and three hundred three of the latter. There is in the Indian Office a small manuscript index to the Special Cases and a folio index to the Special Files.

—— Office of Indian Affairs. Letter Books (letters sent). See Abel, *The American Indian as Slaveholder and Secessionist*, pp. 363-364.

—— Office of Indian Affairs. Letters Registered (abstract of letters received), *ibid.*, p. 364.

—— Office of Indian Affairs, Miscellaneous Records, vol. viii, April, 1852 to July, 1861; vol. ix, July, 1861 to January 22, 1887.

UNITED STATES OF AMERICA. Office of Indian Affairs. Parker Letter Book. Letters to E. S. Parker, Commissioner of Indian Affairs, and others, 1869 to 1870.

—— Office of Indian Affairs. *Report Books*, Reports of the Commissioner of Indian Affairs to the Secretary of the Interior. See Abel, *The American Indian as Slaveholder and Secessionist*, p. 365.

UNITED STATES SENATE, Report of the Committee on the Conduct of the War, 37th congress, third session, no. 108 (1863), 3 vols.; 38th congress, second session, no. 142 (1865), 3 vols. and Supplemental Report (1866), 2 vols.

—— Committee Reports, no. 278, 36th congress, first session, being testimony before a Select Committee of the Senate, appointed to inquire into the Harper's Ferry affair.

—— War Department.

Aside from the *Confederate Records*, which are not regular War Department files, papers have been examined there for the Civil War period, although not by any means exhaustively. Enough were examined, however, to show reason for disparaging somewhat the work of the editors of the *Official Records*. Apparently, the editors, half of them northern sympathizers and half of them southern, proceeded upon a principle of selection that necessitated exchanging courtesies of omission.

WAR OF THE REBELLION. Compilation of the official records of the Union and Confederate armies (Washington), 129 serial volumes and an index volume.

The volumes used extensively in the present work were, *first series*, volumes iii, viii, xiii, xxii, parts 1 and 2, xxvi, part 2, xxxiv, parts 1, 2, 3, and 4, xli, parts 1, 2, 3, and 4, xlviii, parts 1 and 2, liii, supplement; *fourth series*, volume iii.

II. ALPHABETICAL LIST OF AUTHORITIES

ABEL, ANNIE HELOISE. American Indian as slaveholder and secessionist (Cleveland, 1915).

—— History of events resulting in Indian consolidation west of the Mississippi.

American Historical Association *Report*, 1906, 233-450.

—— Indian reservations in Kansas and the extinguishment of their titles.

Kansas Historical Society *Collections*, vol. viii, 72-109.

ANDERSON, MRS. MABEL WASHBOURNE. Life of General Stand Watie (Pryor, Oklahoma, 1915), pamphlet.

BADEAU, ADAM. Military history of U. S. Grant (New York, 1868), 3 vols.

BARTLES, WILLIAM LEWIS. Massacre of Confederates by Osage Indians in 1863.
    Kansas Historical Society *Collections*, vol. iii, 62-66.

BIOGRAPHICAL CONGRESSIONAL DIRECTORY, 1774-1903.
    House Documents, 57th congress, second session, no. 458 (Washington, D.C., 1903).

BLACKMAR, FRANK W. Life of Charles Robinson (Topeka, 1902).

BLAINE, JAMES G. Twenty years of Congress, 1860-1880 (Norwich, Connecticut, 1884-1886), 2 vols.

BOGGS, GENERAL WILLIAM ROBERTSON, C.S.A. Military reminiscences (Durham, North Carolina, 1913).

BORLAND, WILLIAM P. General Jo. O. Shelby.
    Missouri *Historical Review*, vol. vii, 10-19.

BOUTWELL, GEORGE SEWALL. Reminiscences of sixty years in public affairs (New York, 1902), 2 vols.

BOYDEN, WILLIAM L. The character of Albert Pike as gleaned from his correspondence.
    New Age Magazine, March 1915, pp. 108-111.

BRADFORD, GAMALIEL. Confederate portraits.
    "Judah P. Benjamin," *Atlantic Monthly*, June, 1913; "Alexander H. Stephens," *ibid.*, July, 1913; "Robert Toombs," *ibid.*, August, 1913.

BRITTON, WILEY. Memoirs of the rebellion on the border, 1863 (Chicago, 1882).

—— The Civil War on the border (New York, 1899), 2 vols.

BROTHERHEAD, WILLIAM. General Frémont and the injustice done him.
    Yale University Library of American Pamphlets, vol. 22.

CAPERS, HENRY D. The life and times of C. G. Memminger (Richmond, 1893).

CARR, LUCIEN. Missouri: a bone of contention, American Commonwealth series (Boston, 1896).

CHADWICK, ADMIRAL FRENCH ENSOR. Causes of the Civil War, American Nation series (New York, 1907), vol. xix.

CLAYTON, POWELL. The aftermath of the Civil War in Arkansas (New York, 1915).

CONNELLEY, WILLIAM E. James Henry Lane: the grim chieftain of Kansas (Topeka, 1899).

—— Quantrill and the border wars (Cedar Rapids, 1910).

CORDLEY, RICHARD. Pioneer days in Kansas (Boston, 1903).

Cox, Jacob Dolson. Military reminiscences of the Civil War (New York, 1900), 2 vols.

Crawford, Samuel J. Kansas in the sixties (Chicago, 1911).

Curry, J. L. M. Civil history of the government of the Confederate States with some personal reminiscences (Richmond, 1901).

Dana, C. A. Recollections of the Civil War (New York, 1898).

Davis, Jefferson. Rise and fall of the Confederate government (New York, 1881), 2 vols.

Davis, John P. Union Pacific Railway (Chicago, 1894).

Dawson, Captain F. W. Reminiscences of Confederate service, 1861-1865 (Charleston, 1882).

Draper, J. W. History of the American Civil War (New York, 1867-1870), 3 vols.

Dyer, Frederick H., compiler. Compendium of the war of the rebellion (Des Moines, 1908).

Eaton, Rachel Caroline. John Ross and the Cherokee Indians (Menasha, Wisconsin, 1914).

Edwards, John Newman. Shelby and his men (Cincinnati, 1867).
—— Noted guerrillas, or the warfare of the border (Chicago, 1877).

Eggleston, George Cary. History of the Confederate war: its causes and conduct (New York, 1910), 2 vols.

Evans, General Clement A., editor. Confederate military history (Atlanta, 1899), 10 vols.

Fisher, Sydney G. Suspension of habaes corpus during the war of the rebellion.
Political Science Quarterly, vol. iii, 454-488.

Fiske, John. Mississippi Valley in the Civil War (Boston, 1900).

Fite, Emerson David. Social and industrial conditions in the North during the Civil War (New York, 1910).

Formby, John. American Civil War (New York, 1910).

Forney, J. W. Anecdotes of public men (New York, 1873-1881), 2 vols.

Foulke, William Dudley. Oliver P. Morton, life and important speeches (Indianapolis, 1899), 2 vols.

Gordon, General John B. Reminiscences of the Civil War (New York, 1903).

Gorham, George C. Life and public services of Edwin M. Stanton (New York, 1899), 2 vols.

GRANT, ULYSSES SIMPSON. Personal memoirs (New York, 1895), 2 vols., new edition, revised.

GREENE, FRANCIS VINTON. Mississippi, Campaigns of the Civil War series (New York, 1882).

GROVER, CAPTAIN GEORGE S. Shelby raid, 1863.
Missouri *Historical Review*, vol. vi, 107-126.

—— The Price campaign of 1864.
Missouri *Historical Review*, vol. vi, 167-181.

HALLUM, JOHN. Biographical and pictorial history of Arkansas (Albany, 1887).

HODGE, DAVID M. Argument before the Committee of Indian Affairs of the United States Senate, March 10, 1880, in support of Senate Bill, no. 1145, providing for the payment of awards made to the Creek Indians who enlisted in the Federal army, loyal refugees, and freedmen (Washington, D.C., 1880), pamphlet.

—— Is-ha-he-char, and Co-we Harjo. To the Committee on Indian Affairs of the House of Representatives of the 51st congress in the matter of the claims of the loyal Creeks for losses sustained during the late rebellion (Washington, D.C.), pamphlet.

HOSMER, JAMES KENDALL. Appeal to arms, American Nation series (New York, 1907), vol. xx.

——Outcome of the Civil War, American Nation series (New York, 1907), vol. xxi.

HOUCK, LOUIS. History of Missouri (Chicago, 1908), 3 vols.

HULL, AUGUSTUS LONGSTREET. Campaigns of the Confederate army (Atlanta, 1901).

HUMPHREY, SETH K. The Indian dispossessed (Boston, 1906), revised edition.

HUNTER, MOSES H., editor. Report of the military services of General David Hunter, U.S.A., during the war of the rebellion. (New York, 1873), second edition.

JOHNSON, ROBERT UNDERWOOD and Clarence Clough Buel, editors. Battles and leaders of the Civil War (New York, 1887), 4 vols.

JOHNSTON, GENERAL JOSEPH E. Narrative of military operations during the late war (New York, 1874).

JOHNSTON, COLONEL WILLIAM PRESTON. Life of General Albert Sidney Johnston (New York, 1878).

LEWIS, WARNER. Civil War reminiscences.
Missouri *Historical Review*, vol. ii, 221-232.

LIVERMORE, WILLIAM ROSCOE. The story of the Civil War (New York, 1913), part iii, books 1 and 2.

LOVE, WILLIAM DELOSS. Wisconsin in the war of the rebellion (Chicago, 1866).

LOWMAN, HOVEY E. Narrative of the Lawrence massacre [Lawrence, 1864], pamphlet.

LUBBOCK, F. R. Six decades in Texas, or memoirs, edited by C. W. Raines (Austin, 1890).

McCLURE, A. K. Abraham Lincoln and men of war times (Philadelphia, 1892), fourth edition.

McDOUGAL, JUDGE H. C. A decade of Missouri politics, 1860 to 1870, from a Republican Viewpoint.
  Missouri *Historical Review*, vol. iii, 126-153.

McKIM, RANDOLPH H. Numerical strength of the Confederate army (New York, 1912).

McLAUGHLIN, JAMES. My friend, the Indian (Boston, 1910).

MANNING, EDWIN C. Biographical, historical, and miscellaneous selections (Cedar Rapids, 1911).

MARTIN, GEORGE W. First two years of Kansas (Topeka, 1907), pamphlet.

MERRIAM, G. S. Life and times of Samuel Bowles (New York, 1885).

NOBLE, JOHN W. Battle of Pea Ridge, or Elk Horn tavern (St. Louis, 1892).
  War papers and personal recollections, 1861-1865, published by the Commandery of the State of Missouri.

PELZER, LOUIS. Marches of the dragoons in the Mississippi Valley (Iowa City, 1917).

PHILLIPS, JUDGE JOHN F. Hamilton Rowan Gamble and the provisional government of Missouri.
  Missouri *Historical Review*, vol. v, 1-14.

PHISTERER, FREDERICK, compiler. Statistical record of the armies of the United States (New York, 1890).

PUMPELLY, RAPHAEL. Across America and Asia (New York, 1870), third edition, revised.

REAGAN, JOHN H. Memoirs with special reference to secession and the Civil War, edited by W. F. McCaleb (New York, 1906).

REYNOLDS, JOHN HUGH. Makers of Arkansas, Stories of the States series (New York, 1905).

—— Presidential reconstruction in Arkansas.
  Arkansas Historical Association *Publications*, vol. i, 352-361.

RHODES, JAMES FORD. History of the United States from the compromise of 1850 (New York, 1893-1906), 7 vols.

RIDDLE, ALBERT GALLATIN. Recollections of war times (New York, 1895).

ROBINSON, CHARLES. Kansas conflict (Lawrence, 1898).

ROMAN, ALFRED. Military operations of General Beauregard (New York, 1884), 2 vols.

ROPES, JOHN C. Story of the Civil War (New York, 1895-1905), parts 1 and 2.

ROSENGARTEN, JOSEPH GEORGE. The German soldier in the wars of the United States (Philadelphia, 1886).

ROSS, MRS. W. P. Life and times of William P. Ross (Fort Smith, 1893).

SCHOFIELD, JOHN MCALLISTER. Forty-six years in the army (New York, 1897).

SCHURZ, CARL. Reminiscences (New York, 1909), 3 vols.

SHEA, JOHN C. Reminiscences of Quantrill's raid upon the city of Lawrence, Kansas (Kansas City, Mo., 1879), pamphlet.

SHERIDAN, PHILIP H. Personal memoirs (New York, 1888), 2 vols.

SHERMAN, GENERAL WILLIAM T. Home letters, edited by M. A. DeWolfe Howe (New York, 1909).

—— Memoirs (New York, 1875), 2 vols.

SHINN, JOSEPH H. History of education in Arkansas (Washington, D.C., 1900).
United States Bureau of Education, *Publications*.

SHOEMAKER, FLOYD C. Story of the Civil War in northeast Missouri.
Missouri *Historical Review*, vol. vii, 63-75, 113-131.

SMITH, GUSTAVUS W. Confederate war papers (New York, 1884), second edition.

SMITH, WILLIAM HENRY. Political history of slavery (New York, 1903), 2 vols.

SNEAD, THOMAS L. Fight for Missouri (New York, 1886).

SPEER, JOHN. Life of Gen. James H. Lane, "the liberator of Kansas." (Garden City, Kansas, 1896).

SPRING, LEVERETT. Career of a Kansas politician (James H. Lane).
American Historical Review, vol. iv, 80-104.

—— Kansas: the prelude to the war for the union, American Commonwealth series (Boston, 1892).

STANTON, R. L. Church and the rebellion (New York, 1864).

STEARNS, FRANK PRESTON. Life and public services of George Luther Stearns (Philadelphia, 1907).

STEPHENS, ALEXANDER H. Constitutional view of the late war between the states (Philadelphia, 1870), 2 vols.

STOREY, MOORFIELD. Charles Sumner, American Statesmen series (Boston, 1900).

SUMNER, CHARLES. Works (Boston, 1874-1883), 15 vols.

TENNEY, WILLIAM J. Military and naval history of the rebellion in the United States (New York, 1866).

THAYER, WILLIAM ROSCOE. Life and letters of John Hay (Boston, 1915), 2 vols.

THORNDIKE, RACHAEL SHERMAN, editor. Sherman letters (New York, 1894).

TODD, ALBERT. Campaigns of the rebellion (Manhattan, Kansas, 1884).

VAN DEVENTER, HORACE. Albert Pike (Knoxville, 1909).

VIOLETTE, E. M. Battle of Kirksville, August 6, 1862. *Missouri Historical Review*, vol. v, 94-112.

VICTOR, ORVILLE J., editor. Incidents and anecdotes of the war (New York, 1862).

VILLARD, HENRY. Memoirs (Boston, 1904), 2 vols.

VILLARD, OSWALD GARRISON. John Brown, 1800-1859 (Boston, 1910).

WHITFORD, WILLIAM CLARKE. Colorado volunteers in the Civil War (Denver, 1906).

WIGHT, S. A. General Jo. O. Shelby. *Missouri Historical Review*, vol. vii, 146-148.

WILDER, DANIEL W. Annals of Kansas (Topeka, 1875).

WILLIAMS, CHARLES R. Rutherford Birchard Hayes (Boston, 1914), 2 vols.

WILLIAMS, R. H. With the border ruffians: memoirs of the far west, 1852-1868, edited by E. W. Williams (London, 1908).

WILSON, CALVIN D. Negroes who owned slaves (*Popular Science Monthly*, vol. lxxxi, no. 5, 483-494).

WILSON, HILL P. John Brown: soldier of fortune (Lawrence, 1913).

WOODBURN, JAMES ALBERT. Life of Thaddeus Stevens (Indianapolis, 1913).

WRIGHT, MARCUS J. General officers of the Confederate army (New York, 1911).

INDEX

Abbott, James B: 204, *footnote*, 236, *footnote*
Abel, Annie Heloise: work cited in *footnotes* on pages 14, 57, 75, 85, 172, 183, 190, 226, 241, 260
Absentee Shawnees: 205, *footnote*
Acadians: removal of, 304, *footnote*
Adair, W. P: 268, *footnote*, 277, *footnote*, 326 and *footnote*
Adams, C. W: 333
Ah-pi-noh-to-me: 108, *footnote*
Aldrich, Cyrus: 225, *footnote*, 229, *footnote*
Alexander, A. M: 267, *footnote*
Allen's Battery: 146
Allen County (Kans.): 82, *footnote*
Aluktustenuke: 94, *footnote*, 108, *footnote*
Amnesty Proclamation: 322
Anderson, Mrs. Mabel Washbourne: work cited in *footnotes* on pages 127, 130, 138, 194, 197, 271, 272, 288
Anderson, S. S: 265, *footnote*
Arapahoes: 274, *footnote*
Arizona Territory: 61-62
Arkadelphia (Ark.): 261
Arkansans: circulate malicious stories about Pike, 160, *footnote*; lawless, 264; unable to decide arbitrarily about Indian movements, 326
Arkansas: regards McCulloch as defender, 15; Van Dorn's requisition for troops, 25; Federals occupy northern, 34; Pike to call for aid, 36; attack from direction of, expected, 48; left in miserable plight by Van Dorn, 128; army men exploited Pike's command, 150; R. W. Johnson serves as delegate from, 175; R. W. Johnson

becomes senator from in the First Congress, 176; Thomas B. Hanly, representative from, introduces bill for establishment of Indian superintendency, 176; disagreeable experiences of Indians in, 177; Pike recommends separation of Indian Territory from both Texas and, 179; unsafe to leave interests of Indian Territory subordinated to those of, 246; political squabbles in, 249, *footnote*; Indian Home Guards not intended for use in, 259; privilege of writ of *habeas corpus* suspended, 269; Blunt and Curtis want possession of western counties, 325
Arkansas and Red River Superintendency: 181; territorial limits, 177; officials, 177-178; restrictions upon Indians and white men, 178; Pike recommends organization, 179; Cooper seeks appointment as superintendent, 179
Arkansas Military Board: 15, 16
Arkansas Post (Ark.): loss of, 270
Arkansas River: mentioned, 165, 192, 194, 216, 268, *footnote*, 272, *footnote*, 295; Pike's headquarters near junction with Verdigris, 22; Pike to call troops to prevent descent, 36; Indian refugees reach, 85; Indians flee across, 135; Campbell to examine alleged position of enemy south, 136; Federals in possession of country north of, 198; Stand Watie and Cooper pushed below, 220; Phillips to hold line of, 251; Schofield desires control of entire length of course, 260; Blunt patrolling, 293; Stand Watie to move down, to vicinity of Fort Smith,